Conflict and Consensus

Conflict and Consensus

A study of values and attitudes in the Republic of Ireland and Northern Ireland

Tony Fahey

Bernadette C. Hayes

Richard Sinnott

IPA
INSTITUTE OF PUBLIC ADMINISTRATION

First published in 2005
by the Institute of Public Administration
57-61 Lansdowne Road
Dublin 4
Ireland

www.ipa.ie

ISBN 1 904541 18 6

British Library cataloguing-in-publication data
A catalogue record for this book is available from the British Library

Cover design by Slick Fish Design, Dublin
Typesetting by Desktop Print & Design, Dublin
Printed in Ireland by Colour Books Ltd., Dublin

Contents

Notes on Authors

Tony Fahey is a sociologist and is Research Professor in the Economic and Social Research Institute, Dublin.

Formerly of the School of Sociology and Social Policy at Queen's University, Belfast, Bernadette C. Hayes is now Professor in the Department of Sociology, University of Aberdeen.

Professor Richard Sinnott is a member of the Politics Department and director of the Public Opinion and Political Behaviour Research Programme at the Geary Institute, University College Dublin.

Acknowledgements

Support for the writing of this book was provided by Atlantic Philanthropies and by the authors' home institutions – the Economic and Social Research Institute, Dublin; Queen's University, Belfast; and University College, Dublin (UCD). The 1999-2000 wave of the European Values Study survey was conducted with the assistance of grants provided by Atlantic Philanthropies, which funded the survey in the Republic of Ireland, and by the Economic and Social Research Council in the United Kingdom, which funded the survey in Northern Ireland (grant no. R000222959). The first round of the European Social Survey (2002-2003) was conducted in the Republic of Ireland with the assistance of funding provided to the Institute for the Study of Social Change at UCD by the Higher Education Authority through its Programme for Research in the Third-Level Institutions (PRTLI) and, in Northern Ireland, with the assistance of a grant from the Economic and Social Research Council and additional funding from the Northern Ireland Office of First Minister and Deputy First Minister. Participants in a Consultative Seminar on the European Values Study held in UCD in January 2001 under the auspices of the Institute for British-Irish Studies provided valuable comment on some of the material included in this book. Assistance in preparing the manuscript for publication was provided by Daphne McNamara-Lancha of the ESRI. The authors thank all the above for their generous support.

List of Tables

List of Figures

1

Introduction

Ireland has a clearly drawn political boundary that separates the Republic of Ireland from Northern Ireland and a less precise but equally real boundary between the Catholic-nationalist and the Protestant-unionist traditions. This book seeks to assess the nature and extent of conflict and consensus in values and attitudes within and across these boundaries. We are particularly interested in the possibility that there may be certain domains of values and attitudes where conflict is the dominant theme – collective identity and attitudes towards constitutional arrangements on the island, for example – and other areas where similarity of outlook may be more common and where it may be possible to speak of varying degrees of consensus. The book will also critically examine the terms 'Catholic nationalist' and 'Protestant unionist' as characterisations of the opposing polarities of political conflict in the island of Ireland.

In addressing these topics, the study tackles an issue that has surfaced periodically in analyses of the 'Irish problem' – the role played by cultural differences in nationalist-unionist conflict. A major historian of this subject has attributed division on the island to the crowding together of too many cultures in a small space, leading to what he called a 'collision of cultures' that had lethal consequences (Lyons 1979). There are, indeed, many exponents of the view that the present conflict in Northern Ireland is fundamentally religious in character, a 'holy war' which can be regarded as a twentieth-century leftover from the seventeenth century encounter between Reformation and Counter-reformation (for different perspectives within this broad approach see, e.g. Heslinga, 1979; Bruce, 1986; O'Malley, 1990, 1995).

Others deny that cultural cleavage is all that pervasive or, if it is present, that it is a significant contributor to the causes of conflict. Akenson (1988), for example, set out to examine nineteenth-century behavioural and cultural patterns among Catholics and Protestants in Ireland. Using indicators drawn from three areas of life – occupational hierarchy, family structure and the treatment of women – he could find only small differences between them. Richard Rose (1971) similarly found much by way of a common culture between Catholics and Protestants in Northern Ireland in the 1960s. Even at the height of the troubles in the North, as McGarry and O'Leary (1995: 253) point out, the two sides of the divide were culturally so similar to each other – in language, dress, and everyday life-style – that outsiders had to become well-versed in the nuances of names, addresses and schools attended before being able to tell them apart. These perspectives suggest that in spite of the depth of ethnonational division between them the two traditions may also be characterised by elements of an underlying consensus.

Our contribution to the debate on these questions here is a simple one – to use data on values and attitudes gathered by sample survey techniques to provide a detailed empirical assessment of contemporary cultural similarities and differences between and within the two major ethnonational traditions on the island of Ireland and between and within Northern Ireland and the Republic. This exercise may not resolve the debate about the contribution of cultural difference to the causes of conflict in Ireland, but it may help place that debate on a firmer empirical foundation.

Distinctive features

As a contribution to survey-based analysis of values and attitudes in Ireland, this study has four distinctive features. The first, as implied earlier, is its all-Ireland scope. While, as Rottman (1999: 9) notes, both parts of Ireland have been compared to a wide, even exotic range of countries, they have rarely been compared to each other. The political boundary between North and South has effectively partitioned social science research, so that scholars on either side have tended not to regard the other side as offering a useful or appropriate point of comparison. There are some exceptions to this rule – for example, the volume of papers to which Rottman's essay forms the introduction (Heath *et al.*, 1999), Heslinga's (1979) examination of the border as a cultural divide and in the specific area of research pursued here, the Davis and Sinnott (1979) and Moxon-Browne (1983) analyses of the 1978 Republic of Ireland and Northern Ireland attitude surveys. But these exceptions are rare. The present study addresses this gap by placing cross-border comparisons at the centre of attention and aiming for an account of attitudes and values on the island as a whole as well as in each part of it.

A second feature of the study is that it includes Protestants in the Republic as a distinct group. With the formation of the Irish Free State in 1922, the already precarious unity of the Protestant community on the island was weakened. Losses suffered in the First World War and post-independence emigration to Britain and other parts of the empire among the more unionist-minded Protestants in the South caused a sharp decline in the southern Protestant population. Between 1911 and 1926, it fell from almost 10 per cent of the population in the area that became the Free State to just below 7 per cent. Subsequently, a combination of factors caused it to decline steadily to 3 per cent by 1991 (Sexton and O'Leary, 1996). The common perception is that, with this decline, the Protestant community in the Republic, while remaining confessionally distinct, merged into the culture and identity of the larger population (Bowen, 1983; Coakley, 1998; Acheson, 2002: 233-34, 260). However, the very smallness of the Protestant community in the Republic has made it difficult to measure this transition with any precision using quantitative social science methods. The reason is that typical survey samples in the Republic of Ireland contain too few Protestants to allow them to be analysed separately. In the present study, we have dealt with this problem by including a special additional sample of Protestants in the Republic in the European Values Study for 1999-2000. This sample (which numbers 257 cases – see further description below) enables us to make Protestant-Catholic comparisons in the Republic that parallel similar comparisons in the North and allows us to establish the extent to which the Protestant-Catholic differences found in Northern Ireland extend across the border.

The third distinctive feature of the study arises from the Europe-wide range of the main data sources it draws on. The European data provide a context within which the extent of similarity and difference in values and attitudes in Ireland, North and South, can be evaluated. In the absence of such comparisons, it is difficult to distinguish between differences that may be statistically significant but substantively small in international comparative terms and those that indicate a major cultural divide. This problem arises in all studies lacking a broad comparative range. Take, for example, Andrew Greeley's analysis of religion in the two parts of Ireland. He contends that, in terms of culture and belief, Ireland has, not two religions (Catholicism and Protestantism), but three (southern Catholicism, northern Catholicism and northern Protestantism), or possibly even four (adding a distinction between the Anglican and Presbyterian strands of northern Protestantism) (Greeley, 1999). Greeley's propositions are backed up by statistically significant differences on a range of religious and attitudinal indicators between the religious groupings he identified. However, those differences need to be viewed in a broader comparative context to establish whether they can be considered as substantively large, and it is here that the Europe-wide comparisons that are possible with the data sources we have to hand become especially interesting and revealing.

The fourth distinctive feature of the book is its systematic attempt to pursue relevant comparisons over time. This can be done mainly because the core body of data on which this study is based is the third wave of the European Values Study, previous waves having been carried out in 1981 and 1990. In addition, we have drawn on other surveys and opinion polls as appropriate ranging from the late 1960s to 2003, making particular use of the 2002-2003 European Social Survey. Given the wide range of attitudinal surveys used in the book, an overview of these sources may be helpful at this point.

The data

The EVS is a large-scale programme of survey research focusing on trends in values and attitudes in Europe. It is designed and run on a coordinated basis by universities and academic research institutes around Europe, under the auspices of the European Values Study Foundation which is based in Tilburg University in the Netherlands. It was first carried out in 1981, was repeated in 1990 and again in 1999-2000.

Participation in the EVS has grown from ten European societies in 1981 to twelve in 1990 and 33 in 1999-2000. Most central and eastern European societies were included for the first time in the 1999-2000 wave (for technical details on the 1999-2000 round see Halman 2001).[1] An adapted and extended version of the standard EVS was carried out in Northern Ireland in 1999 and the Republic of Ireland in late 1999 and early 2000, under the direction of the present authors. This version replicated the core elements of the EVS as applied generally in Europe but also included an extensive range of questions on aspects of culture, identity and the constitutional situation that are peculiar to Ireland. Care was taken to ensure consistency in the design and implementation of the survey north and south of the border so as to maximise the comparability of the data.

The 1999-2000 EVS survey was carried out by means of face-to-face interviews with random samples of the adult population (age 18+) in both the North and the Republic. The achieved sample sizes were 1,000 in the North and 1,012 in the Republic (for further details, see the methodological sections in Halman 2001). Survey fieldwork was carried out between October 1999 and February 2000 in the Republic of Ireland and between September and November 1999 in Northern Ireland. The sample for the Republic was weighted by sex, age and education based on population totals from the 1997 Labour Force Survey, while the sample for the North was weighted by household size based on the Northern Ireland 1991 census.

In addition, as an integral part of the conduct of the EVS in Ireland, a special booster sample of 257 Protestants was selected and interviewed in the Republic in the period January to mid-March 2000. This sample was drawn in two stages. First, District Electoral Divisions (DEDs) and urban wards were selected in which Protestants amounted to at least 25 per cent of the population according to the 1991 Census of Population. DEDs are the smallest area units for which Census data are available in rural areas, and wards are the urban equivalent. A combination of random screening of households and 'snowballing' techniques was then used to achieve quota samples of Protestants in these areas (snowballing means that

[1] Some loose coordination takes place between the European Values Study and the World Values Study, the latter being a similar programme of survey research conducted in non-European countries under the direction of scholars at the Institute of Social Research at the University of Michigan. Data from the 1981 and 1990 rounds of the EVS have been integrated into the WVS database held in the University of Michigan, but similar integration of the 1999-2000 data has yet to take place.

targeted individuals or households who have already been contacted are asked where other target individuals or households might be found). The resulting sample of 257 Protestants in the Republic was distributed by county as follows:

	%		%
Carlow	2.8	Monaghan	11.6
Cavan	9.9	Offaly	2.3
Cork County	6.5	Sligo	2.3
Donegal	26.6	Tipperary North Riding	3.1
Dún Laoghaire-Rathdown	4.2	Tipperary South Riding	0.6
Kildare	1.1	Westmeath	0.3
Kilkenny	0.6	Wexford	5.4
Laois	4.5	Wicklow	15.5
Leitrim	2.0		
Mayo	0.8	Total	100.0

The Republic of Ireland participated in the two previous waves of the EVS, with the result that trends over almost two decades on the core indicators in the EVS can be traced using these sources (see Fogarty 1984 and Whelan 1994 for the main results of these earlier surveys). Northern Ireland was included in the 1981 and 1990 round only on the basis of a sub-sample (numbering 250 cases for the whole of Northern Ireland) within a larger sample of the United Kingdom. While these 1981 and 1990 Northern Ireland samples are large enough to produce aggregate measures of attitudes and values in Northern Ireland as a whole, they are too small to allow for the detailed breakdowns between sub-populations that are of central interest here.

In order to fill the gaps in potential cross-time comparisons, we have trawled through the wide variety of surveys conducted in Northern Ireland and the Republic since the late 1960s and, on this basis, we can trace the evolution of at least some of the attitudes and values we are interested in. We have also brought our time line forward from the date of the main survey with which we are concerned (late 1999 early 2000) by incorporating the results of subsequent surveys. These include the Northern Ireland Life and Times surveys (1999-2003), the Irish Social and Political Attitudes Survey conducted in late 2001 to early 2002, and especially the European Social Survey as conducted in both the North and the Republic in 2002-2003. Further details on these and other surveys used in our study and on the locations from which the datasets may be obtained are provided in Appendix 1.

2
Historical legacies and contemporary attitudes: a North-South comparison

Introduction

This chapter has two objectives. The first is to place the development of the values and attitudes that are the subject matter of the book in historical and comparative context. The second objective is, in the light of the historical analysis, to develop and test some broad hypotheses regarding the shape of contemporary attitudes in Ireland, North and South. As the evidence to be used in the test will be taken from the 1999-2000 European Values Survey, achievement of this second objective will provide an overview of the main dimensions of values and attitudes covered in the survey that is at the core of this book. This in turn will help to structure the presentation and interpretation of the evidence in the chapters to follow.

Examination of the historical context requires a suitable framework, preferably one that has a comparative dimension capable of linking developments in Ireland to similar or contrasting developments elsewhere. Fortunately, it is possible to build on a body of knowledge and insight that has been accumulated over recent decades, during which time both parts of Ireland have attracted more than their fair share of theoretical and comparative dissection. The reason the Republic of Ireland has attracted the critical attention of comparativists is that its institutions, political processes, attitudes and values have seemed to many to be exceptional. While the reasons Northern Ireland has attracted comparative attention are, by and large, less happy ones, this very fact has given a sharper edge to the theoretical discussions involved.

To review all of the ensuing theoretical and comparative literature would be beyond the scope of this chapter. Instead we draw on a number of works that criticise and synthesise prevailing ideas and propose broad comparative schemas.

We begin with the notion of cleavage and cleavage structures, locating the analysis of cleavage in a historical state-building perspective. Were we analysing cleavages in the Republic of Ireland only, that broad state-building perspective might be sufficient. However, the cleavages in Northern Ireland are no ordinary cleavages and, in order to capture the complexities and intensities of the Northern Ireland conflict, we incorporate certain features that are specific to the situation in Northern Ireland. Having briefly considered the historical development of both societies in the light of the framework put forward, the chapter specifies the expectations one would have regarding the nature and structure of contemporary cleavages in Ireland, North and South. These expectations are then tested by means of a factor analysis of the relevant data in the EVS. The final section of the chapter uses the results of this analysis to provide a sketch-map of the topics and themes that will be pursued in the chapters that follow.

Political culture and political cleavage

Beneath the ebb and flow of public reaction to the events and topics of the day, there is a more fundamental level of attitudes, beliefs, identities, aspirations and predispositions that have been moulded by historical developments and experiences. These are sometimes referred to as values (hence the name European Values Study). However, this usage, while conventional and perhaps convenient, is ultimately unsatisfactory. As van Deth and Scarbrough, after a thorough review of the literature, put it: 'There does not ... seem to be a general or common understanding of the value concept in the social sciences, no dominant or accepted conceptualisation that we can take up' (van Deth and Scarbrough 1995: 23). For good measure they add: 'Even a brief review of the psychological and social-psychological literature shows a lack of consensus comparable to that found among the social sciences.' In lieu of a standard, accepted conceptualisation, van Deth and Scarbrough propose the concept of a 'values-attitudes axis' in which values are thought of as general orientations and attitudes as 'the immediate antecedents of behaviour'. One might push this notion a bit further and add that attitudes are themselves also antecedents, in this case antecedents of opinion, taking the latter terms as referring to immediate responses to specific issues and events. Be that as it may, our basic view is that one should not become too preoccupied with the issue of terminology and that precise definitions will probably continue to elude us. The essential point is that what we want to get at is the substratum of identities, beliefs, ideologies, attitudes and aspirations that go to make up the political cultures of the societies we are concerned with.

In any given society, it is likely that at least some aspects of the political culture are mainly consensual. For example, there is, by and large, agreement in most liberal democracies on the basic rules and procedures that determine how decisions are made. However, in most societies there will also be aspects of the underlying values, attitudes and identities in each society that generate conflict rather than consensus and pit individuals and groups against each other in ways that involve greater or lesser degrees of intensity and polarisation. Such conflicts can be usefully thought of in Lipset and Rokkan's terms as 'cleavages' (Lipset and Rokkan, 1967: 1-3) .

It is perhaps necessary to emphasise that we are using the term cleavage here in its traditional meaning of a sociocultural conflict that may or may not be linked to groups with identifiable social characteristics, and that may or may not be expressed in institutional forms of political conflict such as political parties. This, as we understand it, is the sense in which the term cleavage was originally used by Lipset and Rokkan. Observing that cleavages do not translate themselves into party oppositions as a matter of course, Lipset and Rokkan pose the crucial question: 'How does a sociocultural conflict get translated into an opposition between parties?' We should note, however, that, in contrast to this usage, recent writing has tended to attach much more specific connotations to the term cleavage. For example, drawing upon Bartolini and Mair (1990), Gallagher and his co-authors argue that a cleavage involves a social division, a consciousness of collective identity, and expression in organisational terms (Gallagher *et al.*, 1995: 210-211). In similar vein, Knutsen and Scarborough (1995: 494) state:

> In place of the general notion of cleavages as deep-seated socio-structural conflicts with political significance, our concept of cleavage encompasses three distinct but intertwined phenomena. First, cleavage is rooted in a relatively persistent social division which gives rise to objectively identifiable groups within a society ... Secondly, a cleavage engages some set of values common to members of the group ... Thirdly, a cleavage is institutionalised in some form of organisation – most commonly a political party, but also in churches, unions, and other associational groups.

The problem with these all-embracing conceptions of cleavage is that they obscure the fundamental question of *whether and how* socio-cultural cleavages get translated into oppositions between parties and/or other organised groups. It also obscures the question of how the relationship between cleavages and their organisational or institutional expressions may change over time. In sum, the term cleavage as used here refers to broad socio-cultural conflicts, contrasts or oppositions that are to be found among the mass of people in a society.

Some societies develop multiple cleavages, which may overlap and reinforce each other or may be crosscutting, the usual assumption being that crosscutting cleavages tend to ameliorate conflict. Other societies may develop a cleavage only on a single dimension while having a consensus on other dimensions. The possibility of either a single dominant cleavage or a set of closely coinciding or overlapping cleavages has led many to argue that the most satisfactory approach to the analysis of cleavage is to assume that there is a single dimension of conflict, namely conflict between left and right. The problem is that this unidimensional assumption is even less plausible now than it was for much of the twentieth century when the bipolar international conflict between capitalism and communism gave it some relevance. But even such limited credibility had been questioned by comparative analyses of political cleavages long before the collapse of communism. The most influential such analysis was that of Lipset and Rokkan. They suggested that there were four dimensions of cleavage and that these were a result of large-scale processes involved in the building of national states and the formation of national economies in modern Europe (Lipset and Rokkan, 1967).

An obvious advantage of this framework in the present context is that much of the conflict in Ireland has had to do with precisely one of these two processes, i.e. state-building. Analysing the conflict in Ireland in terms of the broad state-building processes in these islands helps to put what is often regarded as a unique set of Irish circumstances in comparative perspective. Such a state-building or nation-building perspective applies as much to the North as to the perhaps more obvious state-building experience of the Republic. As McGarry and O'Leary (1995: 348) put it, 'Northern Ireland is properly understood as the site of twin nation-building failures, an area with two peoples which the British have been unable to integrate successfully into the British nation and which Irish nationalists have been unable to integrate into the Irish nation.'

In deriving their four dimensions of cleavage, Lipset and Rokkan adopt a broad historical perspective that takes into account the two great revolutions of modern European history: the national revolution and the industrial revolution. The national revolution, the archetype of which was the French revolution, was essentially about building the nation-state. This process tended to generate two cleavages. The first of these – the centre-periphery cleavage – involved the conflict between the centralising efforts of the emerging modern state and the resistance of the territorial periphery that was intent on preserving or expanding its traditional autonomous or semi-autonomous status. In essence, the centre-periphery conflict is a conflict about nationalism – either the state-building nationalism of the centre or the (potentially) secessionist nationalism of the periphery. The second cleavage arose from the struggle between the state-builders and the church, as the latter resolutely defended its traditional privileges.

Of course, both these state-building cleavages were superimposed on the earlier great divides in Europe introduced by the Enlightenment (secular humanism versus the theocratic impulses in Christianity) and the Reformation (Protestant versus Catholic). In Britain and Ireland, the nineteenth-century boundary between the British 'centre' and the Irish 'periphery' lay not along the Irish Sea but along the social and geographical limits that the Reformation had reached in Ireland through the Cromwellian plantations of the 1650s. Within Ireland, the emerging church-state cleavage was transformed into a tension between a Protestant state and a Catholic people.

As these cleavages were working themselves out in Western Europe, the industrial revolution started to transform the national economy, generating two further cleavages. In the first of these, the interests of an emerging industrial economy and society were ranged against the interests of an agrarian economy and society; the second pitted capital against labour or owner against worker, producing what we tend to think of as the distinctively twentieth-century cleavage of (socio-economic) left versus right. The mistake of the unidimensional left-right approach is to think of this fourth cleavage as having entirely superseded the other three. What happened in fact was that the left-right cleavage was superimposed on existing cleavages (as each of the other cleavages itself had been) and the complexity of the cleavage systems of European societies in the twentieth century was due to the timing and shape of these successive superimpositions.

To this fourfold typology of cleavage, Lipset and Rokkan add two propositions. The first is that the period of political mobilisation that accompanied the extension of the suffrage is the defining moment in the development of the present-day political alignments. The second and related proposition is that the cleavages that were dominant at the time of the extension of the franchise became institutionalised and, as a result, have long outlived their origins. Writing in 1967, Lipset and Rokkan argued that the party systems of the 1960s reflected with few changes the cleavage structures that were dominant half-a-century previously. Within a decade of the formulation of this overarching historical interpretation, however, these systems began to look considerably less stable (Bartolini and Mair, 1990). This is a reminder that the stability postulated by the Lipset and Rokkan approach is contingent. Inherited cleavage structures may persist, may wear away, or may be subject to a re-structuring and realignment that establishes a new cleavage and a new alignment. However, before we can get to the point of discussing if and how cleavage structures in Ireland may have begun to change as the twenty-first century and the new millennium approached, it is necessary to examine the specific cleavages that manifested themselves in Ireland in the early decades of the twentieth century.

The dominance of the centre-periphery cleavage

Although electoral reform had been underway in the United Kingdom since the 1830s, the first real broadening of the franchise occurred in 1884. The impact of this on the development of mass political cleavages on the island of Ireland was limited, however, both by the modest extension of the franchise involved and by the restraint on party competition imposed by the extensive territorial segregation of the competing groups (Garvin, 1981: 89-90). The decisive extension of the franchise and the decisive mobilising election occurred in 1918, an election that saw the emergence in Ireland of radical nationalism as an electoral force in the form of a reconstituted Sinn Féin Party. Partly by anticipation and partly in parallel with these developments, the political mass mobilisation of unionism occurred through the Conservative and Unionist Party in the North. As a result, the centre-periphery cleavage (unionism versus nationalism) dominated the politics of the island and, a vital point, did so in the constitutional and political context of the United Kingdom of Great Britain and Ireland. The 1918 general election was, however, the last to be held in that context. Before the next Westminster election was due, southern Ireland had seceded from the Union. The particular form taken by secession had profound effects on the development and institutionalisation of political cleavages on the island of Ireland.

The secession of part of the periphery of the United Kingdom reinforced rather than resolved the centre-periphery or nationalist cleavage. In the South, the question of relations between the centre (London) and the periphery (Dublin) was contested not between nationalists and anti-nationalists but between moderate and extreme nationalists. The fineness of the distinctions that separated the two sides did nothing to soften the conflict, which soon erupted into a civil war between pro-treatyites and anti-treatyites and which, in a modified and constitutional form, went on to become the basis of the division between the two main political parties in the new state, Fianna Fáil and Cumann na nGaedheal (later renamed Fine Gael).

The secession of southern Ireland also reinforced the dominance of the centre-periphery or nationalist conflict within Northern Ireland. It did this by creating a narrow arena in which the lines of conflict were drawn with particular intensity and in which both protagonists could look to actors outside the arena for identification and support. Thus the very existence of the Irish Free State and its successor, the Republic of Ireland, exacerbated the conflict in Northern Ireland by creating a pole of attraction and identification among northern nationalists and a perception of an imminent external threat among northern unionists. On the other side of the conflict, the link with Britain was an essential part of unionist identity and an essential resource in the maintenance of the unionists' dominant position. This notion of the inseparability of the internal and external dimensions of the Northern Ireland problem is emphasised in several theoretical discussions. Thus, Ruane and Todd (1996: 7) regard Northern Ireland as both a 'distinct socio-spatial unit' with its own structures and relationships and as a 'product of a historic system of relationships that in its origins and dynamics operates at the level of the two islands'. Partition, they add, 'restructured this system but did not dissolve it ...' In similar vein, McGarry and O'Leary (1995: 349) emphasise that an explanation of the conflict in Northern Ireland requires 'an understanding of the subtle connections between endogenous and exogenous sources of antagonism, violence and stalemate'. Finally, the recognition of both internal and external dimensions of the problem plays a prominent role in Whyte's magisterial survey of the research literature on Northern Ireland up to 1989 (Whyte, 1990).

Obviously the presence of both internal and external aspects to the conflict in Northern Ireland has challenging implications for any effort to construct an interpretative framework that is at once capable of encompassing the complexity involved while still achieving a degree of parsimony and comparability. Ruane and Todd's response to this challenge is to put forward a framework that posits (a) five dimensions of difference, (b) a structure of dominance, dependence and inequality, and (c) a series of tendencies towards communal polarisation based on the five dimensions of difference. The five dimensions are: religion, ethnicity, settler-native status, ideologies of progress and backwardness, and nationality (Ruane and Todd, 1996: 290). McGarry and O'Leary on the other hand lean towards the parsimonious conclusion that, with certain qualifications, 'the national conflict has been the primary source of antagonism, violence and constitutional stalemate' (McGarry and O'Leary, 1995: 355). This emphasis on the primacy of the nationalist dimension fits with the Lipset and Rokkan interpretation emphasising the centre-periphery conflict. However, the choice between parsimony and complexity is not a strict either/or. Thus, McGarry and O'Leary supplement their emphasis on ethno-nationalism by noting that there are distinct advantages to thinking about the conflict in Northern Ireland as also having a settler-native dimension that stems from the particular way in which the area was colonised in the sixteenth and seventeenth centuries. The essential point in the settler-native perspective is that the introduction of large-scale settlement was 'a sufficient ... condition for interruption of the process of loyalty transformation and legitimation of central administrative authority identified by state-building theorists as necessary for successful state formation' (Lustick, quoted in McGarry and O'Leary, 1995: 332). This perspective leads to the conclusion that '[s]ettler-native zones tend to be especially polarised, replete with antagonistic cultures and socio-economic inequalities' (McGarry and O'Leary, 1995: 351). The overlap of these ideas with some of the categories in the Ruane and Todd framework is quite striking. In summary, and from the point of view of the analysis to be undertaken here, it seems best to regard the main cleavage in Northern Ireland as a nationalist cleavage, but one that must be seen in the light of the role of the two states to which the competing nationalisms orient themselves and in the light of an internal settler-native legacy of long historical lineage that generates significant actual and/or perceived inequalities.

Implications for other cleavages

As well as ensuring the continued predominance of nationalist or centre-periphery conflict, the secession of southern Ireland from the United Kingdom also affected the articulation of the other cleavages postulated by Lipset and Rokkan. This was especially so in the case of religion. In the South, secession created a religiously homogeneous society: the periphery that broke away was overwhelmingly and actively Catholic. The religious homogeneity of the newly independent state, the extremely high degree of religious practice and the close relationship that had existed between the Roman Catholic Church and the nationalist movement prior to secession resulted in a connection between church and state that was at once implicit and intimate. For half a century, this religious homogeneity and this connection ruled out any possibility of the development of a confessional-secular cleavage of the kind found in so many of the European states that were also predominantly Catholic. Religion played a very different role in the cleavage system in Northern Ireland. Whereas in the South conflict related to religion was suffocated by the prevailing religious homogeneity, in Northern Ireland religion as an element in the conflict was pushed to the forefront by the fact that religious denomination was the main ethnic marker that identified the majority unionist and minority nationalist communities.

The other main effect of secession was to sideline the left-right cleavage in both the North and the South, though for different reasons in each case. Given the overwhelmingly agrarian nature of the southern economy, the material basis for any owner-worker cleavage in the newly independent Irish Free State was extremely weak. Moreover, the dominance of an ideologically conservative Catholic Church made the political climate particularly inhospitable to the politics of the left. On top of this, the 1918 election saw the self-exclusion of the Labour movement from what turned out to be the foundation election of the new political order. Given the higher level of industrialisation in the North, the prospects for the emergence of an owner-worker cleavage might have seemed greater there. As events turned out, this particular cleavage was either overshadowed by or subsumed into the all-powerful Protestant-unionist and Catholic-nationalist cleavage described above.

Change and the expected shape of contemporary cleavages

Although particular configurations of cleavages, once they have become institutionalised, are expected to show a substantial degree of stability, that stability can be attenuated, undermined or transformed by economic, social and political change. The possible impact of such changes need to be considered in relation to each of the cleavages, or potential cleavages, in both parts of the island of Ireland. Such consideration will make it possible to draw up a set of expectations regarding the nature and shape of the cleavages in Ireland, North and South, on the eve of the twenty-first century. These expectations – hypotheses, if you like – can then be tested using data for Northern Ireland and the Republic of Ireland from the EVS.

The centre-periphery or nationalist cleavage in the South came under pressure from an early stage mainly as a result of political and constitutional change. This was because a substantial part of what remained of the original centre-periphery conflict after 1922 was subsequently solved by the unilateral constitutional changes effected by the Fianna Fáil governments of the early 1930s, by the Anglo-Irish Treaty of 1938 and by the declaration of the Republic in 1948. Then, the part that was not solved (the Northern Ireland problem) seemed in the mid-1960s to evoke a moderate and modernising response in the Republic of Ireland, as manifested in the proposal to change articles 2 and 3 of the Constitution (Committee on the Constitution, 1967) and in the meeting of Taoiseach Seán Lemass and Prime Minister Terence O'Neill. But all of that was before the eruption of another phase of 'the troubles' in Northern Ireland.

After decades of political stalemate, things might have seemed more promising in Northern Ireland in the mid-1960s. Social, economic and cultural change was underway. A new Catholic middle class emerged as a result of the British post-war educational revolution. In politics, Northern Ireland had a reformist prime minister who seemed committed to change both within Northern Ireland itself and in relations between North and South. As it turned out, however, events quickly overtook the politics of gradualism. The forceful articulation of the demands of the Catholic minority through a series of civil rights marches may have been met at first by a tentatively reformist response from the government of Northern Ireland. This was, however, stymied by the reaction of extremists on the unionist side and rendered irrelevant by the confrontation between a police force that was almost exclusively drawn from the majority community and the civil rights and nationalist demonstrators on the streets. The result was a rapid slide into communal conflict and mutual fear and, in a short time, the emergence or re-emergence of terrorist activity. Unlike previous episodes, this phase of 'the troubles' went on and on – for twenty-five years, leaving more than 3,000 dead and many more injured and bereaved. The troubles did not just reinforce the prevailing nationalist-unionist conflict in Northern Ireland. They created it anew, each terrorist act, each security measure and each failed political initiative adding a fresh basis for grievance and polarisation.

The troubles had an ambiguous effect on attitudes in the Republic. Traditional nationalism was reinforced by events such as Bloody Sunday (1972) and the H-Block hunger strikes in 1981. Generally, however, the effect was the opposite: most of the time and for the majority of people in the Republic, the sheer intractability and bloody-mindedness of the conflict, repeatedly demonstrated in one violent incident after another and in the failure of one political initiative after another, undermined rather than reinforced the demands traditionally associated with Irish nationalism and weakened the position of the centre-periphery conflict in the cleavage system (Hayes and McAllister, 1996).

The wearying destructiveness of the conflict in Northern Ireland and the widespread presumption of its intractability explain the euphoria with which the IRA cease-fire of 1994 and the reciprocal cease-fire called by the main Loyalist terrorist groups were greeted. This transformation in the political situation would have been impossible and would certainly have been insufficient had it not been for the deep involvement since the early 1980s of both the British and Irish governments in a committed, if sometimes fractious, search for a solution. The Anglo Irish Agreement of 1985 and the Framework Document of 1995 were major milestones in this process. The dramatic opening created by the IRA cease-fire and by the changed inter-governmental context led to the all-party negotiations that eventually produced the British-Irish Agreement signed on Good Friday, 10 April 1998 (Mansergh, 2000).

Via the elections to the Northern Ireland Forum of June 1996 (the body set up to provide an all-party negotiating forum, from which the groundwork for the Good Friday Agreement eventually emerged), the public in Northern Ireland had been a marginal but real player at the point of initiation of the all-party negotiations. After the signing of the Agreement, public opinion, North and South, briefly moved to centre-stage, as the Agreement made endorsement by both publics in simultaneous referendums a necessary condition of further progress. That endorsement was forthcoming – by 94 per cent in the Republic and 71 per cent in Northern Ireland.[1]

Taking all of these changes and developments into account, what expectations would one have regarding the shape and status of the centre-periphery or nationalist cleavage in the two parts of Ireland today? Early in the century both states had been founded amidst bloody conflict over nationalist issues. In one of the states, Northern Ireland, conflicts concerning nationalism had reoccurred throughout the century, with the most persistent and virulent reocurrence marking the final quarter of the century. In the other, what is now the Republic of Ireland, a conflict over nationalism gave rise to civil war and became the main division in the party system. This division gradually softened, however, as a combination of bilateral (Anglo-Irish) negotiations and unilateral constitutional change disposed of some of the issues in the 1930s and 1940s and as other and more immediate concerns moved to centre-stage in the succeeding decades. One would, therefore, expect to find a nationalist cleavage in both systems. However, the status of that cleavage is likely to be quite different in each. In the Republic it cannot be expected to be the dominant cleavage it once was, whereas in the North its dominance can be expected to have been reinforced by the struggle and trauma of the most recent round of the troubles and by the on-going difficult search for a means of stabilising

[1] If one takes into account the different rates of turnout in the two societies (81.1 per cent in Northern Ireland as against 56.3 per cent in the Republic) and calculates the 'yes' vote as a proportion of the registered electorate, one finds that the proportion of the population which voted for the Agreement was very similar on both sides of the border.

and building upon the current agreement (Horowitz, 2001). The notion that certain cleavages may be dominant and that the order of dominance may vary over time is emphasised by Lipset and Rokkan: 'There is a hierarchy of cleavage bases in each system and these orders of political primacy not only vary among polities, but also tend to undergo changes over time. Such differences and changes in the political weight of socio-cultural cleavages set fundamental problems for comparative research' (Lipset and Rokkan, 1967: 6).

Turning to expectations regarding the religious versus secular cleavage, the Republic of Ireland, from about 1960 on, has been exposed to the same secularising and liberalising tendencies that affected all advanced industrial democracies. However, the possibility that overt political cleavage would emerge in this area has been blunted by the availability of the referendum device as a means of dealing with the main issues.[2] In short, in respect to this area, one would expect to find in the Republic of Ireland a strong religious versus secular, conservative versus liberal, and confessionalist versus pluralist value cleavage but one that is only partially politicised, i.e. that expresses itself in referendum behaviour but not, perhaps precisely because of referendums, in party choice or party realignment.

The same secularising forces were present in Northern Ireland, perhaps indeed from an earlier stage and more powerfully. However, because the starting point there was different and because religion played a different role in the Northern Ireland cleavage system, these forces were less likely to push a religious-secular cleavage to the forefront; they were also unlikely to weaken the link between religion and national identity. In Northern Ireland, therefore, one would expect religious denomination to be closely aligned with the dominant nationalist-unionist cleavage. Secondly, one would expect religious commitment, or religiosity as such, to be part of a subordinate cleavage dimension that would also include attitudes to moral issues (abortion, divorce, etc).

Throughout the twentieth century there were those, in both the Republic of Ireland and Northern Ireland, who believed that the key to the solution of the problems of both societies lay in the realignment of politics along left-right lines (Bew *et al.,* 1995). As noted above, the left-right cleavage had got off to a bad start in both jurisdictions, though for different reasons in each case. However, around about the mid to late 1960s it seemed that the tide of economic and social change might be about to favour the emergence of class-based politics. In retrospect, one can see that economic developments in the late twentieth century did nothing to improve the prospects of a left-right realignment. With admittedly some bad

---

[2] The initiation of a referendum might be expected to have the effect of heightening the salience of the cleavage and of polarising the protagonists. However, the resolution of successive issues by each referendum tends to insulate the political parties from any pressure to realign along religious-secular or confessionalist-pluralist lines. For a more extended discussion, see Sinnott (1995).

patches along the way, the Republic of Ireland saw the creation of a post-industrial economy that thrived on the basis of a combination of inward investment, an educated workforce and deregulation. Meanwhile, the Northern Ireland economy came to depend increasingly on British subsidies (see Gaffikin and Morrison, 1990). Neither situation was conducive to the late emergence of a dominant left-right cleavage. This would suggest that the left-right cleavage is likely to be subordinate and weakly structured in both societies.

Turning to the potential for the emergence of a new cleavage, contemporary economic and social developments would lead one to expect that environmental concerns might crystallise into an emerging cleavage dimension. Postmaterialist theory argues that such a dimension would be part of a wider phenomenon. The postmaterialist thesis maintains that, in a 'silent revolution', which began in the 1960s, a new, mainly intergenerational, cleavage between materialists and postmaterialists has emerged to compete with and in some cases displace the cleavage legacies of the national and industrial revolutions. According to this view, the value priorities of materialists are economic and physical security and their policy demands focus on economic growth, on controlling inflation and on maintaining internal law and order and external national security. Postmaterialists, in contrast, value personal freedom and fulfilment, quality of life, social and political participation and protection of the environment (Inglehart, 1977: 1990). Accordingly, we have two sub-hypotheses here. The first focuses on the strength and clarity of the environmental dimension and on its position in the hierarchy of cleavages in both jurisdictions. The second relates to whether, in line with the Inglehart thesis, such an environmental dimension is part of a wider set of postmaterialist values. Clearly these are matters that can only be determined by empirical investigation.

Value cleavages North and South: the evidence

The EVS survey in both the Republic and the North included a wide range of questions dealing with the kinds of issues that arise in any discussion of values and political cleavages in the two parts of Ireland. We now examine the responses to these questions in order to provide an overview of the contemporary value cleavages in both societies and to compare what is found to the expectations just outlined. The potential raw material for this analysis consists of a very large number of questionnaire items that cover attitudes to the Northern Ireland problem and to issues such as abortion, divorce, homosexuality and general sexual mores, the role of religion in politics, the role of the state and of the market in the economy, issues of equality, and, finally, environmental and postmaterialist issues. Preliminary analysis of the data resulted in the selection of a set of twenty items regarded as being most likely to capture the hypothesised dimensions. In order to explore the extent of alignment between value cleavages and religious identity and orientation, variables indicating religious denomination (Catholic and Protestant) and degree of religiosity were also included. The same set of twenty-three variables was used for the analysis in both societies; the full wording of the individual questions used is presented in Figures 2.1 to 2.4. Many of these items are explored in detail in subsequent chapters. Here we are concerned with a broad characterisation of the value structures they reveal.

Factor analysis is a widely used statistical technique that is appropriate to the kind of research question just posed. The technique examines the relationships between a given set of variables (in this case the responses to the questionnaire items) in order to discover the common factors or dimensions underlying the pattern of responses. The first thing to be decided in a factor analysis is the number of factors or dimensions that best account for the patterns in the data. As indicated in the foregoing discussion, we have an *a priori* expectation that there will be four factors in each case, though with differences of status or priority attached to particular factors or dimensions. However, part of the purpose in carrying out the analysis is to ascertain whether there are more or fewer factors than hypothesised. The decision as to the number of factors can be made on the basis of a number of statistical criteria; the criterion used in the present analysis is the 'scree test'.[3] In the case of both Northern Ireland and the Republic of Ireland, this test indicated that five rather than four factors should be extracted. The implications of this will

Figure 2.1: Wording of the five attitude items relating to religious and moral issues used in the factor analysis

Please tell me for each of the following statements whether you think it can always be justified, never be justified, or something in between.	• Taking the drug marijuana or hashish • Homosexuality • Abortion (1 ——— 10) Never Always
How much do you agree or disagree with each of the following:	• Politicians who do not believe in God are unfit for public office • It would be better for Ireland (NIrl) if more people with strong religious beliefs held public office (1=Agree Strongly; 5=Disagree Strongly)

Figure 2.2: Wording of the five attitude items relating to left-right issues used in the factor analysis

How would you place your views on this scale?	• Private ownership of business and industry should be increased	Government ownership of business and industry should be increased
	(1 ________	10)
In political matters, people talk of 'the left; and 'the right'. How would you place your views on this scale, generally speaking?	(1 ________ Left	10) Right
How would you place your views on this scale?	• Individuals should take more responsibility for themselves	The state should take more responsibility to ensure that everyone is provided for
	(1 ________	10)
	• Competition is good; it stimulates people to work hard and develop new ideas	Competition is harmful; it brings out the worst in people
	(1 ________	10)
Please tell me for each statement how important it is to you.	• Eliminating big inequalities in income between citizens	
	(1=Very Important; 5=Not at all Important)	

Figure 2.3: Wording of the five attitude items relating to Northern Ireland issues used in the factor analysis

Do you think the long-term policy for Northern Ireland should be for it:	• 1 = To remain part of the United Kingdom 2 = Or, to reunify with the rest of Ireland 3 = Independent state
And, how much say do you think an Irish government of any party should have in the way Northern Ireland is run? Do you think it should have:	• 1 = A great deal of say 2 = Some say 3 = A little say 4 = No say at all
There has been much discussion recently about some of the suggested constitutional and executive changes proposed in the Good Friday Agreement of last year. Looking at a list of some of these changes, could you tell me how you feel about each one?	• The removal of the Republic of Ireland's constitutional claim to Northern Ireland (1=Support Strongly; 5=Oppose Strongly)
Finally, here are some statements that people sometimes make about the situation in Northern Ireland. For each statement could you tell me whether you agree or disagree?	• There will never be peace in Northern Ireland until partition is ended • The British government should declare its intention to withdraw from Northern Ireland at a fixed date in the future (1=Strongly Agree; 5=Strongly Disagree)

Figure 2.4: Wording of the five attitude items/indices relating to environmental and postmaterialist issues used in the factor analysis

I am now going to read out some statements about the environment. For each one read out, can you tell me whether you agree strongly, agree, disagree or strongly disagree?	• I would give part of my income if I were certain that the money would be used to prevent environmental pollution • I would agree to an increase in taxes if the extra money were used to prevent environmental pollution • The Government has to reduce environmental pollution but it should not cost me money (1=Strongly Agree; 4=Strongly Disagree)
There is a lot of talk these days about what Ireland's aims should be for the next ten years. On this card are listed some of the goals to which different people would give top priority. If you had to choose, which of the things on this card would you say is most important? *And which would be the next most important?*	• Maintaining order in the nation • Giving people more say in important government decisions • Fighting rising prices • Protecting freedom of speech (Choices combined to form Inglehart postmaterialism index)
Here is a list of various changes in our way of life that might take place in the near future. Please tell me for each one, if it were to happen whether you think it would be a good thing, a bad thing, or don't you mind?	• Greater emphasis on the development of the individual (1=Good; 2=Don't Mind; 3=Bad)

be considered in the discussion of each factor solution below.

Once the number of factors or dimensions has been determined, they have to be interpreted. This is done by considering the contribution of each variable or questionnaire item to the factor as indicated by the magnitude of the factor 'loading' for that item – the higher the loading, the greater the contribution.[4] The factor loadings and other relevant statistical information for the Republic of Ireland and Northern Ireland are presented in Tables 2.1 and 2.2 respectively.

Republic of Ireland

The first and most important cleavage dimension in the Republic of Ireland is a combination of attitudes to issues of personal morality, the role of religious beliefs in politics, and degree of overall religiosity. The moral issues that load on this factor are not, as might have been expected, confined to issues of sexual morality (homosexuality and abortion) but include also the issue of consumption of marijuana. The substantial loadings on the factor of the items on the desirability of people in public office believing in God and holding strong religious beliefs indicate that moral preferences are seen as not being purely personal but are linked to views about the role of religion that can be summed up as confessionalist (linked to conservative moral views) versus pluralist (linked to liberal moral views). The remaining component of this cleavage is a single index measuring people's overall religious commitment and behaviour. In summary, this first factor or dimension of cleavage in the Republic of Ireland is a complex behavioural and attitudinal spectrum that is characterised at one end by religious commitment, conservative moral views and a confessional attitude to politics and, at the other end, by a secular outlook, liberal moral views and a pluralist conception of politics. As indicated by the order of the factors and the relative proportion of variance explained (see final row of Table 2.1), this is the dominant element in the system of cleavages in the Republic of Ireland as measured by the 1999-2000 EVS.

The second factor in the Republic of Ireland is defined by just three items, all of which tap attitudes to meeting the costs of preventing or reducing environmental pollution: making a direct contribution towards such costs from one's income; paying extra taxes in order to prevent pollution; and leaving it up to the government to reduce pollution but without this resulting in any monetary cost to oneself. It would perhaps be possible to see disagreement with the first two of these items and

[3] Sometimes the results of the scree test are indeterminate. However, Tabachnick and Fidell (2001: 621) note that 'results of the scree test are more obvious and reliable when sample size is large, communality values are high, and each factor has several variables with high loadings.' All these conditions are fulfilled in the present case.

[4] In the analyses that follows, the cut-off point used for considering a loading in the interpretation of a factor is 0.45, which is described as 'fair' on a scale running from excellent (0.71), to very good (0.63), to good (0.55), to fair (0.45), to poor (0.32) (Tabachnik and Fidell 2001: 625).

Table 2.1: Factor analysis of items potentially related to expected cleavages in the Republic of Ireland

	Component				
	1.00	2.00	3.00	4.00	5.00
Catholic	-0.22	0.00	0.00	-0.05	**0.84**
Protestant	-0.05	0.00	0.11	-0.03	**-0.82**
Index of religiosity	**-0.74**	-0.02	0.01	-0.03	0.23
Taking the drug marijuana or hashish can always be justified	**0.58**	-0.19	-0.04	0.04	-0.11
Homosexuality can always be justified	**0.65**	-0.27	0.13	-0.05	0.02
Abortion can always be justified	**0.67**	-0.09	0.03	-0.02	-0.08
Politicians who do not believe in God unfit for public office (1=ag)	**0.63**	0.00	0.04	-0.10	0.07
Better if people with strong religious beliefs held public office (1=ag)	**0.69**	0.09	-0.03	-0.13	0.00
Government ownership of business and industry should be increased	-0.04	0.05	-0.01	**0.76**	0.09
More 'right' than 'left'	-0.34	0.21	-0.01	-0.24	0.09
The state should take more responsibility for providing for people	0.00	0.08	-0.03	**0.72**	-0.07
Competition is harmful, it brings out the worst in people	0.00	0.02	0.02	**0.76**	0.02
Importance of eliminating big inequalities in income between citizens (1=imp)	0.06	-0.12	0.00	-0.04	0.05
Northern Ireland should reunify with the rest of Ireland	-0.05	-0.04	**-0.68**	0.03	0.09
Irish government should have no say in running Northern Ireland	0.01	0.13	**0.61**	-0.13	-0.10
Removal of Republic of Ireland's constitutional claim to Northern Ireland (1=support)	0.17	-0.06	**-0.55**	0.22	0.08
Never be peace in Northern Ireland until partition is ended (1=ag)	0.09	-0.23	**0.58**	0.12	0.20
British government should declare intention to withdraw from Northern Ireland (1=ag)	0.08	-0.24	**0.63**	0.11	0.10
Would give part of income to prevent environmental pollution (1=ag)	-0.07	**0.80**	0.01	0.06	0.16
Would agree to increase in taxes to prevent environmental pollution (1=ag)	0.01	**0.81**	-0.04	0.02	0.14
Environmental pollution should not cost me any money (1=ag)	0.10	**-0.65**	0.08	-0.11	0.03
Post-materialism – Inglehart scale	0.13	-0.16	-0.05	0.00	-0.25
Greater emphasis on development of individual	-0.05	0.04	-0.05	0.13	-0.02
Percent variance explained	12.56	9.04	8.28	8.22	7.23

Source: European Values Study, 1999-2000.

Note: Extraction method – Principal Component Analysis; Rotation method – Varimax with Kaiser Normalization.

Table 2.2: Factor analysis of items potentially related to expected cleavages in Northern Ireland

	Component				
	1.00	2.00	3.00	4.00	5.00
Catholic	**-0.82**	-0.22	-0.01	0.14	-0.01
Protestant	**0.73**	-0.08	-0.02	-0.28	-0.09
Index of religiosity	-0.21	**-0.65**	-0.11	-0.28	-0.08
v228 Taking the drug marijuana or hashish can always be justified	-0.23	**0.71**	-0.08	0.00	0.00
v232 Homosexuality can always be justified	-0.22	**0.73**	-0.07	0.03	0.06
v233 Abortion can always be justified	0.16	**0.76**	-0.03	-0.01	0.03
v129 Politicians who do not believe in God unfit for public office (1=ag)	0.06	0.25	-0.05	**0.72**	-0.08
v131 Better if people with strong religious beliefs held public office (1=ag)	0.02	0.32	-0.01	**0.72**	-0.03
o19 Government ownership of business and industry should be increased	-0.05	0.00	0.10	0.00	**0.70**
v185 More 'right' than 'left'	0.17	0.04	0.02	-0.40	-0.20
v186 The state should take more responsibility for providing for people	0.03	0.04	0.11	0.17	**0.64**
v188 Competition is harmful, it brings out the worst in people	0.03	0.10	-0.07	-0.08	**0.76**
v260 Importance of eliminating big inequalities in income between citizens (1=imp)	0.07	0.14	0.08	**-0.48**	0.01
irl9unit Northern Ireland should reunify with the rest of Ireland	**-0.73**	-0.04	-0.05	0.12	-0.13
irl11 Irish government should have no say in running Northern Ireland	**0.71**	-0.05	0.17	-0.14	-0.02
irl16 Removal of Republic of Ireland's constitutional claim to Northern Ireland (1=support)	**-0.67**	0.14	-0.01	-0.17	0.05
irl22 Never be peace in Northern Ireland until partition is ended (1=ag)	**0.53**	-0.10	0.22	0.31	0.08
irl24 British government should declare intention to withdraw from Northern Ireland (1=ag)	**0.79**	-0.03	0.12	0.09	0.06
v8 Would give part of income to prevent environmental pollution (1=ag)	0.11	-0.03	**0.85**	0.05	-0.01
v9 Would agree to increase in taxes to prevent environmental pollution (1=ag)	0.11	0.04	**0.87**	0.02	0.14
v10 Environmental pollution should not cost me any money (1=ag)	0.00	0.07	**-0.52**	0.15	-0.13
Post-materialism – Inglehart scale	-0.26	0.24	-0.26	0.05	0.04
v195mid Greater emphasis on development of individual	0.10	0.01	0.16	-0.04	0.17
Percent variance explained	16.99	10.32	8.73	7.93	7.07

Source: European Values Study, 1999-2000.

Note: Extraction Method – Principal Component Analysis;
Rotation Method – Varimax with Kaiser Normalization

agreement with the third as compatible with a radical environmentalism which would see all pollution problems being solved by application of the principle that the polluter pays. However, since everybody contributes to the problem of environmental pollution in one way or another and since solutions to the problem are inconceivable without extra cost to the individual either directly or by way of taxation or by way of higher prices, it is probably more realistic to see the three items as measuring the overall degree of commitment of the respondent to dealing with environmental problems. If this is the case and if one accepts the postmaterialist thesis, one would expect these environmental items to be correlated with the general measure of postmaterialism and with other attitudes that are said to be part of the postmaterialist syndrome. Postmaterialism as such is measured in this analysis by the classic Inglehart index. The analysis also includes an item on measuring attitudes to 'greater emphasis on the development of the individual', which is related to the broader conception of postmaterialism. Plausible as the connection between postmaterialism and environmentalism may seem to be, the factor analytic results show quite clearly that environmental and postmaterialist attitudes are simply not connected in the Republic of Ireland sample (see Table 2.1). There is, in other words, some evidence of an environmental attitudinal dimension or cleavage; however, there is no evidence that this has anything to do with a comprehensive postmaterialist ideology or outlook that might inject new life into the system of value cleavages. Indeed there is no evidence of anything resembling a postmaterialist attitudinal syndrome, even one unconnected with environmentalism.

The third factor or dimension in the Republic of Ireland is defined by the five items measuring attitudes to the Northern Ireland problem. These comprise three items measuring traditional nationalist views and aspirations (preference for a united Ireland, the demand for British withdrawal from Northern Ireland and anti-partitionist sentiment) and two items measuring attitudes to the current peace process (attitude to the removal of articles 2 and 3 of the Irish Constitution (Bunreacht na hÉireann) and attitude to the degree of involvement that the Irish government should have in running Northern Ireland). Given the nature of these five items, this third attitudinal dimension can be thought of as pro- versus anti-irredentist nationalism. Thus, the factor analysis confirms the expectation that such a cleavage would exist, while also confirming the expectation that, in the Republic of Ireland, it would no longer be the dominant cleavage it is assumed to have been in the past.

Finally, the analysis included five items that were expected to figure on an anticipated left-right dimension. In the event only three of the five make the cut. As Table 2.1 shows, the three items that are included in the dimension deal with attitudes to competition and to the role of the state in the provision of goods and services. One of the two excluded items deals with attitudes to the elimination of 'big inequalities in income' as an important characteristic of a just society. As is confirmed by more detailed analysis in Chapter 7, egalitarian attitudes and aspirations do not in fact combine with attitudes to the role of the state and the market in a single overall left-right ideological dimension. The failure of the remaining excluded item (the left-right self-placement scale) to load on this dimension is equally significant, confirming as it does that the fourth factor in Table 2.1 is not a comprehensive left-right dimension. The factor captures one aspect of such a dimension but its specificity is better expressed by labelling it 'state versus market'. However, attitudes to equality do not seem to correlate with this state-market dimension in a way that traditional conceptions of left and right would suggest, nor does the self-perception as left or right have a bearing on either the state versus market sub-dimension or on attitudes to equality.

As Table 2.1 indicates, the factor analytic results also suggest the existence of a fifth, unanticipated factor. This is defined by the two denominational variables, Catholic and Protestant. The implications of this fifth factor are interesting for what they indicate is *not* the case. It is at least conceivable that the Catholic-Protestant distinction would have shown up either on the first or the third factor. In other words, being Catholic might have been associated with conservative moral views and being Protestant might have shown up on the opposite, liberal side of this cleavage. Alternatively, it is conceivable that, in sympathy with co-religionists in Northern Ireland, Protestants in the Republic of Ireland would have veered towards the anti-irredentist pole of the third factor, placing Catholics on the irredentist side. The evidence shows that neither of these theoretical possibilities is realised to any degree. Catholics and Protestants in the Republic of Ireland are different but the difference is entirely unrelated to either the main contemporary cleavage (religious-moral-conservatism versus secular-moral-liberalism) or the residue of the main historical cleavage (pro- versus anti-irredentist nationalism) in the society. This *non-alignment* of religious denomination with any of the attitudinal cleavages in the Republic is in sharp contrast to the role played by religious denomination in the analysis of the same set of items in Northern Ireland.

Northern Ireland

The first point to note about cleavages in Northern Ireland is that, as expected and in contrast to the situation in the Republic of Ireland, nationalism is the dominant cleavage (see factor 1 in Table 2.2). Secondly, this dominant cleavage is clearly linked to denominational differences – being Catholic or Protestant is part of the cleavage. The evidence is that this has nothing to do with religion as such. An index of religious commitment was included in the analysis but this shows no linkage either to denominational affiliation or to the unionist-nationalist conflict. Instead, it turns up as part of the conservative versus liberal dimension in the second factor (see below). The lack of connection between religious commitment and unionist or nationalist ideology or preferences is worth emphasising if only because of the not-infrequent characterisation of the problem of Northern Ireland as a religious conflict.

The *second* factor or dimension of cleavage in Northern Ireland mirrors the *first* dimension in the Republic of Ireland with one important difference. Whereas in the South there is evidence of a link between religiosity/moral conservatism, on the one hand, and the view that religious beliefs should play a role in politics, on the other, in Northern Ireland, there is no sign of such linkage. People within Northern Ireland differ from one another on a spectrum that combines degree of religiosity and commitment to conservative versus liberal morality but, in contrast to the Republic, these differences do not spill over into views about the role of religion in politics.

The third factor in Northern Ireland measures pro- versus anti-environmentalism but without any reference to postmaterialism. The results in this respect are very similar to the results in the Republic of Ireland. However, the fourth factor in Northern Ireland is quite distinctive, being built mainly around the two items that deal with the role of religion in politics with a more marginal reference to attitudes to income inequality. The relationship between these attitudes is such that endorsement of an active role for religion in politics is linked to lack of emphasis on the elimination of income inequalities and, more marginally, to self-placement as right-wing on a left-right scale. The really striking point, however, is that endorsement of a role for religion in politics has nothing to do with commitment to a conservative moral agenda (as it has in the Republic). And this is despite the fact that the issue of a conservative versus liberal moral agenda linked to religious commitment does constitute a dimension of cleavage in Northern Ireland.

The fifth and final cleavage dimension in Northern Ireland comprises the state-versus-market items that constituted the fourth dimension in the Republic of Ireland. Again as is the case in the Republic of Ireland, the factor is as significant for what it omits as for what it includes, the significant omission being any reference to equality issues or to left-right self placement.

Conclusion

This chapter set itself the limited objective of identifying the main features of the structure of mass attitudes and values in the Republic of Ireland and in Northern Ireland and of relating those features to the historical development of political culture in Ireland, North and South.

In pursuing these objectives, the chapter has identified certain features that both societies have in common while also turning up certain key differences. The features that both societies have in common are four broadly similar cleavage dimensions, namely a nationalist dimension, a religious and moral conservative dimension, an environmentalist dimension and a truncated left-right dimension. The first key difference in the structure of attitudes in the two societies lies in the order of importance or priority attaching to these cleavages. The religious conservative versus secular liberal dimension is the dominant dimension of attitudes in the Republic of Ireland but plays a subordinate role in Northern Ireland. Conversely, the nationalist dimension is dominant in Northern Ireland and subordinate in the Republic. The second main difference is that the dominant cleavage in each society shows a distinctive element that is not part of that dimension of cleavage in the other society. The distinctive additional element in the religious-moral conservative dimension in the Republic of Ireland is its link to confessionalist attitudes; the distinctive additional element in the nationalist dimension in Northern Ireland is its link to religious denomination.

The striking aspect of the environmentalist and left-right cleavages is what is not included in each. The environmentalist dimension does not connect to any wider set of attitudes but seems to be limited to particular environmental policy issues. It is not, in other words, part of a wider set of materialist versus postmaterialist concerns, with which environmental attitudes have been linked in other European societies. Similarly, the left-right dimension is truncated in the sense that it does not include either attitude to equality or self-identification on a left-right scale.

This account of the overall shape and structure of contemporary attitudes in Ireland, North and South, is consistent with the historical origins and development of each society as outlined at the beginning of this chapter. The account is, however, very broad brush. Its contribution to this book is to define the topics for further research and analysis, while helping to situate them in historical context. The main thrust of the chapters that follow is to pursue these research topics in some detail with a view to teasing out the nature and extent of conflict and consensus within and between the societies, communities and traditions in question. Given the centrality of religion to two of the cleavages identified by the analysis in the present chapter, Chapter 3 starts by focusing on religion and on the attitudes and values associated with it. The chapter examines both religious affiliation (and non-affiliation), practice (and non-practice), belief (and non-belief), thereby establishing the basis for examining, in later chapters, the relationship between religion and political and social attitudes, values and aspirations.

Chapter 4 tackles the nationalist cleavage identified in the present chapter, dealing not just with the Northern Ireland related items considered here but incorporating also evidence from questions on national identity and on the related themes of ethnicity, ethno-nationalism, national pride, and citizenship. The chapter includes detailed examination of the relationship between religious affiliation and national and related identities. Still focusing on the nationalist cleavage, Chapter 5 then examines the preferences regarding constitutional issues that flow from this range of nationalist attitudes and considers the implications of these preferences for the on-going search for a stable solution to the problem in Northern Ireland.

Chapter 6 takes up the other major cleavage identified by the analysis in this chapter, namely the bundle of issues that go to make up the religious-conservative versus secular-liberal dimension. Under this heading we examine what are broadly termed 'family values' as well as the specific issues of sexual morality that are often bundled together under this term. The impact of religion on attitudes in this area is also explored.

This leaves two apparently weaker but potentially powerful attitudinal dimensions – left-right orientations and environmentalism/postmaterialism. In examining attitudes in these areas, Chapter 7 also includes evidence on gender issues and focuses in particular on the problem of the apparent lack of connection between left-right self-identification and classic socio-economic conceptions of left and right. Given this lack of connection, the chapter explores the possibility that left and right may have as much or more to do with the religious-conservative versus secular liberal dimension as with the socio-economic left-right division.

Coming down, as it were, from the high ground of cleavage politics (or the lack thereof), Chapter 8 focuses on the individual in society and on the individual's experience of society, dealing with work experience, life satisfaction and well being and with a topic on which there has been much discussion of late, the incidence, distribution and significance of social capital.

This brings us to the final substantive chapter of the book – that dealing with confidence in political and social institutions and with orientations to political participation. Whether the conflicts that characterise a political system originate at the macro-level of value cleavage or at the individual level of personal interests and life experiences, they must be articulated, aggregated and, ultimately, resolved. The capacity of the political system to do this is in part a function of the legitimacy of the system. Having examined a wide range of evidence related to the nature and extent of the conflicts with which the political institutions must deal, we turn in Chapter 9 to the capacity of the existing political systems to meet these challenges, assessing capacity in terms of confidence in institutions and orientations towards political participation. A key question in this chapter revolves around the effect of the different recent political histories of the two societies on attitudes to political institutions and on citizens' conceptions of their own role in the political process.

The final chapter (chapter 10) summarises the main results of our study and reflects on the implications of our findings.

3

Religion

Background

The Republic of Ireland and Northern Ireland have long stood out in Europe as places where religion and churches matter. In the Republic, the high-point of religious commitment had already passed by the late 1960s and signs of decline had appeared, as shown, for example, by the diminishing authority of the churches in the political sphere and the drying up of vocations to the religious life (Fuller, 2002; Inglis, 1998; Fahey, 1992). In Northern Ireland, the authority of the churches remained stronger, most notably within the ghettoised working-class Catholic population. In fact, its position seemed to some to have strengthened in the province with the emergence of the troubles in the 1970s (O'Connor, 1993: 272-333; Elliott, 2000: 474-475). It was not until the onset of the H-Block protests and hunger strikes of the early 1980s that divisions emerged in public between the Catholic Church and the more militant republican sections of its laity.

At the same time, popular religious commitment remained strong throughout the island of Ireland. Reporting on the 1981 European Values Study, Fogarty (1984: 8) found that: 'every indicator of belief, informal and formal practice and attitudes to the church or churches, shows Irish people, North and South, to be far more inclined to religion than those of other countries in Europe.' By 1990, according to Hornsby-Smith and Whelan (1994), some signs of a shift away from religion could be detected among those aged under 40 years. However, overall, it seemed that Ireland remained exceptionally religious by European standards and there was 'no evidence of a general process of secularisation operating throughout the 1980s' (Hornsby-Smith and Whelan, 1994: 42). Inglehart and Baker's (2000) comparison of 37 mainly western societies in 1990-91 confirmed this view by placing both the Republic and Northern Ireland at the upper edge of the international range in terms of both regular church attendance and the importance people attached to God in their daily lives.

From the point of view of mass attitudes and behaviour, therefore, the two parts of Ireland seemed to present an exception to the secularising trend which many social scientists had long regarded as central to modernisation (Wilson, 1982; Dobbelaere, 1993; Lechner, 1991; Bruce, 1999, 2002; Halman and Riis, 1999). Some researchers sought out special features of the Irish case, such as its history of religious-ethnic conflict and the continuing importance of religiously-based ethnic identity, in order to explain this exceptionalism (Bruce, 1999: 23-26). Paradoxically, *both* the main religious traditions on the island – Catholic and Protestant – could regard themselves as an embattled minority religion in certain contexts, while at the same time asserting their majority status in others (on the importance of minority status as a prop to religious attachment, see Stark and Finke, 2000: 245-6). Historically, Catholicism was a minority religion within the Protestant United Kingdom, even though it was the majority religion on the island of Ireland. Today, Catholics in Northern Ireland echo this historical predicament, in that they are a minority in both the UK and the North but can see themselves as belonging to the Catholic-nationalist majority on the island as a whole. Protestants, correspondingly, form the majority tradition in Northern Ireland and associate with the dominant Protestant tradition in Britain, but often express a sense of being a threatened minority marginalised by the 'pan-nationalist' front that they perceive in the combined Catholic populations of the North and the Republic (McGarry and O'Leary, 1995: 182-185).

Thus, both traditions in some respects have the mentality of an oppressed minority and use religion as a defensive marker of identity. In other respects, they claim an entitlement to a majority status based on that same religious identity. This complex role of religion in defining relations of dominance and subordination between competing cultural traditions on the island, and between Britain and Ireland, has proved deeply enduring and has undoubtedly played a part in maintaining a central place for religion in Irish life.

Some have questioned whether the Irish case is as exceptional as it first appears, mainly on the grounds that there are many instances of societies where religion has persisted – or even revived – in the course of modernisation (Hornsby-Smith, 1992; Fahey, 1992; Greeley, 1999). This approach reflects the view that religion and modernity can co-exist more readily than many social scientists suppose. Such a view has been reinforced in recent years by a new perspective on religion in American social science that queries virtually every aspect of the general thesis that socio-economic development and secularisation go hand in hand (Stark and Finke, 2000; Iannaccone, 1998). This perspective was initially inspired by the continuing vitality of religion, and particularly of Christian fundamentalism, in the United States, but has since been applied more widely. It argues that continuous *fluctuation* rather than persistent decline better describes the history of religious attachment in western countries over the past two centuries. From an Irish perspective, the vitality of religion in the United States is of interest, since as

Inglehart and Baker's (2000) comparative data show, the United States comes closer to the two parts of Ireland on a number of indicators of religious attachment than any European country bar Poland (Malta is also a European outlier, as we shall see further below). In the light of such findings, some have warned against any general expectation that religion would inevitably decline in modernising societies and, in that context, have interpreted the enduring character of Irish religiosity as less contrary to general patterns than it might first appear to be (Greeley, 1999).

Developments in the 1990s in Ireland are of particular interest here, since the social context changed rapidly in this period and the churches themselves, especially the Catholic Church, have been rocked by unprecedented internal shocks (Fuller, 2002; Kenny, 2000). The social context has been transformed by continuing economic modernisation, as reflected especially in the economic boom that began in the Republic in the early 1990s. This transformation would point to an intensification of the type of secularising trends commonly identified by secularisation theory. If such theory is correct, secularisation should have been boosted by the economic leap forward of the 1990s and, because that leap was greater in the Republic than in the North, would be expected to be more pronounced in the South than in the North.

Our expectations must also take account of the politics of North-South and cross-community relations expressed through the Good Friday Agreement and the drive for a settlement of the Northern Ireland conflict. The aim of that development was to ease tensions and conflicts within Northern Ireland. Despite its stop-go implementation, the Agreement has brought about levels of political accommodation and cooperation between the two sides of the political divide in Northern Ireland and between the two parts of Ireland that would have previously been unthinkable (Hayes and McAllister, 2001a). To the extent that tensions across those divides have sustained religious affiliation in Ireland in the past, the likely overall effect of the new situation would be to weaken that particular prop to religion and so increase the tempo of secularisation in the 1990s.

Alongside these structural changes, a series of events within the churches, and especially within the Catholic Church, have added to the pressures on religion in Ireland, and here again the impact would appear to have been greater in the Republic than in the North. The events in question centre on the sex scandals that engulfed the Catholic Church in Ireland from the early 1990s onwards (Fuller, 2002: 251-258). They began in 1992 when it emerged that Eamonn Casey, the Catholic bishop of Galway, had fathered a child some eighteen years previously and had used diocesan funds to support the mother. Matters worsened for the church when stories of physical and sexual abuse of children by priests and members of religious orders – many of them dating back to the 1960s – broke in the media and were confirmed in a series of highly publicised court cases. One of the first of these, which concerned the paedophile Norbertine priest, Brendan

Smyth, gave rise to accusations that authorities within the Catholic Church had known about his activities since the 1960s and had failed to take meaningful action. Allegations of a cover-up of the Smyth affair involving the office of the Attorney General in the Republic led to the fall of the Irish government in late 1994. Taken as a whole, these dramatic events, in one commentator's view, 'marked 1992 as the year when Catholic Ireland began to slide into retreat and decline, the year when Irish Catholicism was seen as being wrong' (Kenny, 2000: 373). Controversies and problems in this area have continued almost without respite since then and have taken new turns as the question of compensation for those abused, sexually or otherwise, by priests and members of religious orders has come to the fore.

However, while the sex scandals uncovered in the 1990s added a new dimension to controversy about the Catholic Church in Ireland, it was not as if controversy on sexual matters had been absent before then. The bruising national debates in the Republic about contraception in the 1970s and abortion and divorce in the 1980s had caused divisions within Catholicism and revealed widening gaps between what the church taught and what significant proportions of the people were willing to accept (Hug, 1999). The sex scandals of the 1990s differed from these earlier controversies in that no grand questions of ideology were at issue, simply a series of sordid revelations for which the church could offer no defence. However, it remains to be established whether they had a more damaging effect on Catholicism than the long-running political tensions about the links between law, the Constitution, sexual morality and Catholic moral doctrine. Despite the shocking character of the sex scandals, one might argue that their relevance to most people's daily lives may be less than the more personal questions of contraception, divorce and abortion. In that perspective, the scandals are likely to be only one among a number of strands of controversy that affect popular religious attitudes and practices.

One of the questions to consider here, therefore, is whether the impact of the sex-scandals on religious attachment might be evident in the 1999-2000 EVS data and how that impact might compare with the influence of longer-term factors. It also is of interest whether they caused more damage to Catholicism in the Republic of Ireland than in Northern Ireland, given that most of the scandals occurred in the Republic. This is not to deny their impact in Northern Ireland, particularly in connection with the Brendan Smyth case, as he was living and working in Belfast at the time the revelations about him came to light. The Protestant churches, both North and South, largely escaped scandals of the type that arose within the Catholic church in this period, and therefore might be expected to have suffered less damage and decline in consequence. This, in itself, has interesting implications, since if Protestant religious affiliation in the 1990s showed broadly similar trends to those found in Catholicism, scandals of the type that affected the Catholic Church might be shown to have less long-term significance for religiosity than the basic social-structural changes that affected both religious traditions equally.

Objectives

Against this background, the purpose of the present chapter is to examine the extent to which the increase in secularisation in Ireland, North and South, that might be expected on *a priori* grounds has in fact come about. Since those *a priori* grounds might also lead one to expect a somewhat stronger secularising trend in the Republic of Ireland than in Northern Ireland, and among Catholics than among Protestants, comparisons between North and South of the border and between Catholics and Protestants become central to the analysis (though it must be recalled that, since time series data are not available for Protestants in the Republic, our analysis of trends over time cannot be extended to include them).

One difficulty in pursuing these objectives is that the concept of secularisation can embrace many different things, which in turn helps account for the on-going academic dispute as to whether secularisation really is taking place in western countries or not. Some versions of the concept point to widespread abandonment of church membership as the core element of secularisation and look to survey data on the numbers who identify themselves as having no religious affiliation (sometimes known in the research literature as 'religious independents') as the key indicator of this process (Sandomirsky and Wilson, 1990; Hayes and McAllister, 1995; Hayes, 2000). Others pay less attention to denominational disaffiliation and focus instead on the degree to which populations continue to practise and believe in traditional institutional forms of religious expression. Typical indicators used for this purpose include falling attendance at church, declining acceptance of formal church teaching, and waning confidence in church leaders or institutions (Hadaway *et al.*, 1993; Bruce, 1999). A third, related approach argues that the central feature of secularisation today is not so much the abandonment of religion as its *privatisation* (Bellah, 1975; Davie, 1994). The key idea here is that a drift away from organised religion may co-exist with a continuing belief in the divine at a personal level. People may 'believe without belonging', in that they abandon churches but continue to believe in God, pray occasionally and attach some importance to the spiritual, but purely as a private matter rather than as a collective expression of faith within a church or denomination (Davie, 1994).

Rather than choose between these alternative concepts and indicators of secularisation, the present chapter ranges selectively over all of them. It first looks at denominational self-identification, or affiliation, with particular emphasis on the growth in the numbers of non-affiliated, that is, those who explicitly identify themselves as having no denominational affiliation. It then looks at conventional indictors of formal religious expression and practice, such as church attendance rates as well as levels of confidence in church leaders and institutions. Finally, indicators of privatised religion, such as a belief in the basic tenets of the Christian faith without the accompaniment of formal religious practice, are then considered.

Religious identification and church membership

The main Christian churches in Ireland have an entry rite in the form of baptism but have no formal mechanisms of membership renewal or registration. Neither do they have informal thresholds of participation that mark the boundary between being in and being out of their organisations. In contrast to the practice in some continental European countries, the state plays no role in identifying or recording church membership among citizens, as is required, for example, in connection with the church tax levied by the state in Germany, Austria, some of the Nordic countries and Switzerland (Bronchi and de Kam, 1999). In consequence, whether or not one 'belongs' to a particular religious denomination in either part of Ireland is as much a matter of subjective perception and identification as of externally observable behaviour.

Accordingly survey-based measures of denominational membership, which usually settle for a straightforward dichotomy between those who say they belong to a religious denomination and those who say they do not, are quite appropriate in the Irish case. The EVS uses a two-part question for this purpose. The first part asks respondents if they belong to a religious denomination and, for those who answer 'yes', the second part asks which one. Other surveys use a slightly different approach that asks respondents which religious denomination they belong to and offers them 'none' or 'no religion' as a response option. The EVS-type question is usually thought to produce somewhat higher estimates of non-affiliation than the alternative, as it offers respondents who are on the margins of a denomination or are unsure about their position a clearer opportunity to say that they do not belong.

We now look at denominational affiliation as reported in the 1999-2000 EVS in the Republic of Ireland and Northern Ireland respectively (see Tables 3.1 and 3.2). Protestant denominations in Northern Ireland are classified into liberal and fundamentalist sub-groups in Table 3.2, since in some contexts that distinction is often thought to have almost as much relevance as that between Catholic and Protestant (Bruce, 1986; Greeley, 1999; McKay, 2000). The data show a continuing high level of denominational affiliation up to 1999-2000 (though as we shall see below there are indications of a downward shift after 2000, especially in the Republic). Over nine out of ten adults in the Republic (91 per cent) and a somewhat smaller proportion in Northern Ireland (85 per cent) still say that they belong to a religious denomination. In the Republic, the vast majority of respondents identify with the Catholic Church (88 per cent), while a small minority (3 per cent) indicate a Protestant affiliation. Those who claim no denominational affiliation (referred to from here on as non-affiliated) – are a further small minority, though at 9 per cent of adults in the Republic, they substantially out-number Protestants.[1]

---

[1] The Census of Population 2002 in the Republic of Ireland produced a similar estimate of the proportion of Catholics in the population to that provided here but the estimate of those with no religion is lower in the Census at 3.5 per cent (Central Statistics Office 2003: 29). The differences arise in part because the census refers to the whole population where the present survey refers only to those aged 18 and over and in part because of differences in question format.

Table 3.1: Religious identification in the Republic of Ireland

	(Percentages)
Catholic	87.8
Protestant	3.4
(Church of Ireland/Episcopalian)	(1.5)
(Presbyterian)	(0.2)
(Methodist)	(0.1)
(Other)	(1.5)
Non-Christian	0.2
Not stated	0.1
Non-affiliated	8.6
Total	100.0
[N]	[1,012]

Question: Do you belong to a religious denomination? [If yes] Which one?
Source: European Values Study, 1999-2000.

Table 3.2: Religious identification in Northern Ireland

	(Percentages)
Catholic	40.3
Liberal Protestant	38.3
(Anglican/Church of Ireland)	(15.0)
(Presbyterian)	(19.0)
(Methodist)	(3.6)
(URC/Congregational)	(0.7)
Fundamental Protestant	5.8
(Baptist)	(1.2)
(Free Presbyterian)	(1.0)
(Brethern)	(0.5)
(Other)	(3.0)
Non-Christian	0.2
Not stated	1.5
Non-affiliated	14.0
Total	100.0
[N]	[1,000]

Question: Do you belong to a religious denomination? [If yes] Which one?
Source: European Values Study, 1999-2000.

In Northern Ireland, the adult population is fairly evenly divided by denomination, with 44 per cent Protestant, 40 per cent Catholic and 14 per cent non-affiliated. Among Protestants, the liberal denominations – Anglicans, Presbyterians, Methodists and Congregationalists – are in the majority, with Anglicans and Presbyterians as the largest groups. The non-affiliated, at 14 per cent of the total, outnumber fundamentalist Protestants (6 per cent), are almost equal in number to Anglicans (15 per cent) and are not far short of the proportion of Presbyterians (19 per cent), the largest Protestant denomination in Northern Ireland.[2]

Religious non-affiliation and secularisation

The proportion of the religiously non-affiliated in the population is often taken as a key indicator of secularisation. This indicator began to rise in Northern Ireland earlier than in the Republic and a gap between the two had opened by the early 1990s (Figure 3.1). After 1995, however, the Republic began to catch up, with a particularly steep rise taking place between 1999-2000 and 2003. The increase in the number of religious independents in the Republic in the 1990s roughly coincides with the emergence of the sex scandals affecting the Catholic Church during this period. However, it also coincides with increases in the strength of other presumed secularising forces and one should be careful, therefore, not to make an argument of the 'post hoc ergo propter hoc' variety.

It is also worth noting that the growth in the number of non-affiliated in Northern Ireland coincided with a decline in the relative size of the two main

Figure 3.1: The growth of the religiously non-affiliated in the Republic of Ireland and Northern Ireland, 1968-2003

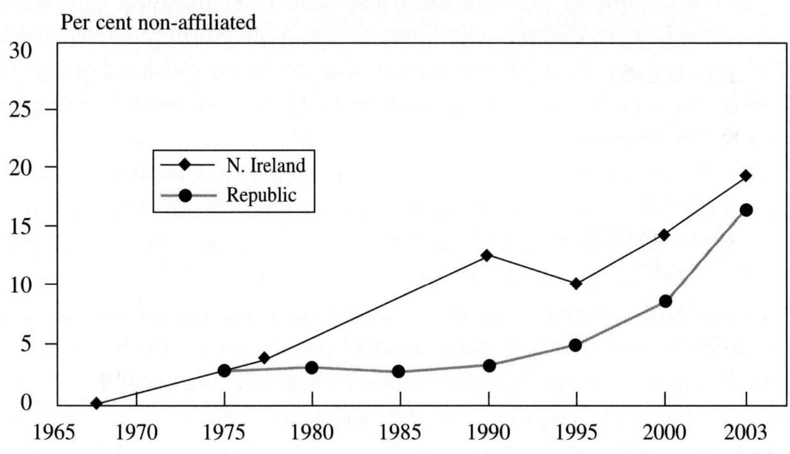

Sources: Republic of Ireland: Eurobarometer Surveys, 1975, 1980, 1985, 1990, 1995, European Values Study, 1999-2000; Northern Ireland: Loyalty Survey, 1968, Social Attitudes Survey, 1978, Northern Ireland Social Attitudes Survey, 1989 and 1995; European Values Study, 1999-2000; European Social Survey, 2003.

2 As in the case of the Republic of Ireland, the recorded estimate of those with no religion is again lower (at 9.7 per cent) in the 2001 Northern Ireland Census.

Figure 3.2: The decline of Anglicans and Presbyterians in Northern Ireland, 1968-2003

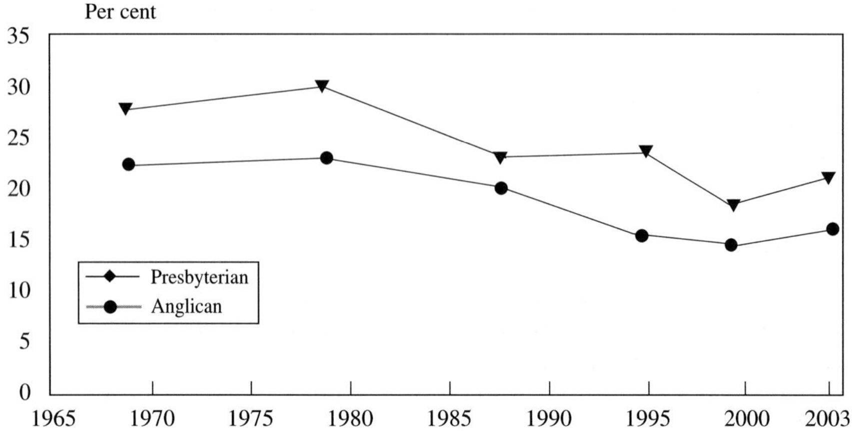

Sources: Loyalty Survey, 1968, Social Attitudes Survey, 1978, Northern Ireland Social Attitudes Survey, 1989 and 1995; European Values Study, 1999-2000, Northern Ireland and Times Survey, 2003.

Protestant denominations – Anglicans and Presbyterians – and seems to have emerged largely at their expense (see Figure 3.2). The Presbyterian share of the adult population dropped from 30 per cent to 23 per cent in the period 1978-1989, the same period in which the share of non-affiliated grew. The Anglican share also declined somewhat, from 23 per cent to 20 per cent. Over the same period, the relative size of the Roman Catholic adult population in the North remained stable, at around 40 per cent of the adult population. Census-based estimates suggested that the Catholic share of the total population in the North rose from 36.8 per cent in 1971 to 40.6 per cent in 1991 (Compton, 1995: 166).

The 1999-2000 EVS asked those who reported that they had no denominational affiliation whether they were formerly members of any denomination. As in previous research (Hayes and McAllister, 1995), the responses to this item, though based on quite small sample numbers, indicate that the non-affiliated in Northern Ireland came disproportionately from Protestant backgrounds (see Table 3.3). There were twice as many ex-Protestants as ex-Catholics among the non-affiliated in Northern Ireland, even though the Protestant-Catholic balance in the total population was more or less even. At the same time, however, a significant proportion of the non-affiliated – over a third in both the Republic and the North – claim to have had no previous denominational affiliation.

This evidence suggests that the growth in denominational non-affiliation in both the Republic of Ireland and Northern Ireland has not been dramatic. Up until the late 1990s, it had disproportionately affected Protestants in Northern Ireland, but since then it has become almost equally evident among Catholics in the Republic.

Table 3.3: Religious origins of the religiously non-affiliated in the Republic of Ireland and Northern Ireland

	(Percentages)	
	Republic of Ireland	Northern Ireland
Anglican	3	20
Presbyterian	0	20
Catholic	61	18
Other	0	7
Non-affiliated	36	35
[N]	[86]	[138]

Question: Were you ever a member of a religious denomination? [If yes] Which one?

Source: European Values Study, 1999-2000.

Denominational non-affiliation in comparative perspective

In the past, the scale of denominational non-affiliation in the populations of Northern Ireland and the Republic was somewhat lower than the norm for Europe and considerably lower than in Britain (Hayes and Hornsby-Smith, 1994; Hayes, 2000). However, at least as far as a European average is concerned, the two parts of Ireland have become less distinctive in recent years, though the range of variation on this indicator is now so wide across Europe that it stretches matters to speak of a European 'norm'. As the data in Figure 3.3 show, the proportion who are non-affiliated in the Republic of Ireland is slightly greater than in some historically Catholic societies (Portugal and Italy) but less than in others (France). Non-affiliation rates in Northern Ireland are now equivalent to those in a number of other mixed Catholic-Protestant societies (e.g. the United States) but are far below those of Britain, where 46 per cent of adults report that they belong to no religious denomination. In fact, of all western industrialised nations, Britain now has one of the highest levels of non-affiliation in western Europe, second only to the Netherlands (61 per cent). On this indicator, therefore, the Republic and Northern Ireland are closer to each other than either is to Britain.

Decline in religious practice

While levels of denominational affiliation remain reasonably high in many countries, including Ireland, recent research in a number of countries points to a rise in 'nominal' adherents – those who claim a religious affiliation but do not regularly attend religious services (Heath *et al.*, 1993; Hornsby-Smith and Whelan, 1994; De Graaf and Need, 2000). Previous evidence also shows that Protestants in

Figure 3.3: Religiously non-affiliated in a cross-national perspective

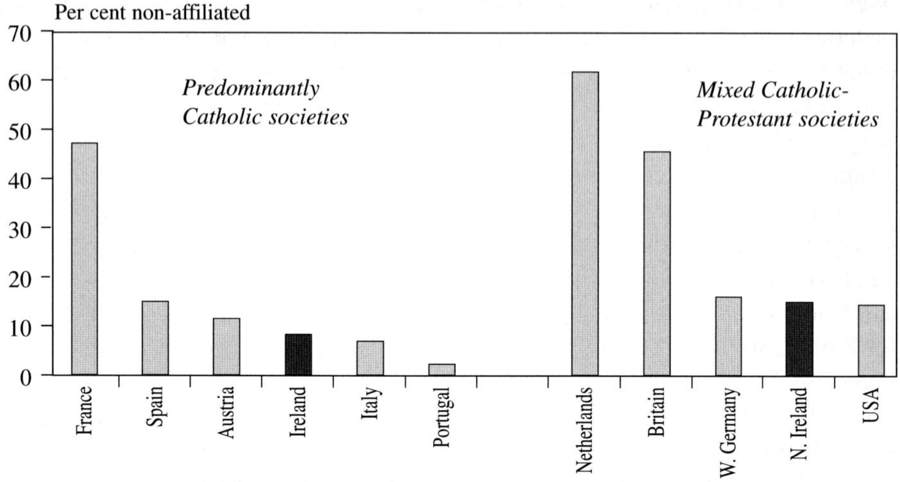

Note: Data for Northern Ireland and the Republic are from the 1999-2000 EVS; data for other countries are from the 1998 ISSP Religion Survey.

Source: ISSP Religion Survey, 1998; European Values Study, 1999-2000.

Northern Ireland stand out as less committed to regular church attendance than Catholics, a phenomenon that is particularly pronounced among liberal Protestants, such as Anglicans (Heath *et al.*, 1993; Hayes and McAllister, 1995). One should note, however, that irregular church attendance is not necessarily as reliable an indicator of nominal adherence among Protestants as it is among Catholics, since frequent church attendance is a less formal requirement in Protestantism than in Catholicism.

Before turning to our data on religious practice, it should be pointed out that doubt has been cast on the reliability of self-reported data on church attendance as collected in sample surveys (Sherkat and Ellison, 1999). In the United States, for example, Presser and Stinson (1998) cite evidence that suggests that over-reporting of church attendance in interviewer-based surveys has risen steadily since the 1960s, mainly because of social desirability bias (the tendency of respondents to give interviewers the answers they think the interviewers would prefer to hear). Presser and Stinson (1998) estimate that actual church attendance in the United States had fallen to about half the levels reported in typical social surveys by the 1990s, the gap between self-reported and actual church attendance having widened steadily over the preceding decades. No similar evidence has yet been provided for Ireland, though anecdotal evidence from parish clergy on actual church attendance levels at weekends would suggest that some degree of over-reporting in social surveys is likely to occur in this country too.

It may be, therefore, that church attendance levels reported in either part of

Ireland, in the EVS or in other surveys, are an indicator of what people think they *ought* to be doing rather than what they actually do. This uncertainty does not undermine the data as much as might be expected, since people's sense of how they ought to behave is of interest in its own right. Even if church attendance levels are over-reported, they indicate a continuing positive orientation towards formal religious observance that is not to be dismissed as irrelevant, and that has all but disappeared in some countries.

Keeping these cautions about the data in mind, Figure 3.4 draws on a range of survey sources to track the level of reported weekly church attendance among all adults (panel A) and the religiously affiliated (panel B) in the Republic of Ireland and Northern Ireland over the past three decades or so. The only estimate available for Protestants in the Republic is that provided by the special sample of Protestants in the 1999-2000 EVS and so time trends are not presented in their case. Looking first at the data for all adults in the Republic, reported weekly church attendance was extraordinarily high in the early 1970s, at over 90 per cent, and was still just above 80 per cent by 1990. Thenceforth, it began to shift consistently downwards, falling below 60 per cent in 1999-2000 and to 50 per cent in 2003. The trend for Northern Ireland shows a much slower downward movement over time but since the starting point was lower than in the Republic, the end-point in 2003 (at 42 per cent) is still below the Republic. The trends for major denominations in panel B in Figure 3.4 show that Catholics in the Republic of Ireland and Northern Ireland had similar attendance levels until the late 1990s but at that point Catholics in the Republic began to drop somewhat below Catholics in Northern Ireland. Protestants in the Republic in 1999-2000 (the only time-point for which we have a measure of religious attendance in their case) were slightly below the level of Catholics in the Republic but above that of Protestants in Northern Ireland. For Protestants in Nothern Ireland, the trend over time was relatively flat over much of the period but showed a sharp downward movement between 1999 and 2003.

Table 3.4 provides full breakdowns on frequency of church attendance by denominational group from the EVS 1999-2000, and also provides an update on the overall levels of attendance from the ESS 2003. Since it is increasingly common in international research to define 'regular' church attendance as monthly or more frequent attendance, a distinction along these lines between regular and irregular attendance is built into the table. The non-affiliated, as might be expected, have very low levels of church attendance – only six per cent in both the Republic and the North attended church on at least a monthly basis in 1999-2000. Just over half (52 per cent) of the non-affiliated in the Republic state that they never attend church, while the equivalent figure in the North is significantly higher at 79 per cent. Thus, for many but not all non-affiliated, a rejection of denominational affiliation is followed through with rejection of

Figure 3.4: Trends in weekly church attendance in the Republic of Ireland and Northern Ireland, 1968-2003

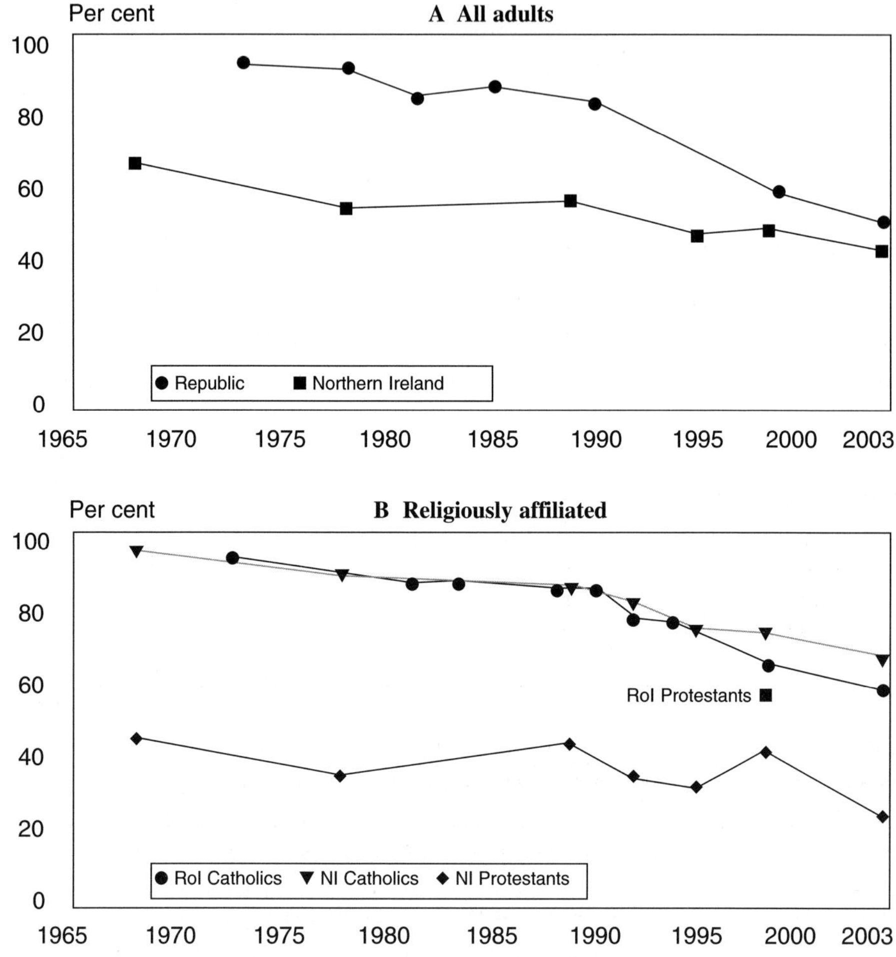

Sources: Republic of Ireland: Eurobarometer Surveys, 1973, 1978, 1985, 1989, 1992 and 1995, European Values Survey, 1999-2000. Northern Ireland: Loyalty Survey, 1968, Social Attitudes Survey, 1978, Northern Ireland Social Attitudes Survey, 1989 and 1995, Northern Ireland Election Survey, 1992, European Values Study, 1999-2000; European Social Survey, 2003.

church attendance. Among those who have a denominational affiliation, nominalism is more common among Northern Protestants (15 per cent) than among Catholics either in the Republic (5 per cent) or in Northern Ireland (4 per cent), (taking the proportions who never attend church as a measure of 'nominal' affiliation). The data from the European Social Survey (ESS) for 2003 show that the proportions who attend church weekly in both the Republic of

Table 3.4: Church attendance by religious identification in the Republic of Ireland and Northern Ireland

(Percentages)

	EVS 1999-2000				ESS 2003
	Catholic	Protestant	Non-affiliated	All	All
			Republic of Ireland		
Regular Attender	76	83	6	70	64
Weekly	*65*	*58*	*5*	*59*	*50*
Monthly	*11*	*25*	*1*	*11*	*14*
Irregular Attender	24	17	94	30	36
Less than monthly	*19*	*12*	*42*	*21*	*24*
Never	*5*	*5*	*52*	*9*	*12*
Total	100	100	100	100	100
[N]	[884]	[253]	[87]	[1,005]	[2,200]
			Northern Ireland		
Regular Attender	87	61	6	64	56
Weekly	*74*	*41*	*2*	*49*	*42*
Monthly	*13*	*20*	*4*	*15*	*14*
Irregular Attender	13	39	94	36	54
Less than monthly	*9*	*24*	*15*	*17*	*36*
Never	*4*	*15*	*79*	*19*	*18*
Total	100	100	100	100	100
[N]	[401]	[438]	[137]	[976]	[775]

Question: Apart from weddings, funerals and christenings, about how often do you attend religious services these days?
Note: Estimates for Protestants in the Republic of Ireland in 1999-2000 are based on the Protestant booster sample; all other estimates are based on the simple random samples for the Republic and the North.

Source: European Values Study, 1999-2000; European Social Survey, 2003.

Ireland and Northern Ireland continued its previous decline but that there was little change in the proportion who say they never attend church. The main movement, therefore, was from very frequent to less frequent attendance rather than to no attendance at all.

Patterns of religious attendance in 1999-2000 are broken down by various socio-demographic variables in Table 3.5. For the Republic of Ireland, these breakdowns indicate particularly sharp contrasts in church attendance by age, in addition to differences by urban-rural location, occupation and gender. Younger adults, particularly in the urban manual occupational category, have especially low levels of weekly church attendance. Among those aged 18-30 years, 27 per cent attend church weekly overall, but this falls to 13 per cent weekly attendance among

Table 3.5: Weekly church attendance by age, occupation and rural-urban location in the Republic of Ireland and Northern Ireland

(Percentages)

	18-30 yrs	31-45 yrs	46-60 yrs	60+ yrs	All
			Republic of Ireland		
Occupation and rural-urban location:					
Non-manual					
Rural	61	69	86	94	76
Urban	24	42	73	91	49
Manual					
Rural	32	63	78	85	63
Urban	13	45	78	82	50
Gender:					
Male	20	46	72	86	51
Female	34	66	81	90	66
All	27	56	77	89	59
[N]	[214]	[270]	[189]	[140]	[813]
			Northern Ireland		
Occupation:					
Non-manual	39	33	59	62	49
Manual	41	35	55	60	48
Gender:					
Male	39	30	55	52	46
Female	40	36	60	67	50
All	40	33	57	60	48
[N]	[225]	[240]	[311]	[224]	[1000]

Question: Apart from weddings, funerals and christenings, about how often do you attend religious services these days?
Source: European Values Study, 1999-2000.

the urban manual working class while it remains above 60 per cent among the rural non-manual group. These figures suggest, though obviously do not prove, that, as the present young adults grow older, decline in weekly churchgoing could become precipitous.

Differences by age, occupation and gender are much less sharp in Northern Ireland than in the Republic. Those aged 45 or under have lower levels of weekly church attendance than those aged over 45, but among the under-45s, the younges – those aged 18-30 – have a slightly *higher* incidence of weekly church-going than t next oldest age-group – those aged 31-45 (40 per cent weekly compared to 33 per cent). This weaker age-gradient in church attendance means that future decline in religious participation in Northern Ireland may be less marked than in the Republic. It is also notable that gender and class differences in church attendance are scarcely present in Northern Ireland, in contrast to the sharp distinctions along these lines found in the Republic.

International comparisons

As mentioned earlier, previous research has indicated that while Catholic-Protestant and North-South differences in church attendance may be significant, they are small by international standards, placing Ireland, North and South, in something of an outlier position in Europe in so far as religious practice is concerned. This pattern is confirmed by the 1999-2000 EVS data on church attendance for 33 societies in western and eastern Europe summarised in Figure 3.5. For comparison, this figure includes data on the main denominational groupings in Ireland, in addition to data for the Republic and Northern Ireland as a whole.

Outside Ireland, as panel A in Figure 3.5 shows, the level of weekly church attendance found in the Republic is exceeded only by Malta and is matched only by Poland. Beyond these, only Italy, Portugal and Slovakia come anywhere in the same range. In other countries, generally below 20 per cent and in some cases below 10 per cent attend church weekly, as compared to almost 60 per cent for the Republic of Ireland as a whole and 65 per cent for Catholics in the Republic. In this context, the overall level of 49 per cent weekly church attendance in Northern Ireland, and 41 per cent among Northern Protestants, though lower than the Republic, is high by European standards. It is also very high by comparison with Britain where only 14 per cent claim to attend church weekly. Even if we were to take into the account the further declines in weekly church attendance that, as we noted earlier, had occurred in the Republic of Ireland and Northern Ireland by 2003, both societies would still remain in the upper range of church attendance rates in Europe.

The proportions who never attend church (Figure 3.5, panel B) are not quite the obverse of those who attend weekly. For one thing, as already noted, there is a greater relative gap between the Republic of Ireland and Northern Ireland on this indicator. Nevertheless, despite the higher level of non-attendance in the North, both the Republic and the North are in the lower reaches of European levels of complete non-attendance at church.

Thus, by European standards, it is not just Catholics but also Protestants in both the Republic and the North who stand out as being relatively religious. Though both groups are less assiduous in church attendance than they were two or three

Figure 3.5: Church attendance in Europe

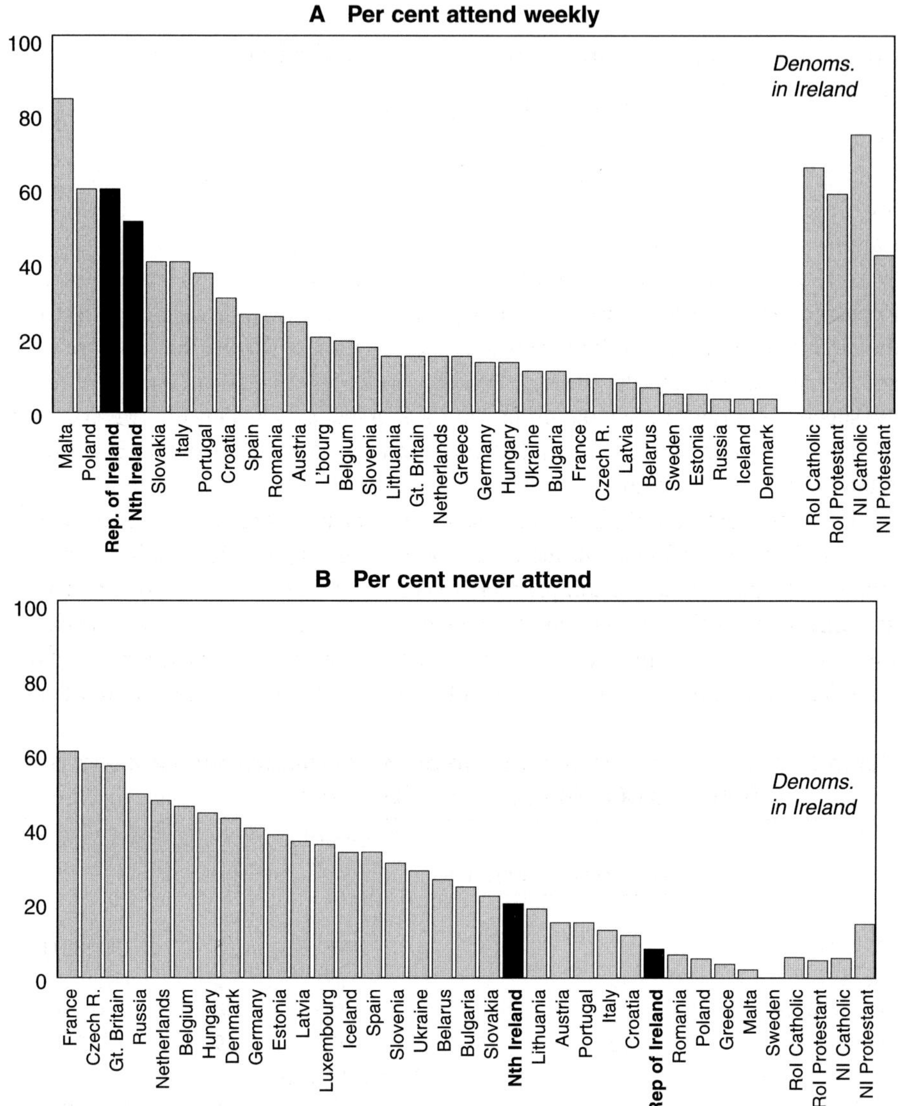

Source: European Values Study, 1999-2000.

decades ago, they have preserved much of the gap that marked them off from other countries on this score in the past. It is impossible to say by how much these church attendance figures are inflated at any point in time by over-reporting. However, even if the reported levels are more accurate as an indication of people's aspirations than of their behaviour, they are still high, despite the decline of recent years. At a minimum, they indicate a cultural valuation of weekly church attendance that is still strong by international standards.

Public attitudes toward the church: a growing disillusionment

High levels of attachment to formal religious practice in Ireland, both North and South, do not necessarily translate into positive attitudes towards the churches. Among the religiously affiliated, Catholics in the Republic stand out as having the lowest levels of confidence in the church (see Table 3.6). Less than a quarter of Catholics in the Republic have a 'great deal' of confidence in the church, compared to over one third of Catholics and Protestants in the North and of Protestants in the Republic. At the same time, even among Catholics in the Republic, confidence in the church on balance is still more positive than negative – those with a 'great deal' and 'quite a lot' of confidence combined amount to 59 per cent. At the other end of the spectrum of confidence, the proportion who have no confidence in the church at all ranges between only 2 and 5 per cent across all groups reporting a denominational affiliation.

Those who are non-affiliated are much more negative: only a tiny minority have a 'great deal' of confidence in the church while the majority have either 'not very much' or 'none'. When we compare those with no affiliation with those who have a denominational affiliation but report irregular (less than monthly) church attendance, we find that the non-affiliated are in somewhat less of an outlier position – Catholic irregular church attenders have a level of lack of confidence in the church that is

Table 3.6: Confidence in the church by religious identification in the Republic of Ireland and Northern Ireland

	Great deal	Quite a lot	Not very much	None	Total [N]
			(Percentages)		
			Republic of Ireland		
Catholic	23	36	36	5	100 [881]
Protestant	36	37	25	2	100 [256]
Non-affiliated	5	7	42	46	100 [84]
All	22	32	37	9	100 [999]
			Northern Ireland		
Catholic	39	36	22	4	100 [399]
Protestant	34	35	26	5	100 [434]
Non-affiliated	4	11	47	38	100 [134]
All	32	32	27	9	100 [967]

Question: Take a look at this card and tell me, for each item listed, how much confidence you have in them, is it a great deal, quite a lot, not very much or none at all?

Note: Estimates for Protestants in the Republic of Ireland are based on the Protestant booster sample; all other estimates are based on the simple random samples for the Republic and the North.

Source: European Values Study, 1999-2000.

Table 3.7: Confidence in the church by differences in religious identification and religious behaviour in the Republic of Ireland and Northern Ireland

(Percentages)

	Republic of Ireland		Northern Ireland	
	Great deal	None	Great deal	None
Catholic	**23**	**5**	**39**	**4**
Regular attender	*29*	*1*	*44*	*1*
Irregular attender	*5*	*18*	*8*	*25*
Protestant	**36**	**2**	**34**	**5**
Regular attender	*42*	*1*	*50*	*1*
Irregular attender	*10*	*10*	*9*	*10*
Non-affiliated	**5**	**46**	**4**	**38**

Note: Regular attender: attended religious services at least once a month. Irregular attender: attended less than once a month or not at all.

Source: European Values Study, 1999-2000.

substantially closer to that found among the non-affiliated (Table 3.7). It is also notable that even among Catholic regular church attenders in the Republic, only 29 per cent say that they have a great deal of confidence in the church. Differences on this item between regular and irregular church attenders are similarly wide among Protestants.

The somewhat low levels of confidence in the church among Catholics in the Republic compared to Protestants and Catholics in the North might seem to indicate that the clerical sex scandals of the 1990s had a particularly severe impact on the standing of the Catholic church in the Republic. However, comparisons with EVS data from 1981 and 1990 indicate that a downward trend in confidence in the Catholic church in the Republic was already well established by 1990 and the trend showed no signs of intensifying as the 1990s unfolded (Figure 3.6). In 1981, 57 per cent of Catholic regular attenders claimed that they had a great deal of confidence in their church. By 1990, this proportion had fallen to 44 per cent, and by 1999-2000 to just 29 per cent, a drop of 13 and 15 percentage points respectively in the earlier and later period. Fogarty (1984) had already detected signs of questioning and criticism of the church among Catholics in the Republic in 1981, so that declining confidence in the church may not have been new even in the 1980s – compare, for example, the reverential respect for the church revealed by Biever's survey of Dublin Catholics in 1962 (Biever, 1976) with the more critical attitudes pointed to by Fogarty (1984). It seems plausible that, as has been suggested earlier, the sex scandals in the Catholic church in the 1990s did not so

Figure 3.6: Declining confidence in the church among regular church attenders in the Republic of Ireland and Northern Ireland, 1981-1999

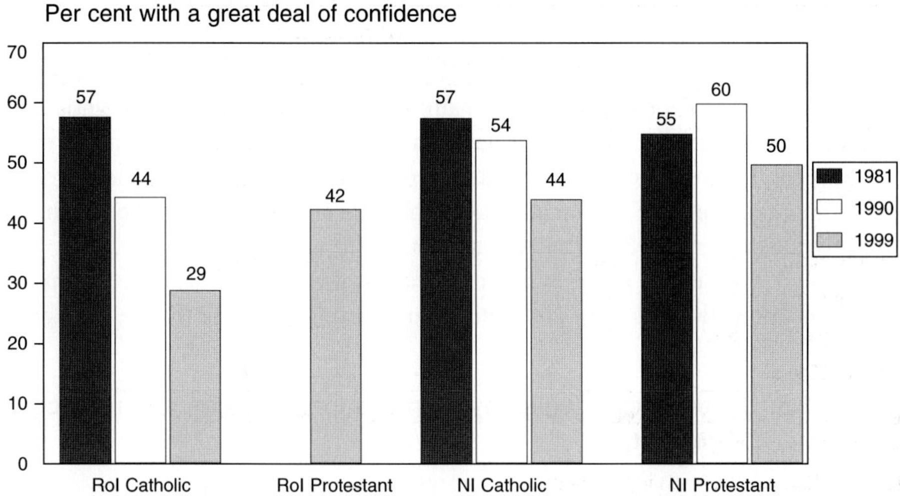

Note: Regular attenders: attended religious services at least once a month. Data for RoI Protestants are available for 1999 only.

Source: European Values Study, 1981, 1990, 1999-2000.

much engender a radical new loss of confidence in the church as carry forward a downward momentum that had begun up to two decades earlier. Among both Catholics and Protestants in Northern Ireland, by contrast, the main decline, amounting to ten percentage points, occurred between 1990 and 1999-2000.

The privatisation of religion: believing without belonging

According to some versions of secularisation theory, the shrinking position of religion in modern societies takes the form not so much of the complete abandonment of religious faith as its privatisation (Bellah, 1975). This perspective suggests that religion may weaken as a public institution but retain a presence in people's private beliefs and day-to-day practices. In other words, to use Davie's expression, people may 'persist in believing (if only in an ordinary God), but see no need to participate with even minimal regularity in their religious institutions' (1994: 2). To what extent is this process occurring in Ireland? We can answer this question by assessing whether, despite the growing number of non-affiliated and marginally attached members of religious denominations, certain forms of religious orientation continue to be held by the adult population in both the Republic and the North (see also Fahey 2002).

Table 3.8 addresses this issue. The data show that key beliefs are more widely accepted among regular church attenders than among others, but they are nevertheless held to a considerable degree even among irregular church attenders and those who are non-affiliated. Belief in God, in particular, is espoused by almost as large a majority of irregular attenders as regular attenders, as well as by over two-thirds of the non-affiliated in the Republic and by over half of the non-affiliated in the North. More people believe in heaven than in hell, but again the proportion who accept these ideas even among the non-affiliated is substantial. For example, 50 per cent of the non-affiliated in the Republic believe in heaven, while 25 per cent believe in hell. The non-affiliated in the Republic have higher levels of belief in God, life after death and heaven than the non-affiliated in the North, but slightly lower levels of belief in hell and sin.

Table 3.9 presents a range of other indicators of religiosity, which confirm that religious orientations of some sort remain quite strong across all the main religious

Table 3.8: Differences in belief by religious identification and religious behaviour

	(Per cent who believe)				
	God	Life After Death	Heaven	Hell	Sin
			Republic of Ireland		
Catholic	**98**	**82**	**90**	**57**	**89**
(Regular attender)	(100)	(86)	(94)	(62)	(92)
(Irregular attender)	(93)	(66)	(76)	(44)	(79)
Protestant	**94**	**72**	**79**	**47**	**84**
(Regular attender)	(98)	(77)	(84)	(54)	(87)
(Irregular attender)	(78)	(46)	(62)	(47)	(69)
Non-affiliated	**68**	**41**	**50**	**25**	**58**
			Northern Ireland		
Catholic	**96**	**74**	**85**	**70**	**91**
(Regular attender)	(99)	(77)	(89)	(73)	(95)
(Irregular attender)	(81)	(51)	(58)	(46)	(70)
Protestant	**93**	**59**	**85**	**68**	**87**
(Regular attender)	(98)	(72)	(95)	(79)	(91)
(Irregular attender)	(85)	(41)	(68)	(50)	(81)
Non-affiliated	**53**	**30**	**36**	**28**	**62**

Question: Which, if any, of the following do you believe in?

Note: Regular attender: attended religious services at least once a month. Irregular attender: attended less than once a month or not at all.

Source: European Values Study, 1999-2000.

categories in Ireland, including the non-affiliated. There is a particularly strong leaning towards what might be called 'rites of passage' religion: almost all Catholics and Protestants and clear majorities of the non-affiliated in both the Republic and Northern Ireland feel that it is important to have religious services at birth, marriage and death. Among the non-affiliated, there is especially strong support (over 70 per cent) for having a religious service at death. Among the other indicators in Table 3.9, the non-affiliated in the Republic show themselves to be more religiously inclined than their counterparts in the North. Almost half of them consider themselves as 'religious persons', compared to 16 per cent in the North; one-third say they get comfort and strength from religion, compared to 17 per cent in the North, and one third also indicate that they consider God to be important in their lives, compared to 18 per cent in the North.

These data generally confirm the view that, in both the Republic of Ireland and Northern Ireland, such incipient secularisation as has occurred has indeed been as much a matter of the privatisation of religion as of a complete shift towards irreligion. Even among those who have abandoned traditional institutional forms of religious attachment, such as membership of a church or regular attendance at religious services, relatively few have embraced out and out atheism. The majority

Table 3.9: Differences in other religious indicators by religious identification

(Percentages)

	Consider it important to have a religious service for[1]			Consider self religious person[2]	Get comfort & strength from religion[3]	Consider God important in life[4]
	Birth	Marriage	Death			
			Republic of Ireland			
Catholic	95	96	98	76	80	71
Protestant	94	95	98	70	78	67
Non-affiliated	55	55	71	45	32	33
All	91	93	96	74	76	67
			Northern Ireland			
Catholic	90	97	98	78	85	77
Protestant	82	92	96	63	71	66
Non-affiliated	53	65	70	16	17	18
All	81	90	93	62	69	63

Question: [1]*Do you personally think it is important to hold a religious service for any of the following events?;* [2]*Independently of whether you go to church or not, would you say that you are ...?;* [3]*Do you find that you get comfort and strength from religion or not?;* [4]*And how important is God in your life?*

Note: Estimates for Protestants in the Republic of Ireland are based on the Protestant booster sample; all other estimates are based on the simple random samples for the Republic and the North.

Source: European Values Study 1999-2000.

of the non-affiliated continue to espouse a general belief in God and feel that religious services have a value as part of the rites of passage associated with birth, marriage and death. Substantial minorities accept a range of other aspects of Christian belief, such as life after death, heaven and sin, and display certain other kinds of religious orientation, such as a feeling that they are religious people or that God is important in their lives. There are some indications in the data that the non-affiliated in the Republic of Ireland are somewhat more religious in these senses, and thus are less secularised, than are their opposite numbers in Northern Ireland. Since the non-affiliated are slightly less common in the Republic than in the North, this is a further indication that secularisation has made somewhat less progress south compared to north of the border, even though, as noted earlier, the gap between the two is not large and appears to be narrowing in recent years.

Pioneers of secularisation

We now take a closer look at the social characteristics of those with different kinds of religious orientation, focusing especially on those who have moved furthest away from traditional forms of religious adherence. Although it has been claimed that the non-affiliated are a highly diverse group (Hadaway, 1989), there are indications from research in a number of western countries that they are reasonably homogenous. Both the non-affiliated and irregular church attenders stand out as being male, better educated, and young (Need and De Graaf, 1996; Hayes, 1996, 2000). They are also less likely to marry, and if they do marry are more likely to be divorced, separated or involved in a remarriage (Sherkat and Wilson, 1995; Hayes, 2000). Finally, some studies suggest that they are also disproportionally drawn from the ranks of the unemployed and the economically marginal but others suggest that this is not so (Need and De Graaf, 1996; Hayes, 2000). The few available studies in the Republic of Ireland and Northern Ireland lend support to some of these findings (Nic Ghiolla Phádraig, 1988; Hornsby-Smith and Whelan, 1994; Hayes and McAllister, 1995). Nic Ghiolla Phádraig (1988) not only found that those who disavow a religious affiliation and/or do not engage in religious practices in the Republic of Ireland were more likely to be young, male, and better educated, but also that they came disproportionately from the ranks of the unemployed. Later research by Hornsby-Smith and Whelan (1994) confirmed these findings.

The results in Table 3.10 provide some further support for these findings. In both the Republic of Ireland and Northern Ireland, both the non-affiliated and irregular church attenders are somewhat more likely to be male, single and young. For example, in the Republic 63 per cent of the non-affiliated and 57 per cent of irregular church attenders were male compared to 46 per cent of regular church attenders, while the corresponding gaps in the North were only slightly narrower. Similarly only a quarter of regular church attenders in the Republic were single, compared to 47 per cent of irregular attenders and 44 per cent of the non-affiliated. Part of this marital status pattern is accounted for by the younger age profile of those who are single. In both the Republic and Northern Ireland, those aged under 45 were in the majority among the non-affiliated and irregular attenders but a minority among regular church attenders.

Multivariate analysis confirms these bivariate findings. In both the Republic of Ireland and Northern Ireland, only age and gender emerged as statistically significant predictors of denominational non-affiliation – males and the young are significantly more likely to disavow a religious affiliation than either females or the old (see Table A3.1 at end of chapter). An identical result emerges when levels of religious conviction are investigated. In both the Republic of Ireland and Northern

Table 3.10: Differences in socio-demographic background between the religiously non-affiliated and affiliated in the Republic of Ireland and Northern Ireland

(Percentages)

		Affiliated	
Socio-demographic background	Non-affiliated	Irregular attenders	Regular attenders
Republic of Ireland:			
Gender (male)	63	57	46*
Marital status (single)	44	47	26*
Age (under 45 years)	78	84	48*
Education (tertiary)	30	12	21
Occupation (service class)	13	15	18
Employment status (unemployed)	33	30	46
Northern Ireland:			
Gender (male)	58	52	43*
Marital status (single)	35	28	21*
Age (under 45 years)	75	52*	38*
Education (tertiary)	20	15	18
Occupation (service class)	17	13	20
Employment status (unemployed)	33	48*	49*

Note: Regular attender: attended religious services at least once a month. Irregular attender: attended less than once a month or not at all. Service class: professional and managerial occupations, supervisors of nonmanual employees and higher-grade technicians.
*Significantly different from the non-affiliated at the 0.05 level.

Source: European Values Study, 1999-2000.

Ireland, only age and gender emerged as significant predictors of religious belief, with males and the young being significantly less likely to accept the main tenets of the Christian faith than either females or the old.

It is important to note, however, that at least as far as the Republic is concerned, there is some evidence to suggest that this lower religious commitment among the young is not just a life cycle effect but represents an overall shift in behaviour over the last decade. As Table 3.11 shows, the number of irregular church attenders increased during the 1990s among both males and females across all age groups, with the exception of males aged 63 years or older. Among women across all age groups, the proportion who were irregular church attenders almost trebled – from just 8 per cent to 22 per cent – between 1990 and 1999, while among males it increased from just 11 per cent in 1990 to 30 per cent in 1999. Thus, where Hornsby-Smith and Whelan (1994: 23) found in 1990 that the decline in attachment over the previous decade was mainly restricted to those aged 18-26 years, the period between 1990 and 1999 has seen a decline in religious commitment across other age groups also.

Conclusion

This chapter has shown that secularisation, formerly so slow to take hold in Ireland, intensified in the 1990s and the early years of this century, both in the North and the Republic. However, its pace is still restrained. At the close of the twentieth century, Ireland as a whole, both North and South, remained among the most

Table 3.11: Gender and age differences among irregular church attenders in the Republic of Ireland

(Per cent who attend church less than monthly)

	Men					Women				
Age	1981	1990	1999	Δ^1	Δ^2	1981	1990	1999	Δ^1	Δ^2
18-26	16	14	45	-2	+31	11	11	42	+0	+31
27-35	21	16	41	-5	+25	16	12	33	-4	+21
36-44	9	16	41	+7	+25	7	2	22	-5	+20
45-53	6	8	19	+2	+11	4	9	13	+5	+4
54-62	10	7	10	-3	+3	0	1	3	+1	+2
63+	4	7	7	+3	+0	1	4	7	+3	+3
All	13	11	30	-2	+17	8	7	22	-1	+14

Note: Δ^1 and Δ^2 shows the net change for each of the gender-specific age groups from 1981 to 1990 and from 1990 to 1999, respectively.

Source: European Values Study, 1981, 1990, 1999-2000.

Christian parts of Europe and among the most committed to institutionalised religious activity. While attachment to organised religion has declined, that decline has been moderate by European standards and leaves Ireland with levels of formal religious adherence that are well above those of other European countries.

The balance between persistence and decline in organised religion is not entirely uniform across the island, though the variation is neither large nor altogether along the lines one would expect. The particularly rapid pace of economic advance in the Republic in the 1990s and the absence of the kind of sectarian tensions that are found in the North might have led one to anticipate a stronger secularising trend in the Republic than in the North in the 1990s. The greater public impact of sex scandals in the Catholic church in the Republic since 1992 would have pointed in the same direction. In fact, allegiance to Catholicism held up somewhat better than allegiance to Protestantism during the 1990s, though this difference declined in the early years of this decade. Protestantism is much stronger in Northern Ireland than in the traditionally Protestant countries of Europe and in that sense still shares an outlier position with Irish Catholicism. But it began to lose adherents somewhat sooner than did Irish Catholicism and has lower levels of formal religious practice. Generally speaking, formal religious adherence has not suffered any greater decline among Catholics in the Republic than it has among either Protestants or Catholics in Northern Ireland.

On only one indicator – confidence in the church – did Catholics in the Republic have significantly lower scores than both Catholics and Protestants in Northern Ireland. Declining confidence in the church among Catholics in the Republic reflects in part the scandals affecting the Catholic church in the 1990s. But an underlying downward trend has been present since the 1970s and therefore cannot be attributed to the events of the 1990s alone. It is likely to be due also to conflicts about moral legislation (on questions of contraception, divorce and abortion) that have recurred periodically over the past three decades and that have generally set Catholic teaching at odds with opinion and practice among substantial sectors of the population in the Republic.

Although Catholics in the Republic may be less assiduous in religious practice and more critical of the Catholic church than in the past, they have been slow to disavow their Catholic connections entirely. Up to the end of the 1990s, only small minorities reported that they never attend religious services or said that they have no confidence whatever in the church, and those minorities had grown only slightly over recent decades. However, there are stronger age and social class differences in levels of religious practice in the Republic than in Northern Ireland. Church attendance, for example, is particularly low among the young urban working class in the Republic. Furthermore, the proportion of the population in the Republic who say they belong to no church grew sharply between the end of the 1990s and 2003 (going from 8.6 per cent to 17 per cent). However, that proportion is still below the level of Northern Ireland and other indicators of disaffiliation, such as the proportion who never attend church, have grown more slowly over the years. Among the minority who now no longer identify with any church, most continue to display various kinds of religious orientation, such as belief in God and a desire to have religious services to mark births, marriages and deaths. The picture is similar for disaffiliated Protestants in Northern Ireland, though with a slightly higher level of rejection of institutional religious affiliation and a slightly stronger leaning towards outright secularism.

Thus, in both the North and the Republic, the typical end-point of decline in religious adherence is not total rejection and indifference towards religion but a shift from strong and highly institutionalised attachment towards more intermittent and lukewarm adherence and towards various forms of privatised belief and commitment.

Table A3.1: Predictors of religious non-affiliation in the Republic of Ireland and Northern Ireland

	(Regression Coefficients)			
	Republic of Ireland		*Northern Ireland*	
	b	Beta	b	Beta
Male	0.01*	0.12	0.01*	0.13
Single	0.01	0.04	-0.01	-0.03
Age (years)	-0.01*	-0.31	-0.01*	-0.25
Education:				
Tertiary[a]	—	—	—	—
Secondary	-0.01	-0.01	0.01	0.01
No qualification	0.01	0.04	0.01	0.02
Class:				
Service[a]	—	—	—	—
Intermediate	0.01	0.08	0.01	0.05
Working	-0.01	-0.02	0.01	0.05
Unemployed	-0.01	-0.05	-0.01	-0.01
Constant	0.297*		0.430*	
R-squared	0.110		0.068	
[N]	[872]		[778]	

Note: *Significant at the 0.001 level or above; [a]Excluded category of comparison.

Source: European Values Study, 1999-2000.

4

Identity

Introduction

Northern Ireland is commonly seen as a society marked by sectarian division between two monolithic religious communities, Protestant and Catholic. The two communities are educated separately, are segregated both residentially and in their work places, and display low levels of religious mobility and inter-marriage (Breen and Hayes, 1996, 1997; Breen and Devine, 1999; Hayes and McAllister, 1999a; Stephen, 2000; O'Connor, 2002). This separation is exacerbated by a degree of social inequality. Despite the substantial progress that has been achieved in the reduction of religious inequalities in educational and occupational attainment over the last two decades, Catholics still remain on average less affluent than Protestants, are under-represented in the higher occupational groups and are substantially more likely to be unemployed (Osborne, 2004; Russell, 2004; Shuttleworth and Green, 2004). During the period from 1922 to 1972, Northern Ireland had its own parliament entirely dominated by representatives of the Protestant community. It has been widely acknowledged that, under this regime, Catholics were subject to discrimination in the labour market, in the operation of the electoral system and in the allocation of public housing (Whyte, 1983).

Differences in territorial allegiance and disagreement about the constitutional position of Northern Ireland remain the main focus of conflict between the two communities. Preferences on these issues are polarised around two competing ethnonational identities: those who identify themselves as British and wish to retain the union between Northern Ireland and Great Britain versus those who identify themselves as Irish and wish to see the two parts of the island of Ireland united. As McGarry and O'Leary (1995: 356) put it, 'the crucial endogenous cause of the conflict has been the presence of two competitive ethnonationalist communities within the same territory.' The conflict is further heightened in that the political cleavage seems to coincide almost exactly with the religious division between Protestant and Catholic (see Chapter 2). The deeply felt and cumulative character of these cleavages gives political life in Northern Ireland its distinctive character (McGarry and O'Leary, 1995; O'Duffy, 1995; White, 1997).

While there is no doubt that the terms 'Protestant' and 'Catholic' serve as important boundary-markers within Northern Ireland, one could argue that it oversimplifies matters to reduce the conflict wholly to religious terms or to a clash between two opposing and uniform ethnonational identities. Both within and between the dominant ethnonational traditions – British-unionist and Irish-nationalist – there are important differences in religious affiliation and state identity (Breen 1996; Trew, 1994, 1996; Duffy and Evans, 1997; Shirlow and McGovern, 1997; Elliott, 2000: 476-482; Coakley, 2002). Previous research has shown that not all Protestants in Northern Ireland perceive themselves as British and/or as unionist, nor do all Catholics identify themselves as either Irish or nationalist. There is also a sizeable minority within the Catholic community who wish to retain the union with Britain.

The situation in the Republic could hardly be more different, characterised as it is by overwhelming uniformity of identity. The national identity forged in the late nineteenth century was based on a strong linkage between 'Irish' and 'Catholic' and in that form provided a powerful bonding force for the majority Catholic population. It had an alienating effect on the Protestant minority in the newly independent Ireland and this was compounded on the Protestant side by a lingering attachment to a sense of Britishness. For the Church of Ireland, the largest Protestant church in the Republic, loyalty to the British crown continued to be strong until the mid-twentieth century (Acheson 2002: 224). However, the Free State strove to be fair to its Protestant minority (Corish 1985: 244). Protestant detachment from the new state and nation gave way to integration as time progressed. After the Second World War, as Acheson (2002: 233) puts it:

> [a] new Church of Ireland generation in the Republic moved away from inherited West Briton loyalties. Tacit acceptance of the state gave way to positive support, and southern church members, particularly in the cities, became more confident in their citizenship.

Gradually, according to the common perception, national identity among Protestants in the Republic became fully Irish, even though they retained a sense of denominational distinctiveness. In a recent biographical investigation of the issue, Murphy and Adair (2002) found that the vast majority of the Protestants they interviewed perceived themselves as 'Irish' and expressed no residual allegiance to Britain. As one voluntary Methodist preacher of fifty years standing stated: 'I have never felt anything other than Irish and have no sense of being British' (Murphy and Adair, 2002: 18). This increasingly widespread acceptance of an Irish identity among the Protestant population in the Republic has been accompanied by a growing sense of distance from Northern Protestants (Milne 2003: 78), and a rejection by southern Protestants of their portrayal by their northern co-religionists as an oppressed minority (Brewer and Higgins 1998: 163). In fact, by the mid-1990s, there was talk in the Church of Ireland of a possible split as its members in the Republic had 'lost all sympathetic understanding of the North' (Acheson 2002: 260). Protestants in the Republic by then, it was said, had 'far more in common with their Catholic fellow-citizens than with their Northern co-religionists' (ibid.). Thus, the expectation today would be that while religious identity among Protestants in the Republic may remain intact, this no longer implies ambivalence about either the Irishness of their national identity or their citizenship in the Irish state. Rather, the expectation would be that, in contrast to the North, the Republic is characterised by homogeneity across denominational groups in identity and uniform attachment to Irish citizenship.

The purpose of the present chapter is to see how far these interpretations and expectations hold true. The 1999-2000 EVS survey examined three different dimensions of collective identity in Ireland, North and South. The first is what we call *national* identity. In the Republic, 'Irish' is more or less the only identity that is relevant in this context, and this is confirmed in responses to an open-ended question, which, having referred to the notion of national identity, asked respondents 'In these terms how do you usually think of yourself?' (for results see below). In Northern Ireland, however, a wide set of options arises, including 'Irish', 'Northern Irish', 'British', and more. In order to take account of this range of options and to maintain comparability with previous research on the topic, the national identity question in Northern Ireland used a closed-ended format, presenting the respondent with a card with five options (see Table 4.1).

The second aspect of identity explored in the EVS data is *citizenship*. This aspect relates to the largely legal question of what citizenship one holds, a question that in practice is usually made concrete by reference to the passport one travels under (or would travel under if one were to travel). Here again, the options are simple in the Republic of Ireland, where Irish citizenship is the dominant possibility. A complication arises in Northern Ireland in that native-born residents are entitled to hold either Irish or British citizenship or both together. Thus the main citizenship options in Northern Ireland are British, Irish and joint British-Irish and this was reflected in the question asked. The third aspect of identity explored in this chapter is political identity in the sense of thinking of oneself in terms of one or other of the main political traditions of unionism and nationalism. Effectively, this aspect arises solely in Northern Ireland and the relevant question was asked there only.

Table 4.1: Religious identification and national identity in the Republic of Ireland and Northern Ireland

	(Percentages)			
	Catholic	Protestant	Non-affiliated	Total
Republic of Ireland:				
Irish	98.9	94.4	94.0	98.3
Other	1.1	5.6	6.0	1.7
[N]	[906]	[257]	[75]	[1,251]
Northern Ireland:				
British	8.0	75.8	52.6	44.7
Irish	63.6	3.0	11.9	29.2
Ulster	1.8	5.1	4.4	3.6
British-Irish*	11.6	6.5	6.7	8.5
Northern Irish	14.3	8.8	21.5	12.8
Other	0.8	0.9	3.0	1.1
[N]	[398]	[434]	[135]	[967]

Question: Most people think of themselves in terms of some national identity, such as American or French or German. In these terms, how do you usually think of yourself (Republic of Ireland)? Looking at this card, could you please tell me which of these best describes the way that you think of yourself (Northern Ireland)?

* 'Sometimes British and sometimes Irish'

Source: European Values Study, 1999-2000.

Religious identification and national identity

Table 4.1 shows the relationship between national identity and religious affiliation in the Republic of Ireland and Northern Ireland.[1] Confirming the common perception referred to above, the data in Table 4.1 show that the Republic of Ireland has a uniformity of national identity across denominational groupings – Catholics, Protestants and the non-affiliated alike overwhelmingly think of themselves as Irish. Only one out of the 257 Protestants in the Republic who were questioned in the survey chose to define themselves as 'Anglo-Irish', while only two defined themselves as British. Thus, as far as Protestants in the Republic of Ireland are concerned, attachment to an Irish identity is more or less universal.

[1] Note that the format of the national identity question used in the Republic of Ireland in the 1999-2000 EVS survey differed from that used for Northern Ireland – the text is reproduced under Table 4.1.

In Northern Ireland, by contrast, national identity is strongly differentiated by denominational group, though it is also far from uniform within each group. On the one hand, as one might expect, Catholics lean strongly towards an Irish identity, Protestants lean towards a British identity, and the non-affiliated are mixed. On the other hand, while almost two-thirds of Catholics in Northern Ireland think of themselves as 'Irish', about 14 per cent see themselves as 'Northern Irish', a slightly smaller proportion prefers a mixed British-Irish identity, and 8 per cent think of themselves as 'British'. Taking the latter two categories together, 20 per cent of Northern Irish Catholics consider themselves wholly or partly British.

Protestants remain strongly committed to a British identity. Three-quarters think of themselves in this way, but again, 9 per cent see themselves as 'Northern Irish' and 7 per cent as mixed British and Irish. Only 3 per cent of Protestants in Northern Ireland think of themselves as 'Irish'. It is notable also that, contrary to the situation in the late 1960s and 1970s, when 32 per cent and 20 per cent of Protestants respectively chose an 'Ulster' identity (Trew, 1996: 142), only 5 per cent chose such an identity in 1999-2000. While this decline may be partly interpreted as a sign of a growing unattractiveness of the 'Ulster' label, a methodological factor may also have been at work in the form of the introduction of a 'Northern Irish' identity as a response category in survey questionnaires since 1989. Once provided for in this way, the 'Northern Irish' label may have been preferred by both Protestants and Catholics as a less contentious alternative to the 'Ulster' label, thus leading to an apparent decline of the latter. As Moxon-Browne (1991: 28) explains:

> As a badge of identity, [the Northern Irish identity] is clearly less divisive than many others. Its attractiveness lies in its ambiguity. Catholics can see the label as referring geographically to the northern part of Ireland ... The interpretation of 'Northern Ireland' avoids any legitimisation of the border; Catholics' Irishness is thus not compromised. Protestants, on the other hand, see the term as adjectivally derived from 'Northern Ireland', the official nomenclature for a part of the United Kingdom; thereby, they do not compromise their British identity.

Trends in identity in Northern Ireland

Figures 4.1 to 4.3 trace the shifts in national identity among Catholics, Protestants, and the non-affiliated in Northern Ireland since 1968, using a range of survey sources. The set of response options provided to respondents in these surveys, though similar in many respects, are not all identical. In particular, as already mentioned, 'Northern Irish' was not included as a response option prior to 1989, and this gives rise to a discontinuity in the trend data in that year.

When one allows for the effect of the introduction of the 'Northern Irish' response category in 1989, there is no strong trend up or down in the choice of either an 'Irish' or 'British' identity among Catholics in Northern Ireland, the former being dominant and the latter being the choice of only about one in ten (Figure 4.1). Apart from the 1999-2000 EVS, the 'Northern Irish' option draws strong support, being usually chosen by about a quarter of Northern Catholics. The lower preference for the 'Northern Irish' identity in 1999-2000, is most likely due to changes in question wording. As already noted in Table 4.1, 12 per cent of the Catholic sample in the EVS survey chose the British-Irish label as their identity. The question-wording effect is confirmed by indications that the preference for the Northern Irish identity recovered in 2000 and in subsequent surveys did not present 'British-Irish' as a response option.

A large shift in identity occurred among Protestants at the beginning of the period under review, that is between 1968 and 1978 (see Figure 4.2). The 'Irish' and 'Ulster' identities declined and the British identity increased. The net effect of these changes was a substantial reduction in the claim to a common Irish identity among Protestants and a polarisation around Irish and British identities along denominational lines. This polarisation coincided with the outbreak of the troubles and the period of intense political violence which occurred in the late 1960s and early 1970s (Hayes and McAllister, 2001a). The shift among Protestants away from an Irish identity towards a British identity has not been reversed since.

As among Catholics, the introduction of a 'Northern Irish' option in surveys

Figure 4.1: National identity among Catholics in Northern Ireland, 1968-2003

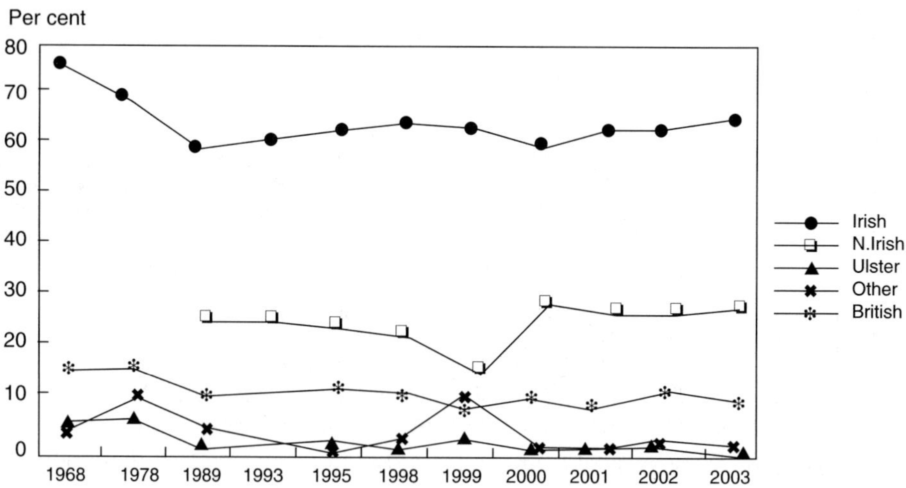

Note: Other includes 'British-Irish' and 'Other'. 'Northern Irish' not given as an option prior to 1989.

Sources: Loyalty Survey, 1968, Social Attitudes Survey, 1978, Northern Ireland Social Attitudes Survey, 1989, 1993 and 1995; Northern Ireland Election and Referendum Study, 1998; European Values Study, 1999-2000; Northern Ireland Life and Times Survey, 2000-2003.

Figure 4.2: National identity among Protestants in Northern Ireland, 1968-2003

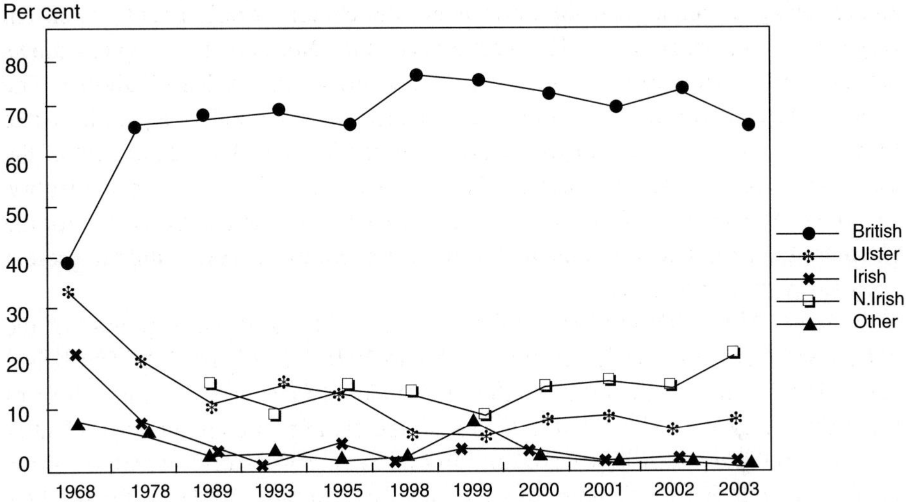

Note: Other includes 'British-Irish' and 'Other'. 'Northern Irish' not given as an option prior to 1989.

Sources: Loyalty Survey, 1968, Social Attitudes Survey, 1978, Northern Ireland Social Attitudes Survey, 1989, 1993 and 1995; Northern Ireland Election and Referendum Study, 1998; European Values Study, 1999-2000; Northern Ireland Life and Times Survey, 2000-2003.

Figure 4.3: National identity among the religiously non-affiliated in Northern Ireland, 1968-2003

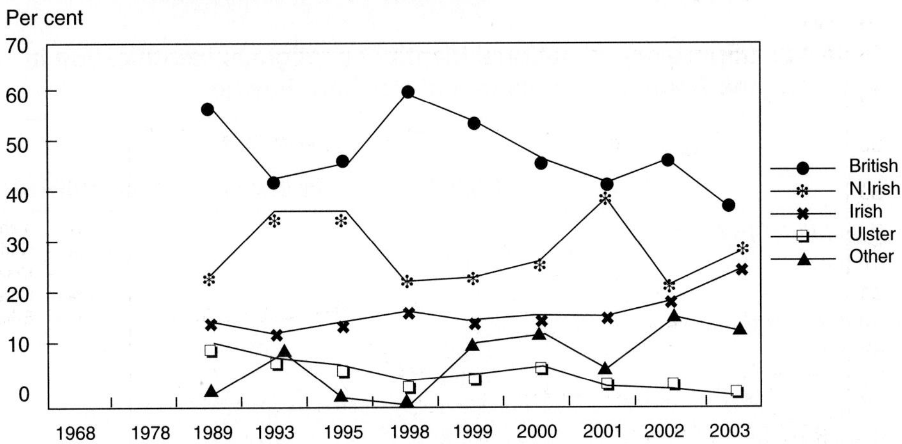

Note: Other includes 'British-Irish' and 'Other'. 'Northern Irish' not given as an option prior to 1989.

Sources: Loyalty Survey, 1968, Social Attitudes Survey, 1978, Northern Ireland Social Attitudes Survey, 1989, 1993 and 1995; Northern Ireland Election and Referendum Study, 1998; European Values Study, 1999-2000; Northern Ireland Life and Times Survey, 2000-2003.

from 1989 onwards resulted in a growth in preference for this label among Protestants, albeit in this instance at the expense of the 'Ulster' identity. Though interpretation of the data is complicated by changes in question wording, there is some evidence of a strengthening of the Northern Irish identity among Protestants in 2003.

The religiously non-affiliated also show this shift towards a Northern Irish identity (Figure 4.3). This adds to the sense of growing support for this identity across all religious identifications.

Importance of identity in the Republic of Ireland and Northern Ireland

Table 4.2 explores patterns of national identity further by setting out the level of importance the different denominational groups attach to the identity they chose for themselves. Data are reported only for those categories for which the sample size was large enough to provide the basis for an estimate. Respondents in the Republic attribute a high level of importance to their Irish identity across denominational groups, though Protestants and the non-affiliated are slightly less emphatic in this regard than Catholics.

In Northern Ireland, the level of importance attached to chosen identities reflects traditional allegiances. For Catholics who define themselves as Irish and for Protestants who define themselves as British, identity is generally regarded as highly important. For those who break away from these dominant identities, the alternatives are less strongly adhered to. Northern Catholics who choose a British or British-Irish identity attach only limited importance to it, and the same is true of

Table 4.2: Importance of national identity by religious identification in the Republic of Ireland and Northern Ireland

		(Means)	
	Catholic	Protestant	Non-affiliated
Republic of Ireland:			
Irish	8.5	7.9	7.9
Northern Ireland:			
British	5.7	8.3	6.8
Irish	8.4	–	–
Ulster	–	–	–
British-Irish*	5.8	5.1	–
Northern Irish	6.0	6.7	6.1

Question: Could you tell me how important it is to you that you are (chosen identity)?

Note: Scale: 1= not important, 10= very important; – , too few cases (less than 25) for an estimate.

*Sometimes British and sometimes Irish.

Source: European Values Study, 1999-2000.

Protestants who choose a British-Irish identity. The 'Northern Irish' identity rates slightly better among both the Catholics and Protestants who hold it than do the varieties of British identity for Catholics or the British-Irish identity for Protestants, but it still falls well below the level of importance attached to the two dominant identities. These patterns suggest that those in Northern Ireland who reject the dominant identity held within their own denominational grouping have not found an alternative identity capable of eliciting the same intensity of feeling.

The intensity of feeling that attached to national identity can also be gauged by looking at pride in national identity. This measure occurs in the Eurobarometer surveys, from which it is possible to trace trends in intensity of national identity over time since 1982 (Table 4.3).[2] The data for Northern Ireland in Table 4.3 are based on small sample sizes (approximately 300 cases in each year) and the relevant question was not framed to take account of the complexities of identity in Northern Ireland. While the evidence in trends in Northern Ireland is therefore less robust than the evidence for the Republic of Ireland, it is of interest nonetheless.

The most striking feature of the patterns revealed in Table 4.3 is the surge in pride in identity in the Republic during the 1990s. In 1988, 55 per cent of respondents in the Republic were 'very proud' of their national identity. By 1997, that had jumped to 72 per cent and it remained more or less at that level up to 2003. Analysis of these trends by age-group, which is not shown here for space reasons, indicates that the main driver of this rise was a sharp increase in pride in identity among younger people – for example, the proportion of 18-24 year olds who said they were 'very proud' of their Irish identity rose from 48 per cent in 1982 to 70 per cent in 1997. Obviously the increase could be due to a number of different factors such as the improvement in the economy, progress towards peace in Northern Ireland, or Irish success on the international stage in sport or popular music.

The picture in Northern Ireland is quite different: the percentages reporting that they were very proud of their national identity were lower than in the Republic and showed no sustained upward trend. Since the early 1980s, the proportion of people in Northern Ireland saying they were 'very proud' of their national identity has fluctuated around 50 per cent. While we need to bear in mind the limitations of the data already noted, the data do seem to suggest that the contested and problematic nature of national identity in Northern Ireland has a dampening effect on feelings about identity in that society.

---

[2] We later look at a related matter, pride in citizenship, but data on this issue are available for only one point in time – the 1999-2000 EVS.

Table 4.3: Pride in national identity in the Republic of Ireland and Northern Ireland, 1982-2003

	(Per cent 'very proud' of national identity)							
	1982	1983	1985	1986	1988	1994	1997	2003
Republic of Ireland	59	54	53	57	55	69	72	71
Northern Ireland	41	51	60	48	46	55	47	52

Source: Mannheim Eurobarometer Trend File 1970-1999; Eurobarometer 60.1, Autumn 2003.

Socio-demographic correlates of national identity in Northern Ireland

Previous research in Northern Ireland has indicated that there are important variations in the demographic characteristics of respondents who identify themselves as Irish, Northern Irish, Ulster and British, and this seems to be particularly the case within the Protestant community. In his analysis of the 1978 Northern Ireland Attitudes Survey, Moxon-Browne (1983) found that what he called 'upper class' Protestants in Northern Ireland were more likely to claim a British identity than their working-class counterparts but that there were no class differences in identity among Catholics. However, later analysis by Trew (1996: 144) found that, irrespective of religious background, both the 'Irish' and 'British' labels were more widely adopted by the less educated, particularly by those with no educational qualifications.

Using the 1999-2000 EVS data, Table 4.4 shows the degree to which support for the two dominant identities – Irish and British – among Catholics and Protestants varies according to the socio-demographic characteristics of respondents. Among Catholics, men are significantly more likely than women to adopt the dominant identity (Irish). However, there is no corresponding gender difference in adoption of a British identity among Protestants. Nor are there any significant age differences in choice of dominant identity among either Catholics or Protestants. However, as in Trew's (1996) findings, there is some evidence that the dominant identity on each side is more strongly endorsed by the socio-economically less privileged, though the evidence is not entirely consistent across all indicators. Those with no educational qualifications are most supportive of the dominant identity among both Catholics and Protestants, while among Catholics the unemployed are significantly more likely to choose an 'Irish' identity than the employed. Among Protestants, the unemployed are slightly *less* likely to choose a British identity than are the employed; however, working class Protestants are significantly more likely to choose that identity than are other social classes.

Table 4.4: Support for dominant religious national identities in Northern Ireland by socio-demographic background

	(Percentages)	
	Catholics who define themselves as Irish	Protestants who define themselves as British
Gender:	#	
Men	70	73
Women	58	79
Church attendance:		
Regular	62	78
Irregular	76	72
Age:		
18-25	64	79
26-35	57	76
36-45	64	79
46-55	67	76
56+	62	75
Education:	#	#
Tertiary	61	59
Secondary	59	75
No qualification	71	84
Employment Status:	#	
Employed	57	77
Unemployed	71	75
Social Class:		#
Service	65	53
Intermediate	56	76
Working	66	89

Note: # Significant group differences at the 0.05 level or above.

Source: European Values Study, 1999-2000.

Multivariate analysis confirms these patterns (see Table A4.1 at end of chapter). For example, within the Protestant population, the key predictor of a British identity is social class. Both the lower non-manual (intermediate) and working class Protestants are significantly more likely to choose a British identity than their service class (higher non-manual) counterparts. Among Catholics, in contrast, the two predictors in accounting for an Irish identity are gender and employment status: males and the unemployed were significantly more likely to claim an Irish identity than either females or the employed.

National identities in Ireland: ethnic or civic?

The theoretical and historical literature on nations and nationalism puts forward a distinction between two types of nationalism and, hence, two types of national identity. The distinction has been variously expressed as territorial versus ethnic (Smith, 1991), nationism versus nationalism (Fishman, 1968), demotic versus ethnic (Francis, 1968) and, perhaps most frequently, ethnic versus civic (Smith, 1991, Hjerm, 1998a, 1998b; Jones and Smith, 2001a, 2001b). The distinction also underlies Habermas's notion of 'constitutional patriotism' (Habermas, 1992). The ethnic model emphasises a community of birth and descent. National identity in this model is more a matter of ascription than of choice: 'whether you stayed in your community or emigrated to another, you remained ineluctably, organically, a member of the community of your birth and were forever stamped by it' (Smith, 1991: 11). A common language and shared religious beliefs have often been regarded as 'markers' of such ethnic identity. The civic model, in contrast, simply implies a common territory, shared political allegiance and acceptance of common laws and political institutions as the basis of sharing a particular identity.

Modern nationalisms and national identities, however, are never entirely consistent with either model. Ethnic and civic identities are ideal types that in practice can exist in one of several combinations and in varying degrees: '... sometimes civic and territorial elements predominate; at other times it is ethnic and vernacular components that are emphasised' (Smith, 1991: 13). This inherent duality often enhances nationalism's appeal as a political ideology and a source of political legitimation and solidarity (Smith, 1991: 15-16).

The issue of the *degree* of endorsement of any of these bases of identity is also very significant. Since identity is multi-faceted, endorsement of an attribute or basis of identity does not necessarily imply that one cannot have the identity without also having the attribute in question. This is why, in the analysis that follows we focus on the proportions saying a particular attribute is 'very important'. This still does not imply that the identity is regarded as being exclusive to those who possess the attribute; rather it enables us to identify *tendencies* towards particular conceptions of national identity.

Such tendencies were measured in the 1999-2000 EVS by presenting respondents with a list of possible bases of identity and asking them to rate the importance of each (see Table 4.5). The ethnic dimension was tapped with items on the importance for national identity of language (Irish or English) and of religion (Catholic or Protestant), while the civic dimension was tapped by items dealing with respect for the country's institutions and laws, with possession of citizenship and with the subjective feeling of being Irish or British. (In regard to each of the attributes or bases of identity, respondents were also offered a 'can't choose' option.) In analyses of this type, the main focus is on people's perceptions of the bases of their own identities, or at least of the identities which are dominant in their own communities. While this is our main concern here also, the EVS survey in Northern Ireland asked respondents about their perceptions of the bases of both Irish and British identity, irrespective of what identity they chose for themselves. In the case of Northern Ireland, therefore, it is possible to establish people's perceptions of the bases of identity across the community divide, that is, where Catholics give their views on British as well as Irish identity and Protestants give their views on Irish as well as British identity. We will touch on this aspect of the findings briefly below.

Table 4.5 sets out the perceived characteristics of Irish identity broken down by denominational groups in the Republic of Ireland and in Northern Ireland. In the case of the conception of identity among Catholics in the Republic, civic features (citizenship, feeling and respect for institutions/laws) predominate, being regarded as 'very important' characteristics of Irish identity by between 40 and 60 per cent. Ethnic characteristics lag far behind. Despite the long association between Catholicism and nationalism, less than 30 per cent regard being a

Table 4.5: Religious identification and perceptions of the foundations of Irish identity in the Republic of Ireland and Northern Ireland

	(Per cent who say 'very important')			
	Catholic	Protestant	Non-affiliated	Total
Ethnic Dimension:		Republic of Ireland		
Be a Catholic	28	2	8	26
Able to speak Irish	13	3	8	13
Civic Dimension:				
Feel Irish	47	29	37	46
Irish citizenship	62	50	57	61
Respect Ireland's political institutions & laws	45	40	24	43
Ethnic Dimension:		Northern Ireland		
Be a Catholic	20	3	7	11
Able to speak Irish	9	3	4	6
Civic Dimension:				
Feel Irish	34	16	22	25
Irish citizenship	33	26	25	29
Respect the country's political institution and laws	37	33	25	34

Question: Some people say that the following things are important for being truly Irish. Others say that they are not important. How important do you think each of the following is?

Source: European Values Study, 1999-2000.

Catholic as very important for being fully Irish. And notwithstanding the carefully nurtured relationship between the Irish language and the nation (recall Pearse's 'not free merely but Gaelic as well; not Gaelic merely but free as well'), only 13 per cent regard ability to speak Irish as a very important attribute of Irish identity.

Irish identity shows a similar tendency towards a civic rather than an ethnic conception among Catholics in Northern Ireland, with only 20 per cent regarding being a Catholic as very important and only 9 per cent taking this view in relation to the Irish language. It is notable, however, that the civic features of identity also receive less endorsement among Catholics in Northern Ireland than among Catholics in the Republic. This reinforces observations we have already made about the degree of hesitancy and uncertainty that attaches to the question of identity in Northern Ireland.

Turning to the perceived bases of British identity in Northern Ireland (Table 4.6), religion again plays a minor part – only 30 per cent of Northern Ireland Protestants regard being a Protestant as a very important part of being British. Civic attributes, while not as high as markers of identity as in the Republic of Ireland, range from 47 to 54 per cent. Given the similarity in the proportions of people in the Republic and in Northern Ireland who strongly endorse religion as a basis of national identity, it is worth looking around for a comparative yardstick with which to assess the figures found in Ireland. While these measures of the bases of national identity were only used in the version of the EVS conducted in Northern Ireland and the Republic, the question is part of the ISSP national identity survey. Analysing these comparative data from 23 countries, Jones and Smith (2001b) found that one in five respondents

Table 4.6: Religious identification and perceptions of the foundations of British identity in Northern Ireland

	(Per cent who say 'very important')			
	Catholic	Protestant	Non-affiliated	Total
Ethnic Dimension:				
Be a Protestant	2	30	11	16
Able to speak English	21	46	29	34
Civic Dimension:				
Feel British	14	47	26	31
British citizenship	17	53	32	36
Respect the country's political institution and laws	27	54	29	40

Question: Some people say that the following things are important for being truly British. Others say that they are not important. How important do you think each of the following is?

Source: European Values Study, 1999-2000.

rated religion as 'very important' for national identity. This puts both Ireland and Northern Ireland closer to the norm in this regard than many might have anticipated and certainly closer to the norm than interpretations of the Northern Ireland conflict as a religious struggle would suggest.

There is one striking difference between responses to this question among the various groups we have been examining. This is the difference between the proportion of Protestants in Northern Ireland who regard ability to speak English as being very important to being fully British (46 per cent) and the proportion of Catholics in the Republic who regard ability to speak Irish as similarly important in regard to Irish identity (13 per cent). In one sense, there is a simple explanation for this contrast. English is the language of the vast majority of the population of Britain whereas Irish is actually spoken by a very small minority of the population of the Republic of Ireland (or of the island of Ireland) and, thus, people's response to this question is simply a reflection of the unequal status of the two languages. Even taking that into account, however, the significance of the proportion of responses that make language a 'very important' marker of identity should not be underestimated. It is possible that the emphasis occurs because ability to speak English is almost universal in Britain and in Northern Ireland and is simply a practical skill that is necessary for full participation in British (civic) society. It is also possible, however, that the quite widespread emphasis on ability to speak English is an indication of endorsement of a cultural or ethnic characteristic that, if it is not possessed, must be painstakingly acquired before an individual can be truly (ethnically) British.

As mentioned earlier, Catholics in Northern Ireland were asked about the bases of British as well as Irish identity and Protestants were asked about Irish as well as British identity. The data on these questions are included in Tables 4.5 and 4.6. The main issue here is whether people on either side of the community divide in Northern Ireland are more likely to characterise the opposing dominant identity in ethnic terms than they are their own. In view of the low priority accorded to religion as a basis of their own identities by both sides, it is of particular interest to note whether they are more likely to ascribe sectarian bases to the opposing dominant identity. We see from the data, however, that such a tendency is absent: neither Catholics nor Protestants in Northern Ireland ascribe an ethnic character to the opposing identity, and in particular there is virtually no support for the idea that religion is important to the opposing identity.

Returning to the question posed in the heading to this section of this chapter, we can conclude that Irish and British identities as seen by Protestants and Catholics in Northern Ireland and in the Republic tend to be civic rather than ethnic.[3] Relatively small minorities (just under one-third of the relevant groups)

[3] We have also analysed the data on bases of identity by focusing on those who endorse a given identity rather than focusing on Protestants and Catholics. The findings remain the same whichever basis of comparison is used.

show a tendency to define the identity associated with their group in religiously based ethnic terms. But this is not all that different from the one-in-five showing a similar tendency across a range of 23 countries referred to by Jones and Smith (2001b). The closest any of the groups in question come to a possible ethnic definition of identity is indicated by the 46 per cent of Northern Protestants who say that ability to speak English is a very important criterion of being British. However, the significance of this finding is open to contrary interpretations and, in any event, is not a factor in the conflict in Northern Ireland.

The small role attributed to religion as a foundation of identity by respondents on all sides may be regarded as paradoxical. As we have seen in the previous section, choice of identity in Northern Ireland is not wholly dictated by whether one is Protestant or Catholic, but denomination is the factor most closely linked with identity. Yet, when respondents are asked to rate the importance of various features of identity, religion comes at the bottom of the list. This may reflect wishful thinking, the view that in some sense religion *ought not to* matter for national identity even if in the present reality in Northern Ireland it matters a great deal. The other explanation lies in the difference between religion as an ethnic marker and religion *per se*. When respondents are asked the question that produced the evidence we have been considering, they may be thinking primarily in terms of the substance of religion. The lack of connection between religion in that sense and identity does not disprove the *de facto* connection between religious denomination and which community one belongs to nor that between religious denomination and the political aspirations one holds.

Citizenship

As suggested earlier, patterns of citizenship in the Republic of Ireland are straightforward, in that the vast majority of the population are Irish citizens and there is no real difference across denominational groups in this respect (Table 4.7). However, when we go beyond the status of citizenship to look at the subjective feeling attached to that status, a notable difference in emphasis appears. As we saw earlier, people in the Republic of Ireland as a whole have high levels of pride in their national identity and Table 4.7 shows that this carries through into a high level of pride in Irish citizenship. However, Protestants in the Republic are significantly less enthusiastic on this front than Catholics: only 49 per cent of Protestants say they are very proud of their Irish citizenship (compared to 75 per cent of Catholics). This is an indication that Irish citizenship may mean something different to Protestants than it does to Catholics, even if the two groups are equally clear that their citizenship is, in fact, Irish.

Table 4.8 turns to the more complex picture in Northern Ireland. This table classifies citizenship not only between Catholics and Protestants but also within each denominational group between those who adopt the dominant national

Table 4.7: Citizenship and pride in citizenship in the Republic of Ireland

	(Percentages) Catholic	Protestant
% who are Irish citizens	99	95
Pride in Irish citizenship:		
Very Proud	75	49
Quite Proud	24	44
Not Very Proud	1	6
Not at all Proud	0	2
[N]	[1,103]	[257]

Question: Are you a citizen of the Republic of Ireland? How proud are you to be an Irish citizen?
Source: European Values Study, 1999-2000.

identity of their group (Irish in the case of Catholics, British in the case of Protestants) and those who do not. This cross-classification enables us to see the interaction between claimed citizenship and sense of national identity. Looking first at the data for all Catholics and all Protestants in Table 4.8, we can see that citizenship in Northern Ireland is substantially, but by no means completely, differentiated along denominational lines. The vast majority of Protestants (86 per cent) declare themselves to be British citizens, while almost all of the remainder declare themselves to be joint British-Irish citizens. Almost none say that they have

Table 4.8: Citizenship, religious identification and national identity in Northern Ireland

	Catholic Identity (Percentages)			Protestant Identity		
	Catholic-Irish	Catholic-Other	All	Protestant-British	Protestant-Other	All
Citizenship:						
Britain	5	29	14	93	64	86
Ireland	46	13	33	0	4	1
Both	49	59	53	7	32	13
[N]	[211]	[126]	[337]	[321]	[99]	[420]

Question: Individuals in Northern Ireland are entitled to claim both British and Irish citizenship. In terms of your own personal choice, do you regard yourself as a citizen of Britain, the Republic of Ireland, or both Britain and the Republic of Ireland?

Source: European Values Study, 1999-2000.

solely Irish citizenship. While far from being the reverse image of this, the picture among Catholics in Northern Ireland is very different. This is because, quite strikingly, a majority of Catholics (53 per cent) regard themselves as having joint British and Irish citizenship.

When we distinguish by national identity within the Catholic and Protestant samples in Northern Ireland, we find that even among those Catholics who define their *identity* as Irish, there are marginally more who see themselves as British-Irish citizens than as Irish citizens (49 per cent as opposed to 46 per cent). Among those Catholics who define their national identity as something other than Irish, the proportion who declare themselves to be Irish citizens falls to 13 per cent and the proportion who define themselves as British citizens rises to 29 per cent. In contrast to the heterogeneity of citizenship on the Catholic side, the overwhelming majority (93 per cent) of those Protestants who define their national identity as British follow through by choosing British citizenship. Even among the small proportion who chose an alternative or mixed identity, a clear majority (64 per cent) also claim British citizenship, while only 32 per cent of this alternative or mixed identity group report having mixed or British-Irish citizenship. These patterns, then, confirm that, as with national identity, citizenship in Northern Ireland breaks down along denominational lines but, because of extensive variation within the Catholic community, the lines are not at all as tightly drawn as might have been expected.

Table 4.9 turns to the question of how proud people in Northern Ireland are of the citizenship they claim for themselves.[4] The first notable feature of the results on this issue is that levels of pride in citizenship are lower overall in Northern Ireland than in the Republic. Taking all citizenship categories together, only 33 per cent are 'very proud' of their citizenship in Northern Ireland, which compares to the 75 per cent among Catholics and 49 per cent among Protestants that was reported for the Republic of Ireland earlier. The second notable feature is the surprising differences in pride in citizenship within Northern Ireland itself across the citizenship categories. Protestants who claim British citizenship are substantially less proud of their citizenship than are Catholics who claim Irish citizenship (40 per cent of the former are 'very proud' of their citizenship compared to 57 per cent of the latter). However, Catholics who claim a joint British-Irish citizenship have significantly lower levels of pride (only 20 per cent being 'very proud').

These results should not be taken to suggest that either Protestants or Catholics in Northern Ireland have *negative* views of their citizenship – the negative responses on this item ('not very proud' and 'not at all proud') are subscribed to by very few respondents in any of the citizenship categories in Table 4.9. They do suggest,

4 We have already dealt with the issue of pride in national identity but, because the Eurobarometer data on which that discussion was based do not include variables on religious denomination it was not possible to explore Protestant-Catholic differences on the issue (see Table 4.3).

Table 4.9: Pride in citizenship in Northern Ireland

(Percentages)

	Catholic			Protestant			All
	British	Irish	Joint	British	Irish	Joint	
Very proud	2	57	20	40	–	17	33
Quite proud	72	40	57	52	–	57	53
Not very proud	23	4	18	7	–	17	12
Not at all proud	2	0	4	1	–	9	3
N	[43]	[111]	[142]	[340]	[4]	[35]	[787]

Note: – too few cases for an estimate
Source: European Values Study, 1999-2000.

though, that enthusiasm for the various forms of citizenship is restrained in Northern Ireland. That may reflect a degree of ambivalence about all of the citizenship options on offer, itself a historical by-product of the contested nature of identity within this society. To the extent that such ambivalence occurs, its presence among Protestants in regard to British citizenship seems to be greater than among Catholics in regard to Irish citizenship, or at least among those Catholics whose primary citizenship orientation is towards Ireland.

As a final note on this issue, it is worth drawing a brief comparison between levels of pride in citizenship in both the Republic of Ireland and Northern Ireland and the other societies covered by the 1999-2000 EVS. Figure 4.4 does so by showing the percentages who are 'very proud' of their citizenship across the full range of countries. As in previous EVS data (Dalton, 1999: 73) the Republic of Ireland emerges from this comparison as having high levels of pride in citizenship while Northern Ireland is low, though by no means the lowest. The former West Germany comes out at the bottom of the comparison, reflecting a burden of guilt arising from its twentieth-century history (Dalton, 1996: 277), but the Netherlands is also extremely low, as are Belgium and a number of former communist countries. Other cross-national investigations using World Values Survey (WVS) data from the early to mid-1990s confirm these findings (Klingemann, 1999: 42-43; Inglehart, 1997: 302-305).

Political identity in Northern Ireland

Divergent national identities in Northern Ireland are important because they express themselves in conflicting *political* identities, that is, people's identification of themselves as unionist or nationalist. The intimate relationship between national and political identity – the ethnonationalist basis of politics – is frequently seen as the main cause of conflict in the North. Thus, McGarry and O'Leary (1995: 354) argue that 'the conflict in Northern Ireland is ethnonational, a systematic quarrel between the political organisations of two [ethnic] communities who want their state to be ruled by their nation, or who want what they perceive as "their" state to protect their nation.' As discussed earlier, however, the linkages are not complete – not all Protestants in Northern Ireland perceive themselves as British and unionist, nor do all Catholics identify themselves as either Irish and nationalist.

To investigate this matter further, Table 4.10 examines the degree to which support for the two dominant political identities – unionist versus nationalist – varies by religious background. Corroborating the findings of previous research, the present results show that while there is considerable polarisation between Catholics and Protestants around nationalist and unionist political identities there is also a substantial middle ground in both denominational groups comprised of those who do not place themselves under either political label.[5] On the one hand, as one might expect, Catholics lean towards a nationalist political identity, Protestants lean towards a unionist political identity, and the non-affiliated reject both labels in favour of the intermediate 'neither' position. However, although 58 per cent of Catholics define themselves as 'nationalist', 42 per cent define themselves as 'neither'. And, while two-thirds of Protestants define themselves as unionist, one-third define themselves as 'neither'. There is a marked unwillingness on the part of either Catholics or Protestants to cross traditional boundaries and adopt the opposing identity. There are almost no Catholics who are willing to call themselves unionist and no Protestants who are willing to call themselves nationalist. This point is significant, especially in regard to Catholics, since as we will see in the next

Table 4.10: Religious identification and political identity in Northern Ireland

	(Percentages)			
	Catholic	Protestant	Non-affiliated	Total
Unionist	0.5	66.0	28.1	33.7
Nationalist	57.7	0.7	6.7	25.0
Neither	41.8	33.3	65.2	41.3
[N]	[388]	[421]	[135]	[944]

Question: Generally speaking, do you think of yourself as a unionist, a nationalist or neither?

Source: European Values Study, 1999-2000.

5 Evidence from other indicators not reported here suggests that a small minority of those who label themselves 'neither nationalist nor unionist' may belong to the extremes rather than the middle ground, for example, in that they might think of themselves as 'loyalists' or 'republicans' rather than 'unionists' or 'nationalists'. Nevertheless, this minority is likely to be small enough for it to be reasonable to refer to the 'neither' category as a middle-ground group.

Figure 4.4: Per cent 'very proud' of citizenship in European countries

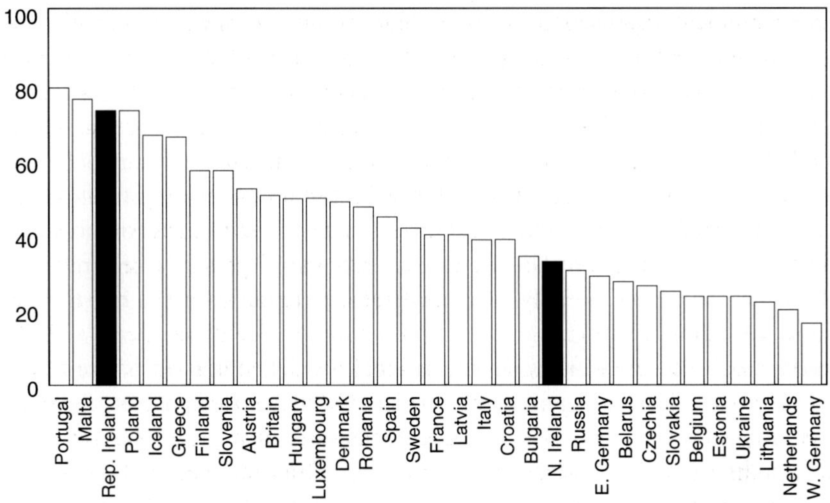

Source: European Values Study, 1999-2000.

chapter, there are quite a few Catholics who lean towards the unionist position on major constitutional questions concerning Northern Ireland.

Trends in political identity

Figures 4.5 to 4.7 trace the shifts in political identity among Catholics, Protestants and those without a religious affiliation in Northern Ireland since 1989, drawing on a range of survey sources. Among Catholics, the general trend up to 1996 was to divide more or less equally between those who viewed themselves as nationalists and those who considered themselves neither nationalist nor unionist, though there were some short-term fluctuations around this trend, especially in the earlier years (Figure 4.5). Between 1996 and 1998, the proportion of Catholics who identified themselves as nationalist increased sharply – from 47 per cent to 66 per cent – most likely reflecting a surge in support for the nationalist position around the time of the ratification of the Good Friday Agreement in 1998 (Hayes and McAllister, 1999b: 39). While there has been some fluctuation since then, the new level established in 1998 has been more or less maintained.

Since the late 1980s political identity among Protestants in Northern Ireland has tended to be more stable than it has been among Catholics (Figure 4.6). In successive surveys, over 70 per cent of Protestants identified themselves as unionist, though a significant minority, approximately one-quarter across all survey years, declined to identify themselves as either unionist or nationalist. The trend in

Protestant support for the unionist label remained flat up until 1999, when it dipped slightly, only to return to 70 per cent or above in subsequent surveys.

Those without any denominational affiliation show a strong tendency to place themselves in the 'neither unionist nor nationalist' camp throughout the period since 1989 (Figure 4.7). This indicates that religious non-affiliation tends to be accompanied by a degree of political dis-engagement, at least as far as the traditional identities with unionism or nationalism are concerned. We cannot be sure whether there is a causal connection between these two forms of non-affiliation, nor in what direction such a causal link might run if it is there. Since many of those who retain their religious affiliation also place themselves in the 'neither' camp, religious disaffiliation is clearly not the only, nor even the most important, route into the lack of political affiliation.

In summary, political identity, in the sense in which this term is used here, remains sharply divided along religious lines in Northern Ireland. Yet, there are many within each of the two main religious communities who see themselves as 'neither unionist nor nationalist', and the tendency to do so is even stronger among those who see themselves as belonging to no religious denomination. Nevertheless, for the majority, the traditional picture holds: Catholicism and Protestantism are closely bound up with the traditional allegiances to nationalist and unionist political identities. While it is true that not all Catholics are nationalist and not all Protestants unionist, it is equally true that Catholics who are willing to call themselves unionist and Protestants who are willing to call themselves nationalist are so thin on the ground that they barely register in sample surveys. The tight interconnection between religion and political identity in Northern Ireland has not been enough to prevent leakage into a middle ground between the two traditional camps but it has prevented the development of cross-cutting membership where people would belong to one side on the religious dimension and the opposing side on the political identity dimension.

Overlap in religious, national and political identity

So far we have looked at the three forms of collective identity (national identity, citizenship, and political identity) separately and at the extent to which each divides along denominational lines. We now turn to the relationships between them and ask to what extent these identities are congruent with each other. To simplify the analysis, we focus on two dimensions – national identity and political identity.

The data (see Table 4.11) show that congruence between religious affiliation is far from complete. A bare majority of Protestants (54 per cent) identified themselves as *both* British and unionist. An even smaller proportion of Catholics (45 per cent) claimed to be *both* Irish and nationalist. Thus, for a majority of Catholics (55 per cent), the relationship between national and political identity is far from coterminous.

Figure 4.8 traces the trends in the extent of congruence in identities on the two

Figure 4.5: Political identity among Catholics in Northern Ireland, 1989-2003

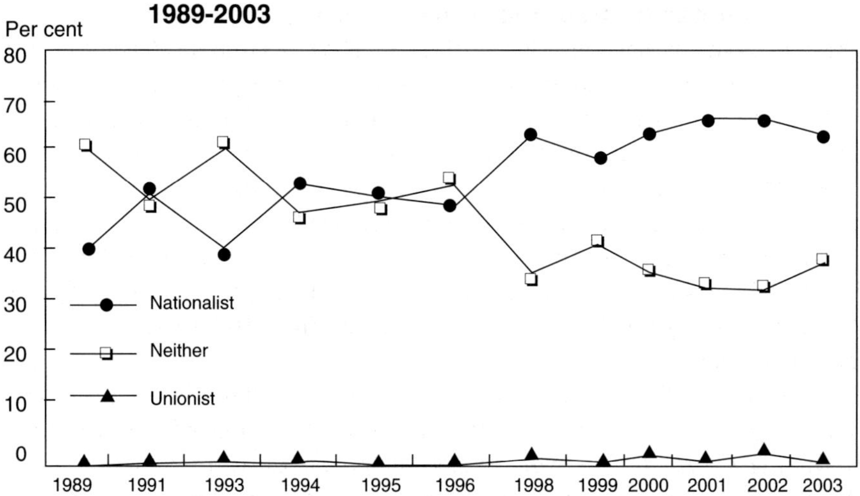

Sources: Northern Ireland Social Attitudes Survey, 1989, 1991, 1993-1996; Northern Ireland Referendum and Election Survey, 1998; European Values Study, 1999-2000. Northern Ireland Life and Times Survey, 2000-2003.

Figure 4.6: Political identity among Protestants in Northern Ireland, 1989-2003

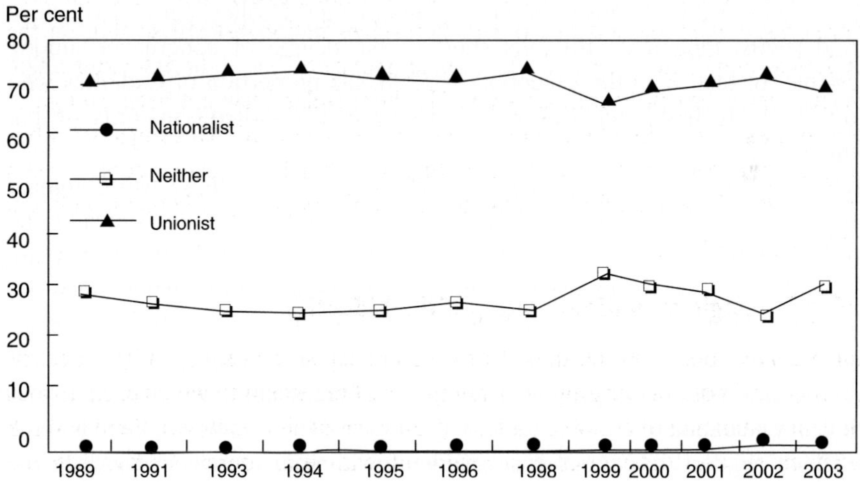

Sources: Northern Ireland Social Attitudes Survey, 1989, 1991, 1993-1996; Northern Ireland Referendum and Election Survey, 1998; European Values Study, 1999-2000; Northern Ireland Life and Times Survey, 2000-2003.

sides of the divide in Northern Ireland since 1989, that is in the proportion of Catholics who define themselves as Irish and nationalist and the proportion of Protestants who define themselves as British and unionist. The level of such congruence among Protestants has remained relatively stable since the late 1980s,

Figure 4.7: Political identity among the religiously non-affiliated in Northern Ireland, 1989-2003

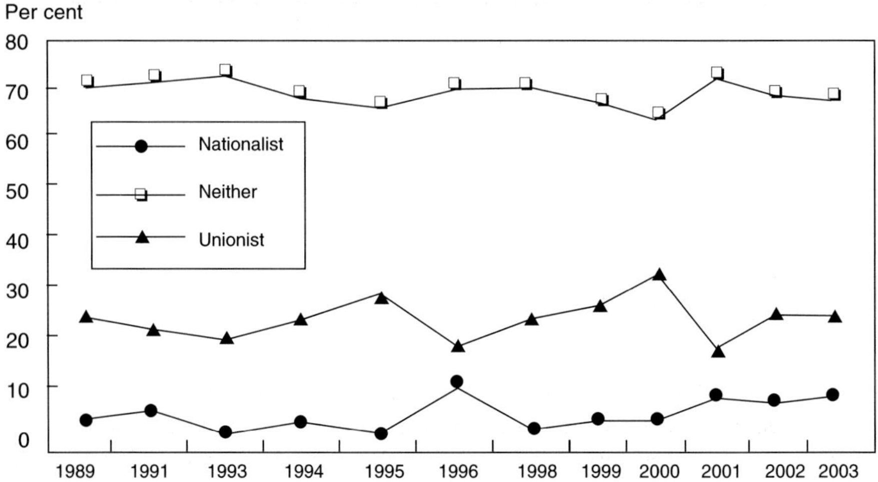

Sources: Northern Ireland Social Attitudes Survey, 1989, 1991, 1993-1996; Northern Ireland Referendum and Election Survey, 1998; European Values Study, 1999-2000; Northern Ireland Life and Times Survey, 2000-2003.

scarcely shifting by more than five percentage points over the period. In contrast, congruence in identity seems to be increasing among Catholics, particularly since the mid-1990s, though it still falls short of the degree of congruence among Protestants. In fact, with the exception of 1998, the proportion of Catholics who claim to be both 'Irish' and 'Nationalist' has never constituted a majority of that community.

Table 4.12 examines the degree to which congruence in these two dominant identities – national and political – among Catholics and Protestants varies by the socio-demographic characteristics of respondents. Among Catholics, men are significantly more likely to have a congruent Irish-nationalist identity than are women, but there is no corresponding gender difference in adopting a British-unionist identity among Protestants. Nor are there any significant age differences in relation to this issue among either Catholics or Protestants. However, as in our previous investigation of national identity itself (see Table 4.4 above), there is some evidence to suggest that congruence in identity is more pronounced among the socio-economically less privileged in each denominational grouping, though the evidence is not consistent across all indicators. Among Catholics, those with no educational qualifications and the unemployed are significantly more likely to be Irish and nationalist in identity, while among Protestants the working class are more likely to be British and unionist.

Multivariate analysis confirms these observations (see Table A4.2). For example, among the Protestant population, the key predictor of a British-unionist identity is

Table 4.11: Relationship between religious affiliation and national and political identity in Northern Ireland

	(Percentages)
Catholic:	
Irish	64
Nationalist	58
Irish-Nationalist	45
Protestant:	
British	76
Unionist	66
British-Unionist	54

Source: European Values Study, 1999-2000.

social class. Both lower, non-manual (intermediate) and working class Protestants are significantly more likely to choose this dual identity status (British-unionist) than their service class (upper non-manual) counterparts. Among Catholics, in contrast, the three key predictors of an Irish-nationalist identity are gender, education and class: males, the uneducated, and the working class are significantly more likely to claim an Irish-nationalist identity than either females, the better educated, or their non-manual class counterparts.

Figure 4.8: Congruence in religious, national and political identity in Northern Ireland, 1989-1999

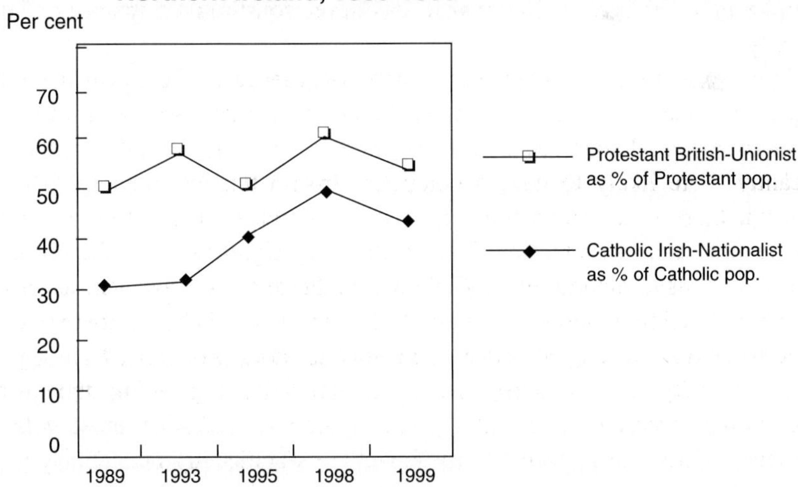

Note: Congruent identities are defined as (a) Catholics who identify themselves as Irish and nationalist and (b) Protestants who identify themselves as British and unionist.

Source: Northern Ireland Social Attitudes Survey, 1989, 1993, 1995; Northern Ireland Referendum and Election Survey, 1998; European Values Study, 1999-2000.

Table 4.12: Socio-demographic background and congruence in religious, national and political identity in Northern Ireland

(Percentages)

	Catholic Irish-Nationalist	Protestant British-Unionist
Gender:	#	
Men	55	56
Women	37	52
Church attendance:	#	#
Regular	43	55
Irregular	59	45
Age:		
18-25	48	61
26-35	41	50
36-45	47	49
46-55	46	45
56+	42	58
Education:	#	
Tertiary	43	42
Secondary	40	54
No qualification	53	58
Employment Status:	#	
Employed	37	52
Unemployed	53	57
Social Class:		#
Service	53	40
Intermediate	40	56
Working	41	62

Significant group differences at the 0.05 level or above.

Source: European Values Study, 1999-2000.

Conclusion

Our comparisons of patterns of collective identity between the two parts of Ireland, North and South, have revealed two strongly contrasting identity profiles. In the Republic of Ireland, identity is simply and strongly based on a common sense of Irishness. This identity is important to people, they are hugely proud of it, their pride in their identity increased during the 1990s, and the level of positive feeling about their identity is now one of the highest in Europe. Little residue can be found of the historic Catholic-Protestant divide in patterns of identity in the Republic: a general sense of being Irish by both identity and citizenship is as clearly present among

Protestants as among Catholics. However, Protestants in the Republic are less emphatic in their pride in Irish citizenship than Catholics.[6]

While collective identity is strong, coherent and uncontested in the Republic of Ireland it is divided and, in certain aspects, weaker in Northern Ireland. As is evident from everyday life in the North, denominational boundaries underpin much of the division in identity: Catholicism is strongly linked to Irish nationalist identity and Protestantism to British unionist identity. Within both the Catholic and Protestant communities, there is some variation by social class, gender and other social categories in the link with the dominant identity, but these variations are modest compared with the overwhelming influence of religious affiliation.

Yet this is not the whole story, since the proportion of the population embracing the dominant identities falls far short of 100 per cent. Just under two-thirds of Catholics in Northern Ireland define themselves as Irish while three-quarters of Protestants define themselves as British. Fewer than half (45 per cent) of Catholics define themselves as *both* Irish and nationalist, and the proportion of Protestants who define themselves as both British and unionist is only slightly larger (at 53 per cent).

There is therefore a large middle ground occupied by those who detach themselves in various ways from the dominant poles of identity. The intermediate identities that characterise that middle ground are captured for the most part by labels such as 'Northern Irish' as a national identity, British-Irish as a citizenship category, or 'neither nationalist nor unionist' as a political identity. Catholics are more drawn to these intermediate identities than are Protestants. For example, 42 per cent of Catholics consider themselves neither nationalist nor unionist, compared to 33 per cent of Protestants, while 53 per cent of Catholics consider themselves as having joint British and Irish citizenship, compared to only 13 per cent of Protestants. However, while many Catholics and some Protestants would appear willing to move towards these intermediate identities, there appears to be little tendency to cross over to the identity of the other side. This is indicated especially by the almost total absence of Catholics who are willing to call themselves unionist or of Protestants who are willing to call themselves nationalist. (The reluctance of Catholics to label themselves as unionist is all the more notable since, as we shall see in the next chapter, substantial minorities of Catholics support retention of the union with Britain and so could be regarded as at least quasi-unionist in their constitutional preferences.)

Apart from the substantial minorities who distance themselves from the Catholic-nationalist and Protestant-unionist poles of identity in Northern Ireland, there is another more subtle sense in which these identities lack the dominance they

[6] This issue will be pursued further in the next chapter, where it will become clear that the sense of being Irish held by Protestants in the Republic, while unambiguous, does not carry quite the same political connotations as it does for Catholics.

seem to possess from the outside. This is the lower level of positive feeling they evoke from those who espouse them, particularly as contrasted with the very high levels of positive feeling towards Irishness found in the Republic. Among Catholics in Northern Ireland, who identify their citizenship as Irish, only 57 per cent say they are 'very proud' of their citizenship, compared to 75 per cent in the Republic. Among northern Protestants, pride in British citizenship is lower still: only 40 per cent of northern Protestants who define their citizenship as British say they are 'very proud' of that citizenship. Lowest of all are those with joint British-Irish citizenship, among whom only one in five say they are 'very proud' of their citizenship. These results do not mean that a negative view of citizenship is common in Northern Ireland, since negative responses to the pride in citizenship question ('not very proud', 'not proud at all') are reported by very few. Furthermore, eleven of the 33 European societies surveyed in the EVS 1999-2000 had lower levels of pride in citizenship than Northern Ireland. Yet, the present results indicate that, in comparison to the Republic, there is a notably lukewarm feeling about identity in Northern Ireland.

Some paradoxes emerge when we explore people's perceptions of the bases of the main identities considered in this chapter. When Catholics in both Northern Ireland and the Republic were asked about the importance of various potential bases of Irish national identity, 'being a Catholic' came next to bottom of a list of five possible items ('ability to speak Irish' was at the bottom). When Protestants in Northern Ireland were asked about the bases of British identity, they placed 'being a Protestant' at the bottom. Thus, although religion is objectively closely related to national identity in both traditions in Ireland, both Catholics and Protestants are hesitant about acknowledging the importance of this link. The implications of this hesitation are taken up in the next chapter, which deals with attitudes North and South, among Protestants and Catholics, British and Irish, unionists and nationalists to the constitutional question in Northern Ireland, with particular emphasis on issues dealt with in the Good Friday Agreement.

Table A4.1: Socio-demographic background and congruence in religious and national identity in Northern Ireland

	(Regression Coefficients)			
	Catholics who define themselves as Irish		Protestants who define themselves as British	
Socio-demographic background:				
Gender (male)	.15*	(.15)	-.01	(-.06)
Church attendance (attender)	-.15	(-.07)	.11	(.09)
Age (years)	-.01	(-.10)	-.01	(-.02)
Education:				
Tertiary (omitted category)	---		---	
Secondary	-.01	(-.01)	.01	(.03)
No qualification	.14	(.14)	.01	(.09)
Class				
Service (omitted category)	---		---	
Intermediate	-.01	(-.09)	.19**	(.23)
Working	-.01	(-.08)	.34**	(.38)
Employment (employed)	-.17**	(-.18)	.01	(.05)
Constant	0.929**		0.477**	
R-Squared	0.070		0.108	
[N]	[302]		[347]	

Note: Congruence is here dichotomised as 1 (congruent) and 0 (not congruent). Standardised regression coefficients are in parentheses.
* significant at the 0.05 level; ** significant at the 0.01 level.

Source: European Values Study, 1999-2000.

Table A4.2: Socio-demographic background and congruence in religious, national and political identity in Northern Ireland

	(Regression Coefficients)			
	Catholics Irish-Nationalist		Protestants British-Unionist	
Socio-demographic background:				
Gender (male)	.24**	(.24)	.01	(.07)
Church attendance (attender)	-.15	(-.07)	.22**	(.16)
Age (years)	-.01*	(-.13)	-.01	(-.01)
Education:				
Tertiary (omitted category)	---	---	---	---
Secondary	.01	(.03)	.01	(.05)
No qualification	.23*	(.22)	.01	(.05)
Class				
Service (omitted category)	---	---	---	---
Intermediate	-.13	(-.13)	.18*	(.18)
Working	.27**	(.27)	.23*	(.22)
Employment (employed)				
Constant	0.809**		0.191	
R-Squared	0.124		0.054	
[N]	[302]		[347]	

Note: Congruence is here dichotomised as 1 (congruent) and 0 (not congruent). Standardised regression coefficients are in parentheses.
* significant at the 0.05 level; ** significant at the 0.01 level.

Source: European Values Study, 1999-2000.

5

The constitutional question

Introduction

For much of the twentieth century, the constitutional question of Northern Ireland turned on what many people saw as a simple choice between continued political union with Britain and re-unification with the rest of Ireland. By the time the Good Friday Agreement was concluded in April 1998, however, that simple choice had turned into a complex compromise consisting of many elements. The fundamental breakthrough the Agreement represented was that, for the first time, it brought all the main political parties in Northern Ireland – those linked with paramilitary groups as well as those commited solely to constitutional means – into the same negotiating forum and obtained their common endorsement of a new set of arrangements for democratic governance in Northern Ireland. It thus took a major step towards reconciling the physical force and constitutional strands of politics in the North. The shared purpose was to end violence and find a political compromise which would accord 'parity of esteem' to both the unionist and nationalist political traditions on the island.

To express that parity of esteem in political institutions, the Agreement organised the institutional arrangements into three strands. Strand One involved the election of an Assembly in Northern Ireland with a power-sharing executive; decisions of the Assembly require a majority of both unionist and nationalist representatives before they can be passed. Strand Two provided for the creation of a North-South Ministerial Council to bring together government ministers from the Republic of Ireland and Northern Ireland in order 'to develop consultation, cooperation and action … on matters of mutual interest'. Twelve possible areas for North-South cooperation were listed in the Agreement, ranging from agriculture and education to health and urban and rural development. Strand Three provided for the creation of a British-Irish Council that would bring together representatives from all parts of Britain and Ireland in order to 'exchange information, discuss, consult and use best endeavours to reach agreement on co-operation on matters of mutual interest'. Strand Three also provided for a British-Irish Intergovernmental Conference that, 'in recognition of the Irish government's special interest in Northern Ireland' would allow the Irish government to put forward views and proposals on Northern Ireland matters. Other parts of the Agreement provided for the decommissioning of paramilitary weapons, the scaling down of the British Army's presence in Northern Ireland, the release of paramilitary prisoners, and an inquiry into policing in Northern Ireland (see Wilford, 2001, for a comprehensive overview of the terms of the Agreement).

Each of these strands represented a trade-off between unionist and nationalist aspirations (Hayes and McAllister, 1999b). In return for the fulfilment of nationalist demands for the creation of cross-border bodies, nationalists accepted the unionist objective of a return to devolved government and the creation of an elected assembly. To make the creation of cross-border bodies more acceptable to unionists, the north-south dimension was complemented by an east-west dimension via the establishment of the British-Irish Council. For nationalists, in return, the elected assembly was based on the principle of proportionality with a power-sharing executive composed of all the major groups within the assembly.

The most significant compromises were achieved on the constitutional issue of Northern Ireland. For unionists there was, for the first time, a formal recognition by both the British and Irish governments of Northern Ireland's current constitutional status within the United Kingdom. Furthermore, this recognition was accompanied by a commitment on the part of the Irish government to amend Articles 2 and 3 of the Irish constitution and thereby replace the Republic's formal territorial claim to Northern Ireland with a more aspirational statement of 'the firm will of the Irish nation … to unite all the people who share the territory of the island of Ireland', subject to the consent of a majority of the people in both jurisdictions on the island.

Objectives

The purpose of the present chapter is to provide an overview of attitudes in Northern Ireland and in the Republic to issues connected with the constitutional status of Northern Ireland and to the main elements of the Good Friday Agreement. The 1999-2000 EVS as adapted for Northern Ireland and the Republic of Ireland included a number of items tapping public thinking both on the broad constitutional position of Northern Ireland and on a range of specific topics dealt with by the Agreement, such as the Northern Ireland Assembly, the power sharing Executive, the role of the British and Irish governments in Northern Ireland, cross-border bodies, the freeing of paramilitary prisoners, and so on.

The analysis also draws on additional data sources both for the decades prior to the Agreement and for the period since. In regard to the more recent period, the Northern Ireland Life and Times Survey, which was fielded annually between 2001 and 2003, had many questions that are directly comparable with those in the EVS. The first round of the European Social Survey 2002-2003 also contains a number of relevant items. These sources are used to bring the analysis of trends in attitudes up to 2003.

Constitutional preferences

Table 5.1 shows the relationship between constitutional preferences regarding Northern Ireland and religious identification in both the Republic of Ireland and Northern Ireland in 1999-2000. In the Republic, a bare majority of respondents (54 per cent) favoured a united Ireland and the next most popular choice was an independent Northern Ireland (32 per cent), followed by retention of Northern Ireland within the UK (10 per cent). This *order* of preferences is found in each of the three main religious categories in the Republic distinguished in Table 5.1: for Protestants as well as Catholics and the non-affiliated, the nationalist option – a united Ireland – draws the most support, and an independent Northern Ireland comes second. However, there are differences in levels of support for each option. This is so especially in that Protestants are somewhat more likely to opt for Northern Ireland remaining in the UK than are Catholics or the non-affiliated: almost one in four Protestants prefer this outcome compared to one in ten among the other two groups. We should not overstate the extent of this difference, since for all three groups, retention of the link with Britain is only third in the list of preferred options. Nevertheless, the somewhat different weighting given to the various options across the three religious groupings indicates that opinion on Northern Ireland among Protestants in the Republic is not identical to that of Catholics but shows a slightly stronger leaning towards historical unionist preferences.

Denominational differences in Northern Ireland on this basic constitutional question are much starker than in the Republic.[1] In 1999-2000, Protestants in the North overwhelmingly favoured remaining in the UK (88 per cent). For Catholics, a united Ireland was the dominant preference (65 per cent); remaining in the UK came a distant second (21 per cent). It is notable that while an independent Northern Ireland was the second most widely supported option in the Republic, it attracted little support in Northern Ireland. It was most favoured

[1] In making comparisons between the Republic and Northern Ireland on constitutional issues, it should be recalled that the salience of these issues differs dramatically from one side of the border to the other. In the Republic, these issues are usually no more than a secondary concern and are often quite remote from people's daily experience, whereas in the North they are a dominant feature of the daily political landscape.

Table 5.1: Religious identification and constitutional preferences in the Republic of Ireland and Northern Ireland

	(Percentages)			
	Catholic	Protestant	Non-affiliated	All
Republic of Ireland:				
Remain in UK	9.1	23.3	15.8	9.9
United Ireland	54.9	41.9	57.9	54.4
Independent N. Ireland	32.5	27.9	26.3	32.1
Other	3.5	7.0	0.0	3.6
Total	100	100	100	100
[N]	[909]	[257]	[19]	[971]
Northern Ireland:				
Remain in UK	21.1	87.7	75.7	59.6
United Ireland	65.0	3.8	12.1	29.3
Independent N. Ireland	11.2	5.1	8.4	8.0
Other	2.7	3.3	3.7	3.1
Total	100	100	100	100
[N]	[331]	[391]	[107]	[829]

Question: Do you think that the long-term policy for Northern Ireland should be for it (1) to remain part of the United Kingdom, (2) to re-unify with the rest of Ireland, (3) become an independent state, (4) other.

Source: European Values Study, 1999-2000.

by Catholics but even in their case only 11 per cent opted for an independent Northern Ireland.

The constitutional preferences in 1999-2000 just presented are the outcome of considerable change over time. While opinion surveys have regularly tracked these preferences since the 1970s, it is not possible to read the resulting data as consistent time series. Surveys tended to reflect constitutional options that were being discussed when the surveys were taken or that were of particular interest to particular research projects, and so vary in their question wording. Responses can be aggregated into categories that have some consistency of meaning over time, but even here the continuity in the data should not be overstated (see Hayes and McAllister 1996 for a discussion). In Table 5.2, views on three broad options – a united Ireland, Northern Ireland as an independent state, and Northern Ireland remaining in the UK – are presented for the Republic of Ireland. In some of the surveys underlying this table, a united Ireland was presented as a response option with no further elaboration, while in others respondents were offered two variants – a unitary state and a federal state (see footnote to table). Likewise, 'remain in the UK' was presented in some surveys as a single straightforward option, while in others direct rule and a devolved parliament were included as possibilities. Some surveys included joint control of Northern Ireland by the British and Irish governments as an option while others did not.

Clearly, variations over time in levels of support for the broad options presented in Table 5.2 are in part the product of such changes in question format between surveys. Nevertheless, a close reading of the data suggests that some real shifts in opinion can be detected. It seems likely that there was some genuine rise in support for a united Ireland between the early 1970s and mid-1980s, and it is likely also that support for that option declined after 1985 as the prospect of a settlement along the lines later agreed in the Good Friday Agreement began to emerge. The 1985 Anglo-Irish Agreement was an important turning point in this regard, as it provided the basis for partnership between the Irish and British governments in Northern Ireland and diluted the traditional nationalist claim to a united Ireland in the Republic. It thus led to the emergence of a new moderate consensus on Northern Ireland among political parties in the South (Girvin 1999: 380-3). The resurgence in support for a united Ireland between 1999 and 2003 suggested in Table 5.2 (when support for this

Table 5.2: Constitutional preferences in the Republic of Ireland, 1973-2003

	(Percentages)		
	United Ireland	Independent State	Remain in UK
1973	37	17	14
1977	42	13	19
1978	68	10	9
1984	72	2	5
1991	41	16	23
1996	38	17	9
1999	44	26	8
2003	59	—	16

Note: Data do not form a consistent series because of changes in question wording across surveys (see text; also Hayes and McAllister 1996a).

Questions: Various solutions have been suggested for the future of Northern Ireland. Which of these proposed solutions would you prefer: Northern Ireland to remain part of the United Kingdom; Northern Ireland to become part of the Republic of Ireland; A Northern Ireland State Independent of both the UK and the Republic of Ireland; or Joint Control of Northern Ireland by Great Britain and the Republic of Ireland? [1973, 1977, 1978, 1984, 1991; 1996]: Do you think that the long-terms policy for Northern Ireland should be for it: To remain part of the United Kingdom; To reunify with the rest of Ireland; Independent State; or Other [1999]; Do you think that the long-term policy for Northern Ireland should be for it: To remain part of the United Kingdom; Or reunify with the rest of Ireland? [2003].

Changes in response options included the following: In 1973, 1977, 1978, 1984, 1991 and 1996 the 'remain in UK' response option was split in two: remain in UK under direct rule or with a devolved parliament. In 1979, 1984 and 1996, the 'united Ireland' option was split in two: united Ireland with one central government or with a federal system. In 1991 and 1996, the Joint Control option by Great Britain and the Republic of Ireland was further qualified in terms of whether respondents preferred Northern Ireland to be governed with or without its own parliament. All reported options are calculated on the total n and, therefore unlike Table 5.1, they do not exclude those who either failed to respond or were undecided.

Source: Irish Marketing Surveys, 1973, 1977; Davis and Sinnott, 1979; Market Research Bureau of Ireland, 1984; Gallup Political and Economic Index, 1991; ISSP National Identity and Role of Government Survey in Ireland, 1996; European Values Study, 1999-2000; European Social Survey, 2003.

option rose from 44 per cent to 59 per cent) is likely to reflect a combination of question wording effect (the 'independent state' option for Northern Ireland was not included in the ESS on which the latter estimate is based) and short term fluctuation.

Reduction in support for re-unification in the Republic of Ireland from the mid-1980s onwards coincided with decline in support for the retention of Articles 2 and 3 of the Irish constitution, though again we have to be careful not to overstate the continuity of survey data on this issue (see Table 5.3). The territorial claim over Northern Ireland contained in these articles was, in effect, significantly reduced by the Anglo-Irish Agreement in 1985 and was modified via the referendum on the Good Friday Agreement held in the Republic in April 1998 (Hayes and McAllister, 2001a). The survey data reflect the gradual movement in public opinion away from the constitutional claim that accompanied these changes. This is particularly so from 1992 onward, when a qualification linking change in the constitution to a political settlement in Northern Ireland was introduced into questions on this topic in opinion poll surveys. In this instance, changes in question format in opinion surveys could be said to have reflected and captured real changes in the contemporary political context. By May 1998, just after the issue had been voted on in the referendum of the previous month, only 15 per cent of the Irish public were in favour of retaining the two articles, in contrast to 71 per cent in 1984.

Table 5.3: Trends in attitudes towards Articles 2 and 3 of the Irish Constitution in the Republic of Ireland, 1978-1998

	(Percentages)			
	Retain	Change	No Opinion	(N)
1978	65	23	14	(1,295)
1984	71	14	15	(1,317)
1991	58	25	17	(1,000)
1992	41	39	20	(1,000)
1993	28	51	21	(1,000)
1995	20	60	20	(1,000)
1998	15	58	27	(1,107)

Note: Data do not form a consistent series because of changes in question wording across surveys (see text; also Hayes and McAllister 1996a).

Prior to 1992, individuals were asked if they approved of (1978) or favoured (1991) the Irish government's constitutional claim to Northern Ireland, or, if this claim should be withdrawn (1984) or removed (1979). In 1993, the question was again slightly modified in that the proposed aspirational change to Articles 2 and 3 of the Irish constitution was linked to the prospect of a political settlement in Northern Ireland. In 1998, this link became even more explicit when individuals were asked if they were in favour of amending Articles 2 and 3 as part of their contribution to the Northern Ireland Agreement.

Source: Hayes and McAllister, 1996; Irish Market Survey, 1998 (18/5/1998: Irish Political Studies; 1999:230/Q10)

Discontinuities in the data on constitutional preferences over time are also present in Northern Ireland and make it equally difficult to identify precise trends. The data in Table 5.4 suggest that retention of the union with Britain was the preferred option of a large majority in Northern Ireland – 76 per cent – in 1978. However, support for that option was bolstered among nationalists in the survey from which the data are taken by the inclusion of a devolved parliament organised on a power sharing basis as a variant of the continued union. By the late 1980s, after two decades of civil unrest and the Republican hunger strikes of 1981, Northern Irish opinion as a whole had begun to shift towards an increased preference for Irish unity and declining support for the retention of the union. By 1989, support for Irish unity was measured at 25 per cent and it remained above that level since then. Support for maintaining the link with Britain declined from 72 per cent in 1989 to around 60 per cent over the period 1999 to 2003.

Table 5.4: Trends in constitutional preferences in Northern Ireland, 1978-2003

(Percentages)

	United Ireland	Independent State	Other	Remain in UK	(N)
1978	17	3	4	76	(1,264)
1989	25	1	2	72	(830)
1995	29	1	2	68	(700)
1999	29	8	3	60	(829)
2001	32	7	3	58	(1,543)
2002	26	7	4	63	(1,556)
2003	27	8	2	63	(1,578)

Note: Data do not form a consistent series because of changes in question wording across surveys (see text; also Hayes and McAllister 1996a).

Questions: There has been a lot of talk about the solutions to the present problem in Northern Ireland. Now I want you to leave aside what you would like to see in an ideal world, and tell me which of the following is the most workable and acceptable to you as a solution: Northern Ireland to remain part of the UK; Northern Ireland to become part of the Republic of Ireland; A Northern Ireland State Independent of both the UK and the Republic of Ireland; or Joint Control of Northern Ireland by Great Britain and the Republic of Ireland with a devolved government of its own? [1978]. Do you think that the long-term policy for Northern Ireland should be for it: To remain part of the United Kingdom; To reunify with the rest of Ireland; Independent State; or Other? [1989-2003]

In 1978 maintenance of the link with Britain was further qualified in terms of whether respondents wished Northern Ireland to remain part of the UK under direct rule or have its own devolved parliament either based on majority rule or a power-sharing basis. The United Ireland option was further qualified in terms of whether respondents favoured one central government or a federal system.

Source: Social Attitudes Survey, 1978, Northern Ireland Social Attitudes Survey, 1989 and 1995; European Values Study, 1999-2000; Northern Ireland Life and Times Survey, 2001-2003.

We have seen earlier that constitutional preferences in Northern Ireland are strongly related to religious identification. Table 5.5 also shows that the trends in constitutional preferences in Northern Ireland just outlined have a strong denominational basis; this is mainly due to the fact that most of the change has been caused by shifts in attitudes among Catholics (keeping in mind also that the question format underlying the data for 1978 just noted would have tended to raise reported preferences for remaining in the UK among Catholics). Among Protestants in Northern Ireland, constitutional preferences have changed little over time: the level of support for retaining the union with Britain has hovered just above or below 90 per cent since the late 1970s.

Table 5.5: Religious identification and attitudes towards constitutional preferences in Northern Ireland, 1978-2003

	(Percentages)						
	1978	1989	1995	1999	2001	2002	2003
Catholic:							
United Ireland	39	61	60	65	71	58	61
Remain in UK	50	35	36	21	18	27	26
Protestant:							
United Ireland	6	3	6	4	5	4	5
Remain in UK	89	95	92	88	88	89	88

Note: Data do not form a consistent series because of changes in question wording across surveys (see text; also Hayes and McAllister 1996a).

Source: Social Attitudes Survey, 1978, Northern Ireland Social Attitudes Survey, 1989 and 1995; European Values Survey, 1999-2000; Northern Ireland Life and Times Survey, 2001-2003

Socio-demographic characteristics, identity and constitutional preferences in Northern Ireland

Although constitutional preferences in Northern Ireland remain strongly related to religious identification, previous research has also pointed to important divisions that exist within each of the two communities. The minorities on both sides of the religious divide who are at odds with the constitutional view that is dominant in their own community can be distinguished in part in socio-demographic terms (Moxon-Browne, 1983; Rose, 1971; Trew, 1996; Hayes and McAllister, 1999a). For example, previous research has shown that the minority of Catholics who support the union with Britain are disproportionately female, better educated and older (Breen, 1996; Trew, 1996). Our concern here is to explore the relative importance of socio-demographic factors and identity in explaining differences in constitutional preferences.

Table 5.6 deals with this issue by focusing on preference for retention of the union with Britain as an indicator of constitutional attitudes and examining

Table 5.6: Intra-religious differences in constitutional preferences in Northern Ireland

	(Percentage who wish to retain Union with Britain)			
	All	Catholic	Protestant	Non-affiliated
Socio-demographic background:				
Gender		#		
Male	64	19	97	84
Female	70	30	95	89
Church attendance	#			
Regular	59	26	96	100
Irregular	80	17	96	85
Age	#	#		
18-25	49	14	92	78
26-35	77	27	98	92
36-45	60	13	98	84
46-55	66	32	91	87
56+	75	33	98	90
Education	#		#	
Tertiary	59	21	88	81
Secondary	66	24	95	85
No qualification	72	28	100	92
Employment status				
Labour active	68	21	97	89
Non-labour active	66	26	95	84
Social Class			#	
Service	59	11	92	77
Intermediate	68	23	94	88
Working	70	27	100	92
Identity:				
National identity	#	#	#	#
British	98	77	98	100
Other	65	40	89	70
Irish	18	15	63	50
Political identity	#	#	#	#
Unionist	98	---	98	97
Neither	71	40	90	89
Nationalist	15	15	---	38

Note: Includes all Catholics, Protestants and Independents who prefer retention of the Union or a united Ireland. #, Significant intra-religious group differences at the 0.05 level or above.

Source: European Values Study, 1999-2000.

differences in this indicator by socio-demographic characteristics and collective identity in Northern Ireland. The most striking aspect of Table 5.6 is that relationships between socio-demographic background and constitutional preference in Northern Ireland are either absent or modest. The main instances where such relationships can be found are in connection with gender (Catholic men are significantly more likely to favour a united Ireland than are Catholic women) and education where, for Protestants, possession of a university degree is associated with lower levels of support for maintenance of the union. Identity is a different matter: there is a clear relationship between constitutional preference and both national and political identity. As might be expected, Protestants who identify themselves as British or unionist are overwhelmingly in favour of retaining the union with Britain (98 per cent support this option). Catholics who identify themselves as Irish or nationalists are almost but not quite the reverse: 15 per cent of these favour retaining the union. The latter are a small minority but nevertheless are numerous enough to indicate that Catholic-Irish-nationalists are not quite as monolithic in their opinions on this issue as are Protestant-British-unionists.

There is a telling contrast in Table 5.6 between Catholics and Protestants in Northern Ireland who adopt identities that are intermediate between the two dominant poles – that is, who define their national identity as something other than British or Irish (see Table 4.1 in previous chapter) and their political identity as neither unionist nor nationalist (see Table 4.10 in previous chapter). Catholics with these intermediate identities come close to an intermediate position in regard to retention of the union with Britain: 40 per cent choose retention of the union as their favoured constitutional option. This is a considerably more favourable attitude towards the union than is shown by Catholics who adopt the dominant identities of Irish and nationalist. Protestants who adopt the same intermediate identities, by contrast, come nowhere near to an intermediate position in regard to retention of the union with Britain: more or less 90 per cent support the latter option, which is only a slightly lower level of support than is shown by Protestants who adopt the dominant identity of British and unionist. This suggests that Protestants who distance themselves from the dominant British-unionist identity nevertheless share the dominant British-unionist constitutional preference for Northern Ireland. The extent to which they are really intermediate is thus somewhat open to question.

Multivariate analysis confirms these bivariate findings (see Table A5.1 at the end of this chapter). Irrespective of religious background, the key predictors of constitutional preferences are national and political identity. Individuals who identify themselves as British and hold a unionist identity are significantly more likely to support the link with Britain than those who consider themselves Irish and/or hold a nationalist political identity. The minority of Catholics who either disavow an Irish identity and/or consider themselves as neither nationalist nor unionist are also more likely to support the union. Socio-economic background, in contrast, is of little importance in explaining intra-religious differences in constitutional preference in Northern Ireland. It is worth noting in particular that, once religious identification has been taken into account, church attendance, which can be considered an indicator of secularisation, has no impact on constitutional preferences. This would suggest that the link between religious denomination and constitutional preference is likely to be uninfluenced by trends towards secularisation, since it is mediated wholly through religious denomination as a marker of identity rather than through intensity of religious commitment.

The road to compromise: support for the Good Friday Agreement

The Good Friday Agreement was signed on 10 April 1998 and was ratified in both parts of Ireland by referendums held on 22 May 1998. In advance of those referendums, there was little doubt that the Agreement would win overwhelming support in the Republic of Ireland and among Catholics in Northern Ireland, but the reaction of Protestants in Northern Ireland was much more uncertain. The largest party, the Ulster Unionist Party (UUP), was split on the issue, with its new leader, David Trimble, supporting the Agreement but encountering strong opposition from many of his senior colleagues. The then second largest Protestant party, the Democratic Unionist Party (DUP) led by Ian Paisley, opposed the Agreement on the grounds that it would undermine Northern Ireland's position within the United Kingdom. Just one week prior to the referendum in Northern Ireland, opinion polls were showing that the Protestant community was deeply divided on the issue, with a large number of undecided voters (Hayes and McAllister, 2001a: 78-79).

In the event, around seven out of every ten voters (71 per cent) supported the Agreement in Northern Ireland, compared with 94 per cent of voters in the Irish Republic[2] (see Table A5.2 at end of chapter). Although the yes vote in Northern Ireland was decisive, it also indicated deep divisions among unionists. The Northern Referendum and Election Study – a nationally representative post-election survey of all adults conducted after the Northern Ireland Assembly elections in June 1998 – found that 57 per cent of Protestants voted yes, while 43 per cent voted no (see Table 5.7). This finding replicated that of an exit poll taken on the day of the referendum, which showed that 55 per cent of Protestants who voted supported the Agreement, and 45 per cent opposed it. Among Catholic voters, in contrast, the yes vote was almost unanimous, with 99 per cent in favour of the Agreement and only one per cent opposed.

[2] But, as noted in footnote 1 in Chapter 2, the different rates of turnout in Northern Ireland and in the Republic meant that the proportions of the total population which supported the Agreement was in fact identical on both sides of the border.

Table 5.7: Religion and the referendum vote in Northern Ireland, 1998

	(Percentages)			
	Catholic	Protestant	Non-affiliated	Total
Did you vote?				
Yes	84	85	79	84
No	16	15	21	16
[N]	[335]	[472]	[72]	[880]
[If yes] How did you vote?				
Yes	99	57	81	75
No	1	43	19	25
[N]	[277]	[371]	[54]	[702]

Question: Now I would like to ask you some questions about the recent referendum that was held on May 22nd when people were asked if they supported the Agreement reached by the politicians on Good Friday. Talking to people, we found that some people did not manage to vote. How about you, did you manage to vote in the Referendum? How did you vote?

Source: Northern Ireland Referendum & Election Survey, 1998.

Table 5.8 deals with attitudes towards eight specific elements of the Good Friday Agreement. These attitudes can be summarised by dividing the eight elements into three groups – (1) those receiving majority support across all communities (positive consensus items); (2) those lacking majority support in one or two communities (divisive items); and (3) those lacking majority support in all communities (negative consensus items). The positive consensus items are decommissioning of paramilitary weapons, the guarantee that Northern Ireland will remain in the United Kingdom, the creation of a Northern Ireland assembly, and the establishment of a power-sharing executive. While the levels of support for these proposals varied between the different religious groupings, each obtained majority support in all groups, Protestant, Catholic and non-affiliated. Not surprisingly, the greatest contrast in support for these four proposals occurred in relation to the guarantee that Northern Ireland would remain in the United Kingdom; support for this key aspect of the Good Friday Agreement was 94 per cent among Northern Ireland Protestants compared to 61 per cent among Northern Ireland Catholics. Nevertheless, 61 per cent among Northern Catholics is a clear majority.

This brings us to the three divisive issues – those that obtained majority support in some but not in all the communities involved. These issues were the reform of the RUC (approximately 70 per cent support among Catholics, North and South versus 17 per cent support among Northern Protestants); the establishment of North-South bodies (76 to 81 per cent support among Catholics, North and South, versus 46 per cent support among Northern Protestants); and, the third item in this category, the removal of the Republic of Ireland's constitutional claim to Northern

Ireland (76 per cent support among Northern Protestants versus 36 to 40 per cent support among Catholics, North and South).

The third category (negative consensus items) in fact comprises only a single item – the release of paramilitary prisoners. The maximum levels of support for this proposal were found among Catholics in the North and the Republic (37 and 34 per cent respectively) and among the non-affiliated in the South (42 per cent). This compares to 12 per cent among the non-affiliated and 6 per cent support among Protestants in Northern Ireland. In other words, while there are differences in the extent of opposition to this policy proposal, at the same time there is a majority consensus against it.

A striking feature of the responses in Table 5.8 is the similarity of attitudes as between Catholics in Northern Ireland and Catholics in the Republic, the maximum difference between them on any issue being 7 percentage points. In

Table 5.8: Support for elements of the Good Friday Agreement

(Per cent 'support strongly' or 'support')

	Republic of Ireland			Northern Ireland		
	Catholic	Protestant	Non-affiliated	Catholic	Protestant	Non-affiliated
Positive consensus items:						
Decommissioning	82	83	74	83	96	85
NI remain part of UK	62	70	55	61	94	82
Establish an Assembly	75	67	60	82	68	62
Power-sharing Executive	79	69	60	86	58	58
Divisive items:						
Reform of RUC	70	45	61	74	17	32
Create North-South bodies	76	69	58	81	46	53
Remove Republic's constitutional claim	40	58	37	36	76	56
Negative consensus item:						
Early release of prisoners	34	21	42	37	6	12
[Base N]	[899]	[257]	[72]	[366]	[459]	[173]

Question: There has been much discussion recently about some of the suggested constitutional and executive changes proposed in the Good Friday Agreement of last year. Looking at a list of some of these changes on this card, could you tell me how you feel about each one?: a) The guarantee that Northern Ireland will remain part of the UK for as long as a majority of people in Northern Ireland wish it to be so; b) The creation of North-South bodies; c) The establishment of a Northern Ireland assembly; d) The requirement that the new Executive be based on power-sharing; e) The removal of the Republic of Ireland's constitutional claim to Northern Ireland; f) Reform of the RUC; g) The de-commissioning of paramilitary weapons; and h) The release of paramilitary prisoners.

Response options were: Support strongly, support, neither support nor oppose, oppose, oppose strongly, don't know.

Source: European Values Study, 1999-2000.

contrast to this harmony of view, Protestants in Northern Ireland and Protestants in the Republic show substantial differences on a majority of the issues, the greatest differences occurring in relation to reform of the RUC, the guarantee that Northern Ireland will remain in the United Kingdom and the creation of North-South bodies. On the first of these – reform of the RUC – Protestants in the Republic are about half-way between their co-religionists in the North and their Catholic fellow citizens in the Republic. On the other two, they are substantially closer to their fellow citizens in the Republic.

Table 5.9 turns to a more general issue underpinning the Good Friday Agreement by investigating public attitudes towards the proper extent of both the Westminster and Dublin governments' role in Northern Ireland. The main contrast in views in this area arises among Northern Protestants, who widely support for a role for the Westminster government in Northern Ireland (80 per cent say it should have either a great deal or some say in the North) but who show little support for a role for the Dublin government (16 per cent say it should have a great deal or some say in the North). Catholics in the Republic are slightly less favourable towards the Westminster government's role than are Catholics in the North (49 per cent versus 53 per cent respectively say it should have a great deal or some say), but otherwise attitudes among Catholics on the two sides of the border are similar: they are more supportive of Dublin's than of Westminster's role in the North but levels of support for Westminster's role are still reasonably high. Protestants in the Republic occupy an intermediate position between Catholics on either side of the border on the one hand and Protestants in the North on the other. However, on the question of the Dublin government's role in the North, they are closer to the Catholic position than to that of Northern Protestants. This again indicates that while Protestants in the Republic share much of the political outlook of Catholics in the Republic, their position on constitutional issues has certain nuances that echo the position held by their Northern co-religionists.

Since its inception, controversy and uncertainty have plagued the Agreement and its accompanying institutions, most notably in relation to the Northern Ireland Assembly. In fact, since its formal establishment on 30 November 1999, the British government has suspended the Assembly and re-introduced direct rule on four separate occasions (Hayes and McAllister, 2004). These events point to the need for an examination of the changing nature of support for the Agreement in the two main religious communities in Northern Ireland.

Trends in support for the Good Friday Agreement in Northern Ireland

Although the Good Friday Agreement was formally endorsed by a majority of the Catholics and Protestants in Northern Ireland in 1998, subsequent surveys point to a growing disillusionment with the Agreement among Protestants (Dixon, 2001; Aughey, 2002; Hughes and Donnelly, 2003). In fact, recent electoral results, as

Table 5.9: Religious identification and public attitudes in the Republic of Ireland and Northern Ireland toward the influence of the British and Irish governments in Northern Ireland

(Percentages)

	Republic of Ireland			Northern Ireland		
	Catholic	Protestant	Non-affiliated	Catholic	Protestant	Non-affiliated
Westminster Government:						
A great deal of say	8	18	5	11	29	19
Some say	41	51	37	42	51	60
A little say	26	20	13	30	16	13
No say at all	25	11	44	16	4	8
[N]	[791]	[218]	[75]	[367]	[404]	[120]
Irish Government:						
A great deal of say	26	12	40	21	1	9
Some say	48	50	33	53	15	39
A little say	18	24	10	21	30	18
No say at all	8	13	17	5	54	34
[N]	[808]	[229]	[78]	[372]	[398]	[121]

Questions: How much say do you think the Westminster government of any party should have in the way Northern Ireland is run? And, how much do you think an Irish government of any party should have in the way Northern Ireland is run?

Source: European Values Study, 1999-2000

evidenced by the success of the anti-Agreement unionist party, the DUP, suggest that, whatever its perceived benefits in the past, a majority of Protestants no longer support the Agreement or its new institutions of governance (Mitchell *et al.*, 2002; Hayes and McAllister, 2004).

Recent opinion poll data are in accord with this interpretation of the electoral results. By 1999, as Table 5.10 shows, survey data showed that if a referendum on the Agreement were held again, a slight majority of Protestant (51 per cent) would vote no. A similar level of rejection of the Agreement was recorded among Protestants in surveys held in each year up to 2002, and in 2003 it rose to 60 per cent. This is in contrast to the situation among Catholics, the vast majority of whom (over 95 per cent in all years except 1999) continued to indicate that they would vote in favour. These surveys provide little indication that there would be differences in turnout between the two religious communities. For example, in the 2003 Northern Ireland Life and Times Survey 86 per cent of Catholics and 81 per cent of Protestants claimed that they would vote if a referendum on the Agreement was undertaken again. Thus, the differing trends in voting intention that had occurred by the early years of this decade, as measured in this hypothetical way, cannot be understood as simply a by-product of differential turnout.

The results in Table 5.11 provide further evidence on how voting intentions

Table 5.10: Religion and change in referendum voting, 1998-2003

(Percentages)

	Protestants		Catholics	
	Yes	No	Yes	No
1998	57	43	99	1
1999	49	51	88	12
2000	46	54	98	2
2001	49	51	96	4
2002	48	52	97	3
2003	40	60	95	5

Questions: Talking to people, we found that some people did not manage to vote. How about you did you manage to vote in the referendum? How did you vote? [1998] If the referendum was held again today how would you vote? [1999] If the vote on the Good Friday Agreement was held again today, how would you vote? [2000-2003]

Source: Northern Ireland Referendum and Election Survey, 1998; Queen's University/Rowntree Trust Opinion Poll, 1999; Northern Ireland Life and Times Survey, 2000-2003.

changed over time. Respondents in 2003 were asked how they had actually voted in the referendum in 1998 and how they would vote if the referendum were held again at the time of the survey. Thirty per cent of Protestants who had voted said that they would change their vote, compared to only six per cent of Catholics. More importantly, of the Protestants who would change, well over half said that they would move from a yes to a no vote. A similar pattern emerges when previously non-voting Protestants are considered: 59 per cent of these said they would abstain again, but of those who said they would vote well over half said that they would now vote no. Among Catholic non-voters, by contrast, a large majority of those who said they would vote in a new referendum indicated that they would vote yes.

Explanations for increasing Protestant disillusionment with the Agreement

What can explain these growing differences in support for the Agreement between the two main religious communities and why, in particular, did anti-Agreement sentiment strengthen so much within the Protestant community?

Some indications of the reasons for this development are provided in Table 5.12 which shows the changes between 1998 and 2000 in support for specific aspects of the Good Friday Agreement. The aspects of the Agreement are arranged into the three categories of positive consensus items, divisive items and negative consensus items identified earlier. Protestant support for all aspects of the Agreement bar decommissioning of paramilitary weapons declined over the period. The largest decline was in regard to the power-sharing executive: the Protestant majority in support of this item in 1998 changed into a minority by 2000, thus changing it from being a positive consensus item in 1998 to a divisive item in 2000. Protestant

Table 5.11: Religious differences in change from actual to hypothetical referendum vote in Northern Ireland, 2003

	(Percentages)			
	Catholic	Protestant	Non-affiliated	Total
Vote change (voters only)				
No – would not change	93.7	69.5	79.8	80.2
Yes – would change	6.3	30.5	20.2	19.8
(Yes voters now vote no)	(2.1)	(23.3)	(11.9)	(13.8)
(Yes voters now not vote)	(4.2)	(4.5)	(7.1)	(4.6)
(No voters now vote yes)	(0.0)	(1.2)	(0.0)	(0.6)
(No voters now not vote)	(0.0)	(1.5)	(1.2)	(0.8)
[N]	[475]	[596]	[84]	[1,155]
Vote change (non-voters only)				
Would not vote	47.4	59.2	67.6	55.6
Would vote	52.6	40.8	32.4	44.4
(non-voters now vote no)	(9.8)	(22.9)	(5.4)	(16.0)
(non-voters now vote yes)	(42.8)	(17.9)	(27.0)	(28.4)
[N]	[133]	[179]	[37]	[349]

Question: If a vote was on the Good Friday Agreement was held again today, how would you vote? And how did you vote in 1998 when the referendum on the Agreement was held?

Note: The 100 individuals who were not registered to vote in 1998 but were registered to vote in 2003 are included in the non-voters category. Their voting intentions were as follows: 52 (yes); 19 (no) and 29 (would not vote). The 29 individuals who were not registered to vote in 1998 but said they would now not vote have been included in the no change category.

Source: Northern Ireland Life & Times Survey, 2003.

support for the Northern Ireland Assembly also declined considerably (from 83 per cent to 67 per cent) but nevertheless support remained the majority position even in 2000.

Although most of the disenchantment with the Agreement arose on the Protestant side, there was also some increase in concern among Catholics, contributing to a further erosion of the fragile consensus that underlay the Agreement (Table 5.13). The major focus of this concern was the constitutional status of Northern Ireland within the United Kingdom. Where 75 per cent of Catholics supported maintaining the link with Britain just after the Assembly elections in June 1998, that proportion had dropped to 53 per cent by 2000. This moved the issue perilously close to the 50 per cent threshold at which it would move out of the category of consensus issues and into that of divisive issues. In a related shift, support for removing the Republic's constitutional claim fell from 48 to 27 per cent, making this policy issue (by then, of course a *fait accompli*) one of the most divisive aspects of the Agreement.

Table 5.12: Decreasing support among Protestants in Northern Ireland for aspects of the Good Friday Agreement, 1998-2000

	(Per cent support)			
	1998	1999	2000	% change
Positive consensus items:				
Decommissioning	95	98	96	+1
NI remain part of UK	98	95	92	-6
Establish an Assembly	83	72	67	-16
Power-Sharing Executive	65	63	44	-21
Divisive items:				
Reform of RUC	34	18	28	-6
Create North-South bodies	50	49	40	-10
Remove Republic's constitutional claim	83	79	78	-5
Negative consensus item:				
Early release of prisoners	7	7	3	-4

Question: Now I would like to ask you about your own views on some of the proposals contained in the Good Friday Agreement [1998]; Looking back at the proposals contained in the Good Friday Agreement, could you tell me how you now feel about each of these [1999, 2000]?

Note: Excludes don't know and no opinion responses.

Source: Northern Ireland Referendum & Election Survey, 1998; European Values Study, 1999-2000; Northern Ireland Life & Times Survey, 2000.

Perceptions of which side of the political divide gained most from the Good Friday Agreement provide another way of examining changing attitudes to the Agreement in Northern Ireland. Throughout the referendum campaign, both the Irish and British governments had stressed the economic as well as political advantages of the Agreement. The American government and the European Commission had also promised that, in the event of a successful passage of the referendum, funding would become available to support economic regeneration within Northern Ireland – a regeneration, it was claimed, which would be of benefit to Protestants and Catholics equally. Previous research points to the importance of the potential political and economic benefits in explaining Protestant support for the Agreement (Hayes and McAllister, 2001a). A clear majority of Protestant 'yes' voters (67 per cent) stated that they thought that the Agreement would bring about economic prosperity, compared to 29 per cent of Protestant 'no' voters. Sixty-one per cent of Protestant 'yes' voters thought it would break the political deadlock in Northern Ireland, compared to 21 per cent of Protestant 'no' voters (Hayes and McAllister, 2001a: 82).

In the aftermath of the Agreement, however, it became clear that Protestants in Northern Ireland generally believed that nationalists had gained most from the Agreement, and the proportion of Protestants who felt that way increased with the

Table 5.13: Decreasing support among Catholics in Northern Ireland for aspects of the Good Friday Agreement, 1998-2000

	(Per cent support)			
	1998	1999	2000	% change
Positive consensus items:				
Decommissioning	87	86	81	-6
NI remain part of UK	75	64	53	-22
Establish an Assembly	94	85	86	-8
Power-Sharing Executive	93	90	82	-11
Divisive items:				
Reform of RUC	85	78	73	-12
Create North-South bodies	91	86	83	-8
Remove Republic's constitutional claim	48	39	27	-21
Negative consensus item:				
Early release of prisoners	38	38	33	-5

Question: Now I would like to ask you about your own views on some of the proposals contained in the Good Friday Agreement [1998]; Looking back at the proposals contained in the Good Friday Agreement, could you tell me how you now feel about each of these [1999, 2000]?

Note: Excludes don't know and no opinion responses.

Source: Northern Ireland Referendum & Election Survey, 1998; European Values Study, 1999-2000; Northern Ireland Life & Times Survey, 2000.

passage of time (Figure 5.1). In 1998, shortly after the referendum on the Agreement, 59 per cent of Protestants believed that nationalists had benefited more from the Agreement than had unionists, while only 37 per cent believed that both sides had benefited equally. By 2003, the proportion of Protestants who believed that nationalists had benefited more had risen to 85 per cent and the proportion who believed that the benefits were equal had fallen to 14 per cent. Almost no Protestants by then believed that unionists had benefited more from the Agreement than nationalists.

Catholics have been much more inclined to think that the Agreement was of equal benefit to both sides – 74 per cent held this view in 1998 (see Figure 5.2). While Catholics who thought that nationalists had benefited more were in a minority (17 per cent in 1998), they easily outnumbered Catholics who thought that unionists had benefited more and they increased as a proportion of all Catholics as the years passed. By 2003, 27 per cent of Catholics had come to believe that nationalists had benefited more from the Agreement than unionists. Thus the *trend* in Catholic perceptions on this issue was in the same direction as that of Protestants, in that as time passed both communities increasingly saw the Agreement as weighted towards the nationalist side, even though this view

Figure 5.1: Who benefited most from the Good Friday Agreement? Perceptions among Protestants in Northern Ireland, 1998-2003

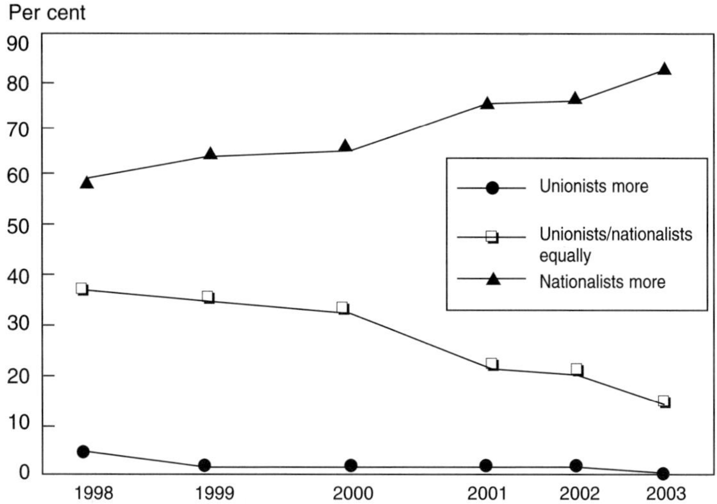

Question: Thinking [about the] back to the Good Friday Agreement now, would you say that it has benefited unionists more than nationalists, nationalists more than unionists, or that unionists and nationalists have benefited equally? [1998, 1999, 2000, 2001, 2002, 2003]

Source: Northern Ireland Referendum & Election Survey, 1998; Northern Ireland Life & Times Survey, 1999-2002, European Social Survey, 2003.

continued to be much less widespread among Catholics than among Protestants.[3]

The views of the non-affiliated in Northern Ireland were in between those of Protestants and Catholics on this issue and showed a less linear trend (Figure 5.3). They started out in 1998 with a majority view (58 per cent) that the Agreement gave equal benefit to both sides, they then shifted to a slight majority view that nationalists had gained more over the next two years, shifted back to the view (51 per cent) that both sides had benefited equally, before changing again to the view (63 per cent) that nationalists had gained more.

The foregoing suggests that there are two levels at which Protestant perceptions of the Agreement can be examined. The first relates to their support or lack of it for specific elements of the Agreement and the second to their more general view as to whether nationalists or unionists benefited more from the Agreement. To what

[3] The ESS in 2003 posed this question to respondents in the Republic of Ireland for the first time. Their views on this question echoed those of Catholics in Northern Ireland, though with some differences. As among Catholics in Northern Ireland, a majority of respondents in the Republic thought that unionist and nationalists had gained equally from the Agreement, but the majority was smaller in the Republic than among Catholics in the North – 54 per cent compared to 67 per cent. Respondents in the Republic were also just about as likely as Catholics in the North to think that nationalists had benefited more from the Agreement – 29 per cent and 27 per cent respectively held this view – but respondents in the Republic were somewhat more inclined than Catholics in the North to think that unionists had gained more – 17 per cent compared to 7 per cent.

Figure 5.2: Who benefited most from the Good Friday Agreement? Perceptions among Catholics in Northern Ireland, 1998-2003

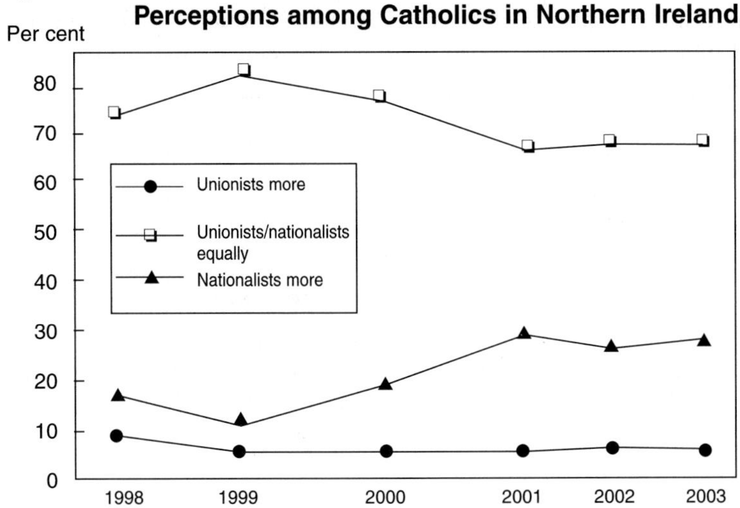

Question: Thinking [about the] back to the Good Friday Agreement now, would you say that it has benefited unionists more than nationalists, nationalists more than unionists, or that unionists and nationalists have benefited equally? [1998, 1999, 2000, 2001, 2002, 2003]

Source: Northern Ireland Referendum & Election Survey, 1998; Northern Ireland Life & Times Survey, 1999-2002, European Social Survey, 2003.

Figure 5.3: Who benefited most from the Good Friday Agreement? Perceptions among the religiously non-affiliated in Northern Ireland, 1998-2003

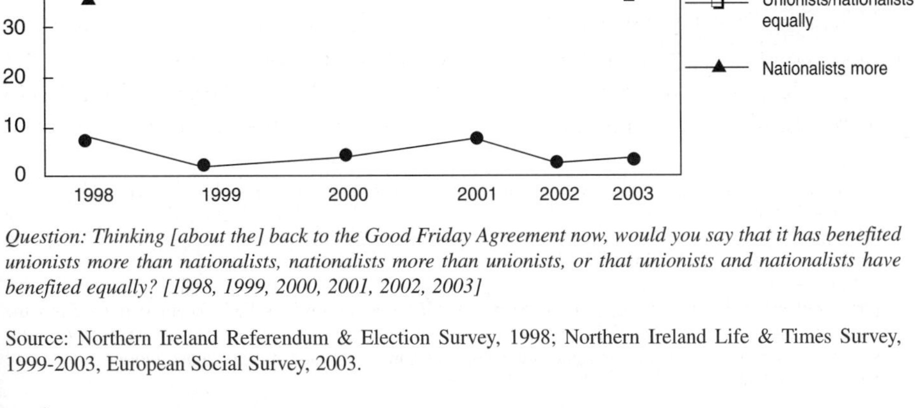

Question: Thinking [about the] back to the Good Friday Agreement now, would you say that it has benefited unionists more than nationalists, nationalists more than unionists, or that unionists and nationalists have benefited equally? [1998, 1999, 2000, 2001, 2002, 2003]

Source: Northern Ireland Referendum & Election Survey, 1998; Northern Ireland Life & Times Survey, 1999-2003, European Social Survey, 2003.

extent are these two levels of perception linked to patterns of persistence and decline in support for the Agreement among Protestants? Table 5.14 addresses this question by examining which perceptions of the Agreement among Protestants were most likely to be associated with their tendency to continue to see themselves as 'yes' voters. The analysis is based on the 2000 Life and Times Survey (see Table A5.4 for an examination of religious differences in change in referendum vote in 2000).

Section A of the table takes those who say they support each element of the Agreement and in each case shows the percentages who say they would persist as 'yes' voters or would change to a 'no' or abstain. The results here indicate that those Protestants willing to accept some of the more divisive elements of the Agreement, particularly those that were difficult for Protestants to accept such as reform of the RUC and North-South bodies, were more likely to continue as 'yes' voters. Support for positive consensus items, on the other hand, was somewhat less influential in determining persistence as a 'yes' voter. Section B of the table looks at Protestants who felt either that nationalists and unionists had benefited more

Table 5.14: Change in referendum vote and support for aspects of the Agreement, and perceptions of beneficiaries of the Agreement among Protestants

	(Row Percentages)		
	Stable Yes	No/Abstain	Total
A. Support for Elements of the Agreement:			
Positive consensus items:			
Decommissioning	70	30	100
NI remain part of UK	69	31	100
Establish an Assembly	75	25	100
Power-Sharing Executive	78	22	100
Divisive items:			
Reform of RUC	81	19	100
Create North-South bodies	82	18	100
Remove Republic's constitutional claim	66	34	100
Negative consensus item:			
Early release of prisoners	–	–	–
B. Perception of Benefits:			
Unionists more	–	–	–
Unionists/Nationalists benefit equally	87	13	100
Nationalists more	52	48	100

– too few cases for a reliable estimate.

Source: Northern Ireland Life & Times Survey, 2000.

from the Agreement or that nationalists had benefited more. Not surprisingly, those Protestants who felt the benefits were equal were more likely to persist as 'yes' voters than those who felt the Agreement was weighted towards nationalists. However, it might be considered surprising that the differences in this regard were not sharper. Protestants who considered the benefits equal were not thereby universally persuaded to continue as 'yes' voters: 13 per cent said they would switch to a 'no' or abstain. More strikingly, Protestants who felt that nationalists had gained more from the Agreement were not universally inclined to switch to a 'no' vote or abstain: 52 per cent said they would continue to vote 'yes'. This indicates again the depth of reservations about the Agreement that were found even among those Protestants who, in the years after the Agreement was signed, said they would continue to vote for it.

Conclusion

This chapter has examined attitudes towards the major constitutional issues affecting Northern Ireland, taking the Good Friday Agreement as the focus for identifying those issues. The results of this analysis suggest that constitutional preferences in Northern Ireland remain strongly related to religious identification, though the link is stronger among Protestants than Catholics. Retention of the union with Britain is currently the preferred option for the vast majority (88 per cent) of Protestants and has been so with little change since the 1970s. Only 5 per cent of Protestants in Northern Ireland support a united Ireland. A majority of Catholics (61 per cent) support Irish unity, but this leaves substantial minorities of Catholics with other preferences. While support for Irish unity is particularly strong among those Catholics in Northern Ireland who consider themselves 'Irish' or 'nationalist', even in their case just under a fifth wish to retain the link with Britain. Among Catholics who disavow the nationalist label, two-fifths are in favour of retention of the union with Britain. Although trends in constitutional preferences are difficult to track because of changes in the phrasing of survey questions that provide evidence on this issue, it appears that support for a united Ireland among Northern Catholics has grown since the 1970s though with some fluctuations. Taking account of present mixed views among Catholics on basic constitutional issues and the way those views have changed over time, Catholic nationalism in Northern Ireland emerges as less homogenous and more changeable in its outlook on the constitutional question than does Protestant unionism.

Support for a united Ireland is the majority position in the Republic of Ireland, though only barely so (54 per cent). One-third prefer an independent Northern Ireland, a much higher level of support for this option than is found in Northern Ireland, where only 8 per cent prefer it. Religious distinctions do not predict constitutional preferences in the Republic as they do in Northern Ireland, but neither are such contrasts wholly absent. For Protestants as for Catholics in the

Republic, the re-unification of Ireland is the dominant preference for solving the Northern Ireland problem in the long-term, but Protestant support for this solution (42 per cent) is somewhat lower than Catholic support (55 per cent). Conversely, support among Protestants in the Republic for keeping Northern Ireland within the UK is somewhat higher than it is among Catholics in the Republic (23 per cent versus 9 per cent). There are several other issues connected with the Good Friday Agreement where the position of Protestants in the Republic is more or less half way between that of Catholics, North and South, on the one hand and Protestants in the North on the other. Protestants in the Republic are therefore partly drawn in the direction of the nationalist view of the situation but they also show some support for the northern unionist position. This indicates that, while, as we saw in the previous chapter, Protestants in the Republic unambiguously identify themselves as Irish, that identity does not have the same connotations in the realm of constitutional politics as it does for Catholics – though neither does it mean that they fully share the views of their northern co-religionists.

While the majority of Protestants in Northern Ireland voted 'yes' in the referendum on the Good Friday Agreement in May 1998, support for the Agreement at that time was weaker and more ambivalent among Protestants than among Catholics. Some elements of the agreement received majority support across all religious communities and so could be classed as positive consensus items. These were the decommissioning of paramilitary weapons, the guarantee that Northern Ireland would remain in the United Kingdom, the Northern Ireland assembly, and the power-sharing executive. Three elements of the Agreement could be classed as divisive issues, in that they received a mixture of support and opposition across the religious communities. These were the reform of the RUC, the establishment of North-South bodies, and the removal of the Republic of Ireland's constitutional claim to Northern Ireland. There was one negative consensus item – release of paramilitary prisoners – which was opposed by all religious groupings.

In the years after 1998, doubts among Protestants in Northern Ireland about the Agreement increased while Catholic support for it remained high. As time passed, Protestants increasingly believed that nationalists had gained more from the Agreement than had unionists, a trend which has continued up to 2003. Catholics were not only more supportive of the basic principles of the Agreement but were also more inclined to believe that both sides had gained equally from it. Very few Catholics felt that unionists had gained more from the Agreement, and the proportion who felt that nationalists had gained more, while in the minority, increased over time.

Thus the trend in perceptions of the Agreement on both sides is towards seeing it as being to the advantage of nationalists. This may be taken either as an indication of a real weighting of the Agreement towards the nationalist agenda or as an indication that nationalist aspirations was easier to satisfy. It may also reflect the fact that Catholic views on the underlying constitutional issues were less homogenous and unchangeable than those of Protestants. In any event, the growing Protestant perception that the Agreement favours nationalists must be regarded as problematic.

Table A5.1: Predictors of support for retention of the Union with Britain in Northern Ireland

	(Regression Coefficients)							
	All		Catholics		Protestants		Non-affiliated	
Socio-demographic background:								
Gender (male)	-.01	(-.02)	-.01	(-.04)	.01	(.02)	-.01	(-.06)
Church attendance (attender)	-.13**	(-.08)	-.01	(-.03)	-.01	(-.02)	.12	(.08)
Age (years)	.01**	(.09)	.01*	(.16)	.01	(.01)	-.01	(-.03)
Education:								
Tertiary	---		---		---		---	
Secondary	.01	(.05)	-.01	(-.06)	.01	(.12)	-.01	(-.01)
No qualification	.01	(.08)	-.01	(-.04)	.01*	(.23)	.01	(.05)
Class:								
Service	---		---		---		---	
Intermediate	.01	(.01)	.15	(.17)	-.01	(-.11)	.01	(.08)
Working	.01	(.03)	.18	(.19)	-.01	(-.02)	.14	(.19)
Employment (employed)	.01	(.01)	-.01	(-.03)	.01	(.08)	.01	(.10)
Identity:								
National identity:								
British	---		---		---		---	
Other	-.22**	(-.21)	-.19	(-.20)	-.01*	(-.15)	-.23**	(-.32)
Irish	-.49**	(-.47)	-.39**	(-.44)	-.27**	(-.23)	-.32*	(-.30)
Political identity:								
Unionist	---		N/A		---		---	
Neither	-.16**	(-.17)	---		-.01	(-.11)	-.01	(-.08)
Nationalist	-.48**	(-.44)	-.19**	(-.21)	N/A		-.49**	(-.37)
Constant	0.942**		0.448*		0.942**		0.965**	
R-Squared	0.647		0.238		0.146		0.407	
[N]	[737]		[285]		[347]		[94]	

Note:Standardised regression coefficients are in parentheses. *, significant at the 0.05 level; **, significant at the 0.01 level; ---, reference category; N/A, no cases in cell.

Source: European Values Study, 1999-2000.

Table A5.2: The result of the referendums, 22 May 1998

	Northern Ireland		Republic of Ireland	
	N	Per cent	N	Per cent
Yes	676,966	71.1	1,442,583	94.4
No	274,879	28.9	85,748	5.6
Total valid votes	951,845	100.0	1,528,331	
Spoiled votes	1,738		17,064	
(Turnout)		(81.1)		(56.3)

Note: In Northern Ireland, the question was: 'Do you support the agreement reached in the multi-party talks on Northern Ireland and set out in Command Paper 3883?'; In the Republic of Ireland, the question was: 'Do you approve of the proposal to amend the constitution contained in the undermentioned Bill, the Nineteenth Amendment of the Constitution Bill, 1998?'

Source: Hayes and McAllister, 2001a.

Table A5.3: Decreasing support among the religiously non-affiliated for aspects of the Good Friday Agreement in Northern Ireland, 1998-2000

	(Per cent support)			
	1998	1999	2000	% change
Positive consensus items:				
Decommissioning	99	88	90	-9
NI remain part of UK	89	84	76	-13
Establish an Assembly	84	66	66	-18
Power-Sharing Executive	86	65	50	-36
Divisive items:				
Reform of the RUC	55	34	45	-10
Create North-South bodies	73	58	48	-25
Remove Republic's constitutional claim	58	60	57	-1
Negative consensus item:				
Early release of prisoners	18	12	8	-10

Question: Now I would like to ask you about your own views on some of the proposals contained in the Good Friday Agreement [1998]; Looking back at the proposals contained in the Good Friday Agreement, could you tell me how you now feel about each of these [1999, 2000]?

Note: Excludes don't know and no opinion responses.

Source: Northern Ireland Referendum & Election Survey, 1998; European Values Study, 1999-2000; Northern Ireland Life & Times Survey, 2000.

Table A5.4: Religious differences in change in referendum vote in Northern Ireland, 2000

(Percentages)

	Protestant	Catholic	Non-affiliated	Total
Vote change (voters only)				
No	79.9	96.2	83.6	86.1
(Yes voters now vote yes)	(41.8)	(95.5)	(56.0)	(62.4)
(No voters now vote no)	(38.1)	(0.7)	(27.6)	(23.7)
Yes	20.1	3.8	16.4	13.9
(Yes voters now vote no)	(13.7)	(0.8)	(5.6)	(8.2)
(Yes voters now not vote)	(3.8)	(2.7)	(5.2)	(3.6)
(No voters now vote yes)	(0.9)	(0.3)	(3.6)	(0.9)
(No voters now not vote)	(1.7)	(0.0)	(2.0)	(1.2)
[N]	[699]	[462]	[132]	[1,292]

Question: If a vote on the Good Friday Agreement was held again today, how would you vote? And how did you vote in 1998 when the referendum on the Agreement was held?

Source: Northern Ireland Life & Times Survey, 2000.

6

The liberal-conservative divide: Family and sexual morality

Introduction

So far in this book we have focused on contemporary manifestations of that combination of religion, identity and political aspiration that has been the defining feature of conflict in Ireland over not decades but centuries. However, the analysis in Chapter 2 tells us that this is not the only dimension of conflict/consensus between or within the communities with which we are concerned. Accordingly, in the present chapter, we examine the liberal-conservative/secular-religious divide that, again according to the evidence in Chapter 2, is the dominant socio-cultural cleavage in the South and a prominent source of difference in the North. In doing so, we compare attitudes to family and sexual morality between Protestants and Catholics, between the religiously committed and the secular and between the younger and the older generations in both jurisdictions. Pursuing the question of additional or alternative lines of conflict and consensus, Chapter 7 turns to the left-right divide, which many political activists and commentators had thought would enable Northern Ireland to transcend its 'sectarian' politics and allow the Republic to escape the worn-out strait jacket of 'civil war politics'. Chapter 2 hinted that the left-right divide was neither very robust nor very coherent. Chapter 7 explores the issue and the possible emergence of other aspects of a 'new politics' in some depth.

In the past, differences in family and sexual morality were often associated with Catholic and Protestant cultural differences and have given rise to considerable finger-pointing as a result (see Akenson 1988 for an historical perspective on this issue). Northern unionists have pointed to legal impediments to the sale of contraceptives in the Republic (which were fully removed only in 1989) and a constitutional ban on divorce (which lasted until 1995) as evidence of 'Rome rule' in public life in the South and as one of many reasons for resisting unification with the Republic (see Hug 1999 on the recent political controversies on these subjects in the Republic). The main Protestant churches, by contrast, have tended to such questions as matters of individual choice and historically have favoured a more permissive legal regime on both contraception and divorce. This led many Catholics in the past to think of Protestants as regrettably lax on these issues (Akenson, 1988: 29-30).

Today, however, liberalism on questions of family and sexual morality is not something that is widely associated with Protestantism in Northern Ireland, no more than it is with Catholicism in the Republic. The continuing religious vitality of both denominations would be expected to reinforce conservative family values. In the face of the liberalising tide which is sweeping through family and sexual morality in Europe (Inglehart, 1997: 267-292, Greeley, 2004: 75-87), this vitality may well draw the two denominations together on the basis of a common Christian heritage. It is here, therefore, more than in any other area, that one might expect the North and the Republic, and the Catholic and Protestant traditions on the island, to be more similar in outlook and perhaps to have more in common with each other than with the more secularised cultures found elsewhere in Europe.

This is not to say that one should expect the Republic and Northern Ireland to be immovably attached to traditional morality. There is abundant evidence, both from previous research and everyday experience, that family and sexual culture in both parts of Ireland is undergoing radical change and has much in common with standard European norms (Whelan, 1994; Cairns, 1991; Inglehart, 1997: 267-292; Widmer *et al.,* 1998; Greeley, 2004: 155-187). At least some of the former behavioural patterns that set Ireland apart, or that differentiated the two main cultural traditions within Ireland from each other, have dissolved and have merged with a common European mainstream. Thus, for example, the Republic of Ireland in the past had exceptionally high fertility rates but these declined steadily since the 1960s, fell below those of Northern Ireland for a time in the mid-1980s and are now within the range common in Europe (Coleman, 1999; Fahey and Russell, 2001). Similarly, within Northern Ireland, Catholic fertility had been much higher than Protestant fertility for much of the twentieth century, but a strong trend towards convergence between the two set in from the 1960s onwards (Ó Gráda and Walsh, 1995). The share of births occurring outside marriage is similar in the North and the Republic, at just about 30 per cent in both cases in 1999-2000, and both are now little different from the average for the European Union (Fahey and Russell, 2001). Although the legalisation of abortion has been resisted with particular vehemence in both the Republic and the North, women from both jurisdictions make extensive use of abortion facilities in Britain. Data on abortions on Irish women carried out in England and Wales suggest that while abortion was rarer among women from the Republic than from the North in the 1970s, the Republic caught up with the North in the 1980s and exceeded it in the 1990s. In 1996 there were over 90 abortions carried out in England/Wales per 1,000 live births in the Republic, compared to 65 per 1,000 live births in Northern Ireland (Coleman, 1999: 89-90).

While change in the way people behave in their private lives may indicate that differences between either part of Ireland and the rest of Europe have narrowed, expressions of values in the public sphere, as reflected, for example, in public debate over legislative change, show how bumpy the course of cultural change has been. Many of the moves to liberalise the law on family and sexual issues over the past four decades met with considerable resistance both in Northern Ireland and in the Republic. In Northern Ireland, for example, when the 1967 Abortion Act was passed in Britain, the Stormont parliament had jurisdiction over the issue in the province but declined to act. In spite of the legal ambiguity that continues to surround the issue,[1] the Northern Ireland Assembly, having considered the possible extension of the 1967 Abortion Act to Northern Ireland in June 2002, voted overwhelmingly against it.

Legislation on same-sex relations in Northern Ireland has also frequently lagged behind that in Britain. The 1967 liberalisation of the British law on this issue was not initially extended to Northern Ireland. However, on foot of a case taken by a Northern Ireland citizen, the European Court of Human Rights ruled in 1981 that the law in Northern Ireland was in breach of the European Convention on Human Rights. The Democratic Unionist party leader, Ian Paisley, famously reacted to this ruling by launching his 'Save Ulster from Sodomy' campaign (Conrad, 1999); nevertheless, in 1982, the British government extended the British legislation to Northern Ireland. However, when the age-limit for legal same-sex relations was reduced to 16 years in Britain in 2001, it was left at 17 in Northern Ireland, the same age limit as prevailed in the Republic (Rose, 1994). The reduction of the age limit in Britain in 2001 was strongly opposed by Catholic and Protestant religious leaders in Northern Ireland. As the reduction in the age limit was being debated in the House of Commons, Ian Paisley led a delegation of churchmen to hand in an 18,000-name petition to Downing Street protesting against it.

Legislation on divorce in Northern Ireland has also remained more restrictive than in the rest of the UK (Conrad, 1999; Hill, 2003). A law enabling divorce on the grounds of irreconcilability was passed in Northern Ireland only in 1978 (compared to 1968 in Britain) and even then the procedures were made more costly and time-consuming than in Britain.

Controversy over some of these issues has, if anything, been more intense in the Republic, partly because of the frequency with which those issues have been the subject of constitutional referendums. The legalisation of artificial contraceptives

[1] As it currently stands, the law on abortion in Northern Ireland is as it was in Britain before 1967 and is governed by the two statutes and one court ruling: the 1861 Offences Against the Person Act, which makes all abortions illegal; the 1929 Infant Life (Preservation) Act, as extended to Northern Ireland in 1945, which allows abortions to preserve a mother's life; and the *Rex v. Bourne* ruling in 1939, which allows abortion in circumstances of risk to the mental or physical health of the mother (Simpson, 1995). The Standing Advisory Commission on Human Rights in 1994 said that the legal position in relation to abortion in Northern Ireland was so uncertain that it would not withstand a challenge if a case was taken to the European Court of Human Rights.

was the big issue of the 1970s, and different aspects of this issue continued to cause controversy up to the 1990s (Hug 1999: 76-144). A constitutional amendment to allow the introduction of divorce was defeated in a national referendum in 1986. A revised amendment was accepted by the voters nine years later, but the margin of victory could scarcely have been tighter (50.56 per cent in favour and 49.44 per cent against).

Abortion as an issue first came into the spotlight in the Republic because of a move initiated by conservative Catholic lobby groups to underpin the already strict legal prohibition of abortion by means of a constitutional amendment affirming the right to life of the unborn, with due regard to the equal right to life of the mother. A constitutional ban on abortion along these lines was accepted in a national referendum in 1983, with a 66.9 per cent majority in favour, and the matter seemed to be closed. However, in February 1992 the Supreme Court made a controversial ruling in the famous X case, which related to the right of a 14-year-old to travel to Britain to terminate a pregnancy that had resulted from a rape. The Court decided that it was permissible for her to do so. This decision threw the issue of abortion wide open, as it seemed to point the way to a radical liberalisation of abortion law in Ireland. There followed a tumultuous public debate on the implications of the X case ruling, and a further three referendums on abortion were held simultaneously in November 1992 to deal with some of these implications. In these referendums constitutional amendments safeguarding the right to information on abortion and the right to travel to another jurisdiction for an abortion were passed but a third amendment seeking to row back on the apparently liberal implications of the Supreme Court ruling in the X case was defeated.[2] A number of Catholic groups continued to campaign over the following years to have the X case ruling reversed by means of a further constitutional amendment. They succeeded in precipitating a referendum in 2002 but, just as in 1992, the moderately conservative amendment was defeated by an alliance of conservatives (who thought the amendment was too liberal) and liberals (who thought the amendment was too conservative). The technical position at present is that, on foot of the X case ruling, abortion is legal on certain health-related grounds in the Republic, but in practice, because of restrictive guidelines adopted by the medical profession, no abortions are carried out in the country.

The law on homosexuality was liberalised more quietly in the Republic. As in Northern Ireland, the European Court of Human Rights played an important role in moving matters along, this time through a ruling issued in 1988 (for the most part, the ruling related to the same nineteenth-century legislation which had been the subject of the 1981 ruling relating to Northern Ireland). It was not until 1993 that the implications of this ruling were incoporated into Irish law, but the

2 For an analysis of the outcome of these three referendums and their implications for our understanding of attitudes in the Republic, see Sinnott, Walsh and Whelan, 1995 and Sinnott, 1995.

legislation then passed, which fully decriminalised homosexuality, was adopted without a vote in the Dáil and without a great deal of public controversy (Hug, 1999: 228).

Objectives

The slow and often tortuous pace of legislative change in both the North and the Republic as just outlined gives an indication of the conservative cast to family values on the island and the possible common role of the two main religious traditions in sustaining that conservativism. This chapter first outlines the nature and direction of change in family and sexual values in the Republic of Ireland and Northern Ireland over the past two decades, as revealed by data from the 1981, 1990 and 1999-2000 rounds of the European Values Study. It then compares the distribution of these values and attitudes across the political-religious divide, asking how similar or different the Republic and the North, and Catholics and Protestants, are to each other on these issues. Following that, it places these values in a European context by means of a brief comparison of Irish patterns, North and South, with those of other European countries. In comparing Catholics and Protestants within both the Republic of Ireland and Northern Ireland, attention is also paid to the growing minorities who report that they belong to no religious denomination.

In pursuing these objectives, the chapter is faced with an embarrassment of riches. The EVS gathered so much data on the domain of family and sexuality that this subject would justify a book-length study in its own right. Given the constraints of space, we have to limit our attention here to a number of indicative items. The analysis begins with an account of the value people attach to family and describes attitudes towards various aspects of marriage and joint parenthood. It then deals with three key 'moral' topics that have generated varying degrees of controversy in a number of countries in recent times – abortion, divorce and homosexuality – and looks in particular at attitudes to abortion in various circumstances (as a means of birth control, where the baby may have a physical defect, etc.). Following that, it examines the impact of secularisation on family values and sexual morality.

The importance of family, marriage and joint parenthood

In spite of the foregoing indications of rapid change in values and attitudes on family and sexual matters, Irish people of all denominational hues still place a very high value on the family – as indeed do most Europeans (van den Akker 1993: 106-7). In both the Republic and the North, nine out of ten rate the family as 'very important' in their lives, and similar proportions consider that 'more emphasis on family life' would be a good thing for the future (Table 6.1). No other broad domain

Table 6.1: Religious identification and importance of family

(Percentages)

	Republic of Ireland			Northern Ireland		
	Catholic	Protestant	Non-affiliated	Catholic	Protestant	Non-affiliated
Family very important in their life	93	90	80	91	89	79
More emphasis on family life good thing for the future	96	95	89	92	94	79
[N]	[899]	[257]	[72]	[366]	[459]	[173]

Questions: Please say for each of the following [Family], how important it is in your life? Here is a list of changes in our way of life that might take place in the future. Please tell me for each one [More emphasis on family life], if it were to happen whether you think it would be a good thing, a bad thing, or don't you mind?

Source: European Values Study, 1999-2000.

of life – work, friends and acquaintances, leisure time, politics, religion – is accorded such a degree of importance. Thus, for example, less than half of respondents in the North and the Republic consider either work or religion to be very important in their lives. In both the North and the Republic, those without any religious affiliation are slightly less enthusiastic about the family than are either Catholics or Protestants, but the difference is small and, even among this group, there is a strikingly high level of positive evaluation of the family.

While positive evaluation of the family as such is unwavering, the picture for marriage is more mixed. Marriage was formerly seen as the only legitimate avenue to sexual relations but that attitude is now rare. As recently as the early 1970s, a survey of moral attitudes in the Republic showed strong disapproval of sex before marriage – in 1973 almost three out of four Irish people aged 31-50 felt that it was 'always wrong' (Nic Ghiolla Phádraig, 1976). Twenty years later, in the early 1990s, the proportion of 31-50 year olds who felt that way had plummeted to one in five (Fahey, 1999: 62).

Marriage, however, continues to be highly valued in other respects. In both the Republic and Northern Ireland, less than a quarter of respondents in the 1999-2000 EVS agreed with the proposition that 'marriage is an outdated institution'. This was a significant increase in the dismissal of marriage compared to 1981 and 1990 but it still amounted to a minority view (Table 6.2). There was also strong and more-or-less unchanging support for the ideal of marital fidelity. Large majorities in 1999-2000 disapproved of married men and women having an affair, and there was no consistent sign of diminution in the size of that majority since 1990 or 1981.

Other aspects of the traditional ideals of marriage, however, have lost out quite substantially. Opposition to divorce in the Republic of Ireland was still quite high in 1981 – 52 per cent felt that it was never justified – but, by 1999-2000 and two referendums later, only 29 per cent in the Republic felt that way, a figure similar to that for Northern Ireland. The similarity between the Republic and the North on this issue is notable, given that voters in the Republic held out against divorce until 1995 – and then voters agreed to allow it only by the narrowest of margins.

Disapproval of the idea that a woman might decide to have a child without having a stable relationship with a man has also declined. Majorities of the EVS samples in both the Republic and Northern Ireland expressed such disapproval in 1981 and 1990, but by 1999-2000 less than 40 per cent did so. On the other hand, over two-thirds of the 1999-2000 samples in the North and the Republic agreed that 'a child needs a home with both a father and a mother to grow up happily', and these proportions were little different to the corresponding proportions in 1981.

Table 6.2: Attitudes to marriage and joint parenthood, 1981-1999

	(Percentages)					
	Republic of Ireland			Northern Ireland		
	1981	1990	1999	1981	1990	1999
Agree that 'marriage is an outdated institution'	12	10	21	14	14	23
Feel that married men/women having an affair is never justified*	77	78	77	76	84	81
Feel that divorce is never justified*	52	35	29	40	31	27
Disapprove of premeditated lone motherhood	57	61	35	51	58	39
Agree that 'a child needs a home with both a father and a mother to grow up happily'	68	83	65	76	81	70
[N]	[1,217]	[1,000]	[1,012]	[312]	[298]	[1,000]

Questions: Do you agree or disagree with the following statement? Marriage is an outdated institution. Please tell me for each of the following statements [married men/women having an affair; divorce] whether you think it can always be justified, never be justified, or something in between? If a woman wanted a child as a single parent, but she didn't want to have a stable relationship with a man, would you approve or disapprove? If someone were to say that a child needs a home with both a father and a mother to grow up happily, would you tend to agree or disagree?

Notes: *Responses 1 or 2 on ten-point response scale where 1=never justified, 10=always justified.

Source: European Values Study, 1981, 1990, 1999-2000.

From these latter two items it would appear that a majority would now accept the right of women to have a child in the absence of a stable partnership even though a majority would also regard joint parenthood as better for the welfare of the child.

The trends just looked at suggest that North-South differences in attitudes to marriage are not very great and that, where they were present in the past (as in the case of support for divorce), they had narrowed by 1999-2000. But what of differences between the main religious denominations, North and South?

Religious differences in attitudes toward marriage and joint parenthood

A general item on the value of marriage – whether marriage or a long-term stable relationship is necessary to be happy – included in the 1999-2000 EVS showed only modest variation by denomination (Table 6.3). On the 'marriage is an outdated institution' item, only about one-fifth of Catholics and Protestants agreed, with little difference between the two groups. However, among the non-affiliated agreement rose to almost a half in the Republic and well over one-third in the North. As is the case in other countries (Greeley, 2004: 82), disapproval of married men and women having an affair is high across all groups, but again, the non-affiliated stand somewhat apart in that their level of disapproval is not quite as high as that of Catholics or Protestants. Attitudes to divorce show a Catholic-Protestant-non-affiliated gradient: Catholics are the most disapproving (though at quite a low level by historical standards), Protestants somewhat less so and the non-affiliated least of all. A similar gradient has been found in previous international research (Hayes and Hornsby-Smith, 1994; Jagodzinski and Dobbelaere, 1995).

On the idea that a woman might choose to have a child as a single parent without wanting to have a stable relationship with a man, there are some inter-denominational differences. In the North, Catholics were somewhat less disapproving than Protestants, with both Catholics and Protestants in the Republic lying between these two positions. Again, however, it is the non-affiliated who stand out. Broadly speaking, their level of disapproval is only about half that of Catholics or Protestants both in the North and the Republic.

Homosexuality and abortion

Homosexuality and abortion have emerged in recent decades as touchstone issues in the culture wars over personal and sexual morality in western societies (Hunter, 1991). Many of the changes in sexual norms which have taken place since the 1960s have been absorbed relatively smoothly. But questions about abortion and homosexuality still have the capacity to generate passionate debate and political controversy. Abortion can be more of an issue than homosexuality in some countries, while the reverse is true in others (Widmer *et al.*, 1998; Frank and McEneaney, 1999). Yet, together, these issues provide potent indices of cultural

Table 6.3: Religious identification and attitudes to marriage and joint parenthood

(Percentages)

	Republic of Ireland			Northern Ireland		
	Catholic	Protestant	Non-affiliated	Catholic	Protestant	Non-affiliated
Agree or agree strongly that 'a marriage or long-term stable relationship is necessary to be happy'	39	45	32	39	33	27
Agree that 'marriage is an outdated institution'	19	19	47	23	19	38
Feel that married men/women having an affair is never justified*	82	79	63	84	80	68
Feel that divorce is never justified*	30	22	13	33	23	19
Disapprove of premeditated unmarried motherhood	40	44	19	37	50	23
[N]	[899]	[257]	[72]	[366]	[459]	[173]

Notes: * Responses 1 or 2 on ten-point response scale, where 1=never justified and 10=always justified.

Source: European Values Study, 1999-2000.

divergence within and between societies across the contemporary developed world (Inglehart and Baker, 2000).

EVS data from 1981, 1990 and 1999-2000 indicate that, in the Republic, opposition to homosexuality and abortion has declined since 1981, though with abortion eliciting consistently higher levels of opposition than homosexuality (Table 7.4). In 1999-2000, 38 per cent in the Republic expressed strongly negative attitudes to homosexuality, compared to 62 per cent in 1981. Sixty per cent in 1999-2000 had similarly negative attitudes towards abortion, as compared to 83 per cent in 1981.

The North is somewhat different in that homosexuality evoked more opposition than abortion in 1981 and 1990. However, the proportion in the North with strong negative attitudes towards same-sex relations declined from 66 per cent in 1990 to 45 per cent in 1999-2000, while the corresponding measure of opposition to abortion remained constant at just over 50 per cent. The consequence was that abortion marginally superseded homosexuality as an object of disapproval in the North by 1999-2000, thus reversing the pattern of earlier years.

As has been found in previous research (Hayes and McAllister, 1995; Hayes,

Table 6.4: Attitudes to homosexuality and abortion, 1981-1999

	(Percentages)					
	Republic of Ireland			Northern Ireland		
	1981	1990	1999	1981	1990	1999
Homosexuality never justified*	62	56	38	69	66	45
Abortion never justified*	83	66	60	50	52	51
[N]	[1,217]	[1,000]	[1,012]	[312]	[298]	[1,000]

Questions: Please tell me for each of the following statements [homosexuality; abortion] whether you think it can always be justified, never be justified, or something in between?

Note: *Responses 1 or 2 on ten-point response scale where 1=never justified, 10=always justified.

Source: European Values Study, 1981, 1990, 1999-2000.

1997; Greeley, 2004: 82), North-South differences on attitudes to homosexuality and abortion are mainly a reflection of denominational differences (Table 6.5). Protestants in the North are more disapproving of same-sex relations than Catholics, but Catholics are more disapproving of abortion than Protestants either in the Republic or in the North. The non-affiliated are less opposed to homosexuality and abortion than either Protestants or Catholics in the North and the Republic. It is notable, however, that the non-affiliated in the North and in the Republic generally echo denominational differences on these issues: in the Republic, they show greater disapproval for abortion than homosexuality, while in the North they show the reverse. This reflects the finding in Chapter 3 that the religiously non-affiliated in the Republic are overwhelmingly ex-Catholic, while in the North they are mainly ex-Protestant.

In addition to general attitudes to moral questions just examined, the EVS explored approval or disapproval of abortion under certain conditions. The data on these questions from the 1981, 1990 and 1999-2000 rounds of the EVS do not form a consistent series because of differences in the format of the items in 1999-2000 compared to the 1981 and 1990 rounds. Apart from certain changes in the wording of items, the response categories presented to respondents differed in 1999-2000 in that they allowed for a 'don't know' option where the 1990 and 1981 rounds allowed only 'approve' and 'disapprove' responses. The inclusion of this extra response option in 1999-2000 is likely to have reduced both the 'approve' and 'disapprove' responses over what they would have been in its absence (by 10-15 per cent combined, as these are the proportions which responded 'don't know' in 1999-2000). Despite these variations, the 1999-2000 data on these items can be used to provide lower bound estimates of the levels of approval and disapproval of

Table 6.5: Religious identification and attitudes to homosexuality and abortion

(Per cent considering item never justified*)

	Republic of Ireland			Northern Ireland		
	Catholic	Protestant	Non-affiliated	Catholic	Protestant	Non-affiliated
Homosexuality	42	52	27	43	57	40
Abortion	66	52	39	72	51	32
[N]	[899]	[257]	[75]	[366]	[459]	[175]

Note: * Responses 1 or 2 on ten-point response scale where 1=never justified, 10=always justified
Source: European Values Study, 1999-2000.

abortion as measured in 1981 and 1990, and it is on that basis that they are included with data for 1981 and 1990 in Table 6.6.

Research in other countries has shown that approval or disapproval of abortion is not unconditional but varies quite strongly according to the circumstances of the pregnancy and the abortion (Ashford and Timms, 1992; Dalton, 1996; Scott, 1998). Table 6.6 shows that this holds also in both the Republic and the North. In the Republic, approval of abortion for general fertility control purposes – that is, where the woman was not married or where a married couple wanted to avoid having more children or could not afford them – was negligible in 1981, and increased only slightly up to 1999-2000. In the North, approval of abortion for these purposes was higher, albeit only marginally so, and showed an equally slow tendency to increase over time. Approval levels were much higher (especially in the North) where the mother's health was at risk. This was the only circumstance in which a clear majority in favour of abortion had emerged in the Republic by 1990 (this item was not asked in 1999-2000). The majorities in favour of abortion in this circumstance were a good deal larger in Northern Ireland, and were present in 1981 as well as 1990. In cases where the pregnancy was the result of rape (a circumstance posed to respondents in the 1999-2000 survey only), a bare 50 per cent approved of abortion in the Republic, compared to 74 per cent in the North. The likelihood of defects in the baby was cause for approval of abortion only for about one-third of respondents in the Republic in 1999-2000 and under half in the North – with some indication from the data that support for abortion on this ground in the North had declined since 1981.

Comparisons by religious grouping in 1999-2000 show that those without any denominational affiliation are generally more tolerant of abortion than either Protestants or Catholics (Table 6.7). Divergence between Catholics and Protestants in both the Republic and the North is particularly marked in connection with two grounds for abortion examined in the 1999-2000 EVS, that is, where there is a strong chance of a serious defect in the baby and where the pregnancy is the result

Table 6.6: Conditional attitudes to abortion, 1981-1999

	(Per cent approving*)					
	Republic of Ireland			Northern Ireland		
	1981	1990	1999	1981	1990	1999
Where the woman is not married	6	8	14	12	16	21
Where a married couple do not want more children	5	8	12	14	17	17
Where a married couple cannot afford more children	—	—	15	—	—	20
Where the mother's health is at risk by the pregnancy	48	65	—	77	78	—
Where it is likely that the child would be born physically handicapped**	26	32	33	62	50	48
Where the pregnancy is the result of rape	—	—	50	—	—	74
[N]	[1,217]	[1,000]	[1,012]	[312]	[298]	[1,000]

Questions: Do you approve or disapprove of abortion under the following circumstances? When the woman is not married; When a married couple does not want to have more children; When a married couple cannot afford any more children; When the mother's health is at risk by pregnancy; When it is likely that the child would be born physically handicapped/When there is a strong chance of serious defect in the baby; Where the woman has become pregnant as the result of rape.

Notes: * Response categories in 1981 and 1990 were 'approve' and 'disapprove'; in 1999 a 'don't know' response category was added, thus reducing the likelihood that respondents would select either the 'approve' or 'disapprove' responses (see text); ** In 1999: 'Where there is a strong chance of a serious defect in the baby'.

Source: European Values Study, 1981, 1990, 1999-2000.

of rape. In both those cases, a majority of Protestants approve of abortion compared to a minority of Catholics.

Abortion and homosexuality thus emerge as issues on which we find some degree of Catholic-Protestant and North-South divergence. Catholics are more opposed to abortion than Protestants in both the Republic and the North, but Protestants are more opposed to homosexuality than Catholics in the North. This means that there is greater opposition to abortion in the Republic than in the North, and greater opposition to homosexuality in the North than in the Republic. These divergences need to be explored further, particularly by reference to other dimensions of variation with which they may be compounded, such as age, education and levels of religious commitment. We now turn to an examination of these issues.

Table 6.7: Religious identification and conditional attitudes to abortion

(Per cent approve)

	Republic of Ireland			Northern Ireland		
	Catholic	Protestant	Non-affiliated	Catholic	Protestant	Non-affiliated
Where the woman is not married	12	21	43	11	24	37
Where a married couple do not want more children	11	15	38	9	16	35
Where a married couple cannot afford more children	13	22	40	12	21	38
Where there is a strong chance of a serious defect in the baby	31	63	57	33	53	68
Where the pregnancy is the result of rape	47	73	71	36	64	80
[N]	[899]	[257]	[75]	[366]	[459]	[175]

Questions: Do you approve or disapprove of abortion under the following circumstances? When the woman is not married; When a married couple does not want to have more children; When a married couple cannot afford any more children; When there is a strong chance of serious defect in the baby; Where the woman has become pregnant as the result of rape.

Source: European Values Study, 1999-2000.

The impact of age and education

It is an almost invariant finding of social research on values and attitudes that the young are more liberal than the old. However, it is harder to say how much of this is a life-cycle effect, where the young become more conservative as they grow older, and how much of it is a cohort effect, where each succeeding generation is more liberal than the one that preceded it.

Figure 6.1 looks at this question for the Republic of Ireland over the years 1981, 1990 and 1999-2000 in connection with disapproval of divorce, abortion and homosexuality (the data for Northern Ireland could not be included in this analysis because the sample sizes in 1981 and 1990 were too small to allow for a detailed breakdown by age). In the graphs in Figure 6.1, the solid lines plot differences between age-groups in each round of the EVS survey (that is, in 1981, 1990 and 1999-2000). These lines generally slope upwards, which shows that, in each survey, the old were more conservative than the young (that is, had higher levels of disapproval). Note that the solid line for each round of the EVS falls below that for the previous round; this registers the decline in disapproval of each item in each successive wave of the survey, indicating a cohort shift towards liberalism. The dotted lines trace the attitudes of specific age-groups over time (for example, in the graph on divorce, a dotted line connects 25-34 year-olds in 1981 with 35-44 year-olds in 1990 and 45-54 year-olds in 1999-2000 and thus shows the level of disapproval of divorce in what is approximately the same age-group as it matures through three different ages in a twenty-year period (1981 to 1999-2000). The dotted lines thus show life-cycle effects in so far as that is made possible by comparison between the three survey samples. It is striking that these lines generally sloped downwards between 1981 and 1990, which indicates that people tended to become less disapproving (that is, more liberal) as they aged during this period. In some instances, however, the slope turned upwards between 1990 and 1999-2000, which suggests a life-cycle move back towards a conservative position.

The graph for divorce in Figure 6.1 also shows that in 1981, those aged over 45-54 were more than twice as likely to consider that divorce was never justified as those aged under 25 (66 per cent versus 30 per cent). By 1999-2000, the gap between the two age-groups was narrower but it was also at a much lower level (23 per cent versus 17 per cent felt that divorce was never justified). The dotted lines show that each age cohort had softened its opposition to divorce in the 1981-1990 period, though among older cohorts some resurgence of opposition occurred during the 1990s. Among the cohort aged 25-34 in 1981, 42 per cent thought that divorce was never justified. By 1990 (when approximately the same cohort was aged 35-44) only 25 per cent thought so, while by 1999-2000 (when they were aged approximately 45-54), 23 per cent did so. Among those aged 35-44 in 1981, a similar softening in opposition to divorce occurred up to 1990 (that is, among the 45-54 age cohort in that year) but among the same cohort a rise in opposition occurred between 1990 and 1999-2000 (that is, among those aged 55-64 in the latter year).

Opposition to abortion as plotted in Figure 6.1 followed the same general pattern, though at a higher overall level and with a less steep age gradient in the earlier years. Again, as with divorce, the 1980s rather than the 1990s was the decade of greatest reduction in opposition to abortion. The 1990s were characterised by a widening of the gap in attitudes between the young and the old. Opposition to abortion continued to decline among the young between 1990 and 1999-2000, while it rose among the older age-cohorts – though not to the extent that opposition among the older cohorts returned to the levels of 1981.

The graph for homosexuality in Figure 6.1 shows that little change in attitudes occurred during the 1980s – the age-gradient for 1990 is only slightly below that of 1981. Furthermore, the dotted lines connecting 1981 and 1990 generally slope upwards, which indicates that older age-cohorts had become more disapproving of homosexuality as they aged. Between 1990 and 1990-2000, however, the level of opposition to homosexuality almost halved in all but the oldest age-groups.

The effect of age on attitudes is inevitably confounded with the effect of education, since the young on average are better educated than the old. Table 6.8

Figure 6.1: Opposition to divorce, abortion and homosexuality by age group and age cohort in the Republic of Ireland, 1981-1999

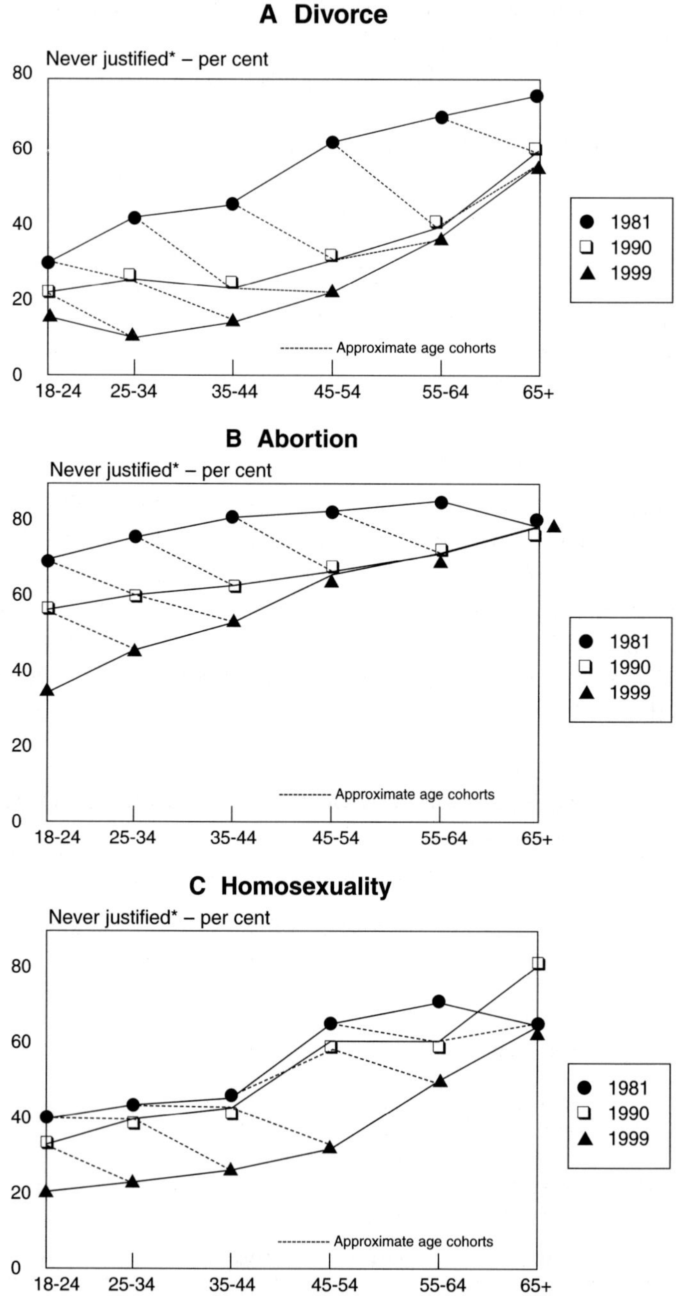

Note: * Scores 1 and 2 on 10-point scale, where 1=never justified, 10=always justified

Source: European Values Study 1981, 1990, 1999-2000.

indicates, however, that controlling for age, education still has a separate effect. This table compares attitudes at the two extremes of the educational spectrum – those with incomplete second level education and those with third level education – among those aged under and over 45 years.

The results show a wide gulf in attitudes between the two educational categories in each age group, both in the Republic and the North: the less educated are more conservative than the highly educated. The one exception is in connection with attitudes to abortion among the over-45 year olds in the Republic, where the gap between the two educational categories shown is narrow. Otherwise, the widest contrasts are between the well-educated aged under 45 years and the poorly educated aged over 45 years. Thus, for example, 72 per cent of those in the older age group who had incomplete second level education or less thought that homosexuality was never justified, compared to only 11 per cent of those in the younger age group who had university education.

The impact of secularisation

We have already seen that the strongest inter-denominational difference in family and sexual attitudes in Ireland arises not between Catholics and Protestants but between Catholics or Protestants on the one hand and those who are neither – that is, the non-affiliated – on the other. As Chapter 3 above showed, the non-affiliated tend to be former Catholics in the Republic and former Protestants in the North. Their distinct value orientations point to a link between secularisation and cultural change – those who have disaffiliated from their former churches think differently

Table 6.8: Opposition to divorce, abortion and homosexuality by age and education

(Per cent considering item never justified*)

		Republic of Ireland		Northern Ireland	
	Age	Incomplete second level	Third level	Incomplete second level	Third level
Divorce	Under 45	28	8	20	12
	45 and over	51	37	37	16
Abortion	Under 45	60	36	57	33
	45 and over	82	74	71	39
Homosexuality	Under 45	51	11	42	23
	45 and over	72	36	65	39
[Base N]		[312]	[198]	[475]	[166]

Note: * Responses 1 or 2 on ten-point response scale where 1=never justified, 10=always justified.

Source: European Values Study, 1999-2000.

about the issues we are examining here than those who have remained as members. However, as Chapter 3 also showed, among those who identify themselves as members of churches there is wide variation in the intensity of commitment to religious faith and practice, ranging from the strongly committed to the nominal. This raises the possibility that creeping secularisation may be affecting the attitudes of those who currently hold a denominational affiliation and not just the attitudes of those who reject a denominational affiliation.

A first indication that this is so is presented in Table 6.9 which contrasts the attitudes of regular and irregular church attenders within the two main denominational groupings, Catholic and Protestant (frequency of church attendance being used in this context as an indicator of intensity of religious commitment). The first point to note is that even among regular church attenders, adherence to their church's teaching on these moral issues is far from complete. In the case of homosexuality, for example, only 47 per cent of Catholic regular attenders and 57 per cent of Protestant regular attenders in the Republic think that homosexuality is never justified (levels of opposition in the North are somewhat higher among Protestants but only slightly so). Around a third of Catholics and Protestants in both the North and the Republic who are regular church attenders think that divorce is never justified. Only on the question of abortion does opposition among Catholic regular attenders rise to the kind of levels that one would expect on the basis of adherence to Catholic moral teaching.

The second point to note is the high level of variation *within* denominations (especially within Catholicism) compared to *between* denominations. In regard to homosexuality, the level of opposition among Catholic regular church attenders is 23 percentage points higher than that of Catholic irregular attenders in the Republic and 31 percentage points higher for the same comparison in Northern Ireland. This is a considerably wider gap than that between Catholic and Protestant regular attenders, which is ten percentage points in the Republic and 19 percentage points in the North. This means that, while devout Catholics are not totally similar to devout Protestants in their level of opposition to homosexuality, they have more in common with them than they have with the less committed members of their own church.

These patterns of variation within and between denominations recur in a broadly similar way in connection with abortion and divorce, though certain features of the patterns are issue-specific. In the case of abortion the issue-specific feature, as noted earlier, is the higher opposition among Catholics compared to Protestants. But, as Table 6.9 shows, internal differentiation among Catholics is so wide that Catholic irregular attenders are less opposed to abortion than Protestant regular attenders. A similar pattern is evident in connection with divorce: the difference in attitudes between regular and irregular attenders in the Catholic population is greater than that between

Table 6.9: Opposition to divorce, abortion and homosexuality by church attendance and denomination, Republic of Ireland and Northern Ireland

		(Per cent considering item never justified*)			
	Church attendance	Republic of Ireland		Northern Ireland	
		Catholic	Protestant	Catholic	Protestant
Homosexuality	Regular attender	47	57	44	63
	Irregular attender	24	34	13	44
Abortion	Regular attender	70	58	77	58
	Irregular attender	39	25	31	38
Divorce	Regular attender	33	27	34	35
	Irregular attender	20	8	10	11
[Base N]		[899]	[257]	[376]	[459]

Note: Regular church attenders are people who said that they attended religious services at least once a month. Irregular church attenders are people who reported that they attended religious services less often than once a month.
* Responses 1 or 2 on ten-point response scale where 1=never justified, 10=always justified.

Source: European Values Study, 1999-2000.

Catholics and Protestants. Internal differences within Protestantism are also quite wide on this issue.

Two preliminary conclusions emerge from these patterns. One is that traditional Christian moral teaching is losing its hold even among regularly practising Catholics and Protestants in Ireland, North and South. In the case of Catholics, this is particularly true in connection with homosexuality and divorce, while it is less true of abortion. Secondly, even though regular practitioners are less than whole-heartedly committed to traditional Christian moral teaching, irregular practitioners are even less so. This gives rise to quite wide attitudinal gaps on family and sexual issues between the devout and the nominal, especially in the case of Catholics. In fact, there is a considerably larger attitudinal gap of this kind *within* both Catholicism and Protestantism than there is *between* Catholics and Protestants.

Thus, the loosening hold of religion on Irish life, North and South, is giving rise not only to a general liberalising of family and sexual values but also to a greater diversity of attitudes within denominations as religious attachment weakens faster among some groups than others. To pursue this line of analysis further, we need to consider how the factors looked at so far jointly influence family and sexual attitudes and thereby try to isolate and quantify the denominational effects more clearly.

A common consensus?

A central question raised at the beginning of this chapter was whether the Republic of Ireland and Northern Ireland, and Catholics and Protestants in both parts of the island, could be said to share a common consensus on family and sexual matters. In one sense, the analysis so far would suggest that this is an overly simplistic way of posing the issue since, as we have seen, there is much diversity within the Catholic and Protestant communities in both parts of the island on these issues. However, the question remains valid if we think of it in overarching terms: taking into account all the other dimensions of variation (age, education, secularisation, and so on), is there a substantial Protestant/Catholic or North/South divide in family and sexual attitudes?

We can provide a more systematic answer to these questions than has been attempted so far by using multivariate analysis. The object is to assess whether substantial denominational and North/South differences in family and sexual attitudes still remain when other major correlates of such attitudes are controlled for. The analysis set out in Table A6 (at end of chapter) does this in connection with acceptance of divorce, conditional approval of abortion, and acceptance of homosexuality. Conditional approval of abortion is measured using a summed scale based on the five items reported in Tables 6.6 and 6.7, while acceptance of divorce and homosexuality is based on single items.

Of the socio-demographic control variables included in the regressions, the effect of age is the most consistent – being the only socio-demographic variable to have a significant effect on all three dependent variables. Education has a liberalising effect on attitudes to homosexuality, but, contrary to the impression gained from the cross-tabulation in Table 6.8, has no effect on attitudes to divorce or abortion. Being male has no effect on attitudes to abortion but, as in previous research (Hayes, 1997), is associated with lower levels of acceptance of homosexuality.

Given the main question we are pursuing here, the important findings in Table A6 relate to religious denomination and the two measures of religious adherence included in the regressions – frequency of attendance at church and importance of God in the respondent's life. The results confirm the Catholic-Protestant differences identified earlier. Protestants in the North and the Republic are more likely to approve of abortion than are Catholics in the North or in the Republic but less likely to consider that homosexuality is justified. In regard to divorce, there is no difference between Protestant and Catholic levels of approval, once other factors are controlled for.

The second pattern emerging from the results is that the effect of religious commitment and its obverse, secularisation, is marked and in general is stronger than the denominational effect – again confirming the findings of the bivariate analysis. The two religious commitment variables – frequency of attendance at church and the importance of God in respondents' lives – have an effect across all the attitudes examined here, while denomination affects only some. Of the two religious commitment variables, the importance of God in one's life has a stronger influence than church attendance, and indeed is the strongest single predictor of attitudes on all three dependent variables in the table (as indicated by its relatively large standardised regression coefficients for all three dependent variables).

It is also notable that the apparent differences between those with and those without a denominational affiliation, which in our earlier bivariate analysis appeared to be strong, become much weaker, or are even reversed, when controls for religiosity are introduced. Only in the case of attitudes to abortion is the coefficient for the non-affiliated in the Republic of Ireland significant. The non-significance of the coefficients for this group for divorce and homosexuality means that the attitudes of the non-affiliated in the Republic on these issues are quite similar to the attitudes of those Catholics in the Republic who have low levels of religious practice and belief.

The coefficients for the non-affiliated in Northern Ireland are even more striking: they are significant for all three items but for two of the three (divorce and homosexuality) they are *negative* (-0.88 and -1.19 respectively). This means that when the non-affiliated in Northern Ireland are compared with Catholics in the Republic who have similarly low levels of religiosity (that is, broadly speaking, the 'nominal' Catholics referred to earlier), the non-affiliated show *lower* levels of support for both divorce and homosexuality. In other words, Catholics in the Republic who are on the fringes of participation in their church are more liberal on divorce and homosexuality than people with no religious affiliation in the North – though they are *not* more liberal on abortion. These patterns reinforce a point made in Chapter 3 above about the greater reluctance of Catholics (either in the North or the Republic) to disaffiliate from their church compared to Protestants in the North. We now see one of the consequences of that: Catholics in the Republic who have weak religious commitment and are liberal on certain moral questions are nevertheless likely to continue to identify themselves as Catholics while former Protestants in Northern Ireland with a similar religious and attitudinal profile are more likely to identify themselves as no longer belonging to any church. This is to reiterate a point made in Chapter 3 that the non-affiliated are best thought of, not as a clearly distinct group, but as part of a loose cluster located towards one end of the continuum that ranges from the highly devout at one extreme to the religiously indifferent at the other.

Is Ireland different?

How do family and sexual attitudes in Ireland, North and South, compare with those in other European countries? Are denominational North/South differences on these issues large or small when looked at from an international perspective? To

..se questions thoroughly would require a lengthy analysis in its own right, but we can provide a summary answer by comparing scores on attitudes to a number of indicative items across the 31 European countries included in the 1999-2000 EVS in which this question was asked.

Figure 6.2 summarises the data, which indicate how tolerant the samples in the countries covered were towards divorce, abortion, homosexuality and premeditated single parenthood – the deliberate choice by a woman to have a child in the absence of a stable relationship with a man. As well as showing the scores on these issues for Northern Ireland and the Republic (bars highlighted in black), scores are also shown for the main denominational categories within the island (bars highlighted in grey).

The most striking feature of the results is that on all four issues, Northern Ireland and the Republic of Ireland lie very close to each other. It is only in the case of divorce that they are other than side by side, and in that case only one country – Lithuania – comes between them. It is also notable that on none of the issues does Northern Ireland lie alongside, or even particularly close to, Britain. These patterns are not to imply that Northern Ireland and the Republic are identical, but that the value spread between them is small by European standards. This is particularly notable in the case of attitudes to abortion and homosexuality, since, as we saw earlier, these were issues in which either Catholic/Protestant or North/South differences in Ireland were widest. Though these differences seemed quite substantial when looked at in a purely Irish context, altering the focus to include the broader European picture makes them look small.

This point holds even when we look at differences between major denominational groups in the two parts of Ireland. Again, attitudes to abortion are most revealing here since abortion was the one issue on which a clear Catholic-Protestant divergence could be found in both Northern Ireland and the Republic. This divergence is evident in the representation of denominational groups in Ireland, North and South, on the abortion issue in Figure 6.2. Though more accepting of abortion than Catholics in either part of Ireland, Protestants in both Northern Ireland and the Republic stand apart from the other countries for their low level of acceptance of abortion. They are more similar to Catholics in Ireland on this issue than to any other national population in Europe, with Poland being the next closest country. They are particularly far removed on this question from the predominantly Protestant countries of Europe, including Britain, and are less accepting of abortion even than several of the historically Catholic countries such as Portugal, Spain and Italy.

A somewhat similar, though not identical, pattern arises in connection with homosexuality. The distinctive feature here is that many eastern European countries (along with Portugal and Malta in western Europe) are quite intolerant of same-sex relations, so that both the Republic of Ireland and Northern Ireland occupy an intermediate position between eastern and western Europe on this issue. However, the range of variation across Europe is so great that the North/South

Figure 6.2: Attitudes to divorce, abortion, homosexuality and pre-meditated single parenthood in European societies

A Divorce

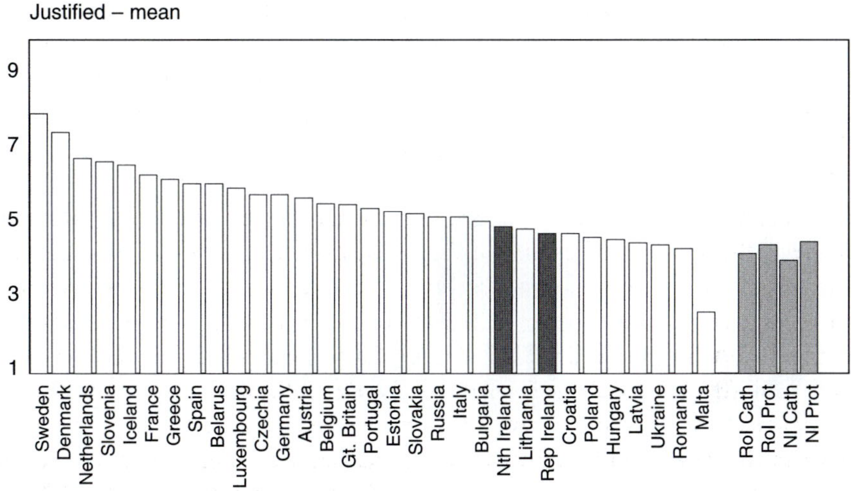

Question: Please tell me for each of the following, whether you think it can always be justified, never justified, or something in between ... Divorce.
Response: 10-point scale where 1=never justified, 10=always justified.

B Abortion

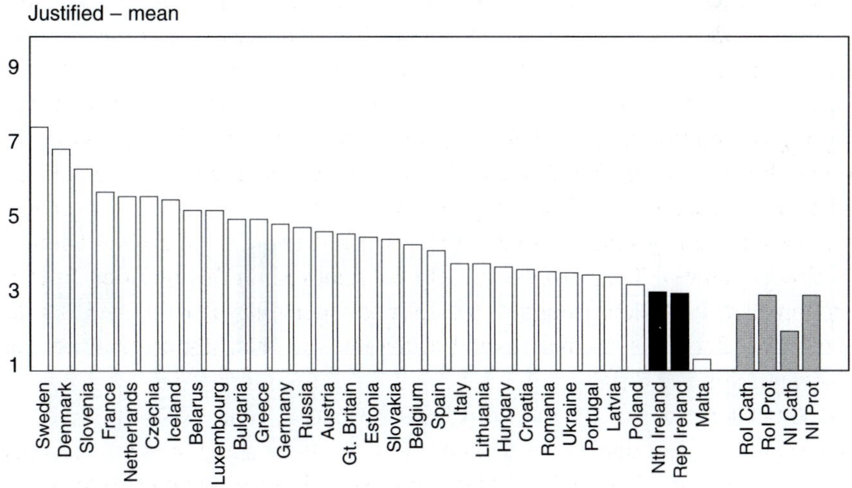

Question: Please tell me for each of the following, whether you think it can always be justified, never justified, or something in between ... Abortion.
Response: 10-point scale, where 1=never justified, 10=always justified.

Figure 6.2: (cont.)

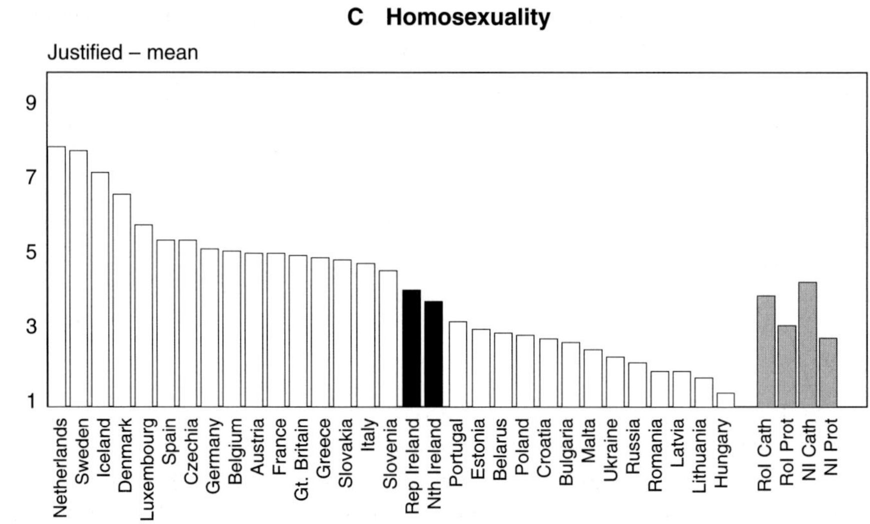

Question: Please tell me for each of the following, whether you think it can always be justified, never justified, or something in between … Homosexuality.
Response: 10 point scale, where 1=never justified, 10=always justified

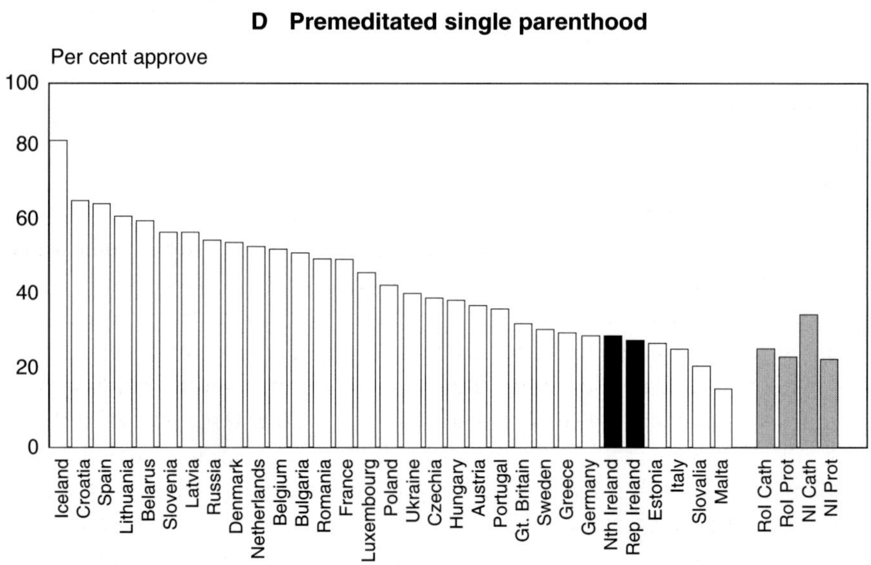

Question: If a woman wanted to have a child as a single parent, but she didn't want to have a stable relationship with a man, would you approve or disapprove?
Response: Approve, Disapprove, It depends. Source: European Values Study, 1999-2000.

difference within Ireland seems insignificant, and even the somewhat stronger denominational differences seem small.

A further point to note is that across the issues examined both the Republic of Ireland and Northern Ireland lie towards the conservative end of the range of attitudes found in Europe, with Malta being the only country occupying a consistently more conservative position. In regard to divorce, this is true primarily in comparison to the western European countries – some of the eastern European countries are as unenthusiastic or less enthusiastic about divorce as both parts of Ireland, a pattern which is even more marked in regard to homosexuality. However, both Northern Ireland and the Republic are on the margins of all of Europe (again excepting Malta) as far as opposition to abortion is concerned.

Conclusion

The findings of the chapter confirm that considerable change has occurred in family and sexual culture in Ireland, North and South, in the last two decades. On nearly all of the issues examined, a substantial shift towards the liberal positions common in most other European countries is evident from the 1981, 1990 and 1999-2000 rounds of the EVS. There are some issues on which little change has taken place: the family is still as highly valued as in the past, and marital infidelity is still widely disapproved of. But on other issues the evidence indicates change, albeit in varying degrees. The institution of marriage has lost some standing, though not to the point where a majority thinks it is outdated. Unmarried parenthood has become more widely accepted, though majorities still regard joint parenthood as better for children's welfare. Opposition to abortion and homosexuality has declined, but is still quite high, especially among Catholics in the case of abortion and among Protestants in the case of homosexuality.

The findings also show, however, that these cultural changes co-exist with a substantial degree of cultural similarity on family and sexual values between Catholics and Protestants, and between the Republic and the North. Some value differences are evident on the issues of abortion and same-sex relations: Catholics in both parts of Ireland are more opposed to abortion than are Protestants, while Northerners in general and Protestants in the Republic are more opposed to homosexuality than Catholics in the Republic. However, viewed in a European context, these differences are small. On all major issues, the Republic and Northern Ireland, and Protestants and Catholics within both parts of Ireland, are closer to each other than to most other national populations in Europe. It is particularly notable that Northern Ireland as a whole, and Protestants within Northern Ireland, are at quite a remove from Britain on these issues. On the major aspects of family and sexual values examined in this chapter, Northern Protestants have more in common with the Catholic population on the island of Ireland than they do with the rest of the United Kingdom.

This account of a substantial degree of consensus that cuts across religious and political boundaries in Ireland has to be qualified by recognising the internal diversity that can be found within the communities and traditions created by those boundaries. The emphasis on consensus and similarity needs to be qualified in particular by recognising the influence of secularisation in generating that diversity. Thus, the denominational differences inherited from the past are being overtaken by secularisation differences emerging in the present as sources of value diversity in this area. Neither Catholic nor Protestant moral teaching has as much influence on family and sexual matters as it had in the past, not only because increasing numbers have abandoned the faith but also because many believers have become more selective in what they accept of their church's moral doctrines. However, although the more strongly committed in each denomination fall short of strict orthodoxy in their family and sexual attitudes, they are considerably more conservative than those with weaker commitment or no commitment at all.

Thus, in the field of family and sexual values, the disaffiliation of significant segments of the population of Ireland, both North and South, from the churches they were born into and from the belief systems and practices that those churches seek to inculcate is creating a potent axis of cultural differentiation along religious-secular and conservative-liberal lines. This development was reflected in the analysis in chapter 2 in which just such an axis was the first attitudinal dimension identified in the Republic and the second identified in Northern Ireland. The fact that this cleavage has not expressed itself in party-political terms does not make it any less real. This is apparent when we take account of the forces and processes inhibiting such expression.[3] What is above all apparent, however, is that, in both Northern Ireland and the Republic of Ireland, the distinction between the religiously committed and non-committed has replaced the Protestant/Catholic dichotomy as the principal religious element in the cultural cleavage relating to family and sexual morality.

[3] These are, in Northern Ireland, the overwhelming nature of the nationalist-unionist conflict and, in the Republic, the fact that such issues tend to be dealt with by means of referendums in a process in which the referendum acts as a channel that prevents the divisiveness of the issues spilling over and infecting the party system (for a discussion of this aspect of role of referendums in the Republic, see Sinnott, 1995 and 2002).

Table A6: Correlates of family and sexual morality

	(Regression Coefficients)					
	Divorce Justified		Conditional Approval of Abortion[a]		Homosexuality Justified	
Religious grouping:						
RoI Catholic (omitted category)						
RoI Protestant	0.20	(0.02)	0.72***	(0.14)	-0.56*	(-0.05)
RoI non-affiliated	-0.01	(-0.01)	0.61**	(0.07)	0.14	(0.01)
NI Catholic	-0.12	(-0.01)	-0.15	(-0.03)	0.35	(0.04)
NI Protestant	-0.01	(-0.01)	0.44***	(0.11)	-1.17***	(-0.14)
NI non-affiliated	-0.88**	(-0.08)	0.35*	(0.06)	-1.19***	(-0.10)
Church attender	-0.25***	(-0.19)	-0.01**	(-0.08)	-0.12**	(-0.08)
God important in life	-0.22***	(-0.19)	-0.18***	(-0.29)	-0.18***	(-0.15)
Male	-0.27*	(-0.04)	-0.01	(-0.01)	-0.59***	(-0.09)
Age (years)	-0.01***	(-0.16)	-0.01***	(-0.07)	-0.01***	(-0.22)
Age completed education	0.01	(0.01)	-0.01	(-0.03)	0.01***	(0.06)
Constant	9.079***		3.270***		7.842***	
R-squared	0.151		0.190		0.145	
[N]	[2171]		[2197]		[2161]	

Notes: Standardised regression coefficients are in parenthesis; [a] Scale derived from the five items reported in Table 6.7 (alpha reliability=0.85);
* p < 0.05,** p < 0.01,*** p < 0.001

Source: European Values Study, 1999-2000.

7

Left-right divide and 'new issue' politics

Introduction

The Lipset and Rokkan schema outlined in Chapter 2 identified the division between labour and capital as one of the basic historical cleavages in modern European value systems This cleavage is expressed in the left-right divide and is reflected in the role of social class in structuring political orientations and in the 'freezing' of the party systems and voter alignments of many European countries.

As was outlined in Chapter 2, the story was different in the two parts of Ireland. The cleavage that shaped long-term political developments in Ireland was less the labour-capital divide created by nineteenth-century industrialisation than the Protestant-Catholic divide created by the seventeenth-century Reformation. By the time universal suffrage arrived in the early twentieth century, that religious divide had evolved into a centre-periphery cleavage between Protestant unionism and Catholic nationalism. The dominance of the centre-periphery cleavage smothered any possibility that a major opposition between left and right would emerge. In Northern Ireland, ethnonational division fractured the working class: workers failed to unite behind left-wing political programmes because sectarian tensions kept them apart (Hayes and McAllister, 1995; Evans and Duffy, 1997; Evans and Sinnott, 1999). In the Free State, a combination of an intra-nationalist conflict (pro-treaty versus anti-treaty) and the homogenising effects of partition precluded the development of a separate working class identity and working class political mobilisation (Sinnott, 1984, 1995; Mair, 1992; Evans and Sinnott, 1999; Girvin, 1999). In both cases, national and denominational divisions proved to be more potent sources of collective identity and political mobilisation than the cleavage between labour and capital, thus giving rise to the distinctive weakness of left-wing politics in the two parts of the island of Ireland in the twentieth century.

However, the potent mix of religion and nationalism that sustained the inherited cleavage system is under pressure. The sources of this pressure, which have been considered in some detail in Chapter 2, include far-reaching economic and social change, distinctly discernible secularisation and a combination of war-weariness and political negotiations in which national aspirations on both sides have been in part realised and in part redefined. The question in the present context is whether these developments have finally eased the way for the left-right divide to come into its own. Looking beyond the left-right divide, the question can be asked about other aspects of political orientation that are frequently bundled under the label 'new issue' politics, i.e. issues concerning equality between men and women, protection of the physical environment or, more generally, the set of issues that, it has been argued, add up to 'postmaterialism'.

The latter (postmaterialist) hypothesis is worth highlighting. Some researchers – most notably the American political scientist Ronald Inglehart – contend that a cultural shift towards 'postmaterialist' values has emerged in developed western societies in recent decades. This shift, according to Inglehart, is prompted by a new level of economic security and freedom, which frees people to focus on values of self-actualisation and inner development rather than on money and material security. Thus, again according to Inglehart, political issues such as economic security, law and order, and national defence, or the goals of 'material values', have now given way to higher order goals, or 'postmaterial' values, such as individual freedom, self-expression, and participation. This is said to have occurred, albeit to varying degrees, within most established western democracies (see Inglehart, 1977; 1981; 1990; 1997). Political scientists have also described this process as a transition from 'Old Politics' values of economic growth, security, and traditional lifestyles to 'new politics' values of individual freedom, social equality, and quality of life (Baker *et al.,* 1981; Evans, 1993; Knutsen, 1995; Dalton, 1996).

The present chapter tackles this question first in connection with the left-right divide, focusing especially on the weakness of left-wing ideology in Ireland North and South and the impact on left-right differences of declining religious attachment. It then looks at 'new politics' issues – gender roles, attitudes towards the environment and the rise of postmaterialism.

The left-right divide

Survey data indicate that the historical weakness of left-wing politics in Ireland, North and South, is reflected in the prevalence of a 'soft-right' political orientation among voters (Inglehart and Klingemann, 1976; Fogarty, 1984; Hardiman and Whelan, 1994; Sinnott, 1995). Self-placement on a left-right scale is the survey measure commonly used to explore this matter. This measure presents respondents with a 10-point scale where 1 represents the left and 10 represents the right and the numbers in between represent various intermediate left-wing or right-wing positions. Respondents are asked to place themselves/their views on the scale.

Analysing results from this measure in the 1981 EVS, Fogarty (1984: 68) found that 'Irish people, North and South, are much more likely than Europeans in general to identify themselves as being on the political right', with a majority locating themselves 'slightly to the right of centre'. In the 1990 EVS data, Hardiman and Whelan (1994: 153) found that 'the Irish are distinctly less left-wing' than the European average and again noted that they had a particular tendency 'to opt for a position just right of the political centre'. However, the data also suggested that respondents might understand the terms 'left' and 'right' in unconventional ways or might even have hazy views as to what the terms mean. In looking at those who placed themselves on the extreme left in 1981, for example, Fogarty (1984: 72) found that they did not fit the classic picture of the European hard left: they were 'nationalist, to an important extent religious, and by the standards of the classic left not specially radical and somewhat mixed up in their social, economic and political views.' This raises a question about what that self-placement on the scale means in respondents' minds, a question we shall return to below.

Table 7.1 presents results for the left-right self-placement measure from the 1981, 1990 and 1999-2000 rounds of the EVS for the Republic and Northern Ireland. The first thing to note is the high level of 'don't know' responses to this item, especially in 1981 and 1999-2000 where 'don't knows' were of the order of one-fifth of the sample. This feature is not peculiar to Ireland – over the entire EVS samples for the 1999-2000 round in Europe, the average non-response to this item was 22 per cent. Such high levels of non-response to this question reinforce the point already made that many people may have difficulty in deciding what left and right means or in summing up their own political position in these terms.

Taking the data at face value, a modest shift towards the centre of the left-right spectrum can be seen to have occurred in both the Republic and Northern Ireland during the 1990s. Recalling that high scores indicate 'right' and low scores indicate 'left', respondents' mean score was above 6 in 1981 and 1990 in both the Republic and the North but, in both cases, dropped to 5.64 in 1999-2000. The shift towards the centre can be illustrated in the case of the Republic where the proportion placing themselves at 7 or above on the scale declined from 35 per cent in 1981 to 22 per cent in 1999-2000, while the proportion placing themselves at 5 increased from 23 per cent to 44 per cent. In neither the Republic nor the North was there any great change in the proportions placing themselves in decidedly left-wing positions, that is, at 4 or below on the scale.

Table 7.2 classifies left-right self-placement scores by religious identification, social class, age and gender for the Republic and the North. In the Republic, Catholics and Protestants showed no significant differences, both being slightly to the right, but the non-affiliated were slightly to the left. This suggests a possible link between secularisation and left-leaning political outlooks which, as we shall

Table 7.1: Self-placement on left-right scale in the Republic of Ireland and Northern Ireland, 1981-1999

(Percentages)

		Republic of Ireland			Northern Ireland		
		1981	1990	1999	1981	1990	1999
Left	1	1	1	1	1	0	2
	2	1	1	1	2	1	3
	3	4	4	5	5	4	6
	4	7	6	7	7	5	9
	5	23	30	44	28	35	36
	6	27	25	19	22	21	17
	7	12	10	10	13	14	15
	8	13	12	5	12	11	7
	9	6	7	2	5	3	2
Right	10	4	5	5	5	4	5
Total		100	100	100	100	100	100
Mean		6.11	6.08	5.64	6.05	6.02	5.64
Don't know as % of N		26	10	18	19	8	21
[N]		[1,217]	[1,000]	[1,012]	[312]	[304]	[1,000]

Question: In political matters, people talk of 'the left' and 'the right'. How would you place your views on this scale, generally speaking?

Note: The calculated percentages showing the left-right distribution of values for both the Republic of Ireland and Northern Ireland exclude the 'don't knows', who are presented as a separate category at the bottom of the table.

Source: European Values Study, 1981, 1990, 1992-2000.

see further below, gives an important clue to what respondents in the Republic mean when they say they are on the left. In the North, the link with secularisation was absent – the non-affiliated were no more left-wing than Catholics, while Protestants stood out from the other two religious groupings as being somewhat to the right. The slightly left-wing position of Catholics in the North provides the main contrast with the evidence from the Republic.

Note also the finding in Table 7.2 indicating the absence of any relationship between social class and left-right self-identification. The manual social classes in both the Republic and Northern Ireland were just as likely to place themselves to the right-of-centre as the professional/managerial class and the lower non-manual category.

Age differences in left-right self-placement were as one might expect in the Republic: the old were more right-wing than the young, though the differences were not great and the young on average would be better described as centrist rather than left-wing. Again, the North was different in that there the young (those aged 18-30) were the most right-wing.

International comparisons

How do the two parts of Ireland look from an international perspective? Figure 7.1 compares mean national scores on the left-right self-placement scale across the 33 European societies in the 1999-2000 EVS (the graph orders the societies according to descending scores on the left-right scale, that is, from most right-wing to most left-wing). Mean scores for the main denominational groups within Ireland, North and South, are also shown.

The two parts of Ireland are located next to each other and one-third of the way across from the most right-wing of the 33 societies. Most of the societies that are

Table 7.2: Self-placement on left-right scale by religious identification, age-group and gender, Republic of Ireland and Northern Ireland

	(Mean scores on a 10-point scale)	
	Republic of Ireland	Northern Ireland
Religious identification:		
Catholic (comparison category)	5.7	5.4
Protestant	5.7	6.0***
Non-affiliated	4.7***	5.1
Social class:		
Prof/managerial (comparison category)	5.5	5.6
Other non-manual/small proprietors	5.8	5.7
Manual	5.7	5.7
Age-group:		
18-30 (comparison category)	5.3	5.9
31-45	5.5	5.4*
46-60	5.7**	5.6
60+	6.1***	5.7
Gender:		
Male	5.6	5.7
Female	5.7	5.6

Notes: Low scores indicate 'left' self-placement, high scores indicate 'right' self-placement; mid-point on scale = 5.5.

Significant difference from comparison category: *$p<0.05$; **$p<0.01$; ***$p<0.001$.

Source: European Values Study, 1999-2000

further to the right than both the Republic and Northern Ireland are former eastern bloc countries, though Malta and Finland also lie to the right of Northern Ireland while Denmark is extremely close to the Republic of Ireland. The similar positions on the scale of Finland and Denmark – two countries which belong to the Nordic group of social democracies – and the two parts of Ireland emphasise the difficulty of interpreting these data. If the citizens of two exemplars of social democracy think of themselves as right wing, what can the concept of 'right wing' mean? Despite this uncertainty (which we will return to in a moment), it is worth noting that Great Britain is located much more to the left than either Northern Ireland or the Republic. Protestants in Northern Ireland – who, as we have seen in Chapter 4 are most likely to identify themselves as British – define their positions on this scale in a way which makes them the most right-wing of any of the denominational groups in either part of Ireland, North or South, and furthest removed from the relatively left-leaning self-definition of people in Britain.

Socio-economic policy preferences

In addition to the left-right self-placement scale, the 1999-2000 EVS measured people's preferences on a range of social and economic policy issues that are frequently assumed to have left-right connotations. The question presented respondents with pairs of opposing statements and for each pair asked respondents to locate themselves on a 10-point scale, where 1 indicated full agreement with one of side of the opposing pair and 10 indicated full agreement with its opposite. Table 7.3 presents the pairs of statements and the mean scores on each scale for the Republic of Ireland, Northern Ireland and the rest of Europe. In all the statement-pairs except the fifth, a low score (that is, a score less than 5.5, the mid-point on the scale) indicates what would conventionally be regarded as a right-wing point of view and a high score indicates a left-wing point of view. In the case of the fifth pair of statements, the opposite is the case, where a low score indicates a left-wing position and a high score indicates the opposing or right-wing point of view.

Most of the items confirm the 'right-of-centre' position of the two parts of Ireland on social and economic policy preferences, both in absolute terms and in comparison with the average for the rest of Europe. In both the North and the Republic, people lean towards individual rather than state responsibility for providing for people, towards greater competition, towards more freedom for firms from state control, towards greater incentive for individual effort rather than equalisation of incomes, and towards private rather than state ownership of business and industry. This position to the right of the European average holds for all but one of the six issues – whether or not the unemployed should have the right to refuse jobs they do not want. On this issue, respondents in the Republic adopt what might be considered a more accommodating, or socially solidaristic, attitude than is the norm for Europe. Recalling that 5.5 is the mid-point of the

Figure 7.1: Self-placement on left-right scale in Europe

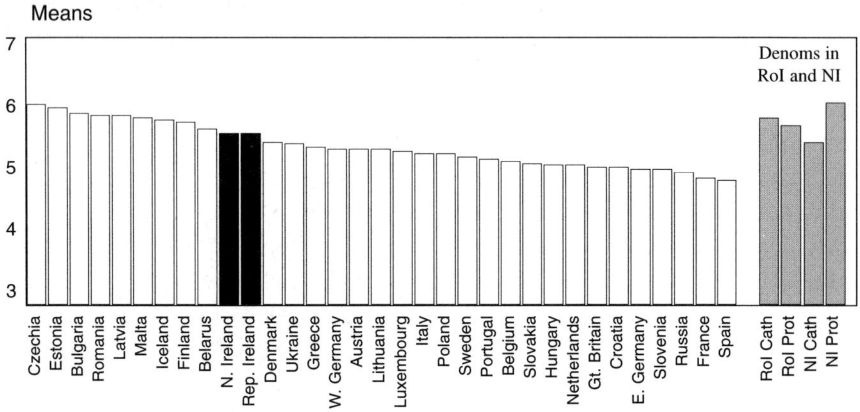

Source: European Values Study, 1999-2000.

scale, their score of 5.62 indicates that they lean slightly in favour of the view that 'people who are unemployed should have the right to refuse a job they do not want' and against the view that 'people who are unemployed should have to take any job available or lose their unemployment benefits'. Respondents in the North, by contrast, lean slightly in the opposite or right-wing direction on this particular item, and the average for the rest of Europe is even further to the right. How one might explain this more accommodating attitude towards the unemployed found in the Republic of Ireland is difficult to say, other than that it may be a consequence of the long history of poor employment prospects that characterised the Irish economy prior to the economic boom of the 1990s.

In any event, the point to note here is that this is the only issue on which either the Republic or the North are to the left of the European average. On other socio-economic issues, such as whether incomes should be made more equal or the state should take more responsibility to ensure that everyone is provided for, both the Republic and the North lean towards a more rightist position than the average for the rest of Europe.

The meaning of left and right

We can now turn to the question of what respondents' definition of themselves as being on the left or the right might mean by assessing the degree of consistency between their self-placement on the left-right scale and their attitudes on a range of issues, including the social and economic preferences just looked at. This analysis concentrates on those who unambiguously place themselves on either the left or the right. We therefore omit those scoring 5 or 6 on the ten-point left-right scale and concentrate on those who score either 1-4 (the left) or 7-10 (the

Table 7.3: Self-placement on socio-economic policy preferences in the Republic of Ireland, Northern Ireland and Europe

		(Means)		
	Republic of Ireland	Northern Ireland	Rest of Europe	
(1 2 3	*4 5*	*6*	*7 8*	*9 10)*
1 Individuals should take more responsibility for providing for themselves	4.58	4.57	5.18	The state should take more responsibility to ensure that everyone is provided for
2 People who are unemployed should have to take any job available or lose their unemployment benefits	5.62	5.16	4.82	People who are unemployed should have the right to refuse a job they do not want
3 Competition is good. It stimulates people to work hard and develop new ideas	3.84	3.88	3.88	Competition is harmful, it brings out the worst in people
4 The state should give more freedom to firms	5.01	4.50	5.47	The state should control firms more effectively
5 Incomes should be made more equal	6.07	5.69	5.54	There should be greater incentives for individual effort
6 Private ownership of business and industry should be increased	4.23	4.50	4.71	Government ownership of business and industry should be increased

Question: Now I would like to you to tell me your views on various issues. How would you place your views on this scale?

Note: Means on 10 point scale where 1=full agreement with statement on the left, 10=full agreement with statement on the right and mid-point is 5.5.

Source: European Values Study, 1999-2000.

right). Similarly, we define those who adopt either a left-wing or right-wing view on social and economic policy preferences as those who score either 1-4 or 7-10 on the items reported in Table 7.3 (the designation of these scores as left or right depends on the wording of the statement pairs in Table 7.3, as already outlined).

Table 7.4 sets out the results of this analysis based on a selection of indicative items (analysis of further items indicates broadly similar results and is omitted here for reasons of space). The first two items in this table examine the relationship between respondents' self-placement on the left-right scale and their views on state versus individual responsibility for providing for people and on income equalisation versus greater incentives for individual effort. The evidence shows that there is little or no consistency between self-definition as left or right and stated preferences on standard left-right policy issues: self-defined left-wingers only weakly support leftist policy positions and espouse rightist positions almost to the same degree as do self-defined right-wingers. On the question of state versus individual responsibility for providing for people, for example, only 28 per cent of self-identified left-wingers in the Republic support a leftist position, compared to 42 per cent who support a rightist position. Self-identified right-wingers in the Republic are more or less as likely to support the leftist position (25 per cent) as are self-identified left-wingers (28 per cent), though they are also somewhat more likely to support a rightist position emphasising individual responsibility (56 per cent) than are left-wingers (42 per cent). Patterns on this issue are similar in the North and are repeated for both the North and the Republic on the question of income equalisation versus individual incentives. Thus there is extensive mis-match between respondents' self-definition as left or right and their left-right stance on specific policy preferences. This mis-match indicates that whatever it might mean for survey respondents, both North and South, to say that they are on the left or the right, it has little connection with the classic left-right ideological issues exemplified in the politics of so many other European states.

A clearer sense of what the concepts of left and right might mean to Irish people begins to emerge when we look further down Table 7.4 at the items dealing with religion and family and sexual morality. Here we find that left-wingers and right-wingers do have different attitudes and/or report different behaviours. These differences have to do with social and moral values rather than principles of economic organisation. This is evident first in regard to religion. Among self-defined left-wingers in the Republic, 53 per cent say that they are regular church attenders (that is, they attend church at least monthly). As Fogarty (1984: 72) noted, this makes them unusually religious by the standards of the traditional European left. But it also makes them much less religious than right-wingers in the Republic, among whom 85 per cent claim to attend church regularly. The difference in monthly church attendance rates between left-wingers and right-wingers is less marked in Northern Ireland (61 per cent versus 73 per cent) but is still statistically significant. These differences in self-placement among regular church attenders are paralleled by differences in levels of confidence in the church. The percentage who have a great deal of confidence in the church is much lower among left-wingers than among right-wingers in the Republic (7 per cent versus 39 per cent), while in the North the gap between the two on this item is present but narrower (25 per cent versus 37 per cent).

The next three items in Table 7.4 deal with family and sexual morality – attitudes to homosexuality and to abortion, and support for the view that children need both parents to grow up happy. The data show that self-defined left-wingers

Table 7.4: Value differences between the self-defined left and right in the Republic of Ireland and Northern Ireland

		(Percentages: self-placement on left-right scale)			
		Republic of Ireland		Northern Ireland	
		Left	Right	Left	Right
State versus individual responsibility:	left	28	25	34	26
	right	42	56	43	55
Equal incomes versus individual incentives:	left	31	29	38	37
	right	48	50	42	42
Regular church attender (at least monthly)		53	85	61	73
Confidence in the church (great deal)		7	39	25	37
Homosexuality never justified*		15	37	25	26
Abortion never justified*		53	73	55	54
Children need both parents to grow up happy (agree)		48	80	71	76
Confidence in police (great deal)		19	45	14	23
[Base N]		[116]	[189]	[151]	[220]

Note: Only those who scored 1-4 (defined as left) or 7-10 (defined as right) in terms of their self-placement on the left-right scale are included here; *Score 1-2 on ten-point scale where 1=never justified, 10=always justified.

Source: European Values Study, 1999-2000.

in the Republic have more permissive views on these issues than right-wingers. Thus, for example, 15 per cent of those on the left think that homosexuality is never justified (points one and two on a 10-point scale); this compares to a figure of 37 per cent among those who see themselves as right-wing. Just over half (53 per cent) of those on the left in the Republic believe that abortion is never justified while the proportion taking this view among right-wingers is 73 per cent. In the case of Northern Ireland, the striking feature is that left and right wing identifiers, while somewhat different in terms of the religious indicators in Table 7.4, show little or no difference on attitudes to homosexuality, abortion, or to children needing both parents.

The final item in Table 7.4 is confidence in the police, here considered as an indicator of attitude to the established political order. In the Republic of Ireland, being on the left is associated with lower levels of confidence in the police, while in the North that relationship is present but weaker, mainly because even those on the right have only limited confidence in the police.

Summarising these correlates of left-right self-placement, it is clear that self-definition as left or right is only weakly related to people's views on how the economy should be organised or how resources and rewards should be distributed in society. In other words, it says relatively little about the usual basis on which the left-right distinction is made. People in both the Republic and the North are slightly to the right on the specifics of these policy issues, and this rightist tendency is almost as strong among self-identified left-wingers as it is among self-identified right-wingers (people in Northern Ireland are a little bit more consistent in this respect than people in the Republic). However, this is not to say that the concepts of left and right have no meaning. The point is that their meaning seems to have as much or more to do with liberal versus conservative attitudes on a range of religious, social and moral issues than with classic left-right divisions on economic or distributive policy. In the Republic of Ireland, in particular, those who see themselves as being on the left are generally less religious, show less confidence in the church and are more liberal and permissive on questions of family values and sexual morality than those on the right. In the case of Northern Ireland, left-wing self-placement shows some association with less frequent religious practice and lower confidence in the church but not with attitudes to issues of family and sexual morality.

The findings regarding left-right self-placement reported in this chapter are consistent with the evidence in Chapter 2 pointing to the truncated nature of the left-right dimension in both societies and to the fact that the concepts of left and right were more closely related to issues of religion and politics than to the role of government in the economy or to issues of redistribution or equality. In a wider perspective, all this confirms the expectations put forward in Chapter 2 regarding the weakness of the classic left-right dimension in the Irish case. Putting the matter another way, we have failed to find any evidence that changes in the traditionally dominant forces of religion and nationalism have been accompanied by any signs of the emergence of a coherent socio-economic left-right cleavage. Indeed, the indications are that, to the extent that the terms left and right have any relevance to contemporary politics in Ireland, North or South, that relevance is defined more in secular versus religious and, in the Republic, liberal versus conservative terms than in terms of socialism versus capitalism.

New politics?

As traditional left-right political divisions have seemed to fade in many economically advanced countries (or, as in the Irish case, have never developed), social science has suggested alternative frameworks within which to interpret the values, attitudes, political orientations and lifestyles to be found in countries in the developed world. As outlined above, one influential attempt in this regard is Ronald Inglehart's thesis concerning the rise of postmaterialist values. In a body of writing dating back to the 1970s (Inglehart, 1977, 1990, 1997; Inglehart and Baker, 2000), Inglehart has argued that improving economic conditions in the developed world have led to a global shift from materialist to postmaterialist values: 'the values of western publics have been shifting from an overwhelming emphasis on material well-being and physical security toward greater emphasis on quality of life' (Inglehart, 1990, p. 5). The new value regime, according to Inglehart, arises from western people's increasing insulation from the threats of poverty, war and other material risks and their growing preoccupation with belonging, esteem, and self-realisation.

Many researchers have expressed scepticism about Inglehart's thesis and have been more hesitant about the kind of broad uni-directional trends he has proposed (Haller, 2002; Clarke *et al.*, 1999; Davis and Davenport, 1999; Dutch and Taylor, 1993). Haller (2002) argues that it is just as plausible to argue for a shift towards rather than away from materialist values, as exemplified by the seemingly insatiable consumerism of western culture. Analysis of earlier rounds of the EVS by a Dutch team of researchers, which set out with hypotheses about the growth of individualist values in the course of modernisation, failed to find clear trends or structures and concluded that the only standard feature was a high level of fragmentation and diversity in value systems (Ester *et al.,* 1993; de Moor, 1993).

Before looking at postmaterialism proper, we can first examine two other 'new politics' issues, namely attitudes towards protection of the environment and towards traditional gender roles. Examination of these will enable us to identify the extent to which citizens are now interested in new issues arising from the non-economic concerns often associated with postmaterialist values.

Take the issue of the environment. In earlier periods, economic needs dominated over concerns about the environment. Today, however, many people say they are willing to make financial sacrifices to improve the environment (Dunlap and Scarce, 1991; Inglehart, 1995; Dalton, 1996; Hayes and Marangudakis, 2000). These concerns reflect more than just a growing awareness of the hidden health and economic costs of pollution. In a broad cross-national study of attitudes towards the environment, Ronald Inglehart (1995) notes that citizens in prosperous countries with relatively cleaner environments are the most willing to make sacrifices for the environment. Material success has allowed people in these countries to shift attention to the quality of their lives.

Or take gender roles. Just a generation ago, traditional attitudes to gender roles were deeply entrenched in developed societies. American women faced limited career opportunities and German housewives were expected to devote their efforts to *Kinder*, *Kirche* and *Kuche*. The status of women in Britain, France and other advanced industrial societies was equally constrained. Over the past three decades, however, these traditional attitudes have come under increasing challenge.

Legislation equalising the rights of both sexes has been implemented in both the United States and Europe, the public at large has now become more sensitive to gender issues, and social norms have gradually changed. Most people now express a belief in equal opportunities for men and women within advanced western industrialised nations and are supportive of feminist issues (Wilcox, 1991; Hayes *et al.,* 2000; Inglehart and Norris, 2003). In the case of both Northern Ireland and the Republic, attitudes towards women's and men's roles in the workplace and the home are now less at the centre of public controversy than they were even in the recent past. But they are still far from being matters on which there is full consensus and are regarded by some as a continuing source of fundamental cultural division (Davis and Downey, 1993; Robinson and Heaton, 1997; O'Connor, 1998).

Gender roles

Table 7.5 focuses on a number of items relating to women's roles in the home and the workplace that were common to the 1990 and 1999-2000 EVS surveys[1] and shows the percentages in both the Republic and Northern Ireland who adopted what might be regarded as 'traditional' stances on those items (that is, agreement with statements that leaned in a traditional direction or disagreement with statements that leaned towards newer, more liberal positions). The data indicate that support for traditional attitudes declined sharply over the 1990s, but also that the minorities who continued to support such traditional positions remained substantial. Thus, while the proportion who felt that 'a pre-school child is likely to suffer if his or her mother works outside the home' fell by almost twenty percentage points in the Republic between 1990 and 1999-2000, over a third of respondents in both the Republic and Northern Ireland still agreed with that view in 1999-2000. Furthermore, while attitudes generally shifted towards greater support for an independent economic role for women outside the home, there was a reluctance to dismiss the value of being a housewife – 60 per cent in the Republic and 53 per cent in Northern Ireland in 1999-2000 agreed that 'being a housewife is just as fulfilling as working for pay.' On the other hand, only 19 per cent in the Republic and 13 per cent in Northern Ireland in 1999-2000 disagreed with the idea that both the husband and wife should contribute to household income.

Obviously, differences in the attitudes of women and men are of particular interest in this area and are examined using the 1999 EVS data in Table 7.6.[2] The data show that men are somewhat more supportive of traditional positions than women on some items, particularly in Northern Ireland, but on other items the differences in attitudes

[1] As the 1981 EVS did not deal with this issue, EVS data allow us to trace developments in this area only over the 1990s.

[2] The final two items in this table were asked for the first time in the 1999 EVS in Ireland and do not appear in the 1990 data shown earlier.

Table 7.5: Support for traditional gender role attitudes, 1990-1999

	(Percentages)			
	Republic of Ireland		Northern Ireland	
	1990	1999	1990	1999
A working mother has as secure a relationship with her children as one who does not work outside the home (% disagree)	37	22	29	18
A pre-school child suffers if mother works outside the home (% agree)	53	35	44	35
A job is all right, but what women really want is a home and children (% agree)	59	37	53	36
Being a housewife is just as fulfilling as working for pay (% agree)	72	60	71	53
A job is the best way for a woman to be an independent person (% disagree)	39	28	31	23
Husband and wife should contribute to household income (% disagree)	30	19	18	13
[Base N]	[1,000]	[1,012]	[304]	[1,000]

Questions: A working mother can establish just as warm and secure a relationship with her children as a mother who does not work outside the home; A pre-school child is likely to suffer if his or her mother works outside the home; A job is all right, but what most women really want is a home and children; Being a housewife is just as fulfilling as working for pay; Having a job is the best way for a woman to be an independent person; Both the husband and wife should contribute to household income.

Source: European Values Study, 1990 and 1999-2000.

between men and women are slight or entirely absent. Thus, for example, men are more concerned than women about the possible negative effect of mothers' work outside the home on children's well-being, particularly in Northern Ireland, but there is little or no difference between women's and men's views on the value of women's economic independence. Men are marginally more likely than women to reject the view that fathers are as good as mothers in looking after children, but the proportions of either men or women who do so are quite small.

The final item listed in Table 7.6 – the belief that men are less able to handle emotions in relationships than women – does not fit easily into a traditional-modern opposition, since it is not clear whether the idea of men's relative emotional incompetence within intimate relationships is a particularly modern one. In any event, it is notable that men are less likely to reject this negative view of themselves than are women, particularly in Northern Ireland. It would seem, therefore, that this is one area where women think more highly of men than men themselves do.

Table 7.6: Support for traditional gender role attitudes by gender

	(Percentages)			
	Republic of Ireland		Northern Ireland	
	Women	Men	Women	Men
A working mother has as secure a relationship with her children as one who does not work outside the home (% disagree)	19	24	13	23
A pre-school child suffers if mother works outside the home (% agree)	32	39	27	44
A job is all right, but what women really want is a home and children (% agree)	35	39	34	39
Being a housewife is just as fulfilling as working for pay (% agree)	62	57	54	53
A job is the best way for a woman to be an independent person (% disagree)	28	25	21	24
Husband and wife should contribute to household income (% disagree)	17	21	11	16
Fathers as well suited to look after their children as mothers (% disagree)*	18	27	18	25
Men are less able to handle emotions in relationships than women (% disagree)*	57	47	57	39
[Base N]	[513]	[496]	[528]	[472]

*Questions: *In general fathers are as well suited to look after their children as mothers; Men are less able to handle emotions in relationships than women.*

Source: European Values Study, 1999-2000.

Multiple regression analysis, not shown here, confirms that religious denomination has no significant influence on gender role attitudes, and that consistent North-South differences are also absent. The key variables affecting gender role attitudes are as one might expect – age and gender (being older and being male is linked to more conservative attitudes) and, to a lesser extent, labour force participation (those active in the labour force have more liberal attitudes on gender roles than those who are inactive). It is also worth noting that religious adherence has a small effect in that, for example, even after controlling for age and gender effects, regular church attenders have more conservative attitudes than those who do not attend church. However, this effect is not a dominant one and does not indicate the existence of any major overlap between the religious-secular axis of cultural differentiation and traditional versus liberal attitudes on gender roles.

Environmental protection

Turning now to our second 'new politics' issue, attitudes towards the environment, the first two items in Table 7.7 show how people weigh up their environmental concerns against the potential costs of environmental protection. The results show only a moderate willingness to bear additional financial costs for the sake of the environment in either Northern Ireland or the Republic: slightly over half (54 per cent) of citizens in the Republic of Ireland and slightly less than half (45 per cent) in Northern Ireland say they are willing to give up part of their income to prevent environmental pollution. People in the North, however, are slightly more willing than their counterparts in the Republic to pay higher taxes to prevent pollution, although in both cases those who agree with this statement are in a minority. The third item shows that people are more willing to support anti-pollution policies that have no cost implications for them personally: seven out of ten in both the North and the Republic support such an approach. This implies that, for a very substantial majority of people, environmental protection is a good thing but is not good enough for them to be willing to incur any cost in doing anything about it.

Multiple regression analysis, not shown here, confirms that religious identification has no significant influence on attitudes towards the environment, and that consistent North-South differences are also absent. The key variables affecting environmental attitudes are as one might expect – age and education (being younger and well educated is linked to more pro-environmental attitudes) and, to a lesser extent, gender (males have more pro-environmental views than females in the Republic). It is also worth noting that religious adherence has a small effect in the North in that, even after controlling for age and education effects, regular church attenders are significantly less likely to adopt a pro-environmental stance in relation to this issue than those who do not attend church on a regular basis.

Taking both gender and environmental indicators together, the results so far suggest that, in so far as value differences are present in these areas, they are modest in extent and are shaped by factors such as age, gender and education rather than by religion. There is not much sign here of the development of significant cleavages around 'new politics issues'. Since these issues are related to postmaterialism, this does not augur well for the thesis that materialism versus postmaterialism might provide the stuff of a realigning cleavage. However, such a conclusion would be premature, as we have yet to focus on the evidence related to postmaterialism as such.

Is Ireland postmaterialist?

In asking whether a general shift towards postmaterialist values can be detected in either Northern Ireland or the Republic, we look first at the materialism-

Table 7.7: Support for environmental protection in the Republic of Ireland and Northern Ireland

					(Percentages)
	Strongly Agree	Agree	Disagree	Strongly Disagree	Total [N]
Republic of Ireland:					
Give up part of my income to prevent pollution	8	46	35	11	100 [970]
Pay more taxes if money used to prevent pollution	5	33	47	15	100 [978]
Government has to prevent pollution but not cost me money	31	39	27	4	100 [971]
Northern Ireland:					
Give up part of my income to prevent pollution	4	41	41	14	100 [896]
Pay more taxes if money used to prevent pollution	3	41	40	16	100 [917]
Government has to reduce pollution but not cost me money	27	44	26	3	100 [927]

Questions: Here are some statements about the environment. For each, can you say whether you strongly agree, agree, disagree or strongly disagree: I would give part of my income if I were certain that the money would be used to prevent environmental pollution? I would agree to an increase in taxes if the extra money is used to prevent environmental pollution? The Government has to reduce environmental pollution but it should not cost me any money.

Source: European Values Study, 1999-2000.

postmaterialism scale developed by Inglehart. There are two versions of this scale, a more elaborate one based on a 12-item battery and a simpler one based on a four-item battery (Inglehart 1990: 74-75). As the four-item scale has been much more widely used and has frequently been applied in survey research in Europe (including the Eurobarometer and the EVS), we will concentrate on it here.

The four-item postmaterialism scale is based on a question that asks respondents what they think their country's most important and second most important priorities should be over the next ten years. In answering the question, respondents select from a list of four options: maintaining order in the nation, giving people more say in important government decisions, fighting rising prices, and protecting freedom of speech. In Inglehart's (1990: 74-75) formulation, those who select 'giving people more say in government' and 'protecting freedom of speech' as their top two priorities are said to be postmaterialist, those who select 'the maintenance of order' and 'fighting rising prices' as their top two priorities are said to be materialist, while those who select other combinations are said to be mixed.

Time series data on this scale have been collected for EU member states by the Eurobarometer surveys at 45 time points between 1970 and 1997. Using these data, Figure 7.2 shows the trend in the proportions classified as postmaterialist in the Republic of Ireland, Northern Ireland and two other selected countries – Belgium and Denmark. Denmark and Belgium are included in this picture to indicate the range of trends found in other EU member states – Denmark as an instance of unambiguous increase (from the early 1980s on), Belgium as an instance of slight downward movement (there was no case in the EU of more pronounced downward movement than Belgium's over this period).

For both the Republic of Ireland and Northern Ireland, contrary to what the Inglehart thesis would lead one to expect, it is not possible to detect any clear increase in the proportions who are postmaterialist. Certainly, there are short-term fluctuations but there is no consistent trend. In the Republic of Ireland, for example, the proportion who were postmaterialist showed a significant increase in the late 1980s, but by 1997 it had fallen back more or less to the level of the 1970s. Both parts of Ireland lie closer to the Belgian than to the Danish pattern; making them quite unexceptional among EU countries. In short, it would seem that there is little or no evidence of a rise in postmaterialist values in either part of the island of Ireland over the period 1970 to 1997.

A second indicator of the shift to postmaterialist values emphasised by Inglehart is consistency in the age-gradient on the postmaterialism scale at different points in time, with the level of postmaterialism being higher among the young than the old in each case (Inglehart 1990: 75-76). Figure 7.3 uses the pooled data

Figure 7.2: Trends in postmaterialism in four European societies, 1970-1997

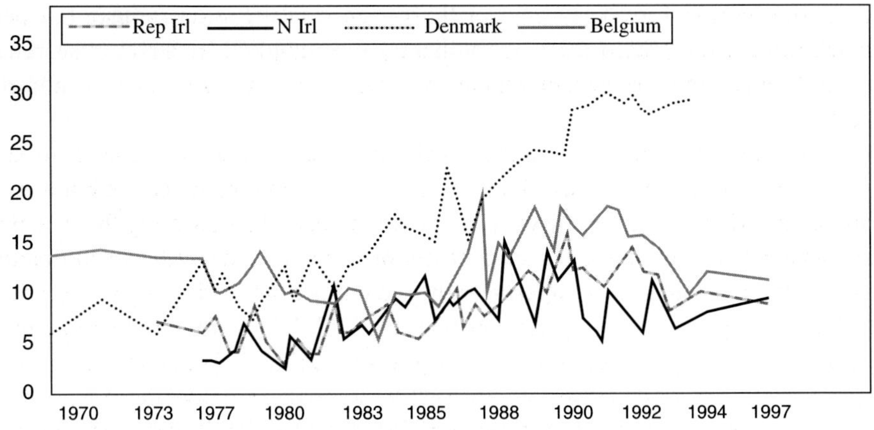

Source: Mannheim Eurobarometer Trend file 1970-1999.

Figure 7.3: Postmaterialism by age-group in the pooled EVS samples for Northern Ireland and the Republic of Ireland, 1981-1999

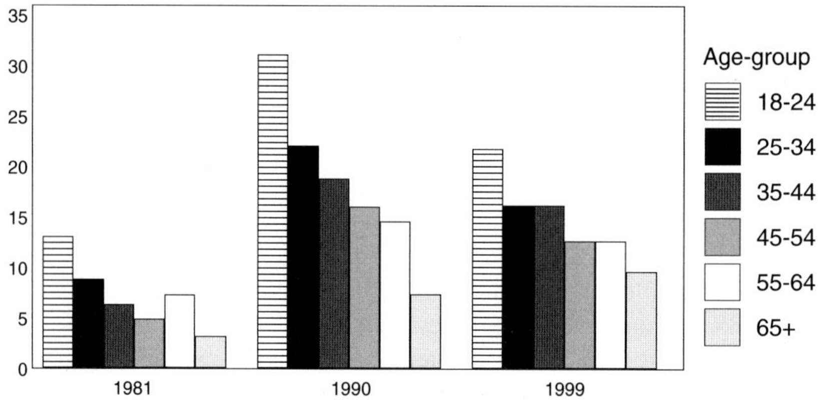

Source: European Values Study, 1981, 1990 and 1999-2000.

for Northern Ireland and the Republic for the three rounds of the EVS to test for the presence of this age-gradient. The results give some support to the Inglehart thesis in that the young are consistently more likely to be postmaterialist than the old. The problem is that the overall trend runs counter to the thesis, as the levels of postmaterialism among younger age-groups are lower in 1999-2000 than in 1990. This again suggests that results in this area are characterised by short-term fluctuations rather than long-term trends.

Figure 7.4 shows that inter-country differences in levels of postmaterialism are closely related to each country's level of development, as measured here by scores on the United Nations Human Development Index.[1] A curvilinear regression of HDI score on the percentage who are postmaterialist in each country accounts for 55 per cent of the variance in the latter indicator, a quite good fit. Croatia (HR) is the main outlier: its postmaterialism score is far higher than its level of development would predict, and Italy and Austria are also overachievers in this sense, though to a lesser degree. Otherwise, across the European countries included here, postmaterialism is reasonably closely related to level of development. Thus, while cross-time comparisons of levels of postmaterialism in Europe provide little support for Inglehart's thesis of a fundamental culture shift in that direction, analysis of cross-country comparisons

[1] The Human Development Index was devised by the United Nations Human Development Programme to measure socio-economic progress across the countries of the world (UNDP 1999). It has three constituent elements: GDP per capita, life expectancy and enrollment in education at primary, secondary and tertiary levels. In the present context, it is worth noting that while the HDI is a better predictor of country-level postmaterialism score, as measured in the 1999-2000 EVS, than GDP per capita, the difference is only marginal – where HDI accounts for 55 per cent of the variance in Figure 7.4, GDP per capita would account for 52 per cent.

Figure 7.4: Postmaterialism and level of development in European countries

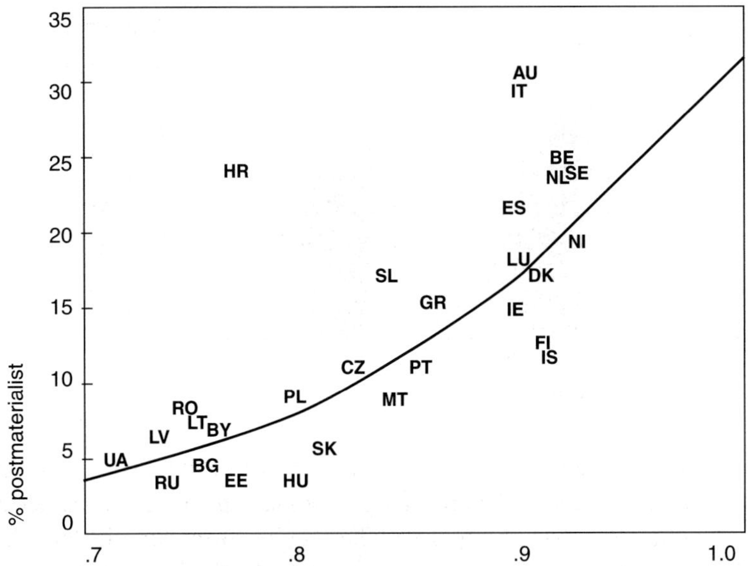

Human Development Index score 1999

Sources: European Values Study, 1999-2000; UNDP, 1999.

in 1999 suggests that the most commonly used indicator of postmaterialism (attributing priority to 'giving people more say in important government decisions' and 'protecting freedom of speech' as the goals of society) is quite closely related to a society's level of development. Accordingly, while the evidence does not show any great signs of an overall postmaterialist revolution, it does suggest that the index is picking up some kind of attitudinal syndrome that is both age-related and reflects variations in levels of socio-economic development.

In the case of Ireland, evidence of a shift towards postmaterialism in Inglehart's sense of the term in either part of the island is at best mixed. Time series data indicate no trend in that direction since the early 1970s, and the age-patterns in postmaterialist values in the 1990s are inconclusive.

In view of these mixed results based on the original Inglehart postmaterialist scale, it is worth looking at some EVS items that explored people's views regarding various changes in both the material aspects of life and certain aspects of human relationships that might take place in the future.

Figure 7.5 sets out the proportions in the Republic of Ireland and Northern Ireland who regarded each of the possible changes as good in 1999-2000. This figure shows that differences between the two parts of Ireland on these items are

Figure 7.5: Preferences for the future, Republic of Ireland and Northern Ireland

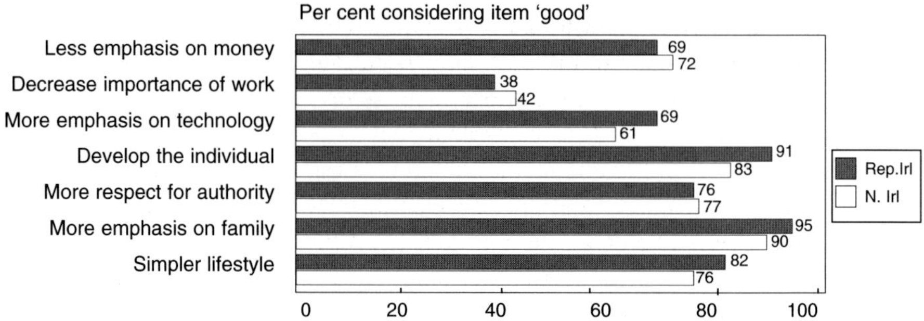

Source: European Values Study, 1999-2000.

not large enough to be considered substantively significant. The general thrust of the evidence indicates a leaning away from materialist conceptions of future progress. 'More emphasis on family life' and 'greater emphasis on the development of the individual' future are the possible changes with the strongest support. 'A simple and more natural lifestyle' and 'less emphasis on money and material possessions' also rate highly. Less than half think that 'decrease in the importance of work in our lives' would be good, but nevertheless the minorities who think that way are large. Comparisons with the same items from previous rounds of the EVS (not presented here) do not show any clear trends, so there is no evidence that the unease with consumerism and materialism, and a tendency to place priority on family and the development of the individual, have increased over the past two decades in either Northern Ireland or the Republic. In assessing the evidence in Figure 7.5 one should also note that three-quarters of both samples took the view that more respect for authority would be a good thing. In the postmaterialist world view this is a decidedly un-postmaterialist attitude.

Conclusion

This chapter has looked at a number of forms of value cleavage that could have the potential either to displace ethnonational or secular-religious differences as a source of division in Northern Ireland or the Republic of Ireland. The classic European cleavage between left and right was the first of these. Our analysis confirmed that the historical failure of the left-right divide to take root in either Northern Ireland or the Republic has continued up to the present: the populations on both sides of the border are alike in placing themselves slightly to the right on the left-right spectrum. Furthermore, there are indications that people now have little grasp of what the classic version of the left-right divide means. People place themselves either to the left or the right and at the same time embrace a somewhat jumbled mix of mildly left-wing and mildly right-wing views on those specific socio-economic issues that historically provided the focus of left-right opposition. This is not to say that the terms 'left' and 'right' have become meaningless. The evidence suggests, rather, that the conception of the 'left' that is most common in the Republic of Ireland and, to a lesser extent in Northern Ireland, relates to a tendency towards secularism on the religious dimension and/or liberalism on sexual and family morality rather than to support for socialist principles. Given the limited coherence of the underlying attitudes and the ambiguity of the terms left and right, the value orientations involved cannot be considered to be a major source of cleavage, potential or otherwise.

Broadly similar patterns emerge when we consider what has sometimes been called the 'new politics' where issues such as gender roles, the environment, and postmaterialist values are the main focus of attention. There has been decisive change in attitudes in some of these areas, most notably in the form of a move away from traditional gender role attitudes. There has been less change in others: evidence in favour of a shift towards postmaterialist values is mixed at best and the evidence of concern for the environment does not add up to a major new value dimension. In short, as has already been suggested in Chapter 2, neither the left-right nor any of these new issues provide a foundation for a new political alignment.

8

Work, subjective well-being and social capital

Introduction

There are many domains of everyday culture in developed societies where religion may once have exerted some sway but where it is now increasingly unlikely that it retains an influence. Yet in the special circumstances of the Republic of Ireland and Northern Ireland, given the cultural force that religion still possesses, the question may be asked whether the vestiges of its influence may still be present in realms of life that in other countries are now rarely thought of in religious terms. More importantly, perhaps, people may believe that such influences are present and may use those beliefs to justify stereotypical representation of cultural differences both within Northern Ireland and between the North and the Republic. It has been said in this regard, for example, that Protestants in Northern Ireland still see themselves as 'an honest, hard-working, straight-talking and law-abiding people', in contrast to Catholics whom they see as 'devious, untrustworthy, lazy, slovenly, happier to "diddle" the state and whinge, than turn an honest penny' (Elliott 2000: 436). Such stereotyping may be dismissed as propaganda, yet its role in collective self-definition on both sides of the divide makes it worthy of investigation, not least because, as post-colonial theorists might argue, even Catholics might tend at some level to believe that it is true.

From the many areas of cultural life where stereotyping of this kind could be tested, this chapter picks out three. The first relates to work. The image of Protestant industry versus Catholic idleness has often surfaced in Irish history (Akenson, 1988). Protestant prosperity in the past was often represented as a product of a Protestant ethic of thrift and hard work that was said to be lacking in the Catholic population. More recently, however, economic boom in the Republic means that one can no longer associate Catholic parts of the island with economic backwardness. A question can therefore be asked whether any differences in Protestant and Catholic attitudes towards work can be found in either part of Ireland today.

A related stereotype of Protestant-Catholic difference in Ireland is that Protestants are dour, grim and private where Catholics are sunny, relaxed and sociable. This contrast might equally be dismissed as too crude to be taken seriously. Yet there is a more plausible version which links aspects of mood and sociability to the recent history of Northern Ireland and asks whether the disturbed political conditions of that society have cast a shadow over the quality of life experienced by its citizens. Questions have also been asked about the quality of life that has emerged in the Republic in the wake of economic boom. An optimistic line of commentary on this question views economic growth and reduced unemployment as obviously beneficial while a more pessimistic interpretation portrays a society where people may have more and do more but somehow feel worse off. The second and third topics dealt with in this chapter take up these issues by exploring two dimensions of quality of life. These are subjective well-being, a feature of life measured in the EVS surveys by reference to how satisfied with life people feel, and social capital, a term which refers to the social connections and relationships of trust and reciprocity that determine how closely people are connected to each other and the society that surrounds them. Here our main interest is to consider similarities and differences between the Republic and Northern Ireland and between Protestants and Catholics in these aspects of life and to assess how far they reflect either an inherited cultural effect or the impact of more recent developments.

Work

The first round of the EVS survey in 1981 found that a positive work ethic was widespread in the Republic of Ireland: Irish people reported themselves more satisfied with and committed to work than the European average, certainly more so than the supposedly work-enamoured Germans (Fogarty 1984: 59-60). Some commentators at the time found it hard to believe this finding (e.g. Lee 1984: 108), but the much-vaunted attractiveness of Irish workers to multinational corporations in the years since then has lent it greater credibility.

The EVS provides a basis for exploring these issues through a number of items in the 1999-2000 survey which tap the degree to which respondents place a positive value on work. One set of such items asked respondents to register their agreement or disagreement with each of the following six statements (a five-point response set was used to record responses – 'strongly agree', 'agree', 'neither agree nor disagree', 'disagree', 'strongly disagree'):

1. *To fully develop your talents, you need to have a job.*
2. *It is humiliating to receive money without having to work for it.*
3. *People who don't work turn lazy.*

4. Work is a duty towards society.
5. People should not have to work if they don't want to.
6. Work should always come first, even if it means less spare time.

Table 8.1 shows the precentage of respondents who either 'strongly agreed' or 'agreed' with each of these statements, classified by religious affiliation. It also shows the mean scores for each religious grouping on a 'pro-work' scale which is derived by averaging responses to the six items. For scaling purpose, disagreement with item 5, which expresses an anti-work sentiment, is counted a pro-work attitude, as is agreement with the other items (the alpha reliability coefficient for the resulting pro-work scale, which is a continuous scale from 1 to 5, is 0.74).

The patterns revealed in Table 8.1 suggest that the level of pro-work sentiment does not vary consistently between Protestants and Catholics but does seem to show a North-South difference, with those in the Republic of Ireland expressing stronger pro-work attitudes than those in the North. On some of the individual items, the gap between Southern and Northern orientations is narrow or is not consistent across religious groupings, but on others (such as the notion that it is humiliating to receive money without working for it or that work is a duty to society), the southern edge in pro-work sentiment is marked and consistent. That

Table 8.1: Work orientations by religious affiliation, Republic of Ireland and Northern Ireland

	Republic of Ireland			Northern Ireland		
	Catholic	Protestant	Non-affiliated	Catholic	Protestant	Non-affiliated
	Per cent 'strongly agree' or 'agree'					
Need job to fully develop talents	61	63	57	61	55	56
Humiliating to receive money without working for it	49	52	47	37	36	29
People who don't work turn lazy	56	61	57	46	50	39
Work is a duty to society	60	70	51	51	50	41
People should not have to work if they don't want to	27	17	34	26	24	27
Work should come first	35	43	24	31	34	24
Mean scores on pro-work scale	3.34	3.45	3.14	3.08*	3.16*	3.00*
[N]	[899]	[257]	[72]	[366]	[459]	[173]

* Significantly different from Catholics in the Republic, $p < 0.01$ (two-tailed t-test)
Source: European Values Study, 1999-2000.

edge is also evident in connection with the combined pro-work scale, where the statistically significant differences arise between the two sides of the border rather than between Protestants and Catholics on either side.

To understand these patterns better, it is worth exploring briefly to what extent cross-border differences in this area might be explained by differences in the profile of the two populations along other dimensions likely to influence work attitudes, such as age, gender, education, urban-rural location and social class. In light of the lack of a consistent denominational effect on work attitudes which we have just outlined, it is also worth including measures of religiosity in this analysis. This is to echo a pattern identified in other chapters in this study where the link between religion and cultural attitudes has been seen to take the form not of a denominational effect but of a religiosity or secularisation effect, that is, where differences *between* Catholics and Protestants are less pronounced than differences *within* each denomination between devout and nominal adherents.

Using multiple regression analysis, we can examine the effects of each of these factors on the pro-work scale while holding the effects of the other factors constant. Two religiosity variables are included in the analysis, one which measures frequency of attendance at church, the other which measures the importance of God in the respondents' lives. These are placed alongside the categorical denominational variables used in Table 8.1. The results of the analysis, as set out in Table 8.2, show that age and gender have the strongest effects: the old have

Table 8.2: Regression on pro-work scale for combined Republic of Ireland and Northern Ireland samples (standardised regression coefficients)

Age	0.135***
Male	0.149***
Unemployed	-0.070**
Rural	0.085***
Attend religious services	0.091**
Importance of God in life	0.108***
Age completed education	0.013
Denomination (ref.=RoI Catholic)	
RoI Protestant	0.056
RoI non-affiliated	0.003
NI Catholic	-0.085***
NI Protestant	-0.037
NI non-affiliated	0.003
Social class (ref: =Manual)	
Professional/executive	-0.012
Other non-manual	0.061**
Farmers/other proprietors	0.090**

*p < 0.05 **p < 0.01 ***p < 0.001

Figure 8.1: Mean scores on pro-work scale in 33 European societies

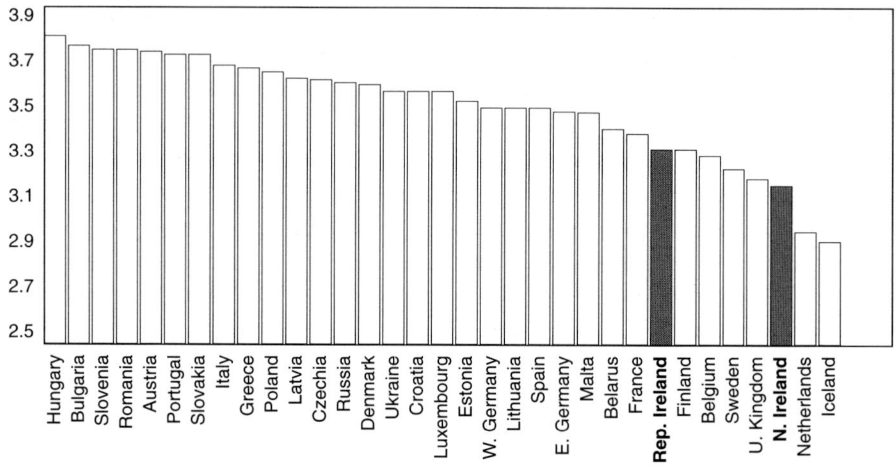

Source: European Values Study, 1999-2000.

stronger pro-work attitudes compared to the young, as do men compared to women. The religiosity variables are the next most influential: those who attend church more often and who attach a high importance to God in their lives have stronger pro-work attitudes than those who don't. The denominational categories are less important: Northern Catholics turn out to be significantly lower on the pro-work scale than sourthern Catholics, but the other elements of the 'northern' effect which appeared in Table 8.1 – the lower pro-work scores of northern Protestants and northern non-affiliated – disappear when the other variables included in the regression are controlled for. The effect of social class is slight: only the farmer/other proprietor category stand out from the other social class groups. These results, in sum, confirm the expectation that consistent denominational differences in work attitudes are absent in Ireland – Protestants do not now have a distinctive Protestant work ethic (which is not to imply that they ever had it in the past either). Catholics in Northern Ireland show weaker pro-work attitudes than other denominational categories, but this cannot be counted as a denominational effect since the contrast groups include Catholics in the Republic as well as Protestants.

However, the findings also suggest that the role of religion in the culture of work goes beyond the denominational question. This is so because of a religiosity effect – those who have strong religious attachment are more committed to pro-work attitudes than those who are less religious. The impact of religiosity is not that great – it is less important than the effects of age and gender. But it does reinforce the pattern pointed to elsewhere in this study which identifies secularisation as a significant axis of differentiation in the culture of everyday life on the island of Ireland, one which, outside the sphere of identity politics, is more important than religious denomination in influencing how people view the world.

To place the level of pro-work sentiment in the two parts of Ireland in a European context, Figure 8.1 shows mean national scores on the pro-work scale for the 33 societies in the 1999-2000 EVS data set. Here it emerges that both Northern Ireland and the Republic rank quite low in Europe on the pro-work scale. There is a broad though not entirely consistent east-west gradient in that the highest-scoring countries on the scale are in central or eastern Europe while the lowest-scoring are in western Europe, though in the middle ranges of the distibution the eastern and western countries are mixed together. These patterns should caution us against expecting to find easily interpretable connections between characteristics of the national economy and attitudes towards work as measured by the attitudinal variables in the EVS.

Measurement of subjective well-being

Although measurement of life satisfaction, happiness and related dimensions of subjective well-being in large-scale surveys has a long tradition in psychology and in certain sub-fields of sociology (Diener *et al.*, 1999; Ryan and Deci, 2001), it has been slow to gain acceptance in the broader social-scientific analysis of human welfare (Frey and Stutzer, 2002; Oswald, 1997). Indicators of subjective well-being have had to struggle against scepticism in the wider research community, where they are often regarded either as liable to 'inauthentic self-reports' from respondents in survey interviews or as reflections of respondents' aspirations rather than their real circumstances in life (Hagerty *et al.,* 2001). However, a case can also be made that such indicators have proved to be highly revealing about the nature of human welfare and the factors that affect it across countries (Fahey and Smyth, 2004). In particular, research which compares subjective well-being across rich and poor countries has shown up a striking regularity: national levels of subjective well-being are strongly and positively related to level of economic development – the populations of poor countries are unhappier and less satisfied with life than the populations of rich countries (Ryan and Deci, 2000; Ingelhart and Klingermann, 2000).

This pattern is particularly evident in the 33 societies covered in the 1999-2000 EVS (see Fahey and Smyth, 2004). Among these are included some societies at low levels of economic development – for example the Ukraine, which in the late 1990s had a GDP per capita of just over $2,000, only one-tenth of the level found in the more developed countries of the EU. Figure 8.2 shows that there are wide differences in the mean level of life satisfaction across this range of European societies and that these differences are closely linked to level of economic development as measured by GDP per capita (expressed in 1997 US$ at purchasing power parities). Broadly speaking, the 'old' EU countries have higher satisfaction levels than do central and eastern European countries while, within the EU, northern countries (including both the Republic of Ireland and Northern Ireland) have higher satisfaction levels than southern countries (such as Greece, Spain, Portugal, Italy and France). Denmark has the highest level of life satisfaction of all the countries, with a mean of 8.24 on the 10-point satisfaction scale, but both the Republic of Ireland and Northern Ireland come close behind (with means of 8.15 and 8.0 respectively). A certain number of countries in central and eastern Europe (Slovenia, East Germany, the Czech Republic, and Croatia) overlap with the southern EU countries, with means between 6.5 and 7.0 on the life satisfaction scale. But the east European countries generally fall well below 6.5 and three countries (Belarus, Russia and the Ukraine) fall below 5.

The curvilinear regression of GDP per capita on country-level mean life satisfaction in Figure 8.2 shows a fit of 84.5 per cent, an exceptionally close level of association. If one were to focus narrowly on the group of 'old' EU countries which cluster closely together in Figure 8.2, Ireland and Denmark would appear to be anomalously high on life satisfaction, Italy and France would appear to be anomalously low, and the overall link with GDP would seem to be weak. However, viewed across the full range of countries, these anomalies hardly seem to be anomalies at all: the richer countries cluster closely together both on GDP and life satisfaction, while across all the 33 societies, it is the consistency and closeness of

Figure 8.2: Mean life satisfaction and GDP per capita in 33 European societies

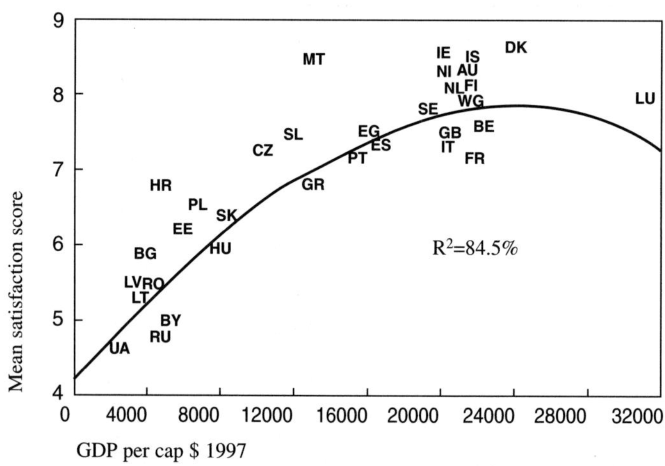

Question: All things considered, how satisfied are you with your life as a whole these days?

*10-point scale where 1=dissatisfied and 10=satisfied.

Source: European Values Study, 1999-2000; World Bank, 2001.

the association between GDP per capita and life satisfaction which stand out. These patterns also suggest that the economic effect plateaus out above a certain threshold. According to the present data, that threshold is located slightly above the level represented by the countries at the lowest levels within the former EU 15 countries as far as mean national GDP per capita is concerned: up to that level increasing GDP has a large effect on life satisfaction but above it the effect tails off sharply so that additional national income makes less and less of a difference to mean national life satisfaction.

To show what these national differences mean in detail, Table 8.3 gives examples of full frequencies for the life satisfaction variable for three sample societies. At the top of the life satisfaction range is the Republic of Ireland, with its mean of 8.2 on the 10-point satisfaction scale. In this case, 70 per cent of respondents score 8 or above and only 8 per cent score 5 or lower. In Greece, an intermediate country, the mean score is 6.7, 41 per cent score 8 or above but 27 per cent score 5 or below. In Belarus, the mean is 4.8, only 14 per cent score 8 or above, while 30 per cent score 3 or below. Thus there is little overlap in satisfaction scores between the two countries at the extremes in this table (Ireland and Belarus): only

Table 8.3: Levels and variance in life satisfaction within the Republic of Ireland, Greece and Belarus

	(Percentages)		
	Ireland	Greece	Belarus
1 dissatisfied	0.8	2.9	7.0
2	0.3	2.3	8.6
3	1.8	4.5	14.7
4	1.4	7.8	14.0
5	3.8	9.4	22.3
6	6.2	12.3	9.2
7	15.3	19.2	10.5
8	22.7	20.9	8.4
9	17.4	14.2	3.4
10 satisfied	30.1	6.4	2.0
Total	100	100	100
Mean	8.2	6.7	4.8
Standard deviation	1.9	2.2	2.2

Source: European Values Study, 1999-2000.

a small minority at the top of the scale in Belarus match the satisfaction levels of the vast majority of Irish people, while the vast majority of Belarusians are less satisfied than all but the most dissatisfied of Irish people.

These patterns do not fully tell us how indicators of subjective well-being should be interpreted, but they argue against the view that indicators of subjective well-being are unresponsive to variations in socio-economic context and are, thus, of limited social-scientific interest. They suggest that a society's location in the international (or at least European) hierarchy of economic development has a strong influence on how members of that society evaluate their personal circumstances. It is possible that this macro-economic effect on life satisfaction at the country level may hide further complexities, since the economic indicators are themselves correlated with other factors. It is notable, for example, that the former EU 15 countries with the lowest life satisfaction – Greece, Spain and Portugal – have the most recent historical experience of non-democratic government, while within central and eastern Europe, the countries which were under communist rule since 1918 generally have lower life satisfaction than those which were brought into the Soviet sphere after 1945 (for further comments along these lines, see Inglehart and Klingemann, 2000). However, the point to note here is that, looking across this range of societies, at least some aspects of their objective situation – whether it be economic or political – have a strong bearing on aggregate life satisfaction and indicate that relativities *between* societies are an important influence on how individuals evaluate the adequacy of their personal situations.

Trends in subjective well-being in Ireland

While life satisfaction levels may vary widely across societies, they seem to vary less across time – at least among those highly developed societies for which time series data on this issue are available. Eurobarometer data, which provide the longest available time series on life satisfaction for EU countries, confirm that this pattern is true in both the Republic of Ireland and Northern Ireland. Using a four-point life satisfaction scale (which is less refined than the 10-point scale used in the EVS), the Eurobarometer measure has been undertaken at 45 time points in the 25 years between 1973 and 1999. Figure 8.3 compares the trend on these data for the two parts of Ireland, North and South, with those for three other EU countries over this period. The comparison countries represent the extremes of variation found within the EU. These countries are the Netherlands, which consistently scores highest or nearly highest in the EU on various measures of subjective well-being, and Italy, which, among the original EU member states, typically scores at or close to the bottom of the EU range on the same measures (though among later entrants, Greece, Spain and Portugal score somewhat lower than Italy).

According to these measures, life satisfaction in Northern Ireland and the Republic of Ireland has fluctuated around a more-or-less flat underlying trend over

Figure 8.3: Mean life satisfaction scores in selected European countries, 1973-1998

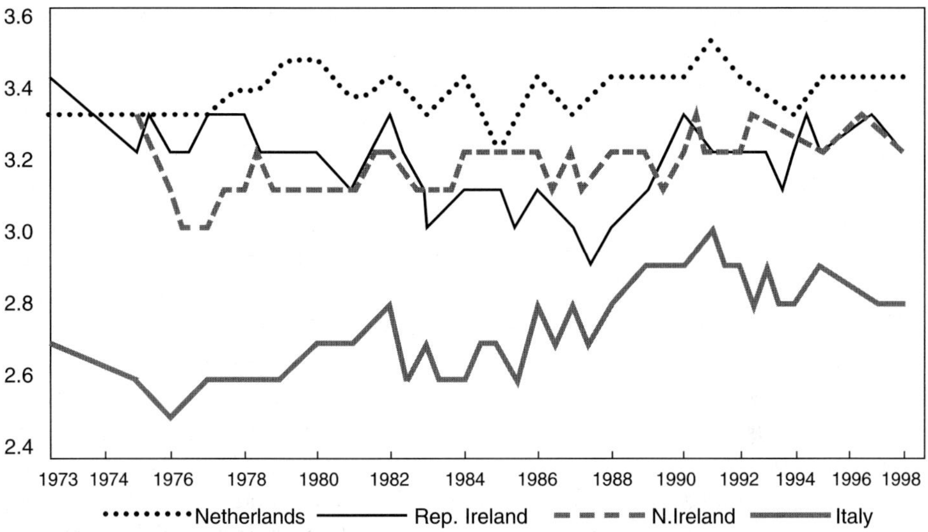

Means are based on a four-point scale where 1=not at all satisfied and 4=very satisfied.

Source: Mannheim Eurobarometer Trend File 1970-1999

the 25-year period. Northern Ireland had somewhat lower scores than the Republic in the 1970s, higher scores in the 1980s, and similar scores in the 1990s, but the difference is nowhere very wide. In Northern Ireland, it is difficult to detect any consistent, substantial effect from the political situation on life satisfaction – the scores are too similar to those of the Republic and too high in comparison with other European countries for a plausible case to be made for such an effect. In the Republic, there is a considerable dip in the mean life satisfaction scores in 1987 and 1988. As this was a period marked by economic recession, high unemployment and the resurgence of high emigration, it is plausible to attribute the dip to the poor state of the economy, particularly since the sense of a crisis in the economy at that time was 'talked up' by the political parties in the context of the general election of 1987 (see Laver *et al.,* 1987). However, following a sharp rise in the scores for the Republic in the period 1987 to 1990, fluctuations around the longer term flat trend resumed. The onset of economic boom in 1994 brought no break in the trend – the surge in the economy did not produce an outbreak of national euphoria. By 1998, although satisfaction scores had risen from the trough of ten years earlier, they were no higher than they had been in the 1970s.

Turning to evidence from the EVS, Table 8.4 presents data on happiness and life satisfaction from the three rounds of the survey (1981, 1990 and 1999-2000) for both the Republic and Northern Ireland. The trend in happiness is more or less as

Table 8.4: Happiness and satisfaction with life in the Republic of Ireland and Northern Ireland, 1981-1999

(Percentages)

	Republic of Ireland			Northern Ireland		
	1981	1990	1999	1981	1990	1999
Very happy	40.7	43.7	42.4	38.6	37.0	46.7
Quite happy	55.3	49.8	54.0	55.0	56.3	49.5
Not very happy	3.4	5.3	3.1	5.0	5.3	2.3
Not at all happy	0.6	1.2	0.6	0.1	1.3	1.5
Total	100	100	100	100	100	100
Mean happiness score[1]	3.4	3.4	3.4	3.3	3.3	3.4
Mean life satisfaction score[2]	7.0	6.8	8.2	6.9	6.7	8.0
[Base N]	[1,217]	[1,000]	[1,012]	[312]	[298]	[1,000]

Question: Taking all things together, would you say you are: very happy, quite happy, not very happy, not at all happy?

Note: [1] Means are based on a four-point scale where 4=very happy and 1=not at all happy'; [2] Means are based on a 10-point scale where 1=dissatisfied and 10=satisfied

Source: European Values Study, 1981, 1990, 1999-2000.

expected, in that it shows no real increase or decrease over the period. Neither is there a significant difference between the Republic and Northern Ireland in any of the three years. There is some movement in the distribution of responses across the four categories of the happiness scale in both the Republic and Northern Ireland, particularly between the 'very happy' and 'quite happy' categories. But the mean of the happiness score is entirely uniform for the three years in the Republic (at 3.4) and is almost so in Northern Ireland (at 3.3 or 3.4).

The trend in life satisfaction is different, in that in both the Republic and Northern Ireland mean satisfaction scores increased between 1990 and 1999. The increase is from 6.8 to 8.2 (on a 10-point scale) in the case of the Republic and from 6.7 to 8.0 in the case of Northern Ireland. This substantial improvement in satisfaction levels during the 1990s is hard to reconcile with the flat trend for the 1990s indicated by the Eurobarometer data just looked at, though it is in keeping with the rise in satisfaction in the Republic which the Eurobarometer data suggest had occurred from 1987 onwards. The differences between the two data sources on this issue could be due to the more refined measurement used in the EVS, which is based on a 10-point satisfaction scale rather than the four-point scale used in the Eurobarometer. Alternatively, it could amount to little more than a normal degree of fluctuation in satisfaction scores in national surveys, where the deviation from the Eurobarometer data can be accounted for by differences in the precise time-points in the year when the data were collected.

Religion, religious denominations and subjective well-being

Given the interest of the present study in cultural cleavages connected to religion, variations in subjective well-being across religious denominations in the two parts of Ireland must be considered. Furthermore, we have seen in earlier chapters that, as far as non-political aspects of cultural outlook are concerned, cultural differences associated with secularisation have emerged as a more important axis of differentiation than those associated with denomination. The question is whether secularisation has any similar relationship with levels of subjective well-being.

We have already seen that there is little or no consistent difference between the Republic of Ireland and Northern Ireland in life satisfaction or happiness, and that fact alone would lead us to expect a similar lack of difference across the main denominational groupings. Table 8.5 generally confirms that this is so. The percentage of Protestants in Northern Ireland who report themselves as very happy is higher than that for any other denominational group, but their higher rating on this item does not carry over into a higher rating on the mean life satisfaction score. In fact they have a marginally lower mean life satisfaction score than Catholics in the North and both Catholics and Protestants in the Republic. It is notable that the non-affiliated score lower on life satisfaction than any category of the religiously affiliated, a pattern that is more marked in the North than in the Republic. This raises a question as to whether religious attachment rather than denomination may be the main aspect of religiosity likely to influence subjective well-being.

Table 8.5: Happiness and life satisfaction by religious identification in the Republic of Ireland and Northern Ireland

(Percentages)

	Republic of Ireland			Northern Ireland		
	Catholic	Protestant	Non-affiliated	Catholic	Protestant	Non-affiliated
Very happy	42.5	40.5	40.8	42.1	50.6	38.1
Not very/not at all happy	3.4	2.3	7.0	4.9	3.3	7.2
Mean happiness score[1]	3.4	3.4	3.3	3.4	3.5	3.3
Mean life satisfaction score[2]	8.20	8.27	7.89	8.11	8.02	7.48
[Base N]	[899]	[257]	[72]	[366]	[459]	[173]

Note: [1] Means are based on four-point scale where 4=very happy and 1=not at all happy'; [2] Means are based on a 10-point scale where 1=dissatisfied and 10=satisfied

Source: European Values Study, 1999-2000.

Table 8.6 offers an additional perspective on this possibility by showing that regular church attenders (i.e. those who attend church monthly or more often) are more likely to say they are very happy and have higher average life satisfaction scores than irregular church attenders (i.e. those who attend church less often than once per month). The relationship is not very strong, but it is consistent across the affective (happiness) and cognitive (life satisfaction) dimensions of subjective well-being and further corroborates the idea that religiosity and subjective well-being are positively related to each other.

Table 8.7 explores the significance of religiosity further by looking at correlations between two measures of religious commitment on the one hand and the two measures of subjective well-being on other. One of the measures of religious commitment is the church attendance scale, where respondents are scored 1 if they never attend church and 8 if they attend church more than once per week. The other is a rating by respondents of how important God is in their lives. As outlined in Chapter 3, this can be regarded as a measure of 'private' religiosity (that is, religious attachment which exists independently of participation in organised religion).

It is of particular interest to note the patterns which arise in the case of the non-affiliated as far as these variables are concerned. As we saw in Chapter 3, the non-affiliated have low levels of attachment to organised religion (reflected here in their low mean scores on the church attendance scale) but they report considerable levels of private religiosity (as reflected here in scores on the 'importance of God in your life' scale which are far from negligible, even if they are well below those of both Catholics and Protestants). Table 8.7 suggests that to the extent that such private religiosity is present among the non-affiliated, it is important for their subjective well-being – the correlations between their 'importance of God' scores and their life satisfaction ratings, in both the Republic and Northern Ireland, are the largest

Table 8.6: Church attendance and subjective well-being in the Republic of Ireland and Northern Ireland

	Republic of Ireland		Northern Ireland	
	% 'very happy'	Mean life satisfaction score[1]	% 'very happy	Mean life satisfaction score[1]
Church attendance:				
Regular attender	45	8.25	50	8.16
Irregular attender	36	7.92	39	7.68
[Base N]	[1,012]	[1,012]	[1,000]	[1,000]

Note: [1] Means are based on a 10-point scale where 1=dissatisfied and 10=satisfied

Source: European Values Study, 1999-2000.

Table 8.7: Religiosity and subjective well-being by religious identification in the Republic of Ireland and Northern Ireland

	Republic of Ireland			Northern Ireland		
	Catholic	Protestant	Non-affiliated	Catholic	Protestant	Non-affiliated
Mean church attendance[1]	6.2	6.2	1.4	6.5	5.1	1.8
Correlations with:						
Life satisfaction	0.12**	0.18*	0.20	0.16**	0.07	0.16*
Happiness	0.11**	0.18*	0.07	0.13*	0.14*	0.22**
Importance of God in your life: mean scores[2]	7.7	7.4	4.9	8.0	7.3	3.8
Correlations with:						
Life satisfaction	0.20**	0.17*	0.32**	0.09	0.11*	0.22**
Happiness	0.12**	0.18*	0.20*	0.16**	0.07	0.19*
[Base N]	[899]	[257]	[72]	[366]	[459]	[173]

Note: [1] Means are based on an eight-point scale where 1=never and 8=more than weekly; [2] Means are based on a 10-point scale where 1=no importance at all and 10=very important; *Statistically associated at the 0.05 level; **Statistically associated at the 0.01 level.

Source: European Values Study, 1999-2000.

in the table. These correlations are not very strong in absolute terms (0.32 in the Republic and 0.22 in the North) but they indicate that private religiosity among the non-affiliated yields some of the psychological benefits that church members draw from their attachment to more organised forms of religion. For the non-affiliated in Northern Ireland, church attendance is also positively linked to both happiness and life satisfaction. This means that while church attendance is uncommon and infrequent among the non-affiliated in Northern Ireland, there nevertheless is a statistically significant gain in subjective well-being among those few who do attend. The other correlations reported in Table 8.7 indicate that religiosity is positively related to subjective well-being across all the denominational groupings, though in a number of instances the relationships are too weak to be statistically significant.

Social correlates of subjective well-being

This brings us to a range of other social and economic factors likely to be connected with subjective well-being. In previous research, much of the attention in this regard has focused on the impact of income on satisfaction. The most consistent finding here is that income makes relatively little difference at the individual level in rich countries (Diener *et al.*, 1999; Ryan and Deci, 2001; Oswald, 1997) though this finding may not apply to poorer countries (Fahey and

Smyth, 2004) and is not universally accepted even for richer countries (Frey and Stutzer, 2002). At the same time, certain other individual-level factors have been found to exert a statistically significant influence, even though together they account for only a small share of the individual-level variance in life satisfaction (Diener *et al.*, 1999; Ryan and Deci, 2001). In most studies, unemployment emerges as the strongest of these (Frey and Stutzer, 2002: 419-21; Oswald, 1997). The unemployed have considerably higher distress, lower life satisfaction and higher rates of suicide than employed persons. Marital status is also usually found to be important – the married have generally been found to be happier (as well as being physically healthier) than those in any other marital status category. Other factors that have often been found to have an impact include health status, age and gender, though findings on age and gender effects are of doubtful consistency and robustness.

Table 8.8 shows variations in both the Republic of Ireland and Northern Ireland in the percentage who are 'very happy' and in mean life satisfaction scores across a number of socio-demographic categories – gender, age, marital status, social class, and employment status. Looking at this table overall, it is clear that two factors stand out as having substantial links with happiness and life satisfaction. These are unemployment and marital status – and under the latter heading, the separated or divorced have particularly low levels of subjective well-being. Among both the unemployed and the separated or divorced in both Northern Ireland and the Republic, only around 20 per cent say they are 'very happy', which is less than half the percentages who are 'very happy' in the samples as a whole. Similarly, their life satisfaction scores are the lowest – they are the only sub-groups to have means below 7.5 on the life satisfaction scale (and in fact in Northern Ireland both sub-groups score below 7.0 on this scale). Thus both the separated/divorced and the unemployed fall substantially below the overall levels of subjective well-being in the sample and do so consistently for both the affective and cognitive dimensions (i.e. happiness and life satisfaction).

Apart from the separated or divorced, the widowed and those who are single also have somewhat lower levels of subjective well-being. They are not as low on the happiness and life satisfaction scales as the separated or divorced, but they fall considerably short of the scores of the married, as well as of the overall samples.

These patterns are in keeping with the findings of international research which, as already noted, consistently show that unemployment negatively affects subjective well-being, while those who are married have on average higher levels of subjective well-being than those in any other marital status category.

Gender is a further factor in Table 8.8 which shows links with both happiness and life satisfaction scales in the Republic and Northern Ireland. Women have higher subjective well-being than men, the difference being slight but consistent. Otherwise, the factors listed in Table 8.8 at most have either weak or inconsistent

Table 8.8: Happiness and life satisfaction by socio-demographic background in the Republic of Ireland and Northern Ireland

	Republic of Ireland		Northern Ireland	
	% 'very happy'	Mean life satisfaction score[1]	% 'very happy	Mean life satisfaction score[1]
Gender:				
Males	39	8.13	43	7.86
Females	45	8.22	47	8.04
Age:				
18-34	40	8.13	49	7.91
35-49	46	8.18	45	7.87
50-64	42	8.17	45	7.95
65+	38	8.20	41	8.13
Marital status:				
Married	49	8.43	53	8.21
Widowed	33	7.98	35	7.77
Separated/divorce	19	7.32	21	6.87
Never married	33	7.73	40	7.80
Social class:				
Professional/managerial	49	8.49	57	8.30
Other non-manual	45	8.27	44	7.98
Manual	42	8.09	41	7.88
Farmers/agric. workers	41	7.92	57	8.30
Employment status:				
At work	44	8.23	48	8.07
Unemployed	22	7.18	21	6.86
Retired	39	8.45	47	8.27
Home duties	46	8.13	49	7.94
Other	33	8.02	43	7.90
Overall sample	42	8.20	47	8.0
[Base N]	[1,012]	[1,012]	[1,000]	[1,000]

Note: [1] Means are based on 10-point scale where 1=dissatisfied and 10=satisfied

Source: European Values Study, 1999-2000.

effects on subjective well-being. The strongest age-effect, for example, is that those aged over 65 are less likely to be 'very happy' than other age-groups, but their mean life satisfaction scores are higher than other age groups.

Social capital

We now turn to the third main topic to be dealt with in this chapter – social capital. Just as much as people want to be happy, it is widely assumed that they also want and need to be engaged in a web of social relations. There is a widespread public concern in many developed societies that the way we live our lives today has reduced our capacity to meet this fundamental need. This concern has recently been captured in Robert Putnam's well known book, *Bowling Alone: The Collapse and Revival of American Community.* Putnam argues that for all the economic and social progress of the past fifty years, Americans have become socially more isolated and have suffered a fundamental decline in quality of life as a result. He uses a wide range of data to argue that Americans spend less time socialising with friends or interacting with neighbours, they trust each other less, they participate less in clubs, trade unions and political activity, and even within the same household are less likely to eat together or watch television in the same room (Putnam, 2000). In short, according to Putnam, social capital in America has steadily eroded from the high levels it had attained in the 1950s and shows no immediate signs of revival.

Putnam's thesis has often been assumed to apply to all developed countries, and the question arises as to whether it is valid for either or both parts of Ireland. It should be said immediately that research in a number of countries outside of the USA gives grounds for scepticism on this matter. Data for Britain, the Netherlands, France, Japan, Australia, Germany and Sweden give some indications of change in the character of associational life and informal socialising but no evidence of overall decline in social capital. In fact for Britain and Germany there is some evidence of an increase, indicating if anything that at least some aspects of social capital are strengthening rather than weakening in these countries (for a comprehensive review see OECD, 2001). Thus, although the idea that social capital is in decline rings true for a lot of people, hard evidence in support of this thesis is not easy to find, at least outside of the United States. There is little *prima facie* indication that Putnam's thesis is valid for developed countries in general and, in consequence, there is no particular basis for assuming that it is likely to be valid in either Northern Ireland or the Republic of Ireland.

Here we can explore this issue by looking at the evidence on trends and correlates of social capital in the two parts of Ireland based on a number of measures drawn from the EVS. There is no widely agreed definition of what social capital means and no standard method for quantifying it. Some of the factors we have dealt with earlier could be counted as important forms of social capital though they are not always considered as such – for example, regular church attendance, participation in family networks or participation in paid work, all of which contribute to the creation of social relationships. In fact, the importance of both marriage and unemployment as influences on subjective well-being and as sources of social interaction could be taken to indicate that the most important forms of social capital are those which arise from having a spouse and having a job. However, certain measures of social capital have become semi-standard in the research literature, referring especially to social capital outside the family and workplace. Some of these are contained in the EVS data and will be examined here under two headings – trust and participation in voluntary organisations.

Trust

Trust is widely regarded as a central element of the social glue that binds people together. It is most commonly thought of in connection with trust in other people and that is what we deal with in this section. It can also be applied to confidence in public institutions, the latter being considered as an indicator of acceptance of and identification with the public sphere. This issue will be taken up in Chapter 9 in connection with political participation.

The item on interpersonal trust contained in the EVS data is based on a survey question which asks respondents whether they agree that 'most people can be trusted'. This is the most widely utilised measure of trust in surveys of this kind. Table 8.9 shows the trend in trust in the Republic of Ireland and Northern Ireland over the years 1981, 1990 and 1999-2000. In the Republic of Ireland, trust showed a substantial decline between 1990 and 1999-2000, though it had risen in the preceding period, from 1981 to 1990. In Northern Ireland, a more modest decline occurred during the 1990s, but without the preceding rise in the 1980s. Thus there is an indication here of a certain decline in trust in others in the 1990s but the rise in this measure in the Republic in the 1980s and its stability in the North in the same decade casts doubt on the likelihood of a long-term downward movement. This evidence does not counter Putnam's thesis of a general decline in this dimension of social capital, but neither does it lend it any great support.

Table 8.10 explores the links between religion and trust by looking at trust across the main religious groupings in 1999-2000. The strongest pattern which emerges here is the lower levels of trust among the non-affiliated. Only 29 per cent of the non-affiliated in both the Republic and Northern Ireland think that most people can be trusted, compared to sample averages of 36 per cent in the Republic and 40 per cent in the North.

Table 8.11 looks at the links between trust and two indicators of religiosity – church attendance and the importance of God in the respondent's life. The links

Table 8.9: Trust in people in the Republic of Ireland and Northern Ireland, 1981-1999

	(Per cent agreeing)					
	Republic of Ireland			Northern Ireland		
	1981	1990	1999	1981	1990	1999
Most people can be trusted	41	47	36	44	44	40
[Base N]	[1,217]	[1,000]	[1,012]	[312]	[298]	[1,000]

Question: Generally speaking, would you say that most people can be trusted or that you can't be too careful in dealing with people?

Source: European Values Study, 1981, 1990, 1999-2000.

Table 8.10: Religious identification and trust in people in the Republic of Ireland and Northern Ireland

	(Per cent agreeing)					
	Republic of Ireland			Northern Ireland		
	Catholic	Protestant	Non-affiliated	Catholic	Protestant	Non-affiliated
Most people can be trusted	36	47	29	44	40	29
[Base N]	[899]	[257]	[72]	[366]	[459]	[173]

Source: European Values Study, 1999-2000.

with church attendance indicate that church members who do not attend regularly have lower levels of trust than those who do – and this relationship applies both in the Republic and the North. In connection with the importance of God in respondents' lives, which we have referred to earlier as an indicator of 'private religiosity', Table 8.11 presents data solely for the non-affiliated, since it is in their case that the impact of private religiosity is of particular interest. The results give a different indication of the impact of religiosity, since those who score high on this measure are less trusting of other people than those who score low. Thus, where private religiosity among the non-affiliated was found above to be linked to higher subjective well-being, its linkages with trust seem to work in the opposite direction, again reinforcing the individualised, or non-collective nature, of this kind of orientation.

Table 8.11: Religiosity and trust in people in the Republic of Ireland and Northern Ireland

	(Per cent who think that most people can be trusted)	
	Republic of Ireland	Northern Ireland
Church attendance (full sample):		
Regular attender	38	43
Irregular attender	30	35
[Base N]	[1,012]	[1,000]
Importance of God (non-affiliated only)		
High importance[a]	22	20
Low importance[a]	37	32
[Base N]	[72]	[161]

Note: [a] The importance of God in your life is a 10-point scale ranging from 1 (not important at all) to 10 (very important). For the purposes of this analysis two categories are distinguished: high importance (individuals who scored 6-10) and low importance (individuals who scored 1-5).

Source: European Values Study, 1999-2000.

Figure 8.4: Trust in people in European countries

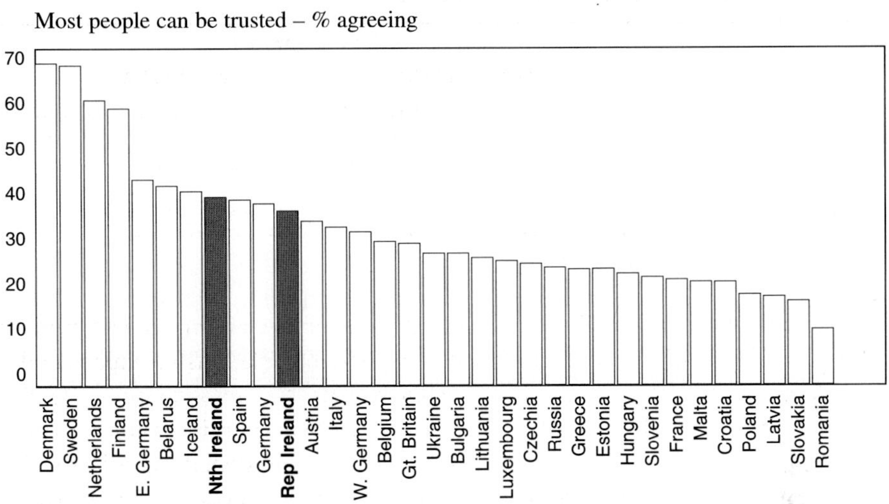

Source: European Values Study, 1999-2000.

Figure 8.4 shows levels of trust in a wider European perspective. Four northern European countries – Denmark, Sweden, the Netherlands and Finland – stand out as having high levels of trust in other people, while the two parts of Ireland fall into the next, somewhat lower, tier in the European range on this issue. A considerable east-west gradient in levels of trust in others is also evident: the lowest scoring countries on this variable are all former communist countries, though France and Malta are also quite far down the range.

Participation in voluntary organisations

A second dimension of social capital we wish to look at here is participation in voluntary organisations. Along with trust, this is often considered a core element of social capital since it relates to a form of social participation outside of family networks that is not motivated by material gain and approximates instead to an altruistic contribution to the welfare of others. This dimension was not examined in the 1981 round of the EVS, so that time comparisons can be made here only with reference to the 1990 and 1999-2000 rounds of the EVS.

Table 8.12 compares two measures of participation in voluntary organisations for 1990 and 1999-2000. One measure shows the percentage of the population who are members of at least one voluntary organisation while the other shows the percentage of the population who reported that they currently did unpaid voluntary work for at least one organisation (other indices of participation in voluntary organisations can be computed from these data, such as the mean number either of

Table 8.12: Participation in voluntary organisations in the Republic of Ireland and Northern Ireland, 1990 and 1999

	(Percentages)			
	Republic of Ireland		Northern Ireland	
	1990	1999	1990	1999
Members of at least one voluntary organisation	49	57	56	46
Do work for at least one voluntary organisation	27	33	26	21
[Base N]	[1,000]	[1,012]	[298]	[1,000]

Question: Please look carefully at the following list of voluntary organisations and activities and say (a) which, if any, do you belong to and (b) which, if any, are you currently doing unpaid voluntary work for?

Source: European Values Study, 1990, 1999-2000.

memberships or of organisations for which respondents do voluntary work, but these indices show similar results and are not reported here). Both of these measures suffer from a certain degree of vagueness. The measure of organisational membership, for example, does not distinguish between nominal and active membership, while the measure of unpaid work for organisations does not specify what is meant by the term 'currently'. Nevertheless, since this vagueness is likely to affect the 1990 and 1999-2000 measures equally, the trend aspect of the data may be considered reasonably reliable. The results show simply that both kinds of participation in voluntary organisations increased in the Republic between 1990 and 1999-2000 and decreased in the North. In 1990, the North had a higher level of organisational membership than the Republic and a similar level of unpaid voluntary work, while in 1999-2000 the Republic had considerably higher levels of both kinds of organisational participation than the North.

Figure 8.5 puts one of these measures in an international context by comparing the percentages who are members of at least one voluntary organisation across European countries. The comparison suggests that both Northern Ireland and the Republic of Ireland are located around the mid-point of the European range on this measure, and taken at face value this would indicate an intermediate level of this kind of social capital in Ireland. However, it is difficult to know what significance should be attached to this measure since idiosyncratic notions of what can be counted as voluntary organisation membership have a large impact on the data in different countries. Thus, for example, the very high level of voluntary organisation membership in Sweden arises in part because over 70 per cent of Swedish respondents reported themselves as members of 'religious or church organisations' (as was also true in Iceland). This seems to mean that in the eyes of most Swedes, to belong to a church (in most cases, the Lutheran church) is to be a member of a

Figure 8.5: Membership of voluntary organisations in European countries

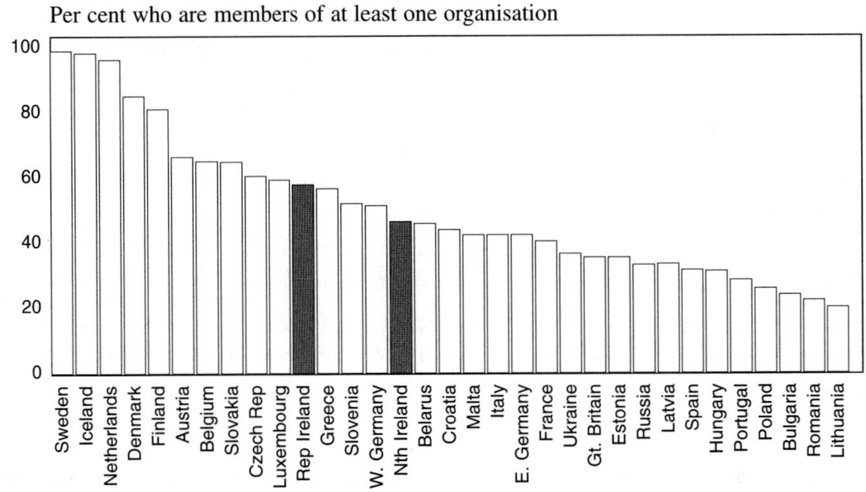

Source: European Values Study, 1999-2000.

'religious or church organisation'. In the Republic of Ireland, by contrast, only 16 per cent report themselves as members of 'religious or church organisations', even though actual church attachment and participation is far higher in Ireland than in Sweden. Thus, Swedish-Irish differences on this measure may well be as much the consequence of different perceptions of what counts as voluntary organisation membership as of actual differences in levels of participation in organisational life.

Conclusion

This chapter has examined three areas where Catholic-Protestant cultural differences have sometimes been argued to exist, though often as much by way of hostile stereotyping as of informed analysis. The first of these had to do with values and attitudes connected with work, with reference especially to the old idea of the 'Protestant work ethic'. The question asked was whether identifiable traces of this ethic could be found among the Protestant communities either in Northern Ireland or the Republic of Ireland today and whether these made present-day work culture among Protestants noticeably different from that found among Catholics. The analysis found that there is no systematic difference between Protestant and Catholic work cultures in Ireland, North or South. There were some indications, however, of a North-South difference: people in the Republic have stronger pro-work sentiments than do their counterparts in Northern Ireland. In Europe as a whole, however, neither the Republic nor Northern Ireland emerge as having particularly strong work ethics, though the precise signficance of data on this issue is difficult to interpret.

The second topic examined in the chapter was subjective well-being, as measured by survey questions on people's levels of life satisfaction and happiness. The underlying pattern here is that in Europe as a whole national levels of prosperity have a substantial effect on subjective well-being: the more prosperous the society, the higher the levels of life satisfaction and happiness. Both Northern Ireland and the Republic of Ireland fit in with this pattern: their scores on subjective well-being variables are quite high and are as would be predicted by their level of GDP per capita. This finding is of particular note in the case of Northern Ireland, as it suggests that the disturbed political atmosphere in that society has not been strong enough in its effects to counterbalance the positive influence on subjective well-being of the high standards of living provided by the Northern Ireland economy and welfare state. There is no consistent denominational difference in either the North or the Republic in levels of subjective well-being though religious adherence does have a modest effect: the religiously devout have higher subjective well-being than those with weaker religious attachment. This corroborates the pattern noted earlier that, outside the spheres of national identity and political allegiance, the major religiously based differences on the island of Ireland today are between believers and non-believers rather than between denominations.

Just as patterns of subjective well-being in Northern Ireland and the Republic of Ireland are unremarkable, so too are levels of social capital, the bonds of trust and social engagement that bind people to each other. The context for this topic is provided by the widely held view that social capital is in decline in western countries. Indicators of social capital contained in the EVS data are limited, but such as they are they provide little support for this belief in the case of Ireland North or South. While certain aspects of social capital have shown some decline, both in the Republic and the North, others have either strengthened or remained stable. It is thus difficult to speak of a clear-cut movement in any direction, and not at all justified to speak of unambiguous decline. This observation brings us directly to the final topic in our analysis, namely confidence in political institutions and political participation.

9

Confidence in political institutions and political participation

Introduction

So far, this book has reviewed a wide range of evidence on social and political values and attitudes in Ireland, North and South. While some aspects of the evidence point to areas of consensus and similarity between North and South and/or between Protestants and Catholics, other aspects identify major conflicts and differences in attitudes and aspirations between the groups and communities in question. We have also seen evidence of attitudes that cut across ethnic and national boundaries, aligning people for or against particular positions on the basis of, for example, degree of religious commitment. The task of resolving these conflicts and differences or, at least, of working out a *modus vivendi* between them falls mainly to each society's political institutions and political system.[1] The ability of any political system to fulfil this task is affected by the attitudes and orientations of the citizens towards the system. Two such attitudes/orientations are crucial – people's confidence in politics and in the political process and people's propensity to become engaged in and participate in politics. Accordingly, now that we have completed our review of the substantive issues that give rise to conflict between various communities and groups on the island of Ireland, it is appropriate to consider the question of confidence and participation in the institutions and practices that make up the political systems involved.

Confidence and participation have been extensively analysed in comparative research in this field (see, for example, Kaase and Newton, 1995; Klingemann

[1] In the case of the unionist-nationalist conflict, of course, progress also depends on cooperation between the authorities in the different political systems involved and on public support for such cooperation.

and Fuchs, 1995; Norris, 1999, 2003). Before turning to the specific circumstances of the two parts of Ireland and how these circumstances might affect either confidence or participation in politics, it is worth briefly considering the issues that have arisen in the comparative literature.

Over recent decades and almost in a cyclical pattern, there has been much speculation and some data-analysis regarding an alleged decline in trust and confidence in the political process in developed countries. One of the key points to emerge both from theoretical reflection and analysis of the data is that trust and confidence in the political process varies depending on how the object of the attitudes in question is defined.[2] Thus Norris and her colleagues in the Critical Citizens project distinguished five objects of what they generically referred to as political support. The five objects, from the most diffuse to the most specific, were (i) political community, (ii) regime principles, (iii) regime performance, (iv) regime institutions and (v) political actors (Norris, 1999: 9-13). Broadly speaking, the various analyses in that project, including one that covered 39 countries, suggested that support for the political system tended to be high in the case of the first two, varied in the case of the third, was on the decline in the case of the fourth and was mixed in regard to the fifth.

In addition to varying levels of confidence relating to different objects or aspects of the political system, there is also uncertainty about what such levels and trends may imply. Low or declining levels of positive attitudes to politics may, on the one hand, signal alienation or apathy, or, on the other hand, may point to the emergence of 'critical citizens who are dissatisfied with established authorities and traditional hierarchical institutions, who feel that existing channels for participation fall short of democratic ideals, and who want to improve and reform the institutional mechanisms of representative democracy' (Norris, 1999: 27). These alternative scenarios bring the discussion directly to the second theme of this chapter, people's propensity to participate in the political process.

Here again it is essential to begin with a number of basic distinctions (for a useful overview, see Kaase and Newton, 1995: 127-45). The first distinction is between types of participation. Four such types can be identified – voting, campaign activity, communal activity and particularised contacts (i.e. contacting officials on personal matters) (Verba *et al.*, 1978: 51-56). Subsequently, Barnes *et al.* (1979) distinguished between conventional and non-conventional participation

[2] Some treatments of the topic regard trust and confidence as quite distinct – see for example the relevant volume of the Beliefs in Government project which devoted separate chapters to trust in politicians and confidence in political institutions (Listaug, 1995; Listaug and Wiberg, 1995). The view taken here is that the distinction between the objects of the attitude is more fundamental and that, once this is clear (or as clear as can be), the attitude may be operationalised either as trust or confidence. Based on this assumption, the discussion towards the end of the chapter compares data from the EVS (1999-2000) and the European Social Survey (2002) even though the former uses confidence as the operationalisation and the latter uses trust.

or behaviour and further work refined this by drawing attention especially to the difference between legal and illegal political action.

Our ability to test these distinctions against the empirical evidence is dependent on the availability of an appropriate range of indicators. The EVS provides a range of items relating to what is often referred to as the repertory of political action and also includes data on citizen orientations that, while not indicating political action in the strict sense, are important forms of political engagement. We refer here to the variables that measure interest in, perceived importance of, attention to and discussion of political matters. Before turning to the data analysis, however, it is necessary to consider how confidence in politics and orientations to political participation/political action might have been affected by the special circumstances prevailing in Ireland, North and South, over recent decades.

Given a quarter of a century of conflict in Northern Ireland and the tortuousness of the current path to a stable solution, one might expect that the impact of recent history on confidence in institutions would be strongly negative in Northern Ireland. On the other hand, relief at the ending of 25 years of violent conflict may have generated a nascent restoration of confidence in politics. One would also anticipate that the deep political divisions in Northern Ireland are reflected in different evaluations of the political system in each of the two communities. The situation in the Republic is also likely to be complex, since recent political experience in the Republic encompasses both remarkable economic success and some remarkable political scandals. It is difficult to decide a *priori* which is likely to have had the greater impact on public attitudes towards the political system.

Furthermore, progress towards a solution to the Northern Ireland problem may well mean that confidence in politics in the Republic of Ireland may have been affected not just by events and developments within the Republic but also by events and developments in Northern Ireland. Finally, one should note that events, particularly events in Northern Ireland, may have affected not just the level of confidence in individual political institutions but the very way in which people see and respond to their political institutions. In other words, the imprint of history may well be discernible in the pattern and structure of attitudes (in this case attitudes of confidence or lack of confidence in political institutions). Accordingly, our examination of the evidence of orientations to politics in Ireland, North and South, begins, in the case of each of the communities involved, with an analysis of the *pattern or structure* of attitudes of confidence or lack of confidence in politics and in the political process.

The structure of confidence in political institutions

The wide range of institutions covered in the 1999-2000 EVS gives us the opportunity to examine the structure of attitudes in this area. At issue here is whether people tend to link areas of the institutional system together in their minds and adopt attitudes to them which differentiate between segments of the system (that is, clusters of institutions) rather than simply between individual institutions. In examining this issue, we focus on four major reference points (the Republic of Ireland, Catholics in Northern Ireland, Protestants in Northern Ireland, and the rest of Europe) and on eight institutions that are central to the state system, that is we exclude aspects of civil society such as the press and the trade unions. The institutions included are the justice system, the political parties, the parliament, the health care system, the social welfare system, the armed forces, the police and the civil service (see the left-hand column of Table 9.1).[3] Factor analysis of these eight items identifies an underlying pattern or structure that is broadly similar across three of our four samples (the Republic of Ireland, Northern Ireland Protestants and the rest of Europe sample). This structure comprises two dimensions: confidence in politics and policies on the one hand and confidence in the security forces on the other. The dimension of confidence in politics and policies takes in six of the eight items (the justice system, the health care system, the social welfare system, the civil service, the national parliament and the political parties). The dimension of 'confidence in the security forces' comprises just two items – the police and the armed forces.

There are some minor variations in the composition of these two dimensions of confidence in political institutions across the three samples in question. In the European sample and among Northern Ireland Protestants, confidence in the civil service is clearly part of the politics and policy dimension, but in the Republic of Ireland confidence in the civil service is associated as much or more with confidence in the security forces. The rest of Europe shows the additional minor variation that confidence in the police is associated partly with the political dimension and partly with the security forces dimension. Having noted these variations, it is important to emphasise that they are minor. The basic pattern is that broadly similar dimensions of confidence in political institutions (i.e. confidence in politics/policy, on the one hand, and confidence in the security forces, on the other) are found in the Republic of Ireland, in the rest of Europe and among Northern Ireland Protestants.

Northern Ireland Catholics see things differently. In place of the 'normal' main dimension of confidence in politics and policies, the dominant dimension in the case of Northern Ireland Catholics is a combination of confidence/lack of confidence in the Westminster Parliament *plus* confidence/lack of confidence in the security forces (army and police), the civil service, and, at a somewhat lower loading, the justice system. In short, the dominant dimension of confidence/lack of confidence in political institutions among Northern Ireland Catholics relates

[3] Unfortunately one of the items (political parties) is not available for the rest of Europe sample.

Table 9.1: Factor analysis of items relating to confidence in aspects of the political system

	Republic of Ireland		Northern Ireland Catholics		Northern Ireland Protestants		Rest of Europe	
	Politics and policies	Security forces and civil service	Institutions of the state	Policies and political parties	Politics and policies	Security forces	Politics and policies	Security forces
The justice system	**0.74**	0.10	**0.50**	**0.59**	**0.61**	0.35	**0.70**	0.24
The political parties	**0.68**	0.10	0.26	**0.52**	**0.53**	0.10	-	-
The Parliament	**0.67**	0.23	**0.77**	0.23	**0.71**	0.22	**0.62**	0.37
The health care system	**0.67**	0.15	-0.11	**0.83**	**0.52**	0.34	**0.76**	-0.02
The social welfare system	**0.63**	0.23	0 .29	**0.73**	**0.79**	0.09	**0.77**	0.04
The army/the armed forces	0.00	**0.85**	**0.83**	0.06	0.07	**0.88**	0.01	**0.90**
The police	0.27	**0.69**	**0.86**	0.14	0.28	**0.81**	**0.51**	**0.54**
The civil service	**0.48**	**0.56**	**0.60**	0.41	**0.77**	0.08	**0.68**	0.29
Percent variance explained	32.46	20.70	35.01	29.08	34.14	21.66	39.65	19.87

Source: European Values Study, 1999-2000

to the core political and security institutions of the state rather than to day-to-day politics and policies. This syndrome of confidence/lack of confidence in the regime creates a somewhat truncated and subordinate 'politics and policy' dimension among Northern Ireland Catholics that is defined mainly in terms of confidence in the health and social welfare systems but also includes reference to the justice system and to the political parties.

Given this identification of differences in the structure of confidence in politics as between Northern Ireland Catholics and the other three samples, the task of comparing the distribution of confidence across our four societies cannot be treated as a simple matter of lining up similarly worded items and looking at the frequencies. For example, on a reading of the individual items, levels of confidence in Parliament in the Republic of Ireland, in the other European countries and among Northern Ireland Catholics are more or less the same (ranging from 28 per cent among Northern Ireland Catholics to 34 per cent in the rest of Europe sample). However, when we look at how attitudes cluster together, we find that, in the case of Northern Ireland Catholics, confidence in (the Westminster) Parliament is part and parcel of an overall attitude to the institutions of the state including, in particular, its security institutions. In contrast, confidence in parliament among people in the Republic of Ireland and the other European states is part of a syndrome of confidence (or lack of confidence) in the ordinary political process and in the policy outputs it produces. Accordingly, the fact that confidence in parliament among Northern Ireland Catholics comes out at 28 per cent has quite different implications from the fact that an almost identical proportion (31 per cent) expresses confidence in parliament in the Republic of Ireland. Similarly, although confidence in the civil service is practically identical between Northern Ireland Catholics and the rest of Europe sample, the attitudinal structure in which the individual item is embedded is quite different in each case. Among Northern Ireland Catholics, confidence in the civil service links back into attitudes to the state as such, whereas in the rest of Europe, the 37 per cent figure for confidence in the civil service simply reflects a low level of confidence in bureaucrats and the bureaucratic process that is closely linked to attitudes to politics and policy outputs.

All of this reinforces the point that, in comparing the *distribution of attitudes*, we must bear in mind the *structure of attitudes*. If we do this (see Table 9.2)[4], we can draw two overall conclusions. The first is that the levels of confidence in politics and policies are broadly similar (in the range of 42-49 per cent) across our four samples. The second conclusion is that *levels of confidence in the security forces* (armed forces and police) are very different across these

[4] In presenting the distribution of levels of confidence, Table 9.2 arranges the individual items according to the underlying structure indicated by the factor analysis.

Table 9.2: Distribution of confidence in aspects of the political system

	(Per cent with a 'great deal' or 'quite a lot' of confidence)							
	Republic of Ireland		**Northern Ireland Catholics**		**Northern Ireland Protestants**		**Rest of Europe**	
	Politics and policies	Security forces and civil service	Institutions of the state	Policies and political parties	Politics and policies	Security forces	Politics and policies	Security forces
The justice system	54		39	39	54		43	
The political parties	18			16	18		-	
The Parliament	31		28		47		34	
The health care system	58			66	69		59	
The social welfare system	56			47	54		47	
The army/the armed forces		58	26			79		54
The police		83	37			83	54	54
The civil service	59	59	41		55		37	
Average level of confidence across items in dimensions (boxed)	46	67	34	42	49	81	46	54
[Average N of Cases]	[1,007]	[1,007]	[425]	[425]	[497]	[499]	[37,683]	[37,721]

Source: European Values Study, 1999-2000.

samples. Thus, the average proportion showing a great deal plus quite a lot of confidence in the security forces as a whole ranges from 81 per cent among Northern Ireland Protestants to 34 per cent among Northern Ireland Catholics, with the Republic of Ireland (67 per cent) and the rest of Europe (54 per cent) occupying intermediate positions. The exceptionally low level of confidence in the security forces among Northern Ireland Catholics takes on an additional significance because, as the factor analysis has shown, it is enmeshed in a syndrome of attitudes to or confidence in the institutions of the state as such.

Two further particular points in Table 9.2 are worth noting. The first is the exceptionally high level of confidence in the police in the Republic of Ireland (83 per cent). This matches the level of confidence in the police among Protestants in Northern Ireland where, at the time of the survey, the issue of policing was a highly partisan and contentious one between the two communities and one on which highly polarised attitudes would have been anticipated. The second particular point is the relatively high level of confidence in the civil service in the Republic of Ireland, compared to the level of confidence in the civil service that is found in the rest of Europe sample (59 per cent in the Republic of Ireland sample compared to 37 per cent in the rest of Europe).

Trends in confidence in institutions

The first round of the EVS carried out in 1981 found that confidence in public institutions in the Republic of Ireland was 'unusually high' by European standards and that, perhaps more surprisingly, confidence in institutions was also reasonably high overall in Northern Ireland (Fogarty 1984: 69, 157). In order to examine the general pattern of trends since then, Figures 9.1 and 9.2 show the trends in confidence levels in a range of political and social institutions. These include those already considered in Table 9.2 for which we have data over time and, in order to broaden the comparison beyond the political system, also includes the press, the educational system and the European Union. Three institutions in the Republic of Ireland showed significant increases in confidence over this period. They are the education system, the trade unions and the Civil Service. The biggest increase was in the education system, where the proportion with a 'great deal' or 'quite a lot' of confidence went from 66 per cent in 1981 to 87 per cent in 1999. The increases in the case of the trade unions and the Civil Service were more modest (up ten percentage points in the case of the former and up seven percentage points in the case of the latter). For all three of these institutions, the increase in confidence may well have had a common basis in the transition from the economic crisis of the late 1970s and 1980s to the economic boom of the 1990s. The contribution of education to economic growth has been a constant refrain among commentators. Similarly, the trade unions may owe their increased confidence rating to their incorporation into a

Figure 9.1: Confidence in individual public institutions, Republic of Ireland, 1981-1999

(% with 'great deal' or 'quite a lot' of confidence)

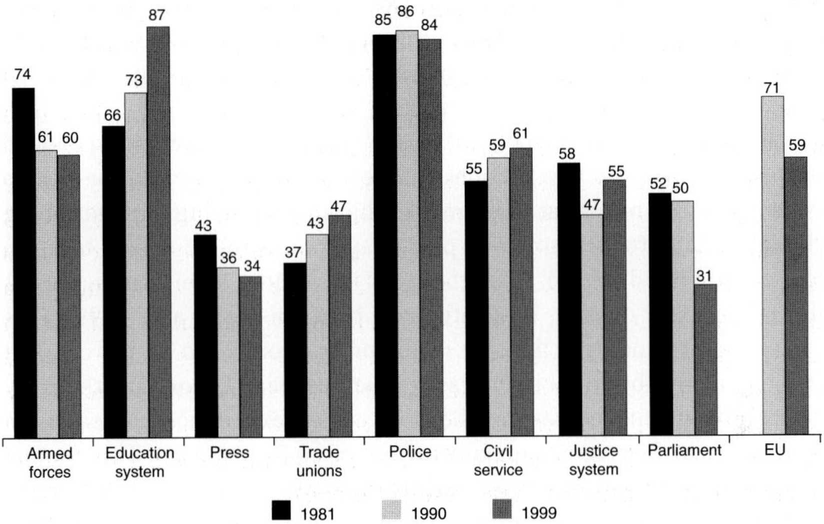

Sources: European Values Study 1981, 1990, 1999-2000.

Figure 9.2: Confidence in individual public institutions, Northern Ireland, 1981-1999

(% with 'great deal' or 'quite a lot' of confidence)

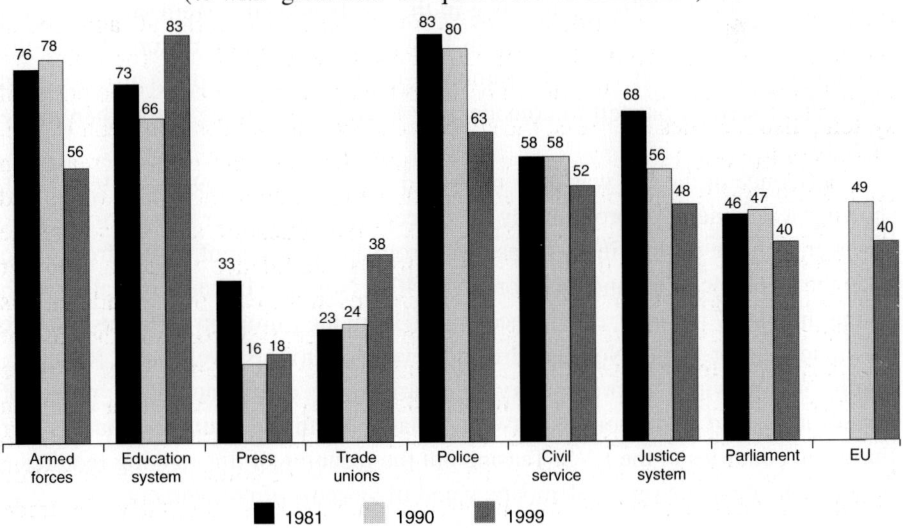

Sources: European Values Study 1981, 1990, 1999-2000.

successful and stable tri-partite or neo-corporatist system of wage and policy negotiation that is frequently seen as one of the underpinnings of the economic boom. Finally, the improved rating of the Civil Service may also be a reflection of the better performance of the economy. Declines in confidence in the armed forces and the press provided counter-balancing downward movement. By 1999-2000, the press had one of the lowest confidence ratings of any of the institutions.

Confidence in the Gardaí (police) in the Republic of Ireland remained remarkably stable over the two decades in question. Confidence in the justice system was also more or less at the same level at the beginning and end of the period though it had dropped some 10 percentage points in the survey taken in the middle of the period (1990). The other four institutions shown in Figure 9.1 suffered a significant decline in confidence between 1981 and 1999. This decline was modest enough in the case of the press (from 43 to 34 per cent). It was somewhat more substantial in the case of the European Union[5] and the army and was very marked in the case of the Dáil, which experienced a decline in public confidence of 21 percentage points (from 52 to 31 per cent). This decline in confidence in the Dáil occurred mainly between 1990 and 1999 and a substantial set of scandals and ensuing inquiries and controversies provide a ready explanation for the change.

In Northern Ireland, the picture is more mixed (Figure 9.2). The education system experienced a rise in the 1990s following decline in the 1980s, while the trade unions experienced a rise in the 1990s following stability in the 1980s. Confidence in both arms of the security system – the army and the police – declined by about 20 percentage points over the period, almost all of the decline taking place in the 1990s. Confidence in the 'justice/legal system' also declined by about 20 percentage points but, in this case, the decline occurred over the whole period (1980-99). As in the Republic, confidence in the press also declined in Northern Ireland but fell to considerably lower levels in the North than in the Republic.

Confidence in the EU was only measured in the EVS in 1990 and 1999-2000, showing a decline of approximately 10 percentage points over that period. Note, however, that the decline in each case was from a very different base – from 71 to 59 in the Republic of Ireland and from 49 to 40 in Northern Ireland. It is also worth noting that, at 37 per cent, confidence in the EU in the European Union as a whole was much closer to the Northern Ireland level than to the level in the Republic. Figure 9.3 provides a preliminary comparison of confidence in a range of organizations and institutions as between Ireland, North and South and the 31 other European countries in the EVS. Teasing out the meaning of this ranking requires a closer look at evaluations of democracy and of systems of government.

[5] Because the EU item was not included in the questionnaire in 1981, trends in confidence in the EU can only be examined for the period 1990-1999.

Figure 9.3: Confidence in public institutions in Europe

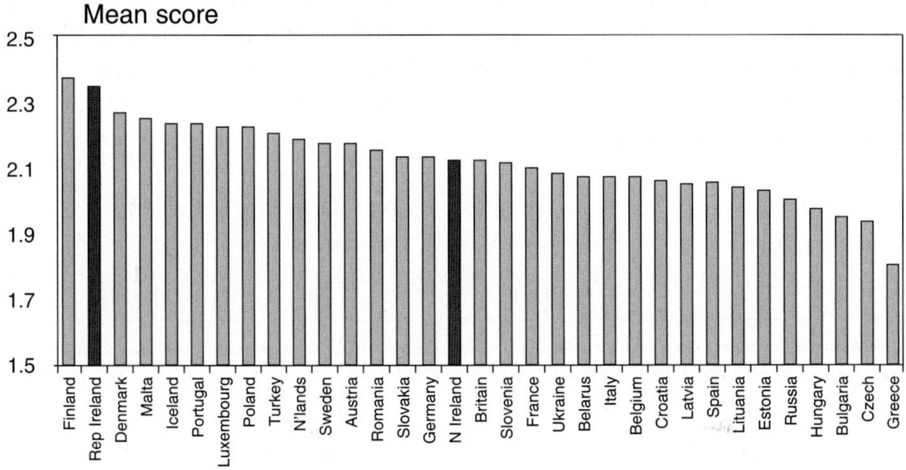

Note: Mean scores are based on a four-point scale ranging from 1 (none at all) to 4 (a great deal). Institutions included: armed forces, education system, the press, trade unions, the police, the civil service.

Source: European Values Study, 1999-2000.

Evaluations of democracy and of the system of government

Obviously, people's attitudes to the political system encompass much more than their confidence in political institutions. In order to obtain a more complete picture of the attitudes of people in Ireland, North and South, to their respective political systems, we turn to three further indicators of their overall orientation to the political system: degree of satisfaction with the way democracy is developing, evaluation of the system of government, and relative evaluation of the system of government as it was in 1999-2000 compared to what it had been 10 years previously.

As Table 9.3 shows, almost two-thirds of people in the Republic of Ireland say they are either very satisfied or rather satisfied with 'the way in which democracy is developing' in their country, whereas less than one-third of people in Northern Ireland take the same view of the way democracy is developing in Northern Ireland. On this item, Northern Ireland is well below the average for the rest of Europe, a situation that may be explained by the contested and still precarious nature of the democratic institutions in Northern Ireland (see Hayes and McAllister, 1996b).

The low rating of the functioning of democracy in Northern Ireland is common to Catholics, Protestants and the non-affiliated. In the Republic, where the working of democracy is rated quite highly, Protestants are even slightly more positive on this issue than Catholics (see Figure 9.4).

Table 9.3: Satisfaction with the way democracy is developing

	(Percentages)		
	Republic of Ireland	Northern Ireland	Rest of Europe
Not at all satisfied	7	19	15
Not very satisfied	29	52	39
Rather satisfied	54	26	41
Very satisfied	10	3	4
[N]	[937]	[879]	[35,354]

Question: On the whole are you very satisfied, rather satisfied, not very satisfied or not at all satisfied with the way democracy is developing in [Ireland/Northern Ireland]?

Source: European Values Study, 1999-2000.

Figure 9.4: Religious identification and satisfaction with the way democracy is developing, Republic of Ireland and Northern Ireland

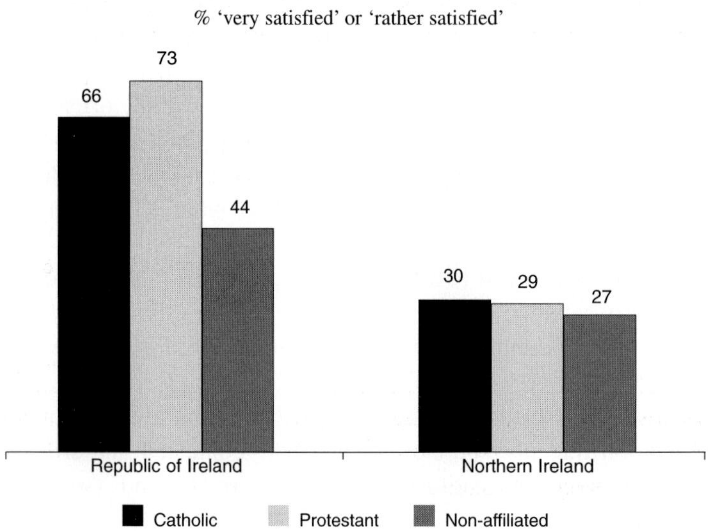

Source: European Values Study 1999-2000.

Our second indicator – the rating of the system of government – gives a different perspective on these contrasts (Table 9.4). We should note here that in the case of Northern Ireland, this question refers to the system of government *in the United Kingdom*, in contrast to the previous item on democracy which referred to the situation in Northern Ireland.[6] Here again, the Republic of Ireland gets a somewhat more positive rating than Northern Ireland: 36 per cent in the Republic give the system of government a rating of seven or better on the 10-point scale, compared to 31 per cent in Northern Ireland. However, both societies are more positive about the system of government than the rest of Europe where only 22 per cent give their system of government a rating of seven or better. Figure 9.5 shows that within Northern Ireland, Protestants are more positive about the system of government in the UK than Catholics, but again one could note here that even among Catholics, the proportion who rate the system of government quite positively (28 per cent at seven or above) is higher than the corresponding proportion for the rest of Europe shown in Table 9.4. It is also higher than in Britain, where only 23 per cent rate the UK government at seven or higher. The relatively positive assessment of the UK government in Northern Ireland may be due to very different

Table 9.4: Assessment of the system of government

(Percentages)

Rating on scale	Republic of Ireland	Northern Ireland	Rest of Europe
1-2 (very bad)	7	10	17
3-4	16	23	26
5	25	21	21
6	15	15	14
7-8	28	26	19
9-10 (very good)	8	5	3
[N]	[998]	[879]	[36,425]

Question: People have different views about the system of government in [Ireland/United Kingdom]. Here is a scale for rating the system of government: 1 means very bad; 10 means very good.

Source: European Values Study, 1999-2000.

6 Questionnaire items about politics and the political system in Northern Ireland are bedevilled by the problem of which is the more appropriate context – Northern Ireland or the United Kingdom – in which to situate or frame a particular question. From a questionnaire-design point of view, the arguments for selecting one context rather than the other can be very finely balanced. After the decision is made, all the researcher can do in interpreting the results is to take careful account of which context is referred to by each question.

Figure 9.5: Religious identification and positive assessment of the system of government, Republic of Ireland and Northern Ireland

(% who rate system of government 7 or above on 10-point scale)

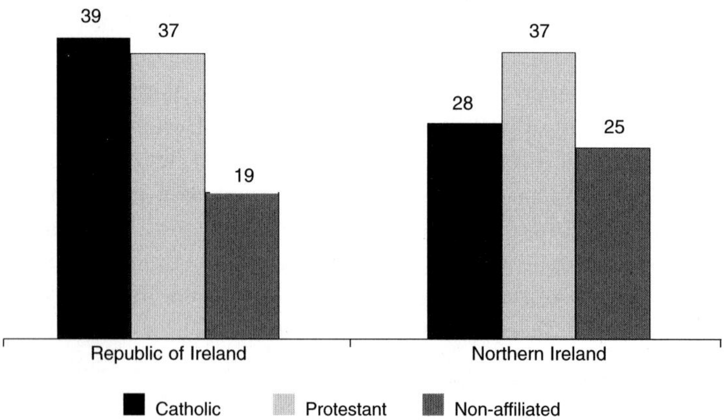

Question: As in Table 9.4.
Sources: European Values Study 1999-2000.

reasons within each community. Among Northern Ireland Protestants, it may be an expression of their continued loyalty to the United Kingdom, while Northern Ireland Catholics may be responding to what could be seen as a greater willingness on the part of the UK government to accommodate their national aspirations than was the case previously. It may also reflect how both communities evaluate the quality of services provided by the government in areas such as health, education, social welfare and so on (see the evidence on confidence in these aspects of the political system already presented in this chapter).

The question on the rating of the system of government was followed by a further question that asked 'Where on this scale would you put the system of government as it was 10 years ago?' A simple subtraction of the second response from the first gives a measure of whether people's evaluation of the system of government as of 1999-2000 was higher or lower than it was ten years previously (Table 9.5). Respondents in the Republic of Ireland were generally positive in this regard. Forty-four per cent of Catholics in the Republic of Ireland felt that the system of government was better in 1999 than it had been ten years previously, while only 20 per cent thought it was worse. The improvement in evaluation of the system of government over time was even larger among Protestants in the Republic and was also substantial among those without any religious affiliation.

The contrasts in perceptions of improvement/disimprovement in the system of government were much sharper in Northern Ireland. Among Northern Ireland Catholics, no fewer than 60 per cent gave the UK system of government as of 1999-

Table 9.5: Religious identification and rating of system of government now compared to ten years ago, Republic of Ireland and Northern Ireland

	(Percentages)	
	Higher rating	Lower rating
Republic of Ireland:		
Catholic	44	20
Protestant	55	11
Non-affiliated	43	27
Northern Ireland:		
Catholic	60	14
Protestant	31	30
Non-affiliated	36	20

Question: (1) People have different views about the system of government in [Ireland/United Kingdom]. Here is a scale for rating the system of government: 1 means very bad; 10 means very good.(2) Where on this scale would you put the system of government as it was ten years ago?

Source: European Values Study, 1999-2000.

2000 a higher rating compared to the system as it was ten years previously and only 14 per cent gave it a lower rating. Among Northern Ireland Protestants, the proportion giving a higher rating was much smaller, at only 31 per cent. Nevertheless, even among Protestants the balance between improvement and disimprovement was still just about positive, since the proportion giving the UK government of 1999-2000 a lower rating than that of ten years previously was 30 per cent, one percentage point less than the proportion giving a higher rating. The non-affiliated in Northern Ireland tended to give a rating that was at an intermediate level between that of Catholics and Protestants.

The contrast within Northern between the very strong improvement in the rating of the system of government among Catholics compared to the ratings given by Protestants echo the views on who were the main winners from the peace process that were discussed in Chapter 5. On the other hand, some support for the view that the peace process is a positive rather than a zero sum game may be taken from the fact that 31 per cent of Northern Ireland Protestants gave a more positive rating to the system of government now as compared to 10 years ago and that a further 40 per cent showed no change in their evaluation of the system of government in the United Kingdom.

Figure 9.6 shows that improved evaluations of the system of government were more the exception than the rule across the 33 societies in the 1999-2000 EVS. In 19 out of the 33 societies, people on average gave a lower rating to the system of government as in 1999-2000 in comparison to the system of government of ten years previously. It is striking that both the Republic of Ireland and Northern

Figure 9.6: Rating of system of government now compared to ten years ago in European Societies

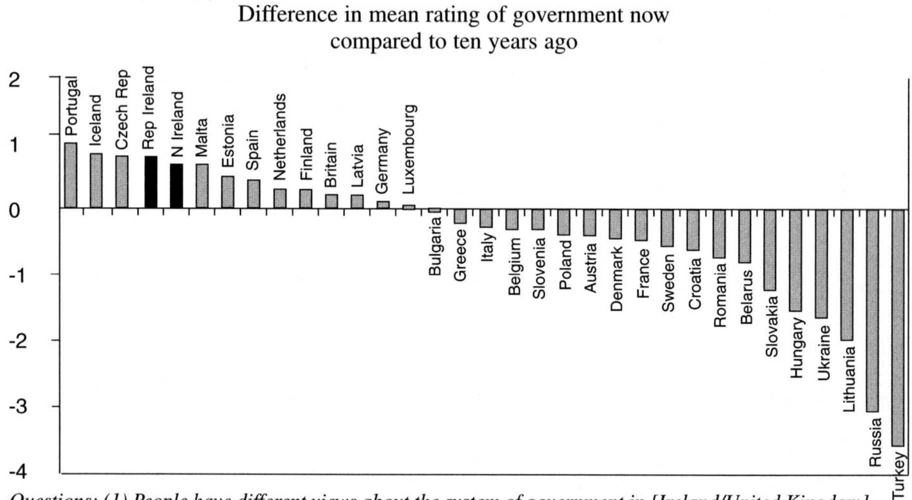

Questions: (1) People have different views about the system of government in [Ireland/United Kingdom]. Here is a scale for rating the system of government: 1 means very bad; 10 means very good. (2) Where on this scale would you put the system of government as it was ten years ago?

Note: Positive values indicate a higher rating of government in 1999-2000 than ten years previously.

Source: European Values Study, 1999-2000.

Ireland come quite high up in the ranking of countries in terms of improvement/disimprovement in evaluation of the system of government over time. It is also notable that Northern Ireland, which is fifth from the top in this regard, is higher up this table than Britain, which lies eleventh from the top.

Orientations to political action and political participation

In analysing orientations to political action and political participation we focus on ten items ranging from interest in politics and involvement in political communication to various forms of direct political action (see left-hand column in Table 9.6). A factor analysis of these ten items shows a very clear-cut structure underlying orientations to political action in the Republic of Ireland and in the rest of Europe and considerable contrasts between this common structure and the structure of orientations to political action in Northern Ireland.

In the Republic of Ireland and in the rest of Europe, attitudes and orientations in this area involve three distinct dimensions. The first dimension comprises interest in politics, rating of the importance of politics, following politics in the news and frequency of discussion of politics. In the Republic of Ireland, this dimension also includes a predisposition to help a party or candidate at election time. As this latter question was not asked in all European countries, we cannot say

Table 9.6: Dimensions of orientations to political action

	Republic of Ireland			Northern Ireland Catholics			Northern Ireland Protestants			Rest of Europe		
	Interest in politics and help party	Approved political protest	Unapproved political protest	Interest in politics	Unapproved political protest (broad definition and help party	Approved political protest	Interest in politics	Unapproved political protest (broad definition)	Approved political protest narrow definition and help party	Interest in politics	Approved political protest	Unapproved political protest
Very/somewhat interested in politics	**0.83**	0.08	0.04	**0.87**	0.10	0.06	**0.80**	0.05	0.29	**0.84**	0.18	0.03
Politics very/quite important	**0.77**	-0.02	0.12	**0.82**	0.09	-0.01	**0.78**	-0.04	0.14	**0.77**	0.08	0.06
Follow politics in the news several times a week/more	**0.72**	0.09	-0.07	**0.77**	0.09	0.11	**0.78**	0.07	-0.15	**0.71**	0.00	-0.01
Frequently discuss politics	**0.71**	0.17	-0.06	**0.67**	0.12	0.02	**0.74**	0.08	0.06	**0.75**	0.13	0.05
Have/might help political party or candidate	**0.51**	0.23	0.20	0.28	**0.57**	0.17	0.19	0.09	**0.60**	-	-	-
Have/might sign a petition	0.10	**0.85**	-0.02	0.03	0.16	**0.90**	-0.01	0.13	**0.81**	0.09	**0.88**	0.02
Have/might attend lawful demonstrations	0.21	**0.70**	0.31	0.19	**0.56**	**0.62**	0.04	**0.49**	**0.60**	0.18	**0.69**	0.34
Have/might join in boycotts	0.08	**0.62**	0.42	0.04	**0.70**	**0.47**	0.03	**0.68**	0.42	0.09	**0.69**	0.33
Have/might occupy buildings or factories	0.03	0.07	**0.86**	0.14	**0.87**	-0.06	0.10	**0.77**	0.09	0.02	0.15	**0.87**
Have/might join unofficial strikes	0.02	0.28	**0.76**	0.00	**0.78**	0.26	0.00	**0.85**	0.06	0.04	0.28	**0.81**
Percent variance explained	26.12	17.81	16.66	26.11	25.65	15.23	24.51	20.61	16.85	26.79	20.86	18.16

Source: European Values Study, 1999-2000.

whether this political party item is or is not part of the overall syndrome of political engagement in the rest of Europe. The second dimension in the Republic of Ireland and in the rest of Europe comprises orientations to generally approved forms of political protest (signing a petition, attending lawful demonstrations and joining in boycotts). The third dimension also has to do with the expression of political views or political protest but focuses on unapproved methods (occupying buildings or factories and joining unofficial strikes).

As Table 9.6 shows, the structure of orientations to political action in both communities in Northern Ireland is quite different from that identified in the case of the Republic of Ireland and the rest of Europe. In the first place, in contrast to the Republic of Ireland, a propensity to help a political party or candidate at election time bears no relationship to the general dimension of interest in politics among either Catholics or Protestants in Northern Ireland. Secondly, the very clear distinction between approved and unapproved protest in the Republic of Ireland and rest of Europe samples breaks down in the case of Northern Ireland. This is partly because there is some overlap in the distribution of items between the factors, i.e. some political-action items figure on more than one factor. More fundamentally, however, it is because two of the political protest items that form the core of the approved political protest dimension in the Republic of Ireland and in the rest of Europe (boycotts and lawful marches and demonstrations) combine with the items relating to occupation of buildings and unofficial strikes to form a more extensive unapproved political protest dimension in Northern Ireland. This blurring of the lines between approved and unapproved political protest is presumably related to the controversies in Northern Ireland over lawful demonstrations and to the use of boycotts in the recent past as part of the ethnonational conflict in Northern Ireland (see Jarman *et al.,* 1998).

The third distinctive feature of the structure of orientations to political action in Northern Ireland has to do with the tendency to help a political party or candidate at election time. As already noted, in contrast to the Republic of Ireland, this orientation to party and electoral politics in Northern Ireland is not associated with general interest in politics and involvement in political communication/discussion. Instead, willingness to be involved with parties or candidates in Northern Ireland is linked with one of the other two dimensions, i.e. either with the dimension of approved forms of political protest or with the dimension of unapproved political protest. In the case of Northern Ireland Catholics, the willingness to help a political party or candidate at election time is associated with the unapproved political protest dimension whereas, in the case of Northern Ireland Protestants, such willingness combines with petition signing and attending lawful demonstrations to form a truncated approved political protest dimension. It seems highly probable that these peculiarities in orientations to political action, in particular the disjunction between engagement in politics and willingness to be involved with parties or candidates at election

Table 9.7: Distribution of orientations to political action

	Republic of Ireland			Northern Ireland Catholics			Northern Ireland Protestants			Rest of Europe		
	Interest in politics and help party	Approved political protest	Unapproved political protest	Interest in politics	Unapproved political protest (broad definition and help party	Approved political protest	Interest in politics	Unapproved political protest (broad definition)	Approved political protest and help party	Interest in politics	Approved political protest	Unapproved political protest
Very/somewhat interested in politics	43			45			38			46		
Politics very/quite important	32			43			32			33		
Follow politics in the news several times a week/more	46			50			49			71		
Frequently/occasionally discuss politics	59			66			70			73		
Have/might help political party or candidate	45				32				24	-		
Have/might sign a petition		84				78			82		71	
Have/might attend lawful demonstrations		63			49	49		52	52		60	
Have/might join in boycotts		42			42	42		37			41	
Have/might occupy buildings or factories			18		16			8				17
Have/might join unofficial strikes			36		33			25				26
Average	45	63	27	51	35	56	47	30	52	56	58	21
Average n of cases	1005	1002	1001	425	425	425	498	499	499	35612	37415	37341

Source: European Values Study, 1999-2000.

time, are the result of the tensions that accompany the party-political and electoral process in Northern Ireland, tensions that also arise from disputes about the legitimacy of the marches and demonstrations that are a prominent feature of politics in Northern Ireland.

As in the case of the evidence of confidence in political institutions, contrasts in the structure of political orientations of the kind just considered must be taken into account when assessing the implications of the distribution of attitudes on individual items. With this in mind, Table 9.7 presents the frequency distribution over the ten items for each of our samples, organising the data and calculating averages for groups of items on the basis of the factor analysis presented in Table 9.6.

Looked at in terms of the distributions over the broad dimensions of attitudes and orientations to political action identified by the factor analysis, there are only quite limited differences between the four samples. Thus the average level of interest/involvement in politics ranges from a low of 45 per cent in the Republic of Ireland to a high of just 56 per cent in the rest of Europe. Likewise, propensity to engage in approved political protest shows quite a narrow range of variation (from 63 per cent in the Republic of Ireland to 52 per cent among Protestants in Northern Ireland). The largest range occurs in the case of unapproved political protest, a positive orientation to which is found among 35 per cent of Northern Ireland Catholics at the top end of the scale and among 21 per cent of the rest of Europe sample at the bottom. The limited range of variation is reflected in the distribution of most of the individual items. There are two exceptions to this generalisation. The first is that willingness to help a party or candidate, which, as we have seen, has different connotations in the Republic of Ireland and in Northern Ireland, varies from a high of 45 per cent in the Republic to a low of 24 per cent among Northern Ireland Protestants. The other substantial difference is between the rest of Europe and the three Irish samples – whereas 71 per cent of other Europeans report that they follow politics in the news several times a week or more, this is true of only between 45 and 50 per cent of people in Ireland, North or South.

Focusing as it does on comparisons between whole societies and whole communities, the foregoing analysis implicitly assumes that all members of a particular society or community are more or less the same. Of course this is by no means the case as differences of generation, gender and social status may well point to different experiences of political institutions and (consequentially or not) different orientations to political action. To carry out an exhaustive analysis of the demography of political confidence in the Republic of Ireland and among Northern Ireland Catholics and Northern Ireland Protestants would require more space than is available in this chapter. However, the matter can be explored by focusing on the Republic of Ireland data and by then noting whether demographic patterns within the two communities in Northern Ireland diverge significantly from those in the South.

Table 9.8 displays gender and age differences for the Republic of Ireland in the two areas with which this chapter has been concerned – confidence in political institutions and propensity to be involved in the political process. The latter ranges from interest in politics through involvement in the electoral process to participation in demonstrations, boycotts and the illegal occupation of buildings. The gender part of the story is simply told. Men and women in the Republic of Ireland show no differences whatsoever in their degree of confidence in political institutions. However, the sexes do show quite significant differences on all but one measure of orientations to political action, women having a generally lower propensity to engage in politics. The exception is propensity to vote in a general election, which is virtually identical between men and women. In sum, gender makes no difference in terms of confidence in politics or of turning out to vote but has significant effects on a range of other forms of political involvement.

Using the Republic of Ireland pattern as a yardstick highlights certain key differences in the gender structure of orientations to politics in Northern Ireland. Among Catholics in Northern Ireland, women show more confidence than men in

Table 9.8: Confidence in political institutions and orientation to political action by gender and age, Republic of Ireland

(Percentages)

	Gender		Age			
	Male	Female	18 to 30 years	31 to 45 years	46 to 60 years	61 years or more
A great deal plus quite a lot of confidence in:						
Political parties	19	19	15	15	21	27
Dáil	32	32	26	30	39	34
Civil service	61	60	58	54	66	64
Gardaí	85	86	81	84	89	89
Health care system	59	57	62	51	59	63
Social welfare system	56	58	50	49	62	69
Political action:						
Very interested or somewhat interested in politics	53	39	39	43	53	46
Have helped or might help a political party	54	40	49	44	51	41
Have occupied or might occupy buildings	21	14	21	20	19	7
Have attended or might attend lawful demonstrations	73	57	73	69	68	46
Follow politics in the media every day or several times a week	57	46	33	49	60	58
Would vote in next election	79	81	69	79	84	87

Source: European Values Study, 1999-2000.

the institutions of the state (parliament, civil service and the police) but, at the same time, the gap between male and female frequency of following politics in the media is greater in the Northern Ireland Catholic community than it is in the Republic. Gender differences among Northern Ireland Protestants add a further refinement to the picture: whereas men and women in the Republic of Ireland show no difference in their confidence in any of the aspects of politics covered, Protestant women in Northern Ireland differ from Protestant men in having more confidence in the civil service while *not* being any less assiduous than their male counterparts in following politics in the media.

Returning to the Republic of Ireland, it is apparent that, in contrast to gender, age makes a difference both to confidence in political institutions and to most orientations to political action. With one or two minor qualifications and with some variations as to the size of the contrasts, younger people show significantly less confidence in political institutions and policy outputs. By and large, 'young' for this purpose can be taken as 45 or less, though stronger contrasts are found if one isolates those aged 18-30 and compares them with the older age groups: for example, only 26 per cent of 18-30 year-olds express confidence in the Dáil as an institution compared to 39 per cent of 46 to 60 year-olds.

When it comes to orientations to political action, young people in the Republic of Ireland are significantly less likely than older people to say they are interested in politics, much less likely to follow politics in the media and substantially less likely to vote. In regard to two of our other forms of political action (occupying buildings and attending lawful demonstrations), however, it is among the oldest age group that, perhaps not surprisingly, the lowest propensities to engage in the actions in question are found. These patterns are by and large replicated among the two communities in Northern Ireland, the main exception being the tendency for young people in the Catholic community to show fewer signs of political disengagement relative to their elders than do young people in either the Republic of Ireland on in the Northern Ireland Protestant community. For example, the gap between younger and older people in interest in politics is only 6 percentage points among Northern Ireland Catholics compared to 14 points among people in the Republic of Ireland and 18 points among Northern Ireland Protestants.

Table 9.9 shows these same two sets of variables broken down by employment status, social class (manual versus non-manual) and education. The unemployed in the Republic of Ireland show less confidence only in relation to the Gardaí and the social welfare system but, with the exception of propensity to occupy buildings, show markedly lower levels of political engagement. For example, interest in politics is shown by only 29 per cent of the unemployed compared to 49 per cent of the rest of the population.

It is quite striking that, among Catholics in Northern Ireland, confidence in the political process/policy outputs is no lower among the unemployed than among the rest of the Catholic population and, in one case (the health care system) confidence

Table 9.9: Confidence in political institutions and orientation to political action by employment status, social class and education, Republic of Ireland

(Percentages)

	Employment status		Social Class		Education		
	Employed	Unemployed	Non-Manual	Manual	Some secondary or less	Completed secondary	Third level
A great deal plus quite a lot of confidence in:							
Political parties	17	16	19	19	20	19	22
Dáil	31	27	33	30	30	31	42
Civil service	58	49	62	60	59	61	64
Gardaí	86	67	87	85	83	88	89
Health care system	54	55	55	62	62	52	60
Social welfare system	52	41	55	61	63	53	54
Political action:							
Very interested or somewhat interested in politics	49	29	51	40	40	44	66
Have helped or might help a political party	52	40	52	43	42	43	63
Have occupied or might occupy buildings	20	25	18	18	14	15	28
Have attended or might attend lawful demonstrations	73	63	70	59	56	70	82
Follow politics in the media every day or several times a week	51	39	76	66	47	49	65
Would vote in next election	78	67	80	80	81	77	84

Source: European Values Study, 1999-2000.

among the unemployed is markedly higher (84 per cent among the unemployed compared to 62 per cent among the rest of the population). There are also fewer differences in the level of political engagement among unemployed Catholics compared to the rest of the Catholic population. In the case of the Protestant community, the higher level of confidence in the health care system among the unemployed is repeated. However, the unemployed show noticeably lower levels of confidence in three core institutions – parliament, the civil service and the police. Finally, the unemployed among the Protestant community in Northern Ireland are quite distinctive in showing no difference from the rest of their community in propensity to engage in politics; in fact, if anything, they show a slightly higher level of engagement.

In the Republic of Ireland, the basic social class distinction (manual/non-manual) behaves rather like the distinction between the sexes, i.e. there are virtually no differences between the two groups in confidence in politics but, with the exception of voting, significant differences exist in several aspects of orientation to political action, those with manual occupations tending to have a somewhat lower propensity to participate (Table 9.9). An exception to this observation occurs in the case of occupying buildings and voting, where the propensity to engage in the action in question is equal between the two groups. The absence of differences in confidence between those with non-manual and manual occupations is replicated in the two communities in Northern Ireland as is the general pattern of contrasts between the social classes in regard to the various forms of political participation.

Turning to our final socio-demographic variable (education) and again focusing first on the Republic of Ireland, it is apparent that, with one exception, education makes relatively little difference to levels of confidence in political institutions. The exception is that those with third level education stand out as having a significantly higher level of confidence in the Dáil as an institution. This is so despite the fact that their view of politicians is just as jaundiced as that of people with lower levels of education. Presumably what is happening here is that those with third level education are better able to distinguish between the incumbents and the institution, with the result that, while only 22 per cent have confidence in politicians, 42 per cent have confidence in the Dáil as an institution.

Education, and especially third level education, makes the biggest difference in terms of the propensity to engage in political action. Those with third level education have a substantially higher propensity to be interested in politics, to help a political party or candidate at election time, to attend lawful demonstrations and to follow politics in the media. On each of these measures, the relationship is linear – highest for those with third level, lower for those with complete second level and lower again for those with incomplete secondary or less, the percentage-point difference between the highest and the lowest level of education being mostly in excess of 20 points. On the other hand, as with all the other demographic variables considered except age, there is no apparent relationship between propensity to vote in an election and level of education.

All of the foregoing analysis of the variables associated with variations in confidence or participation are subject to a serious potential pitfall. The nature of the problem becomes apparent if we look at the relationship between age, education and propensity to participate in politics. Take the following four propositions: (i) older people are more likely to participate in politics; (ii) more educated people are more likely to participate in politics; (iii) older people are more likely to have lower levels of education; (iv) younger people are more likely to have higher levels of education. This series of propositions implies that, among younger and among older people, there may be two effects working in opposite directions. Being young makes individuals *less* likely to participate but being more highly educated makes them *more* likely to participate. Likewise, being older makes individuals *more* likely to participate but being less educated makes them *less* likely to participate. The net impact of these contrary effects are visible in Tables 9.8 and 9.9, but the forces at work behind the scenes, as it were, are undoubtedly more complex and may well be more substantial than suggested by these tables. The problem is here defined in terms of age and education but it could in fact be applied to several subsets of the variables we have been examining. The underlying relationships are more complex than those that can be captured by means of a set of simple bivariate analyses, and it is necessary to turn to multivariate analysis to throw light on these relationships.

Before proceeding along these lines, however, it is worth recalling that the data on the issues we have been discussing so far in this chapter were collected in 1999-2000. The potential implications of this passage of time are perhaps particularly strong in the case of the present chapter in that the very aspects of politics that generate or undermine confidence and that stimulate or dull people's interest in politics and their urge to participate are precisely the aspects that may have changed in the last three or four years. Fortunately, the European Social Survey data collected in late 2002 and early 2003 provide similar measures to those discussed here. There are some differences in question wording and format between the two surveys but these can be taken into account and indeed in one respect help to throw additional light on some of the attitudes we have been considering. For this comparison between 1999/2000 and 2002/2003, the following discussion will concentrate on confidence/trust in three institutions (parliament, the justice/legal system and police).

There were two main differences in the way in which this question was asked in the two surveys. In the first place the basic concept was operationalised in different ways – *as confidence* in the EVS and as *trust* in the European Social Survey. The second difference was that, whereas the EVS offered respondents a four-point response scale, the European Social Survey offered an 11-point scale ranging from zero (no trust at all) to 10 (complete trust). The scale difference is particularly important in that the four-point scale offers no mid-point, while the 11-point ESS scale gives an obvious mid-point at five and one that is visually evident to respondents on the show card used in administering the question. In order to compare the distribution of attitudes using these two different questions, we divide the responses into a set of negative scores, which one can think of as 'tend not to have confidence in/tend not to trust'[7] and positive scores ('tend to have confidence in/tend to trust'),[8] retaining a middle category of don't know/depends, which was a spontaneous response in the EVS method and mainly a displayed response (5 on the 10-point scale) in the ESS approach.

In the case of the Republic of Ireland and looking first at confidence/trust in the

[7] 0 to 4 on the ESS scale; 1 to 2 on the EVS scale.

[8] 6 to 10 on the ESS scale; 3 to 4 on the EVS scale.

Table 9.10: Confidence/trust in selected political institutions, Republic of Ireland, 1999 and 2003

(Percentages)

	Dáil		Justice/legal system		Gardaí	
	EVS 1999	ESS 2003	EVS 1999	ESS 2003	EVS 1999	ESS 2003
Tend to have confidence in/ tend to trust	32	31	55	43	86	69
DK/Depends	2	25	2	21	0	13
Tend not to have confidence in/ tend not to trust	66	44	44	36	14	18
Tend to have confidence/trust minus tend not to have confidence/trust	-33	-13	11	7	72	51
[N]	[1,005]	[2,034]	[1,008]	[2,033]	[1,008]	[2,024]

Sources: European Values Study, 1999-2000; European Social Survey, 2003.

Dáil, the overall positive rating remained at the same low level (about one-third) between 1999 and 2003 but the level of negative evaluation fell by more than 20 percentage points) and the share of mid-point responses went up correspondingly (see Table 9.10). In the case of the justice/legal system[9], the non-committal middle category also increased by about 20 percentage points but this was at the expense of both positive and negative responses (the former being down 12 percentage points and the latter falling by 8 points). In the case of the Gardaí, who, as we have already seen show up as enjoying very high levels of confidence in 1999/2000, there was a significant decline in confidence/trust (down 17 percentage points), a slight rise (4 points) in lack of confidence/trust and a more moderate increase in the middle category (up 13 points).

One can summarise the net effect of the changes across all three objects of confidence/trust by subtracting the proportion who tend not to have confidence/trust from the proportion who tend to have confidence/trust in the objects in question. As indicated by the last row in Table 9.10, this measure shows substantial differences between 1999 and 2003, especially in the case of the political objects. Thus, net confidence in the Dáil comes in at –33 percentage points in 1999 and at only –13 percentage points in 2003. What has occurred in the meantime is less a movement of people from negative to positive than a movement into 'don't know' which, as we have seen, only becomes apparent when such a category is provided, as in the European Social Survey question format.

On this measure of net confidence, the justice/legal system had a more or less similar positive rating at both time points (+11 in 1999-2000 and +7 in 2002-03). In the case of the Gardaí, the change in net confidence/trust was more substantial and in a negative direction (from +72 to +51). This occurred partly because the more recent survey is better at identifying those who hold a middle/noncommittal position. It cannot, however be attributed entirely to this methodological factor; it is also due to a fall in confidence/trust and a (smaller) rise in lack of confidence/trust in the Gardaí over the period in question.

Turning to the parallel data on trends in confidence/trust in institutions in Northern Ireland shows that the effect of using an 11-point scale with a clearly defined mid-point is the same as in the Republic, i.e. a substantial increase in the non-committal responses (Table 9.11). The effect of this clarification of the nature of the general distribution of confidence is, however, quite different in the Catholic and Protestant communities. This can be seen in summary form by looking at the rows of figures that show the net level of confidence/trust obtained by subtracting the proportion that tend to have no confidence/trust from the proportion that tend to have confidence/trust. Between 1999/2000 and 2002/2003 and across all three institutions (Westminster Parliament, the justice/legal system and the police), this net measure improved substantially among Northern Ireland Catholics; among

[9] This item was phrased as 'justice system' in the EVS and as 'legal system' in the ESS.

Table 9.11: Confidence/trust in selected political institutions, Northern Ireland, 1999 and 2003

(Percentages)

	Political parties/politicians		Westminster Parliament		Justice/legal system		Police	
	EVS 1999	ESS 2003	EVS 1999	ESS 2003	EVS 1999	ESS 2003	EVS 1999	ESS 2003
Catholics:								
Tend to have confidence in/tend to trust	17	21	28	29	39	41	36	44
DK/Depends	6	28	8	25	3	23	3	17
Tend not to have confidence in/tend not to trust	77	51	64	46	58	36	61	39
Tend to have confidence/trust minus not tend to have confidence/trust	-60	-30	-35	-18	-19	5	-25	7
[N]	[399]	[244]	[400]	[247]	[399]	[243]	[401]	[247]
Protestants:								
Tend to have confidence in/tend to trust	18	18	48	27	54	46	85	69
DK/Depends	7	16	6	18	6	18	1	15
Tend not to have confidence in/tend not to trust	75	66	46	55	40	36	14	16
Tend to have confidence/trust minus not tend to have confidence/trust	-57	-48	2	-28	14	10	72	53
[N]	[436]	[333]	[434]	[328]	[436]	[326]	[438]	[334]
Non-affiliated:								
Tend to have confidence in/tend to trust	12	14	29	25	37	46	63	55
DK/Depends	10	17	9	17	6	14	0	17
Tend not to have confidence in/tend not to trust	78	69	62	58	57	40	37	28
Tend to have confidence/trust minus not tend to have confidence/trust	-65	-55	-33	-33	-20	5	26	27
[N]	[138]	[148]	[139]	[144]	[139]	[149]	[137]	[151]

Sources: European Values Study, 1999-2000; European Social Survey, 2003.

Northern Ireland Protestants, on the other hand, the net measure disimproved in the case of all three institutions, the disimprovement being substantial in the case of Westminster and the police.

In summary, comparison of the EVS 1999-2000 and the ESS 2002-2003 enables us to refine our account of people's confidence in certain key institutions. Part of this refinement comes from the ESS evidence that shows that there is a larger middle ground on these issues than is apparent from the earlier EVS evidence and that identification of this midde ground tends, for the most part, to reduce the proportion that takes a negative view. But the refinement also suggests substantive movement of opinion between 1999-2000 and 2003, both in Northern Ireland and in the Republic. In the Republic of Ireland this mainly takes the form of a reduction in the very high levels of confidence in the Gardaí. In the case of Northern Ireland, it takes the form of improved confidence in the police among Catholics and reduced confidence in the Westminster Parliament and in the police among Protestants.

A multivariate analysis of political engagement

In the following analysis the dependent variable (political interest) is the propensity of people to engage with the political process in their society as indicated by their subjective assessment of their own involvement in politics and by their reported action or inaction in following politics in the media, in discussing politics, and in taking part in the electoral process.[10] This combination of psychological and behavioural engagement in politics is an essential underpinning of the political process and knowing what causes it to wax or wane is an essential element in our understanding of that process.

Table 9.12 presents an analysis which addresses these issues for both the Republic and Northern Ireland. Model 1 in the analysis focuses on a range of possible background influences on political interest. These include the socio-demographic characteristics of respondents (gender, age, employment status, occupational class and education), their religious identification, and a range of social and political characteristics – whether one has a political identification as left-wing or right-wing, whether one tends to trust other people, and one's frequency of religious practice.

In the Republic of Ireland, age and education are positively related to political engagement, while being female and being in a manual social class position are negatively related. Those who lean towards the right are also more likely to be

[10] The measure of political interest is based on the factor analysis of orientation to political action presented in Table 9.6. It is constructed from the first five items listed in Table 9.6 – interest in politics, importance of politics, follow politics in the news, discuss politics and have helped/might help a political party or candidate at election time. Each item is dichotomised so that 1 indicates interest in politics and 0 indicates lack of interest, the five dichotomies are then summed and the result divided by 5 to give a political engagement scale ranging from 0 to 1.

Table 9.12: Regression of political interest in the Republic of Ireland and Northern Ireland

	(Unstandardised Regression Coefficients)			
	Republic of Ireland		Northern Ireland	
	Model 1	Model 2	Model 1	Model 2
Age	0.01***	0.01***	0.00	0.00
Education	0.09***	0.08***	0.00	-0.01
Female	-0.14***	-0.14***	-0.16***	-0.14***
Manual social class	-0.05**	-0.06**	-0.06	-0.04
Unemployed	-0.02	-0.03	-0.01	-0.03
Religious identification:				
Catholic (reference)				
Protestant	-0.10***	-0.07**	-0.02	-0.03
Non-affiliated	0.00	0.04	-0.10***	-0.14**
Trust people	0.04	0.03	0.09**	0.07**
Regular church attender	0.07**	0.06	0.02	0.03
Lack confidence[1] in:				
armed forces		0.01		-0.02
the police		-0.01		0.00
Parliament		-0.05**		0.01
Civil service		0.01		0.04
social security system		0.05**		-0.01
health care system		0.03		0.08***
justice system		0.01		0.04*
political parties		-0.08***		-0.12***
Constant	0.08	0.19	0.50	0.65
R squared	0.16	0.21	0.11	0.17
[N]	[1,038]	[916]	[899]	[676]

Note: [1] Scale: 1=great deal of confidence, 4=no confidence at all; ***, Significant at the 0.001 level, **, Significant at the 0.01 level, *, Significant at the 0.05 level.

Source: European Values Study, 1999-2000.

interested in politics. However, the most interesting effect of the background variables in the Republic arises with religious identification: Protestants have less interest in politics than either Catholics or the non-affiliated. The size of this effect is not large, so one should be careful not to overstate its importance. Yet it echoes the indications found in the two previous chapters of an element of restraint in Protestants' orientations to the established political order in the Republic: while they clearly identify themselves as Irish, they are less enthusiastic about that identity than are the majority population and are less supportive of the dominant nationalist position on questions related to Northern Ireland.

In Northern Ireland itself, the pattern of relationships between the background variables and political interest is quite different. Of the socio-demographic variables, only being a female has a strong effect on political interest, though being in a manual social class position also has a small negative effect. There are no significant differences in political interest by age, education or religious affiliation, indicating that political interest is more evenly dispersed through society than is the case in the Republic.

Model 2 adds in eight measures of confidence in the political process so that we can isolate which aspects are related to political interest. The results show that most of these confidence items have no effect: in both the Republic and Northern Ireland, five of the eight items have non-significant coefficients. Furthermore, only one item – lack of confidence in political parties – has an effect in both the Republic and Northern Ireland. Of the items that do have an effect, the signs are not all in the same direction: some of the effects are positive, others are negative. Thus, in the Republic, lack of confidence in the political parties and parliament erodes political engagement, but lack of confidence in the health system and in the justice system actually increases it. These finding address the question of whether lack of confidence in politics breeds critical citizens or alienated/apathetic citizens. The answer is that while effects of these kinds seem not to be strong, such effects as are present depend on the aspect of confidence involved. Lack of confidence in political outputs, specifically in regard to the health system and the justice system in Northern Ireland and in regard to the social welfare system in the Republic, leads to increased political engagement but lack of confidence in political institutions and actors (specifically parliament and political parties in the Republic and political parties in Northern Ireland) undermines engagement.

Conclusion

This chapter has identified significant differences in attitudes to politics and political institutions between the Republic of Ireland and Northern Ireland and between the main religious denominations. Broadly speaking, people in the Republic are more positive about politics and political institutions than are the people of Northern Ireland, and Protestants in the Republic are, if anything, even more positive than are

Catholics. On many counts, levels of confidence in the political system in the Republic and satisfaction with its performance rose during the 1990s, and the Republic was one of the minority of European societies where the system of government as of 1999-2000 was rated more highly than was the system of government of ten years before. In comparisons with other countries in Europe, the Republic emerges as one of the societies showing more positive ratings of various aspects of the political system – or perhaps one should say that it is less negative, since negative evaluations of political institutions are more the rule than the exception in Europe. Evidence from the 2002-03 European Social Survey suggest that attitudes to political institutions and actors in the Republic have remained fairly stable since 1999. The ESS data also suggest that attitudes to parliament and to parties/politicians may not be quite as negative as portrayed by the European Values Survey in that a significant proportion of people (one-fifth to one quarter) tend to suspend judgment in regard to confidence in political institutions, a point that was not apparent from the different question format used in the European Values Survey.

At the beginning of this chapter, the question was raised whether evaluations of the political system in the Republic were likely to have turned negative as a result of political scandals in the 1990s or been boosted by the economic leap forward of the Celtic Tiger years and the continuing moves towards a settlement of the Northern Ireland problem. On the balance of evidence presented in the chapter, one would have to opt for the latter: the general direction of movement in public sentiment was slightly upwards, and while indications of cynicism about the system could be found in 1999-2000, there was also a widespread sense that the political process was working better than it had previously.

The picture for Northern Ireland was less positive and more complex than that for the Republic. Ratings of the political system were generally lower than in the Republic and, as might be expected, there were sharp denominational divides in attitudes on certain issues. Division was most evident in connection with attitudes towards the security forces: Catholics were distrustful of the armed forces and the police while Protestants strongly supported them. The balance of feeling was the other way around in assessments of the role of the UK government: Catholics were more positive about how that role had changed during the 1990s than were Protestants, and in this echoed the more positive reception of the Good Friday Agreement among Catholics than among Protestants documented in Chapter 5.

Nevertheless, despite these divisions and negative attitudes towards some aspects of the political system in Northern Ireland, the overall level of confidence is remarkably positive when compared with the picture for other European countries. Despite the long history of political turmoil and instability in Northern Ireland, people's confidence in the political system and evaluations of political institutions were generally at or above the average for Europe. It is particularly notable that overall confidence in political institutions and ratings of the UK system of government were higher in Northern Ireland than in Britain – and even Catholics in Northern Ireland rate the UK system of government more highly than do the people of Britain. Protestants in Northern Ireland may be less satisfied with the way the political system has developed in the past ten years than are Catholics, but even in their case more people see improvement or no change than see disimprovement in this area and in that they are among a minority in Europe. In sum, therefore, while Northern Ireland may be characterised by levels of political division and strife that are out of the ordinary for Europe, it does not show unusual levels of disaffection or alienation from the political system.

The differences in orientations to political action between Northern Ireland and the Republic relate in the main to how each community regards actual or potential involvement in non-conventional modes of political participation. The evidence also points to some differences in levels of political participation in Ireland compared to the rest of Europe (Ireland being somewhat lower). A multivariate analysis shows that political engagement is more evenly present across Northern Ireland society than it is in the Republic. In particular, the fall-off in interest among the young and those with lower education found in the Republic seems to be absent in Northern Ireland. There is also a notably lower level of political interest among Protestants in the Republic than among the rest of the population, and this denominational difference is also absent in Northern Ireland. Finally, political engagement is *stimulated by low levels of confidence in policy outputs* but is *undermined by low levels of confidence in political institutions and political actors*. In this sense, the analysis provides a qualified answer to the question whether low or declining levels of confidence create critical citizens or apathetic citizens. The answer is: it depends. Lack of confidence in political outputs produces critical citizens; lack of confidence in political institutions and political actors breeds apathy.

10

Conclusion

This study set out to examine the nature and extent of conflict and consensus in cultural values and political attitudes on the island of Ireland. Two ethnonational traditions – Catholic-nationalist and Protestant-unionist – are divided by a cleavage in collective identity and political orientation that has dominated the way North-South and Protestant-Catholic relations have evolved. At the same time, the two traditions possess sets of values and attitudes that cut across ethnonational boundaries and go some way towards creating what might be called a common culture. The purpose of the study was to examine these two themes – conflict and consensus – in order to arrive at a more detailed assessment of where precisely the similarities and differences begin and end.

The study was based on surveys of values and attitudes carried out between the 1960s and 2003 but with a particular focus on the European Values Study carried out in 1999-2000. The EVS surveys conducted in the Republic of Ireland and Northern Ireland in 1999-2000 were adapted from the core EVS surveys applied elsewhere in Europe in two ways: questions were added to explore people's views on the political situation on the island of Ireland, and a special booster sample of Protestants was added to the main population sample for the Republic of Ireland so that Protestant-Catholic comparisons could be made for the Republic as well as for the North. The other main pan-European survey drawn upon in the study is the European Social Survey 2002-3. This enabled us to update to 2003 some of the general themes covered in the EVS and also to examine specific Northern Ireland issues by analysing questions added to the ESS survey as part of this project. A major advantage of these pan-European surveys is that the large number of countries covered provides a comparative backdrop against which patterns of similarities and difference in Ireland, North and South, can be assessed.

The starting point of the study was the concept of socio-cultural cleavage developed by Seymour Lipset and Stein Rokkan in the 1960s in their analysis of political alignment in Europe. Application of this framework suggests that political division in Ireland is a particular case of the centre-periphery conflicts that marked the process of nation-building on the European mainland. These conflicts centred on competing nationalisms – the centralising nationalisms of the metropolitan powers versus the separatist nationalisms of the peripheral regions. In the Irish case, the ideology of the centre was expressed in unionism and the ideology of the periphery in Irish nationalism. The dominance of this version of the centre-periphery cleavage and the secession that sought to resolve it meant that other dimensions of cleavage – between state secularism and church authority, between industrial and agrarian interests and between capital and labour – were pushed into the background.

Religion

Religion is fundamental to the paradox of conflict and consensus we are concerned with here and for that reason was the first substantive topic to be examined in our study. On the one hand, religion is one of the key symbols or markers of difference between the two dominant ethnonational traditions. On the other hand, the very fact that religion still matters in both traditions sets them apart in Europe and gives them a paradoxical similarity to each other. While neither Catholics nor Protestants in the North or in the Republic are as attached to their churches as they once were, they are alike in continuing to subscribe to organised religion and orthodox Christian belief to a greater degree than the populations of most other European societies. Religion may constitute a line of division in one way but in another it twins the two traditions as a relatively religious pair in an increasingly secular Europe.

Secularisation has of course advanced in both Northern Ireland and the Republic of Ireland. But the start of that advance was recent compared to other countries in Europe and moved at a more moderate pace. Some people have reduced their formal religious observance to low levels, and others have disavowed membership of any denomination, though many of these continue to adhere to various kinds of private or informal religion. But the majority continue to participate to some degree and there are still very few who are willing to call themselves atheist. The present trend in secularisation in either part of Ireland, therefore, is not towards outright rejection of belief but towards a widespread pattern of active, if often lukewarm, attachment to churchly religion, coupled with a growing amount of independent religious belief that is not connected to any church. Looked at from within the confines of this island, the weakening of religious commitment and church power since the 1960s has been dramatic: by 2003, weekly church attendance among adults had fallen to 50 per cent in the Republic of Ireland and to 42 per cent in Northern Ireland. From a European perspective, however, it is the continuing vitality of religion that stands out: church attendance rates at the levels found in Ireland, North or South, are very much the exception in Europe as a whole. The contrast with Britain in this regard is particularly telling, since Britain is now one of the most secularised countries in the world. The weakness of organised religion in Britain today means that the religious contrast in these islands is not only between Catholicism and Protestantism but also between the vigorous, assertive Protestantism of Northern Ireland and the more quiescent and more marginalised Protestantism found in most of Britain.

In view of the sex scandals and child abuse revelations that have rocked the Catholic church since 1992, not to speak of the increase in materialism which is often assumed to have accompanied the 'Celtic tiger' economy in the Republic over the past decade, it might be expected that Catholicism, especially in the Republic, would have shown greater decline over this period than Protestantism. In fact, Catholicism in both parts of Ireland has held up at least as well, and in some respects slightly better, than has Protestantism in Northern Ireland (we did not have the necessary data on Protestantism over time in the Republic to make comparable statements on trends in their case). Up to the late 1990s, Catholics in both the North and the Republic were more reluctant to depart their church altogether or give up entirely on church attendance than were Protestants in the North, though Catholics in the Republic have closed some of this gap in the early years of the present decade.

Only one indicator – confidence in the church – shows the Catholic church in either the Republic or the North to be in a weaker position than the Protestant churches. Public loss of confidence in the Catholic church should not be overstated: the majority of the Catholic population, North and South, are still more positive than negative in their expressions of confidence in the church. But compared to the very high confidence ratings enjoyed by the Catholic church in the past and the reasonably high standing of the Protestant churches today, the Catholic church is now in a weakened position. The travails of the Catholic church since the early 1990s have undoubtedly contributed to this outcome, though the decline in public confidence in the Catholic church has been underway since the 1970s and was almost as great during the 1980s, before the scandals emerged, as it was in the following turbulent decade.

The weakness of the Catholic church in terms of public confidence contrasts with its relative strength (compared to Protestantism) on other indicators. The Catholic *faith* in Ireland is holding up just as well, if not slightly better, than the Protestant faith, even though the public image of the Catholic *church* has taken the greater battering over the past decade. This in turn indicates that persistence in religious attachment is a complex matter: one dimension of attachment, such as confidence in the church, can decline more rapidly than other dimensions such as belief in church doctrines or attendance at religious services.

Identity

Moving from religion to identity is usually thought to be a short step in Ireland since the two are conventionally seen as closely intertwined. In many respects, this standard perception is correct but in other ways it is not. It is most questionable in the case of the Republic of Ireland, where national identity has shed much of the confessional character it possessed in the past. Catholics and Protestants in the Republic now equally think of themselves as Irish, and the former 'west British' associations of Protestantism are largely gone. The weakening of religious attachment that has occurred in recent decades has had no adverse effect on collective identity in the Republic, and those who have no religious affiliation are just as strong in their sense of Irishness as are those with strong religious commitment.

In Northern Ireland, by contrast, the religious bases of identity remain strong, albeit with some fraying around the edges. The majority of Protestants think of themselves as British by national identity and citizenship and as unionist in political identity. The majority of Catholics in the North think of themselves as Irish and nationalist. The weakening of religious attachment referred to earlier has done nothing to soften the denominational divide in identity and political allegiance: lukewarm Catholics and Protestants are no less polarised in their identities than those with stronger commitment to their faith. The non-affiliated also show signs of being divided in their identity according to whether they are ex-Catholic or ex-Protestant.

However, it oversimplifies matters to portray the two sides as monoliths since there are substantial minorities on both sides, especially on the Catholic side, who distance themselves in one way or another from the dominant identities of their own group. Thus the middle-ground identities of 'Northern Irish' or 'sometimes British, sometimes Irish' are adopted in Northern Ireland by 26 per cent of Catholics, 16 per cent of Protestants and 29 per cent of the non-affiliated. At the same time, the degree to which the monolithic boundaries are breached is limited since the distancing from dominant identities within each group falls short of creating new cross-cutting allegiances: only 8 per cent of Catholics define themselves as British and only 3 per cent of Protestants describe themselves as Irish. The blurring of identity on each side, therefore, tends to entail a move to a neutral middle ground rather than an embrace of the identity of the other side. The neutral middle ground between nationalist and unionist *political* identities in Northern Ireland is occupied by even larger shares of the population: over 40 per cent of Catholics and 33 per cent of Protestants say they are neither nationalist nor unionist (compared to 58 per cent of Catholics who say they are nationalist and 66 per cent of Protestants who say they are unionist). Two-thirds of the non-affiliated say they are neither nationalist nor unionist. Here, however, the lack of crossover to the other side is even starker, especially as between Catholics and Protestants: almost no Catholics define themselves as unionist and no Protestants define themselves as nationalist. The unwillingness of Catholics to define themselves as unionist is particularly notable, since substantial minorities of Catholics hold mildly pro-union constitutional preferences (a point to which we shall return below). Among Catholics in Northern Ireland, a unionist political identity is embraced by virtually none, even though certain aspects of unionist constitutional preferences are partially or wholly accepted by many.

Two further nuances in patterns of identity in the Republic and Northern Ireland are indicated by people's perceptions of the bases of their identities and their level of pride in their identities. Although the association between religion and identity is strong, people play down this association in response to questions about the bases of their identity. When presented with a list of five items that might be considered as potential bases of Irish identity and asked to rate their importance, Catholics in both the Republic and the North placed 'being a Catholic' close to the bottom of the list (only the 'ability to speak Irish' was ranked lower). Catholics in Northern Ireland ranked this item even lower than Catholics in the Republic, though in actuality, as we have seen, religion is more closely linked to identity in the North than in the Republic. When Protestants in Northern Ireland were presented with a similar list of possible foundations of British identity, in which 'being a Catholic' was replaced by 'being a Protestant', they placed the latter very firmly at the bottom of the list. Those without religious affiliation in both the North and the Republic also accorded little importance to religion as a basis for either Irish or British identity. Other 'civic' and ethnic factors, such as respecting a country's political institutions and laws, were accorded much greater importance as foundations of national identity by all religious groups. The striking pattern here, then, is that in Northern Ireland in particular the link between religion and identity which is evident from daily life is pushed to the background in people's own representation of how their identities are constituted. The precise significance of this pattern is difficult to pinpoint, but it does remind us that identity is a complex matter in which nuances of meaning are many, subtle and difficult to interpret.

A different kind of hesitancy about identity in Northern Ireland is indicated by the relatively low levels of pride in identity and citizenship among Northern Ireland respondents, both Catholic and Protestant, especially in contrast to the very high levels of pride found among Catholics in the Republic of Ireland. Less than half of the population in Northern Ireland say they are 'very proud' of their national identity, compared to over 70 per cent in the Republic. Catholics in the Republic stand out as having high levels of pride in citizenship (one of the highest in Europe) but in this they stand in contrast to all other major religious groupings on the island. Among Protestants in Northern Ireland who identify their citizenship as British, only 40 per cent say they are very proud of their citizenship, while 57 per cent of Catholics in Northern Ireland who identify their citizenship as Irish say they are very proud of their citizenship. Those in Northern Ireland who report a joint British-Irish citizenship report even lower pride scores: only 20 per cent of Catholics and 17 per cent of Protestants with joint citizenship are 'very proud' of it. This is not to say that perceptions of identity in Northern Ireland are negative, since very few say they have no pride at all in their identity. It does suggest, however, that the contested nature of identity in Northern Ireland generates a degree of restraint or ambivalence in people's feelings about their chosen identities that is absent among Catholics in the Republic. The middle-ground identity represented by British-Irish citizenship generates a particularly low level of pride. This reinforces the point made earlier that those who distance themselves from the dominant identity in their religious groups are doing so hesitantly and to a limited degree and are not forging a strong new pole of collective identification that effectively transcends historic divisions.

On this subject, the Protestant minority in the Republic is more similar to the Northern population, Catholic and Protestant, than to the Catholic population in the Republic. While almost all Protestants in the Republic define their citizenship as Irish, only 49 per cent say they are 'very proud' of it. This is a slightly higher level of pride in citizenship than is found among Protestants in the North who report a British citizenship (40 per cent very proud) and slightly lower than Northern Catholics with an Irish citizenship (57 per cent very proud) but is far below the 75 per cent of Catholics in the Republic who are very proud of their citizenship. This indicates that, while Protestants in the Republic may have no doubt that their citizenship is Irish, the connotations of that citizenship are different, and somewhat less positive, for them than for Catholics in the Republic.

Constitutional preferences

We can learn more of the implications of identity for different religious groups from their attitudes and preferences regarding the constitutional future for Northern Ireland. Broadly speaking, preferences on the historic constitutional question that has long been at the centre of ethnonational division – whether Northern Ireland in the long-term should re-unite with the rest of Ireland or remain within the United Kingdom – break down along expected religious lines. Among Northern Protestants, there is something approaching unanimity on the issue: 88 per cent support retention of the union with Britain. Those without religious affiliation in the North are close to the Protestant position: 76 per cent are in favour of remaining in the UK. This in part reflects the high proportion of ex-Protestants among those without religious affiliation but also suggests that the ex-Catholics among them show considerable support for the union.

Catholics North and South and the non-affiliated and Protestants in the South have quite mixed views. Among Catholics in Northern Ireland, two-thirds would prefer a united Ireland, but this leaves one-third who would prefer something else. This one-third consists of 21 per cent who favour retention of the union with Britain and 11 per cent who prefer an independent Northern Ireland. In the

Republic of Ireland, the Catholic majority in favour of a united Ireland is even smaller (55 per cent), with 33 per cent preferring an independent Northern Ireland and 9 per cent in favour of the North remaining in the UK. Those without religious affiliation in the Republic are marginally more in favour of a united Ireland than are Catholics in the Republic but again the majority in this position (58 per cent) is relatively small. For Protestants in the Republic, a united Ireland is the most common preference (supported by 43 per cent) and in this they are closer to Catholic preferences, North and South, than to the preferences of their co-religionists in Northern Ireland. However, there is also considerable support among Protestants in the Republic for an independent Northern Ireland (28 per cent) and for the North remaining in the UK (23 per cent). Protestants in the Republic are thus similar to Catholics in Northern Ireland in the frequency with which they support retention of the union with Britain (just over a fifth in both cases).

With the advent of the Good Friday Agreement in 1998, the debate about the constitutional future of Northern Ireland moved beyond a simple choice between preserving the union with Britain and Irish unity. The Agreement put in place a complex set of compromises that attempted to find a new middle way between these two options. At the time of the referendum on the Agreement in April 1998, it was clear from opinion poll data that Protestants in Northern Ireland were less enamoured of many of its provisions than Catholics either in Northern Ireland or the Republic. While a majority of Protestants in the North voted for the Agreement in the referendum, that majority was small (estimated in exit poll data at 55 per cent). There was near unanimous support for the Agreement both among Catholic voters in the North (estimated at 99 per cent in exit poll data) and among all voters in the Republic (where the 'yes' vote was 94.4 per cent).

Subsequent tracking of Protestant opinion in Northern Ireland showed that disenchantment with the Agreement grew after 1998. By 2003, 85 per cent of Protestants, compared to 59 per cent in 1998, had come to believe that nationalists had gained more from the Agreement than unionists. Almost none felt that unionists had gained more than nationalists. Catholics in Northern Ireland had a more positive view of the Agreement. The majority believed that nationalists and unionists had gained equally from the Agreement (65 per cent expressed this view in 2001). Echoing the pattern among Protestants, the proportion of Catholics who felt that nationalists had benefited more from the Agreement grew over time (from 17 per cent in 1998 to 27 per cent in 2003) and was larger than the proportion who felt that unionists had gained more (7 per cent in 2003).

Analysis of attitudes to specific aspects of the Good Friday Agreement shows that issues relating to security were a particularly sore point with Protestants in Northern Ireland. Northern Protestants strongly supported the proposals for decommissioning of paramilitary weapons (96 per cent support) and were very unhappy both with the release of paramilitary prisoners (6 per cent support) and reform of the RUC (17 per cent support). The fact that the first of these failed to come about quickly or fully, while the latter two went ahead more or less as proposed in the Agreement, is likely to have nurtured the growing unhappiness of Protestants in Northern Ireland with the Agreement.

Catholics too in both Northern Ireland and the Republic were concerned about security issues but not as strongly as were Protestants in the North and not always in the same direction. They were almost as supportive of decommissioning (over 80 per cent) as were Protestants in the North and, as with Protestants, a majority were unhappy with the release of paramilitary prisoners. However, the minority of Catholics who were in favour of the release of paramilitary prisoners was quite large (34 per cent in the Republic, 37 per cent in the North). Contrary to the position of Northern Protestants, a majority of Catholics strongly supported reform of the RUC (70 per cent support in the Republic, 74 per cent in the North).

The non-affiliated in Northern Ireland occupy an intermediate position on these issues between Catholics and Protestants, though they are closer to Protestants than Catholics on a number of the items. In the Republic, by contrast, they largely echo the position of Catholics in the Republic, perhaps because they themselves are largely ex-Catholic. In fact, on some issues, they adopt a position that if anything is slightly more nationalist than that of Catholics.

Protestants in the Republic of Ireland displayed attitudes to the elements of the Good Friday Agreement that were generally in between those of Catholics, North and South, on the one hand and Protestants in Northern Ireland on the other. A typical example is provided by attitudes to the guarantee that Northern Ireland will remain in the UK: 70 per cent of Protestants in the Republic support this guarantee, compared to just over 60 per cent of Catholics in the North and the South on one side and 94 per cent of Protestants in the North on the other. Similarly, 45 per cent of southern Protestants support reform of the RUC, compared to over 70 per cent of Catholics on one side and 17 per cent of northern Protestants on the other.

This in-between position of southern Protestants on key constitutional questions is revealing. It suggests that that while they may have adopted an identity that is unquestionably Irish, that Irishness is less nationalist than that of Catholics and is somewhat more in tune with the concerns of Northern Protestants. It is a further indication that while the absorption of southern Protestants into the Irish state may to all intents and purposes be complete, they nevertheless retain a distinct perspective on major issues relating to Northern Ireland. That perspective echoes some elements of Irish nationalism but in other respects approximates more closely to the position of Northern Protestants. It thus places them in a middle ground between nationalism and certain aspects of unionism as far as constitutional questions are concerned.

The liberal-conservative divide: Family and sexual morality

Given the continuing strength, relatively speaking, of religious practice and belief in both parts of Ireland and given the connection between religious commitment and attitudes to the family and to issues of sexual morality, the latter might be expected to provide the most likely base for the emergence of alternative political alignments. The analysis in chapter 2 confirmed that this is indeed an identifiable line of cleavage that cuts across Protestant-Catholic and North-South divisions. In many respects, both the Republic of Ireland and Northern Ireland have moved with the times in these areas and share in the liberalisation of contemporary western values regarding family life and sexual behaviour. We know from demographic data, for example, that family size in both the North and the Republic has fallen to within the range found in the rest of Europe and that the share of births taking place outside of marriage is about average for the EU.

However, several issues in this arena still have the power to divide opinion and inflame public debate. Abortion is one of these, homosexuality is another – though at a milder level – and divorce *was* one in the recent past, at least in the Republic. A shift towards liberalism on these issues is evident both in the Republic of Ireland and Northern Ireland, not just in that the young have become more liberal than the old but also that even those in the middle and older ages have become more liberal than they were at earlier stages in their lives. However, this shift has not gone that far by European standards since both the North and the Republic still remain on the conservative side of the European average and on one issue – abortion – retain an exceptionally conservative outlook. The key observation, however, is that whatever point on the spectrum of opinion the North and the Republic occupy on a given issue in this arena, they are typically located side by side in Europe-wide comparisons. It is particularly notable that Northern Ireland has much more in common with the Republic of Ireland on these questions than it has with the rest of the United Kingdom, so that cultural similarity in this instance is stronger on the island of Ireland than it is between Northern Ireland and Britain.

Indicators of consensus in this area are most evident in the case of abortion. Widespread disapproval of abortion has been repeatedly expressed in the Republic of Ireland in the sequence of referendums on the subject which have taken place since 1983. EVS data show that such disapproval is present in Northern Ireland also and is almost as strong among Protestants as it is among Catholics. In a close-up view, Catholics in both the North and the Republic are more opposed to abortion than Protestants. However, in a wider European perspective, the difference turns out to be small: Protestants North and South stand apart from other countries in Europe by virtue of their low level of acceptance of abortion and are more similar to Catholics in Ireland on this issue than to any other national population in Europe. Their opposition to abortion is stronger even than that of historically Catholic countries in Europe such as Italy, Spain and Portugal.

While the North and the Republic are generally similar to each other in their attitudes to such matters as abortion, homosexuality and divorce, they also are internally diverse. This internal diversity is itself revealing since, along with the usual factors such as age and education, it is shaped by secularisation: those with weak religious attachment are more liberal than the devout and those with no religious affiliation are more liberal than those who still identify with particular churches. This is not an extreme pattern, since even the secular in both the North and the Republic are moderately conservative on some issues (especially abortion) and even the devout have softened or abandoned many of the stricter moral positions of their churches (for example, in regard to homosexuality or non-marital parenthood). Nevertheless, the role of religious commitment in sustaining conservative family and sexual values and moral attitudes helps explain both the similarity of the Republic and the North to each other in this area and their difference from the rest of Europe. It also shows that in so far as religion has a role in creating cultural division on the island of Ireland, at least in the arena of family and sexual morality, that division is structured not by denomination but by secularisation. Neither Catholic nor Protestant morality has as much influence on family and sexual matters as it had in the past, but the more strongly affiliated in each denomination are more conservative and more similar to each other than they are to those with weak attachment or no attachment at all. Thus old differences between Catholics and Protestants have been replaced by new differences between the devout and the lukewarm as axes of cleavage in the culture of family and sexuality in both parts of Ireland.

Left-right divide and 'new politics'

It is often argued that, because of the historical dominance of the nationalist-unionist divide in the politics of both Northern Ireland and the Republic, other lines of cleavage failed to develop. This absence is a significant common feature in the culture of the two societies. An important case in point is the left-right, or labour versus capital, opposition that the Lipset-Rokkan scheme identified as an important dimension of political alignment in Europe since the late nineteenth century. An analysis of EVS data for signs of the left-right divide in the two parts of Ireland confirms its relative unimportance and incoherence. Most people in both the North and the Republic place themselves either in the centre or slightly to the right on a left-right self-placement scale. This locates the two populations beside each other on the European political spectrum in a position somewhat to the right of the average. There are other populations in Europe – mainly in the former communist countries of central and eastern Europe – who place themselves further to the right, but the most common European position is to the left of both Northern Ireland and the Republic.

Further evidence of the weakness of the left-right cleavage in the North and the Republic emerges when we examine more closely what the terms 'left' and 'right' might mean. In both the North and the Republic, there is little fit between people's identification of themselves as left-wing or right-wing and their views on classic left-right policy issues such as the role of the state in the economy, the acceptability of income inequality, or the obligation of the state to provide welfare support for its citizens. Self-defined left wingers are no more likely to adopt old-style left-wing views on these issues than are self-defined right wingers. It emerges, rather, that to be on the left in either part of Ireland has more to do with adopting liberal or mildly anti-establishment attitudes on religious and personal moral issues than with standard socialist views on how the economy should be organised. Even at that, the liberalism of left wingers in this sense in both the North and the Republic is muted: neither part of Ireland is a hotbed of radicalism on any aspect of the liberal social agenda.

The same can be said of new lines of political cleavage that some commentators have proposed as the basis of an emergent new politics in western countries generally. The politics of gender is one such possibility, environmentalism is another and postmaterialism is a third. The evidence from the EVS does not support such expectations: the indications are that while all of these axes of division are to some degree discernible in both the North and the Republic, they are relatively weakly articulated. Furthermore, looking at present attitudinal patterns among young people, there is little ground for expecting that they will become stronger in the immediate future. Here again, the dominant picture for both parts of Ireland is of a moderate conservativism, with some leanings towards more liberal attitudes but no strong shift in that direction.

Work, subjective well-being and social capital

Final possible axes of differentiation across the ethnonational divide and between North and South that this study considered had to do with old stereotypes concerning the Protestant work ethic versus Catholic fecklessness, issues of happiness and satisfaction with life, and broad patterns of sociability (or 'social capital' as it has recently come to be called).

In the past, it was often considered to be an axiom of life in the two parts of Ireland that Protestants were sober, industrious and committed to economic success where Catholics were wayward, easy-going and mired in economic backwardness. Whether or not these old stereotypes were ever true, EVS data show that they have little application to either the Republic or the North today. Direct religious influence on attitudes towards work has diminished and significant Catholic-Protestant differences are rarely found. Where religious influence does show up, it is as likely to arise in a contrast between those with strong religious faith and those with little or none rather than in a contrast between Catholics and Protestants.

People's subjective well-being is also unlikely to vary from one religious denomination to another, but in the particular circumstances of Northern Ireland, it might be thought that civil strife and violence could have cast a shadow over people's feelings of happiness and satisfaction with life. However, in so far as large-scale surveys can measure these things, the European evidence is that prosperous societies – among which both the Republic of Ireland and Northern Ireland are included – provide a benign environment for the pursuit of (subjective) happiness and life satisfaction. Both the Republic and the North score quite highly on the available measures of subjective well-being, as would be predicted by their high levels of GDP per capita. There is little indication in the North that the positive prosperity effect is outweighed to any noticeable degree by a negative effect from the unsettled political environment. These findings would suggest that Northern Ireland is far from being the gloomy place that media reporting of its political problems might lead one to expect.

If people in the Republic of Ireland and Northern Ireland are reasonably satisfied with their lives, they are also reasonably sociable. It has been widely suggested that 'social capital' is in decline in prosperous societies, that is, that the bonds of trust and sociability that bind people together are weakening. Whether or not this trend is present in other societies, there is no consistent evidence that it is occurring in Ireland, North or South. While certain aspects of social capital have shown some decline, both in the Republic and the North, others have either strengthened or remained stable. It is thus difficult to speak of clear-cut movement of social capital in any direction, and not at all justified to speak of unambiguous decline.

Confidence in political trust and participation

There has been much talk of popular disengagement from politics in many developed countries, as evidenced especially by falling turnout at elections. There would be some grounds for expecting disengagement in both the Republic and Northern Ireland too. For example, in the Republic, revelations that have emerged over the past decade of corruption in the planning system and the tribunals of investigation on this and other matters are often said to have tainted the popular perception of politics. In Northern Ireland similar negative effects might be expected from the continued wrangling over the implementation of the Good Friday Agreement. However, there would also be grounds for expecting increased satisfaction with politics, particularly in view of the astonishing success of the economy in the Republic over the past decade and the reduction in political violence in Northern Ireland.

The evidence from the successive rounds of the EVS is that both the Republic and Northern Ireland have long been quite positive about general aspects of the political system in comparison to much of the rest of Europe. Indeed trends in the 1990s, while mixed in some respects, have tended generally to show something of an increase in positive feeling. These features are especially present in the Republic of Ireland, where attitudes towards the political system could be considered almost enthusiastic, especially when set against the glummer attitudes prevailing in many other countries in Europe. The overall level of public confidence in a range of public institutions in the Republic of Ireland is among the highest in Europe, having nudged slightly upwards during the 1990s. Almost two-thirds of people in the Republic are satisfied with the way democracy is developing, compared to less than half in the rest of Europe. Over 40 per cent of people in the Republic think that the system of government today is better than the system of government of ten years ago – double the proportion who think that it is worse. The more common pattern in Europe is the reverse of that in the Republic – more people think that the system of government has worsened than think it has improved over the past ten years.

Northern Ireland has a less positive set of attitudes on these issues but at the same time is by no means particularly negative compared to the rest of Europe. Overall confidence in public institutions is at about the average for Europe and is more or less the same as in Britain. People in Northern Ireland are less satisfied with the way democracy is developing than the average for Europe, but they are more positive in their rating of the system of government and, as in the Republic of Ireland, they are one of the few societies in Europe in which more people think that the system of government has improved than think it has disimproved over the past ten years.

However, as might be expected, the average picture for Northern Ireland is made up of different stances across the main denominational groups, though this is more pronounced on some issues than on others. Catholics have lower levels of confidence in public institutions than do Protestants, though much of the divergence arises in connection with negative Catholic perceptions of the security forces. It is clear from the structure of Catholic attitudes that Northern Catholics think of the security forces in a box apart from other institutions, a feature that is unique to Northern Catholics not only within the island of Ireland but more generally in Europe. In other areas of the state system, such as the health services, confidence among Catholics in the North is reasonably high and is similar to that of Protestants. Northern Catholics' assessment of the UK system of government is less positive than that of Northern Protestants but is not particularly negative compared to the way many populations in Europe rate their own govenments. It is notable in particular that Catholics in Northern Ireland are more likely to give the UK system of government a positive rating than are people in Britain. Northern Catholics are also much more positive about the trend in the system of government than are Northern Protestants – 60 per cent of Catholics think the system of government is better now than it was ten years ago compared to 31 per cent of Protestants. Thus while it might be true to say that Northern Catholics have only limited loyalty towards and identification with the British state, it would be wrong to say that they feel thoroughly disaffected with all aspects of the state system.

Rather, they are quite accepting of many aspects of that system and have become more so over recent years.

Political engagement in Northern Ireland is also reasonably high, and shows less of the fall-off among the young than is found in the Republic. The manner in which political engagement is affected by confidence or lack of confidence in the political system is complex: dissatisfaction with what the system delivers to citizens tends to give rise to higher levels of engagement, while low levels of confidence in political institutions themselves tend to reduce engagement.

Concluding assessment

There is much in the findings of the present study that simply confirms what we already know. In particular, it is no surprise to learn that Northern Ireland is still deeply divided in political terms and that the divide still runs very much along Protestant-Catholic lines. Religious faith may be losing its spiritual hold in the lives of the people, but it still serves as a potent marker of ethnonational difference in Northern Ireland. It was less evident in advance what the corresponding situation in the Republic would be, though again our findings on this question are in line with what many commentators would expect: denominational divisions in identity and political allegiance of the kind found in the North are absent in the Republic. The Protestant minority may not be fully aligned with the majority population in the precise meaning of its sense of Irishness, but for Protestants as for Catholics in the Republic that sense of Irishness is clear and undivided.

The main concern of the study, however, was to place ethnonational divisions against a broader cultural background that encompassed elements of conflict and consensus. Here, the complexity of religion in the cultural life of the island was brought out: religion is a major source of similarity as well as difference. Similarity derives in the first instance from the very fact that religion is still treated with some seriousness in both societies. Northern Ireland and the Republic may be edging towards a post-Christian future, but if so, *edging* may be the appropiate word. They are not rushing to get there – certainly not as fast as other European societies – and the main Christian churches still have a presence in people's lives that is exceptional in Europe. The contrast with Britain, where the post-Christian future has been more fully realised, is particularly striking and highlights the shared distinctiveness created by the extent of religious commitment found in the two parts of Ireland today.

Secondly, a degree of consensus arises in the issue domain in which religious commitment has traditionally exerted much influence, namely, in relation to family and sexual morality. In the past, different approaches to such issues were a cause of divergent views between Catholics and Protestants. Today, the doctrinal standpoints that underpinned those differences have been all but washed away, and now any vestige of a denominational influence is hard to find. However, while people in Ireland both North and South may have thrown off many of the religious influences that so shaped their family and sexual morality in the past, enough of that influence remains to set them off from other countries and make them more similar to each other on certain key moral issues than they are to any other national population in Europe. In so far as differences based on religion now arise in these areas in either part of Ireland, they are based not on denomination but on secularisation, that is, on the degree to which people persist with or abandon their faith.

The evidence in this book does nothing to overturn the prevailing impression of a continued and deep ethno-national conflict in Northern Ireland. It also shows that this conflict is not about religion but rather is one in which religious denomination is the dominant ethnic marker. The evidence confirms that the conflict continues to be expressed in the form of increasingly divergent reactions to the Good Friday Agreement up to and including the most recent year covered by the study (2003).

There are, however, some areas in which the ethno-national conflict in Northern Ireland is softened at the edges, as, for example, in the less monolithic nature of the identity and aspirations of Northern Ireland Catholics. This softening is also evident in how positively Northern Ireland Catholics feel about the UK system of government as of 1999-2000 in comparison to 10 years previously and in the extent to which they acknowledge that they have gained significantly from the Good Friday Agreement. If, however, the conflict were to be seen by the protagonists as a zero-sum game, this perception of benefit by the Catholic/nationalist community could run the risk of stoking further discontent among Protestants and unionists.

Since ethno-national conflict on the island of Ireland is not about religion *per se*, secularisation has done nothing to ease it. But secularisation could play a role in the future in creating cultural divisions that cut across the ethno-national divide and so reduce polarisation. Northern Ireland and the Republic of Ireland are still exceptionally religious compared to the rest of Europe but they have also moved a considerable distance in a secular direction. As a result, they now have a secular-liberal versus religious-conservative divide that was largely absent three or four decades ago. The very fact that that divide is found on both sides of the border and within both traditions in Northern Ireland could, in the future, help it to displace or at least dilute ethno-national tensions with less polarising forms of cultural cleavage.

A second alternative cleavage – left versus right – has been much more talked about but is, in reality, much less evident. Given the historical circumstances, its subordinate role both North and South in the past was, perhaps, inevitable, but there are no signs that it is likely to become any more prominent in the foreseeable future. Once again, what is striking is the degree of similarity in this regard across the two jurisdictions.

The Republic of Ireland and Northern Ireland face both old and new challenges in building inclusive and tolerant societies and there is no doubt that the old challenges facing society in Northern Ireland in this regard are the most pressing and potentially dangerous. However, both societies bring distinct advantages to the task of meeting these challenges. They both enjoy high levels of socio-economic welfare, individual life satisfaction and social capital. As has been repeatedly noted in this book, the two societies and the two traditions are characterised by major similarities as well as by self-evident differences. Put another way, the grounds for consensus within and between the two societies are almost as extensive as the grounds for conflict. Moreover, in managing processes of conflict and consensus, both societies enjoy levels of confidence in political institutions that, relative to other European societies, could be regarded as surprisingly high. In short, looked at from the point of view of social and political culture, there are good reasons to be optimistic about the prospects for positive political developments in Ireland, North and South.

Appendix 1: Data sources

This appendix provides information about the main data sources drawn upon for the present study.

The European Values Study (1981, 1990, 1999-2000). The 1999-2000 wave of the EVS is described briefly in Chapter 1 above and full technical details are available in Halman (2001). Brief accounts of the 1981, 1990 and 1999-2000 waves are available http://www.europeanvalues.nl. The fieldwork for the EVS in 1999-2000 was funded in the Republic of Ireland by American Philanthropies and in Northern Ireland by the Economic and Social Research Council. The core data for the 33 societies participating in the 1999-2000 round are available from the Zentralarchiv in Cologne (Central Archive for Empirical Social Research, University of Cologne) which may be accessed at http://www.gesis.org/en/data_service/topics/50-CD-ROM/index.htm. The full data sets for the Republic of Ireland and Northern Ireland, which contain variables not included in the core data set, are available from the Irish Social Science Data Archive at University College, Dublin (http://www.ucd.ie/issda/). The questionnaires used in the surveys are also available from this source. The Northern Ireland data set is also available from the UK Data Archive at the University of Essex (http://www.data-archive.ac.uk/).

European Social Survey (2002-2003). The ESS is a pan-European survey conducted for the first time in 25 European countries in 2002-2003 (Jowell *et al.*, 2003). This survey is due to be repeated at two-yearly intervals beginning in 2004. The ESS was initiated by the European Science Foundation and is supported by the European Commission's Fifth and Sixth Framework Programme for Research and Technological Development and by national funding agencies. In the Republic of Ireland, national funding came from the Higher Education Authority's PRTLI programme to the Institute for the Study of Social Change, UCD and in Northern Ireland from a grant by the Economic and Social Research Council and additional funding from the Northern Ireland Office of First Minister and Deputy First Minister. Data from the first round of the ESS are currently available from the ESS data website (http://ess.nsd.uib.no). The full data sets for the Republic of Ireland

and Northern Ireland, which contains variables not included in the core data set are available from the Irish Social Science Data Archive at University College, Dublin (http://www.ucd.ie/issda/). The Northern Ireland data set is also available from the UK Data Archive at the University of Essex (http://www.data-archive.ac.uk/).

Eurobarometer Surveys. The Eurobarometer Surveys have been carried out by the European Commission in EU member states since 1972. At least two surveys per year have been fielded since 1975. The surveys deal with a wide range of policy issues of interest to the European Commission, as well as more general social and cultural topics. Data from the surveys may be accessed through the Irish Social Science Data Archive at (http://www.ucd.ie/issda/).

International Social Survey Programme (ISSP) Religion Survey (1998). The ISSP was begun in the mid-1980s by established academic survey organisations in a number of countries with the aim of conducting high quality and directly comparable cross-national surveys of the mass public on selected topics of importance in the social sciences. Since 1984, the membership has grown to thirty-eight nations, including both the Republic of Ireland and Northern Ireland. Each year a drafting committee produces a fifteen-minute questionnaire, which each country appends to its next national survey. The ISSP is normally conducted as a self-completion questionnaire, additional to each organisation's regular social survey. The data are currently available from the Central Archive for Empirical Social Research, University of Cologne (http://www.gesis.org/en/) and various national archives such as the UK Data Archive (UKDA) at the University of Essex (http://www.data-archive.ac.uk/) and the Irish Social Science Data Archive at University College, Dublin (http://www.ucd.ie/issda/).

Loyalty Survey (1968). The principal investigator of this survey was Richard Rose. Funded by the Social Science Research Council in Britain, the data are currently available from the UK Data Archive (UKDA) at the University of Essex (http://www.data-archive.ac.uk).

Northern Ireland Election Survey (1992). The principal investigators of this survey were Sydney Elliott, John Ditch and Edward Moxon-Brown. Funded by the Economic and Social Research Council (ESRC), the data are currently available from the UK Data Archive (UKDA) at the University of Essex (http://www.data-archive.ac.uk/).

Northern Ireland Life and Times Survey (1998-2003). The Northern Ireland Life and Times Survey (NILT) was launched in October 1998. It is an annual survey, which monitors the attitudes of people in Northern Ireland to a wide range of social and political issues. The data, which are publicly available, can be downloaded from the Northern Ireland Social and Political Archive (ARK) website (http://www.ark.ac.uk).

Northern Ireland Referendum and Election Survey (1998). The principal investigators of this survey were John Curtice, Bernadette C. Hayes, Geoffrey Evans and Lizanne Dowds. Carried out immediately after the assembly elections in June 1998, the survey was designed to measure political attitudes and electoral behaviour both at that election and in the previous month's referendum. Funded by the Economic and Social Research Council (ESRC), the data are currently available from the UK Data Archive (UKDA) at the University of Essex (http://www.data-archive.ac.uk/).

Northern Ireland Social Attitudes Survey (1978). The principal investigators of this survey were E. Moxon-Brown in Northern Ireland and Earl E. Davis and Richard Sinnott in the Republic of Ireland. Funded by the Nuffield Foundation, the Ford Foundation, the Committee for Social Science Research in Ireland and the Economic and Social Research Institute (ERSI), Dublin, the data are currently available from the UK Data Archive (UKDA) at the University of Essex (http://www.data-archive.ac.uk/).

Northern Ireland Social Attitudes Surveys (1989-1995). Funded by the Nuffield Foundation and the Northern Ireland Central Community Relations Unit, the data are currently available from the UK Data Archive (UKDA) at the University of Essex (http://www.data-archive.ac.uk/).

Appendix 2:
European Values Study 1999-2000

Questionnaire for Republic of Ireland/Northern Ireland comparative study

Full text of RoI questionnaire plus annexe of questions specific to Northern Ireland

Variable label prefix conventions:

v = core EVS questionnaire item
o = optional EVS questionnaire item
Irl = item for both parts of Ireland
RoI = Republic of Ireland item
Northern Ireland items included separately as annexe

1) Please say, for each of the following, how important it is in your life.

	Very Important	Quite Important	Not Important	Not at all Important	DK	NoAns	
A Work	1	2	3	4	7	9	v1
B Family	1	2	3	4	7	9	v2
C Friends and acquaintances	1	2	3	4	7	9	v3
D Leisure time	1	2	3	4	7	9	v4
E Politics	1	2	3	4	7	9	v5
F Religion	1	2	3	4	7	9	v6

2) When you get together with your friends, would you say you discuss political matters frequently, occasionally or never?

A	Frequently	1	
B	Occasionally	2	
C	Never	3	v7
	Don't Know	7	
	No Answer	9	

SHOW CARD 1

3) I am now going to read out some statements about the environment. For each one read out, can you tell me whether you agree strongly, agree, disagree or strongly disagree? (Read out each statement and code an answer for each)

		Strongly Agree	Agree	Disagree	Strongly Disagree	DK	NoAns	
A	I would give part of my income if I were certain that the money would be used to prevent environmental pollution	1	2	3	4	7	9	v8
B	I would agree to an increase in taxes if the extra money is used to prevent environmental pollution	1	2	3	4	7	9	v9
C	The Government has to reduce environmental pollution but it should not cost me any money	1	2	3	4	7	9	v10

4) Taking all things together, would you say you are:

A	Very Happy	1	
B	Quite Happy	2	
C	Not Very Happy	3	v11
D	Not at all Happy	4	
	Don't Know	7	
	No Answer	9	

SHOW CARD 2

5) Please look carefully at the following list of voluntary organisations and activities and say ...

a) which, if any, do you belong to? (Code all mentioned under (a))

b) which, if any, are you currently doing unpaid voluntary work for? (Code all mentioned under (b))

v12-v29, v30-v47

		A		B	
		Mentioned	**Not Mentioned**	**Mentioned**	**Not Mentioned**
A	Social welfare services for elderly, handicapped or deprived people	1	0	1	0
B	Religious or church organisations	1	0	1	0
C	Education, arts, music or cultural activities	1	0	1	0
D	Trade unions	1	0	1	0
E	Political parties or groups	1	0	1	0
F	Local community action on issues like poverty, employment, housing, racial equality	1	0	1	0
G	Third World development or human rights	1	0	1	0
H	Conservation, the envirnonment, ecology, animal rights	1	0	1	0
I	Professional associations	1	0	1	0
J	Youth work (e.g. scouts, guides, youth clubs etc.)	1	0	1	0
K	Sports or recreation	1	0	1	0
L	Women's groups	1	0	1	0
M	Peace movement	1	0	1	0
N	Voluntary organisations concerned with health	1	0	1	0
O	Other goups	1	0	1	0
	None	1	0	1	0
	Don't Know	1	0	1	0
	No Answer	1	0	1	0

6) I'm going to ask how often you do certain things. For each activity, would you say you do them every week or nearly every week; once or twice a month; only a few times a year; or not at all? (Interviewer: Code 'Not applicable' when respondent is not involved in work, church or club)

v48-v51

		Every Week	**Once or twice a month**	**A few times a year**	**Not at all**	**DK**	**NoAns**	**NAP**
A	Spend time with friends	1	2	3	4	7	9	0
B	Spend time with colleagues from work or your profession outside the workplace	1	2	3	4	7	9	0
C	Spend time with people at your church, mosque or synagogue	1	2	3	4	7	9	0
D	Spend time with people in clubs and voluntary associations (sport, culture, communal)	1	2	3	4	7	9	0

SHOW CARD 3

7) On this list are various groups of people. Could you please indicate any that you would not like to have as neighbours? (Code an answer for each)

		Mentioned	Not Mentioned	
A	People with a criminal record	1	0	v52
B	People of a different race	1	0	v53
C	Left wing extremists	1	0	v54
D	Heavy drinkers	1	0	v55
E	Ring wing extremists	1	0	v56
F	People with large families	1	0	v57
G	Emotionally unstable people	1	0	v58
H	Muslims	1	0	v59
I	Immigrants/foreign workers	1	0	v60
J	People who have AIDS	1	0	v61
K	Drug addicts	1	0	v62
L	Homosexuals	1	0	v63
M	Jews	1	0	v64
N	Gypsies/Romanies	1	0	v65
O	Travellers/itinerants	1	0	Rol1

8) Generally speaking, would you say that most people can be trusted or that you can't be too careful in dealing with people?

A	Most people can be trusted	1	
B	Can't be too careful	2	v66
C	Don't Know	7	
	No Answer	9	

9) Some people feel they have completely free choice and control over their lives, and other people feel that what they do has no real effect on what happens to them. On a scale from 1 to 10, how much freedom of choice and control do you feel you have over the way your life turns out?

1	2	3	4	5	6	7	8	9	10	77	99	
None at all									**A great deal**	**DK**	**NoAns**	v67

10) All things considered, how satisfied are you with your life as a whole these days?

1	2	3	4	5	6	7	8	9	10	77	99	
Dissatisfied									**Satisfied**	**DK**	**NoAns**	v68

SHOW CARD 4

11) Why are there people in Ireland who live in need? Here are four possible reasons. Which one reason do you consider to be most important? (Code one under (a) below)

12) And which reason do you consider to be the second most important? (Code one under (b) below)

		v69	v70
		A	**B**
		Most Important	**Second Most Important**
A	Because they are unlucky	1	1
B	Because of laziness and lack of willpower	2	2
C	Because of injustice in our society	3	3
D	It's an inevitable part of modern progress	4	4
	None of these	5	5
	Don't Know	7	7
	No Answer	9	9

SHOW CARD 5

13) Here are some aspects of a job that people say are important. Please look at them and tell me which ones you personally think are important in a job? (Circle 1 for all mentioned)

		Mentioned	**Not Mentioned**	
A	Good pay	1	0	v71
B	Pleasant people to work with	1	0	v72
C	Not too much pressure	1	0	v73
D	Good job security	1	0	v74
E	Good chances for promotion	1	0	v75
F	A job respected by people in general	1	0	v76
G	Good hours	1	0	v77
H	An opportunity to use initiative	1	0	v78
I	A useful job for society	1	0	v79
J	Generous holidays	1	0	v80
K	Meeting people	1	0	v81
L	A job in which you feel you can achieve something	1	0	v82
M	A responsible job	1	0	v83
N	A job that is interesting	1	0	v84
O	A job that matches one's abilities	1	0	v85
	None of these	1	0	v86

14) Are you yourself employed or not?

Yes	1	→ Go to Q15	
No	2	→ Go to Q17	v87

15) Overall, how satisfied or dissatisfied are you with your job?

1	2	3	4	5	6	7	8	9	10	77	99	0	
Dissatisfied									**Satisfied**	**DK**	**NoAns**	**NAP**	v88

16) How free are you to make decisions in your job? On a scale from 1 to 10 please indicate how much decision-making freedom you feel you have.

1	2	3	4	5	6	7	8	9	10	77	99	0	
None at all									**A great deal**	**DK**	**NoAns**	**NAP**	v89

16a) And how satisfied or dissatisfied are you with your job security? On a scale from 1 to 10 please indicate how satisfied or dissatisfied you are.

1	2	3	4	5	6	7	8	9	10	77	99	0	
Dissatisfied									**Satisfied**	**DK**	**NoAns**	**NAP**	04

ASK ALL

17) How strongly do you agree or disagree with the following statements?

		Agree Strongly	**Agree**	**Neither Agree nor Disagree**	**Disagree**	**Disagree Strongly**	**DK**	**No Ans**	
A	To fully develop your talents, you need to have a job	1	2	3	4	5	7	9	v90
B	It is humiliating to receive money without having to work for it	1	2	3	4	5	7	9	v91
C	People who don't work turn lazy	1	2	3	4	5	7	9	v92
D	Work is a duty towards society	1	2	3	4	5	7	9	v93
E	People should not have to work if they don't want to	1	2	3	4	5	7	9	v94
F	Work should always come first, even if it means less spare time	1	2	3	4	5	7	9	v95

18) Imagine two secretaries, of the same age, doing practically the same job. One finds out that the other earns £30 a week more than she does. The better paid secretary, however, is quicker, more efficient and more reliable at her job.

In your opinion is it fair or not fair that one secretary is paid more than the other?

A	**Fair**	1	
B	**Unfair**	2	v96
	Don't Know	7	
	No Answer	9	

19) People have different ideas about following instruction at work. Some say that one should follow instructions of one's superiors even when one does not fully agree with them. Others say that one should follow one's superior's instructions only when one is convinced that they are right. Which of these two opinions do you agree with?

A	Should follow instructions	1	
B	Must be convinced first	2	
C	Depends	3	v97
	Don't Know	7	
	No Answer	9	

20) Do you agree or disagree with the following statements?

		Agree	Disagree	Neither	DK	NoAns	
A	When jobs are scarce, employers should give priority to Irish people over (non-Irish) immigrants	1	2	3	7	9	v98
B	When jobs are scarce, men have more right to a job than women	1	2	3	7	9	v99

SHOW CARD 6

21) Here are two statements which people sometimes make when discussing good and evil. Of the two which one comes closest to your own point of view?

A There are absolutely clear guidelines about what is good and evil. These always apply to everyone, whatever the circumstances.

B There can never be absolutely clear guidelines about what is good and evil. What is good and evil depends entirely upon the circumstances at the time.

A	**Agree more with statement A**	1	
B	**Agree more with statement B**	2	
C	**Disagree with both**	3	v100
	Don't Know	7	
	No Answer	9	

22) Do you belong to a religious denomination?

Yes	1	→ Go to Q23	v101
No	2	→ Go to Q24a	

23) Which one?

Christian – no denomination	1	→ Go to Q25	
Roman Catholic	2	→ Go to Q25	
Anglican/Church of Ireland/Episcopalian	3	→ Go to Q25	
Baptist	4	→ Go to Q25	
Methodist	5	→ Go to Q25	
Presbyterian	6	→ Go to Q25	
Free Presbyterian	7	→ Go to Q25	
Brethern	8	→ Go to Q25	
URC/Congregational	9	→ Go to Q25	
Other Protestant (WRITE IN)	10	→ Go to Q25	v102
Other Christian denomination (WRITE IN)	11	→ Go to Q25	
Hindu	12	→ Go to Q25	
Jew	13	→ Go to Q25	
Islam/Muslim	14	→ Go to Q25	
Sikh	15	→ Go to Q25	
Buddhist	16	→ Go to Q25	
Other non-christian denomination (WRITE IN)	17	→ Go to Q25	
No Religion	18	→ Go to Q24a	
Don't Know	77	→ Go to Q24a	
Refuse/No Answer	99	→ Go to Q24a	

24a) Were you ever a member of a religious denomination?

Yes	1	→ Go to Q24b	
No	2	→ Go to Q25	v103

24b) Which one?

Christian – no denomination	1	
Roman Catholic	2	
Anglican/Church of Ireland/Episcopalian	3	
Baptist	4	
Methodist	5	
Presbyterian	6	
Free Presbyterian	7	
Brethern	8	
URC/Congregational	9	
Other Protestant (WRITE IN)	10	v104
Other Christian denomination (WRITE IN)	11	
Hindu	12	
Jew	13	
Islam/Muslim	14	
Sikh	15	
Buddhist	16	
Other non-christian denomination (WRITE IN)	17	
No Religion	18	
Don't Know	77	
Refuse/No Answer	99	

25) Apart from weddings, funerals and christenings, about how often do you attend religious services these days?

A	More than once a week	1	
B	Once a week	2	
C	Once a month	3	
D	Christmas/Easter Day	4	
E	Other specific holy days	5	v105
F	Once a year	6	
G	Less often	7	
H	Never, practically never	8	
	Don't Know	77	
	No Answer	99	

26) Apart from weddings, funerals and christenings, about how often did you attend religious services when you were 12 years old?

A	More than once a week	1	
B	Once a week	2	
C	Once a month	3	
D	Christmas/Easter Day	4	
E	Other specific holy days	5	
F	Once a year	6	v106
G	Less often	7	
H	Never, practically never	8	
	Don't Know	77	
	No Answer	99	

27) Do you personally think it is important to hold a religious service for any of the following events?

		Yes	No	DK	NoAns	
A	Birth	1	2	7	9	v107
B	Marriage	1	2	7	9	v108
C	Death	1	2	7	9	v109

28) Independently of whether you go to church or not, would you say you are ...

A	**A religious person**	1	
B	**Not a religious person**	2	
C	**A convinced atheist**	3	v110
	Don't Know	7	
	No Answer	9	

29) Generally speaking, do you think that in Ireland **your** church is/**the** churches are giving adequate answers to ...
(Read out and code one answer for each)

NB: For those belonging to a church or a religious community; ask **YOUR** church/ religious community
For those not belonging to a church or religious community ask: **THE** churches

		Yes	No	DK	NoAns	
A	The moral problems and needs of the individual	1	2	7	9	v111
B	The problems of family life	1	2	7	9	v112
C	People's spiritual needs	1	2	7	9	v113
D	The social problems facing our country today	1	2	7	9	v114
E	The Northern Ireland problem	1	2	7	9	Irl 1

30) Which, if any, of the following do you believe in? (Read out and code one answer for each)

		Yes	No	DK	NoAns	
A	God	1	2	7	9	v115
B	Life after death	1	2	7	9	v116
C	Hell	1	2	7	9	v117
D	Heaven	1	2	7	9	v118
E	Sin	1	2	7	9	v119
F	Telepathy	1	2	7	9	v120

31) Do you believe in re-incarnation, that is, that we are born into this world again?

A	**Yes**	1	
B	**No**	2	v121
	Don't Know	7	
	No Answer	9	

32) Which of these statements comes closest to your beliefs? (Code one answer only)

A	There is a personal God	1	
B	There is some sort of spirit or life force	2	
C	I don't really know what to think	3	v122
D	I don't really think there is any sort of spirit, God or life force	4	
	Don't Know	7	
	No Answer	9	

33) And how important is God in your life? On a scale from 1 to 10 please indicate - 10 means very important and 1 means not at all important.

1	2	3	4	5	6	7	8	9	10	77	99	
None at all									**Very**	**DK**	**NoAns**	v123

34) Do you find that you get comfort and strength from religion or not?

A	**Yes**	1	
B	**No**	2	v124
	Don't Know	7	
	No Answer	9	

35) Do you ever take some moments for prayer, meditation or contemplation or something like that?

A	**Yes**	1
B	**No**	2
	Don't Know	7
	No Answer	9

v125

36) How often do you pray to God outside of religious services? Would you say ....

A	**Every day**	1
B	**More than once a week**	2
C	**Once a week**	3
D	**At least once a month**	4
E	**Several times a year**	5
F	**Less often**	6
G	**Never**	7
	Don't Know	77
	No Answer	99

v126

37) Do you have a lucky charm (such as a mascot or a talisman)?

A	**Yes**	1
B	**No**	2
	Don't Know	7
	No Answer	9

v127

38) Do you believe that a lucky charm such as a mascot or a talisman can protect or help you?

1	2	3	4	5	6	7	8	9	10	77	99	
Definitely not									**Definitely yes**	**DK**	**NoAns**	v128

39) How much do you agree or disagree with each of the following:

v129-132, o12

		Agree Strongly	**Agree**	**Neither Agree nor Disagree**	**Disagree**	**Disagree Strongly**	**DK**	**NoAns**
A	Politicians who do not believe in God are unfit for public office	1	2	3	4	5	7	9
B	Religious leaders should not influence how people vote in elections	1	2	3	4	5	7	9
C	It would be better for Ireland if more people with strong religious beliefs held public office.	1	2	3	4	5	7	9
D	Religious leaders should not influence government decisions	1	2	3	4	5	7	9
E	If a nurse were asked to help perform a legal abortion, she should be allowed to refuse on religious grounds	1	2	3	4	5	7	9

SHOW CARD 7

40) Here is a list of things which some people think make for a successful marriage. Please tell me, for each one, whether you think it is very important, rather important or not very important for a successful marriage? (Read out each item)

		Very	Rather	Not very	DK	NoAns	
A	Faithfulness	1	2	3	7	9	v133
B	An adequate income	1	2	3	7	9	v134
C	Being of the same social background	1	2	3	7	9	v135
D	Mutual respect and appreciation	1	2	3	7	9	v136
E	Shared religious beliefs	1	2	3	7	9	v137
F	Good housing	1	2	3	7	9	v138
G	Agreement on politics	1	2	3	7	9	v139
H	Understanding and tolerance	1	2	3	7	9	v140
I	Living apart from your in-laws	1	2	3	7	9	v141
J	Happy sexual relationship	1	2	3	7	9	v142
K	Sharing household chores	1	2	3	7	9	v143
L	Children	1	2	3	7	9	v144
M	Being willing to discuss the problems that come up between husband and wife	1	2	3	7	9	v145
N	Spending as much time together as possible	1	2	3	7	9	v146
O	Talking a lot about mutual interests	1	2	3	7	9	v147
P	Same ethnic background	1	2	3	7	9	o16

41) If someone were to say that a child needs a home with both a father and a mother to grow up happily, would you tend to agree or disagree?

A	**Tend to agree**	1	
B	**Tend to disagree**	2	v148
	Don't Know	7	
	No Answer	9	

42) Do you think that a woman has to have children in order to be fulfilled or is this not necessary?

A	**Needs children**	1	
B	**Not necessary**	2	v149
	Don't Know	7	
	No Answer	9	

43) Do you agree or disagree with the following statement? (Read out)

	Agree	Disagree	DK	NoAns	
Marriage is an outdated institution	1	2	7	9	v150

44) If a woman wanted to have a child as a single parent, but she didn't want to have a stable relationship with a man, would you approve or disapprove?

A	**Approve**	1	
B	**Disapprove**	2	
C	**Depends**	3	v151
	Don't Know	7	
	No Answer	9	

45) To what extent do you agree or disagree with the following statements?

v152,v153

		Agree Strongly	Agree	Neither Agree nor Disagree	Disagree	Disagree Strongly	DK	NoAns
A	A man has to have children in order to be fulfilled	1	2	3	4	5	7	9
B	A marriage or a long-tem stable relationship is necessary to be happy	1	2	3	4	5	7	9

46) People talk about the changing roles of men and women today. For each of the following statements I read out, can you tell me how much you agree or disagree with each.

v154-v161

		Agree Strongly	Agree	Neither Agree nor Disagree	Disagree	Disagree Strongly	DK	NoAns
A	A working mother can establish just as warm and secure a relationship with her children as a mother who does not work outside the home	1	2	3	4	5	7	9
B	A pre-school child is likely to suffer if his or her mother works outside the home	1	2	3	4	5	7	9
C	A job is alright but what most women really want is a home and children	1	2	3	4	5	7	9
D	Being a housewife is just as fulfilling as working for pay	1	2	3	4	5	7	9
E	Having a job is the best way for a woman to be an independent person	1	2	3	4	5	7	9
F	Both the husband and wife should contribute to the household income	1	2	3	4	5	7	9
G	In general, fathers are as well suited to look after their children as mothers	1	2	3	4	5	7	9
H	Men are less able to handle emotions in relationships than women	1	2	3	4	5	7	9

SHOW CARD 8

47) Which of these two statements do you tend to agree with? (Code one answer only)

A Regardless of what the qualities and faults of one's parents are, one must always love and respect them

B One does not have the duty to respect and love parents who have not earned it by their behaviour and attitudes

A	**Tend to agree with statement A**	1
B	**Tend to agree with statement B**	2
	Don't Know	7
	No Answer	9

v162

SHOW CARD 9

48) Which of the following statements best describes your views about parents' responsibilities to their children? (Code one only)

A	Parents' duty is to do their best for their children even at the expense of their own well-being	1	
B	Parents have a life of their own and should not be asked to sacrifice their own well-being for the sake of their children	2	v163
C	Neither	3	
	Don't Know	7	
	No Answer	9	

SHOW CARD 10

49) Here is a list of qualities which children can be encouraged to learn at home. Which, if any, do you consider to be especially important? Please choose up to five? (Code five only)

		Important	Not Mentioned	
A	Good manners	1	0	v164
B	Independence	1	0	v165
C	Hard work	1	0	v166
D	Feeling of responsibility	1	0	v167
E	Imagination	1	0	v168
F	Tolerance and respect for other people	1	0	v169
G	Thrift, saving money and things	1	0	v170
H	Determination, perseverance	1	0	v171
I	Religious faith	1	0	v172
J	Unselfishness	1	0	v173
K	Obedience	1	0	v174
	Don't Know	1	0	v175
	No Answer	1	0	v176

50) Do you approve or disapprove of abortion under the following circumstances?

v177, v178, Irl2-Irl4

		Approve	Disapprove	DK	NoAns
A	Where the woman is not married	1	2	7	9
B	Where a married couple does not want to have any more children	1	2	7	9
C	Where a married couple cannot afford any more children	1	2	7	9
D	Where there is a strong chance of a serious defect in the baby	1	2	7	9
E	Where the woman has become pregnant as a result of rape	1	2	7	9

SHOW CARD 11

51) Now I'd like you to look at this card. I'm going to read out some different forms of political action that people can take, and I'd like you to tell me, for each one, whether you have actually done any of these things, whether you might do it or would never, under any circumstances, do it.

		Have Done	Might Do	Would Never do	DK	No Ans	
A	Signing a petition	1	2	3	7	9	v179
B	Joining in boycotts	1	2	3	7	9	v180
C	Attending lawful demonstrations	1	2	3	7	9	v181
D	Joining unofficial strikes	1	2	3	7	9	v182
E	Occupying buildings or factories	1	2	3	7	9	v183
F	Helping a political party or candidate at election time	1	2	3	7	9	Irl5

51a) How interested would you say you are in politics?

A	**Very interested**	1	
B	**Somewhat interested**	2	
C	**Not very interested**	3	o17
D	**Not at all interested**	4	
	Don't Know	7	
	No Answer	9	

SHOW CARD 12

52) Which of these two statements comes closest to your own opinion?

A I find that both freedom and equality are important. But if I were to choose one or the other, I would consider personal freedom more important, that is, everyone can live in freedom and develop without hindrance

B Certainly both freedom and equality are important. But if I were to choose one or the other, I would consider equality more important, that is, that nobody is underprivileged and that social class differences are not so strong

A	Agree with statement A	1	
B	Agree with statement B	2	
C	Neither	3	v184
	Don't Know	7	
	No Answer	9	

53) In political matters, people talk of 'the left' and 'the right'. How would you place your views on this scale, generally speaking?

1	2	3	4	5	6	7	8	9	10	77	99	
Left									**Right**	**DK**	**NoAns**	v185

SHOW CARD 13

54) Now I'd like you to tell me your views on various issues. How would you place your views on this scale?

A	1	2	3	4	5	6	7	8	9	10	77	99	v186
	Individuals should take more responsibility for providing for themselves					**The state should take more responsibility to ensure that everyone is provided for**					**DK**	**No Ans**	
B	1	2	3	4	5	6	7	8	9	10	77	99	
	People who are unemployed should have to take any job available or lose their unemployment benefit					**People who are unemployed should have the right to refuse a job they do not want**					**DK**	**No Ans**	v187
C	1	2	3	4	5	6	7	8	9	10	77	99	
	Competition is good. It stimulates people to work hard and develop new ideas					**Competition is harmful. It brings out the worst in people**					**DK**	**No Ans**	v188
D	1	2	3	4	5	6	7	8	9	10	77	99	
	The state should give more freedom to firms					**The state should control firms more effectively**					**DK**	**No Ans**	v189

E	1	2	3	4	5	6	7	8	9	10	77	99	
	Incomes should be made more equal									**There should be greater incentives for individual effort**	**DK**	**NoAns**	o18

F	1	2	3	4	5	6	7	8	9	10	77	99	
	Private ownership of business and industry should be increased									**Government ownership of business and industry should be increased**	**DK**	**NoAns**	o19

SHOW CARD 14

55) There is a lot of talk these days about what Ireland's aims should be for the next ten years. On this card are listed some of the goals to which different people would give top priority. If you had to choose, which of the things on this card would you say is most important? (Code one answer only)

56) And which would be the next most important? (Code one answer only)

		v190 **First Choice**	v191 **Second Choice**
A	Maintaining order in the nation	1	1
B	Giving people more say in important government decisions	2	2
C	Fighting rising prices	3	3
D	Protecting freedom of speech	4	4
	Don't Know	7	7
	No Answer	9	9

SHOW CARD 15

57) Here is a list of various changes in our way of life that might take place in the near future. Please tell me for each one, if it were to happen whether you think it would be a good thing, a bad thing, or don't you mind?

v192-v199

		Good	**Bad**	**Don't Mind**	**DK**	**NoAns**
A	Less emphasis on money and material possessions	1	2	3	7	9
B	Decrease in the importance of work in our lives	1	2	3	7	9
C	More emphasis on the development of technology	1	2	3	7	9
D	Greater emphasis on the development of the individual	1	2	3	7	9
E	Greater respect for authority	1	2	3	7	9
F	More emphasis on family life	1	2	3	7	9
G	A simple and more natural lifestyle	1	2	3	7	9
H	More power to local authorities	1	2	3	7	9

57a) In the long run, do you think the scientific advances we are making will help or harm mankind?

A	**Will help**	1	
B	**Will harm**	2	
C	**Some of each**	3	o25
	Don't Know	7	
	No Answer	9	

SHOW CARD 16

58) Please look at this card and tell me, for each item listed, how much confidence you have in them. Is it a great deal, quite a lot, not very much or none at all?
(Code one answer for each item)

		A great deal	Quite a lot	Not very much	None at all	DK	NoAns	
A	The church	1	2	3	4	7	9	v200
B	The army	1	2	3	4	7	9	v201
C	The education system	1	2	3	4	7	9	v202
D	The press	1	2	3	4	7	9	v203
E	Trade unions	1	2	3	4	7	9	v204
F	The Gardaí	1	2	3	4	7	9	v205
G	The Dáil	1	2	3	4	7	9	v206
H	The Civil service	1	2	3	4	7	9	v207
I	The social welfare system	1	2	3	4	7	9	v208
J	The European Union	1	2	3	4	7	9	v209
L	The United Nations	1	2	3	4	7	9	v210
M	The health care system	1	2	3	4	7	9	v211
N	The justice system	1	2	3	4	7	9	v212
P	The political parties	1	2	3	4	7	9	Irl6

59) On the whole are you very satisfied, rather satisfied, not very satisfied or not at all satisfied with the way democracy is developing in Ireland?

A	**Very satisfied**	1	
B	**Rather satisfied**	2	
C	**Not very satisfied**	3	v213
D	**Not at all satisfied**	4	
	Don't Know	7	
	No Answer	9	

60) People have different views about the system of government in Ireland. Here is a scale for rating the system of government: 1 means very bad; 10 means very good

1	2	3	4	5	6	7	8	9	10	77	99	
Bad									**Very good**	**DK**	**NoAns**	v214

61) Where on this scale would you put the system of government as it was ten years ago?

1	2	3	4	5	6	7	8	9	10	77	99	
Bad									**Very good**	**DK**	**NoAns**	v215

62) I'm going to describe various types of political systems and ask what you think about each as a way of governing Ireland. For each one, would you say it is a very good, fairly good, fairly bad or very bad way of governing this country?

		Very Good	Fairly Good	Fairly Bad	Very Bad	DK	No Ans	
A	Having a strong leader who does not have to bother with parliament and elections	1	2	3	4	7	9	v216
B	Having experts, not government, make decisions according to what they think is best for the country	1	2	3	4	7	9	v217
C	Having the army rule the country	1	2	3	4	7	9	v218
D	Having a democratic political system	1	2	3	4	7	9	v219

63) I'm going to read off some things that people sometimes say about a democratic political system. Could you please tell me if you agree strongly, agree, disagree or disagree strongly, after I read each of them?

		Agree Strongly	Agree	Disagree	Disagree Strongly	DK	No Ans	
A	Democracy may have problems but it's better than any other form of government	1	2	3	4	7	9	v220
B	In a democracy, the economic system runs badly	1	2	3	4	7	9	v221
C	Democracies are indecisive and have too much squabbling	1	2	3	4	7	9	v222
D	Democracies aren't good at maintaining order	1	2	3	4	7	9	v223

64) How much respect is there for individual human rights nowadays in Ireland? Do you feel there is (read out):

A	A lot of respect for individual human rights	1	
B	Some respect	2	
C	Not much respect	3	v224
D	No respect at all	4	
	Don't Know	7	
	No Answer	9	

SHOW CARD 17

64a) In politics, different parties often hold different views. Which do you think is better?

A A party leader should stand firm for what he or she believes, even if others disagree

or

B A party leader should be prepared to cooperate with other groups, even if it means compromising some important beliefs

A	Agree most with statement A	1	
B	Agree most with statement B	2	o31
	Don't Know	7	
	No Answer	9	

SHOW CARD 18

65) Please tell me for each of the following statements whether you think it can always be justified, never be justified, or something in between, using this card. Code one answer for each statement

1	2	3	4	5	6	7	8	9	10	77	99
Never									**Always**	**DK**	**NoAns**

			DK	**NoAns**	
A	Claiming state benefits which you are not entitled to		77	99	v225
B	Cheating on tax if you have the chance		77	99	v226
C	Taking and driving away a car belonging to someone else (joyriding)		77	99	v227
D	Taking the drug marijuana or hashish		77	99	v228
E	Lying in your own interest		77	99	v229
F	Married men/women having an affair		77	99	v230
G	Someone accepting a bribe in the course of their duties		77	99	v231
H	Homosexuality		77	99	v232
I	Abortion		77	99	v233
J	Divorce		77	99	v234
K	Euthanasia (terminating the life of the incurably sick)		77	99	v235
L	Suicide		77	99	v236
M	Throwing away litter in a public place		77	99	v237
N	Driving under the influence of alcohol		77	99	v238
O	Paying cash for services to avoid taxes		77	99	v239
P	Having casual sex		77	99	v240
Q	Smoking in public buildings		77	99	v241
R	Speeding over the limit in built-up areas		77	99	v242
T	Sex under the legal age of consent		77	99	o34
U	Prostitution		77	99	o35
W	Scientific experiments on human embryos		77	99	o37
X	Genetic manipulation of food stuffs		77	99	o38

SHOW CARD 19

66) How many people in Ireland do you think do the following?

		Almost All	**Many**	**Some**	**Almost None**	**DK**	**No Ans**	
A	Claiming state benefits to which they are not entitled	1	2	3	4	7	9	v243
B	Cheating on tax if they have the chance	1	2	3	4	7	9	v244
C	Paying cash for services to avoid taxes	1	2	3	4	7	9	v245
D	Taking the drug marijuana or hashish	1	2	3	4	7	9	v246
E	Throwing away litter in a public place	1	2	3	4	7	9	v247
F	Speeding over the limit in built-up areas	1	2	3	4	7	9	v248
G	Driving under the influence of alcohol	1	2	3	4	7	9	v249
H	Having casual sex	1	2	3	4	7	9	v250

SHOW CARD 20

67) Which of these geographical groups would you say you belong to **first of all**?

68) And the **next**?

69) And which do you belong to **least of all**?

		v251 **Q67 First**	v252 **Q68 Next**	v253 **Q69 The Least**
A	Locality or town where you live	1	1	1
B	County where you live	2	2	2
C	Your country as a whole	3	3	3
D	Europe	4	4	4
E	The world as a whole	5	5	5
	Don't Know	7	7	7
	No Answer	9	9	9

SHOW CARD 21

70a) Most people think of themselves in terms of some national identity, such as American or French or German. In these terms, how do you usually think of yourself?

A	Irish	1	
B	Other (WRITE IN)	2	RoI2
	Don't Know	7	
	No Answer	9	

70b) Could you tell me how important it is to you that you are Irish/other?

1	2	3	4	5	6	7	8	9	10	77	99	
Not Important								**Very Important**		**DK**	**NoAns**	RoI3

70c) Are you a citizen of the Republic of Ireland?

A	Yes	1	→ Go to Q70d	
B	No	2	→ Go to Q71a	v254
	Don't Know	7		
	No Answer	9		

70d) How proud are you to be an Irish citizen?

A	Very Proud	1	
B	Quite Proud	2	
C	Not very Proud	3	
D	Not at all Proud	4	v255
	Don't Know	7	
	No Answer	9	
	Not Applicable	0	

SHOW CARD 22

70e) Some people say the following things are important for being truly Irish. Others say they are not important. How important do you think each of the following is?

		Very Important	Fairly Important	Not very Important	Not at all Important	Can't Choose	
A	To have been born in Ireland	1	2	3	4	7	RoI4
B	To have Irish citizenship	1	2	3	4	7	RoI5
C	To have lived in Ireland for most of one's life	1	2	3	4	7	RoI6
D	To respect Ireland's political institutions and laws	1	2	3	4	7	RoI7
E	To be able to speak Irish	1	2	3	4	7	RoI8
F	To feel Irish	1	2	3	4	7	RoI9
G	To be a Catholic	1	2	3	4	7	RoI10

Ask all

71a) Do you ever think of yourself as European?

A	**Yes**	1	→ Go to Q71b	Irl7
B	**No**	2	→ Go to Q72	

71b) On a scale from 1 to 10 could you tell me how important it is to you that you are European?

1	2	3	4	5	6	7	8	9	10	77	99	
Not Important								**Very Important**		**DK**	**NoAns**	Irl8

SHOW CARD 23

72) If there was a general election tomorrow, which political party would you be most likely to vote for?

Fianna Fáil	1	→ Go to Q74	
Fine Gael	2	→ Go to Q74	
Labour	3	→ Go to Q74	
Progressive Democrats	4	→ Go to Q74	
Sinn Féin	5	→ Go to Q74	
Green Party	6	→ Go to Q74	v256
Independent	7	→ Go to Q74	
Other political party (Specify)	8	→ Go to Q74	
I would not vote	96	→ Go to Q74	
I would cast a blank ballot	97	→ Go to Q74	
Response refused	99	→ Go to Q74	
Don't Know	77	→ Go to Q73	

SHOW CARD 23

73) If don't know in (a): Do you think of yourself as a little closer to one political party than the others?

Fianna Fáil	1	
Fine Gael	2	
Labour	3	
Progressive Democrats	4	
Sinn Féin	5	
Green Party	6	v257
Independent	7	
Other political party (Specify)	8	
I would not vote	96	
I would cast a blank ballot	97	
Response refused	99	
Don't Know	77	

SHOW CARD 24

74) How about people from less developed countries coming here to work? Which one of the following do you think the government should do?

A	Let anyone come who wants to	1	
B	Let people come as long as there are jobs available	2	
C	Put strict limits on the number of foreigners who can come here	3	v258
D	Prohibit people coming here from other countries	4	
	Don't Know	7	
	No Answer	9	

SHOW CARD 25

75) Which of these statements is the nearest to your opinion?

A	For the greater good of society it is better if immigrants maintain their distinct customs and traditions	1	
B	For the greater good of society it is better if immigrants do not maintain their distinct customs and traditions but take on the customs of the country	2	v259
	Don't Know	7	
	No Answer	9	

SHOW CARD 26

76) In order to be considered "just", what should a society provide? Please tell me for each statement how important or unimportant it is to you. 1 means very important; 5 means not important at all.

		Very Important			Not at all Important		DK	No Ans	
A	Eliminating big inequalities in income between citizens	1	2	3	4	5	7	9	v260
B	Guaranteeing that basic needs are met for all, in terms of food, housing, clothes, education, health	1	2	3	4	5	7	9	v261
C	Recognising people on their merits	1	2	3	4	5	7	9	v262

77) How often do you follow politics in the news on television or on the radio or in the papers?

A	Every day	1
B	Several times a week	2
C	Once or twice a week	3
D	Less often	4
E	Never	5
	Don't Know	7
	No Answer	9

v263

78) To what extent do you agree or disagree with the following statements?

v264, v265

		Agree Strongly	Agree	Neither Agree nor Disagree	Disagree	Disagree Strongly	DK	No Ans
A	If someone has information that may help justice be done, generally he or she should give it to authorities	1	2	3	4	5	7	9
B	People should stick to their own affairs and not show too much interest in what others say or do	1	2	3	4	5	7	9

79) To what extent do you feel concerned about the living conditions of:

		Very Much	Much	To a certain extent	Not so much	Not at all	DK	No Ans	
A	Your immediate family	1	2	3	4	5	7	9	v266
B	People in your neighbourhood	1	2	3	4	5	7	9	v267
C	The people of the county you live in	1	2	3	4	5	7	9	v268
D	Your fellow countrymen and women	1	2	3	4	5	7	9	v269
E	Europeans	1	2	3	4	5	7	9	v270
F	Human kind	1	2	3	4	5	7	9	v271

80) To what extent do you feel concerned about the living conditions of:

		Very Much	Much	To a certain extent	Not so much	Not at all	DK	No Ans	
A	Elderly people in your country	1	2	3	4	5	7	9	v272
B	Unemployed people in your country	1	2	3	4	5	7	9	v273
C	Immigrants in your country	1	2	3	4	5	7	9	v274
D	Sick and disabled people in your country	1	2	3	4	5	7	9	v275

81) Would you be prepared to do something practical to improve the conditions of:

v276-v280

		Absolutely Yes	Yes	Maybe Yes/ maybe No	No	Absolutely No	DK	No Ans
A	Your immediate family	1	2	3	4	5	7	9
B	People in your neighbourhood / community	1	2	3	4	5	7	9
C	Elderly people in your country	1	2	3	4	5	7	9
D	Immigrants in your country	1	2	3	4	5	7	9
E	Sick and disabled people in your country	1	2	3	4	5	7	9

Now, I would like to ask you some questions about the current political situation in Northern Ireland

82) Do you think the long-term policy for Northern Ireland should be for it

Irl9

To remain part of the United Kingdom	1
Or, to reunify with the rest of Ireland	2
Independent state	3
Other answer (WRITE IN)	4
Don't Know	7
Refused / No Answer	9

83) How much say do you think a Westminster government of any party should have in the way Northern Ireland is run? Do you think it should have

Irl10

A great deal of say	1
Some say	2
A little say	3
No say at all	4
Don't Know	7
Refused / No Answer	9

84) And, how much say do you think an Irish government of any party should have in the way Northern Ireland is run? Do you think it should have

Irl11

A great deal of say	1
Some say	2
A little say	3
No say at all	4
Don't Know	7
Refused / No Answer	9

SHOW CARD 27

85) There has been much discussion recently about some of the suggested constitutional and executive changes proposed in the Good Friday Agreement of last year. Looking at a list of some of these changes on this card, could you tell me how you feel about each one?

Irl12-Irl19

	Support Strongly	**Support**	**Neither Support nor Oppose**	**Oppose**	**Oppose Strongly**	**DK**	**No Ans**
The guarantee that Northern Ireland will remain part of the UK for as long as a majority of people in Northern Ireland wish it to be so	1	2	3	4	5	7	9
The creation of North-South bodies	1	2	3	4	5	7	9
The establishment of a Northern Ireland assembly	1	2	3	4	5	7	9
The requirement that the new Executive be based on power-sharing	1	2	3	4	5	7	9
The removal of the Republic of Ireland's constitutional claim to Northern Ireland	1	2	3	4	5	7	9
Reform of the RUC	1	2	3	4	5	7	9
The de-commissioning of paramilitary weapons	1	2	3	4	5	7	9
The release of paramilitary prisoners	1	2	3	4	5	7	9

86) Now, thinking about the reasons why some Loyalist groups have used violence during the troubles, would you say that you have any sympathy with the reasons for violence, even if you don't condone the violence itself? Would you say you have

A lot of sympathy	1
A little sympathy	2
Or, No sympathy at all?	3
Don't Know	7
Refused / No Answer	9

Irl20

87) And thinking about the reasons why some Republican groups have used violence during the troubles, would you say that you have any sympathy with the reasons for violence, even if you don't condone the violence itself? Would you say you have

A lot of sympathy	1
A little sympathy	2
Or, No sympathy at all?	3
Don't Know	7
Refused / No Answer	9

Irl21

88) Finally, here are some statements that people sometimes make about the situation in Northern Ireland. For each statement could you tell me whether you agree or disagree?

Irl22-Irl24

	Strongly Agree	Agree	Neither Agree nor Disagree	Disagree	Strongly Disagree	DK	No Ans
There will never be peace in Northern Ireland until partition is ended	1	2	3	4	5	7	9
On the whole, the British treat Catholics and Protestants equally in Northern Ireland	1	2	3	4	5	7	9
The British government should declare its intention to withdraw from Northern Ireland at a fixed date in the future	1	2	3	4	5	7	9

89a) What is the name of the current Taoiseach?

WRITE IN NAME:	
Don't know	7
Refused	9

Rol13

89b) And can you name the current Minister for Finance?

WRITE IN NAME:	
Don't know	7
Refused	9

Rol14

89c) How many seats are there in the Dáil, in other words, how many TDs are there?

WRITE IN no. of seats/TDs:	
Don't know	7
Refused	9

Rol15

89d) How many member states are there in the European Union?

WRITE IN no. of member states:	
Don't know	7
Refused	9

Rol16

DEMOGRAPHICS: ASK ALL RESPONDENTS

90a) Sex of respondent

A	Male	1	v291
B	Female	2	

90b) Have you ever lived outside the Republic of Ireland for more than six months?

A	Yes	1	
B	No	2	Irl25
	Refused / No Answer	9	

91) Can you tell me your year of birth, please 19____ v292

92a) What is your current marital status?

A	Married	1	→ Go to Q92b	
B	Living as married	2	→ Go to Q92c	
C	Widowed	3	→ Go to Q93	v294
D	Separated	4	→ Go to Q93	
E	Divorced	5	→ Go to Q94	
F	Never married	6	→ Go to Q94	
	Refused/No Answer	9		

92b) Did you live with your spouse before you got married?

A	Yes	1	Irl26
B	No	2	

92c) Is your husband/wife/partner the same religion as you?

A	Yes, same religion	1	
B	No, not same religion	2	
	Don't Know	7	Irl27
	Refused / No Answer	9	
	Not applicable (e.g. resp. has no religion)	0	

93) Have you ever been divorced?

A	Yes	1	
B	No	2	v297
	Refused / No Answer	9	

94) How many children, including deceased children, have you yourself ever had?
.... (write in) | | | v298

95) How many people, including yourself, are currently living in your household?

A	Aged 18 and over			v299
B	Aged between 13 and 17			v300
C	Aged between 5 and 12			v301
D	Under 5			v302

96) At what age did you (or will you) complete your full time education, either at school or at an institution of higher education? Please exclude apprenticeships. (Interviewer instruction: If respondent is still at school, ask: at what age do you expect you will have completed your education?) (Write in age) ....

		Years old	v303

SHOW CARD 28

97) What is the highest qualification level you have reached in your education to date (code one only)?

Higher degree	1	
Primary degree or equivalent	2	
Diploma or equivalent from university or RTC	3	
VPT or Post Leaving Cert (PLC)	4	
Completed Leaving Cert or equivalent	5	
Completed Inter/Group/Junior Cert	6	v304
Some 2nd level, no exams completed	7	
Primary Cert or equivalent	8	
Did not finish primary	9	
Special school	10	
No answer	99	

98) Do you live with your parents (EXCLUDE in-laws)?

A	Yes (with both parents)	1	
B	Yes (with one parent)	2	
C	No	3	v305
	Don't Know	7	
	No Answer	9	
	Not Applicable	0	

99a) What is you current employment status?

At work; employee	1	→ Go to Q99b	
At work; self-employed (including farming)	2	→ Go to Q99b	
At work; On Govt training/community employment scheme	3	→ Go to Q99b	
Unemployed	4	→ Go to Q99c	Irl28
Retired / Pensioned	5	→ Go to Q100	
Home duties not otherwise employed	6	→ Go to Q106	
Student	7	→ Go to Q106	
Other (please specify)	9	→ Go to Q106	
Don't Know	77		
No Answer	99		

99b) If currently employed, how many hours a week do you work?

A	30 hours a week or more	1	→ Go to Q100	
B	Less than 30 hours a week	2	→ Go to Q100	Irl29
	Don't Know	7		
	No Answer	9		

99c) If currently unemployed, for how long have you been unemployed (current spell)?

A	Less than half a year	1
B	Between half a year and one year	2
C	One year	3
D	Between one and two years	4
E	Two years	5
F	More than two years	6
	Don't know	7
	No answer	9
	Not applicable	0

v314

100) In your job, do you or did you supervise anyone who is directly responsible to you?

A	Yes	1	
B	No	2	→ Go to 102
	Don't Know	7	
	No Answer	9	

v307

101) How many people do you or did you supervise? ...... (write in number)

v308

102) How many other people usually work for your organisation? .... (write in number)

v309

103) Please describe, as fully as possible, the nature of the job you do. If a civil servant, in the army or Gardaí, please give rank. If a farmer, please state acreage and broad type of farming undertaken (eg dairying, dry-stock, mixed, etc.)

.... v311

If farmer, write in number of acres

acres Irl30

104) Please describe the nature of the business in which you work

.... v30X

106) Are you the chief wage earner in your household?

A	Yes	1	→ Go to Q111
B	No	2	→ Go to Q107

v315

107) Is the chief wage earner employed now or not?

A	Yes	1
B	No	2
	Don't Know	7
	No Answer	9
	Not Applicable	0

v316

108) Please describe, as fully as possible, the nature of the job you do. If a civil servant, in the army or Gardaí, please give rank. If a farmer, please state acreage and broad type of farming undertaken (eg dairying, dry-stock, mixed, etc.) In which profession/industry does/did he (she) work? (Write in)

.... v317

If farmer, what is the size of his/her farm? (Write in number of acres)

				acres

lrl31

109) And, what is/was the nature of the business in which he/she worked?

.... v31X

ASK ALL

SHOW CARD 29

111) Here is a range of incomes and we would like to know in what group your household is, counting all wages, salaries, pensions and other incomes that come in. Just give the number of the group your household falls into, after taxes, social welfare and other deductions.

Under £3,000 per annum (less than £60 per week)	1
£3,000 – £3,999 per annum (£60 - £80 per week)	2
£4,000 – £6,999 per annum (£80 - £135 per week)	3
£7,000 – £9,999 per annum (£135 - £195 per week)	4
£10,000 – £14,999 per annum (£195 - £290 per week)	5
£15,000 – £19,999 per annum (£290 - £385 per week)	6
£20,000 – £25,999 per annum (£385 - £500 per week)	7
£26,000 – £29,999 per annum (£500 - £580 per week)	8
£30,000 – £39,999 per annum (£580 - £770 per week)	9
£40,000 + per annum (£770+ per week)	10
Don't Know	77
No Answer	99

v320

112) Size of area of residence

Open countryside	1
Village/Town Under 2,000	2
2,000 – 4,999	3
5,000 – 9,999	4
10,000 – 19,999	5
20,000 – 49,999	6
50,000 – 99,999	7
100,000 – 499,999	8
500,000 and more	9
Don't Know	77
No Answer	99

v322

Questions specific to Northern Ireland questionnaire

SHOW CARD 30

70a) Looking at this card, could you please tell which of these best describes the way you think of yourself?

A	British	1
B	Irish	2
C	Ulster	3
D	Sometimes British and sometimes Irish	4
E	Northern Irish	5
G	Other (WRITE IN)	6
	Don't Know	7
	No Answer	9

70b) Could you tell me how important it is to you that you are (British/Irish/Ulster/British Irish/Northern Irish)?

1	2	3	4	5	6	7	8	9	10	77	99
Not Important								**Very Important**		**DK**	**NoAns**

SHOW CARD 31a

70c) Some people say the following things are important for being truly British. Others say they are not important. How important do you think each of the following is?

	Very Important	**Fairly Important**	**Not very Important**	**Not at all Important**	**Can't Choose**
A To have been born in the UK	1	2	3	4	7
B To have British citizenship	1	2	3	4	7
C To have lived in the country for most of ones' life	1	2	3	4	7
D To respect its political institutions and laws	1	2	3	4	7
E To be able to speak English	1	2	3	4	7
F To be Protestant	1	2	3	4	7
G To feel British	1	2	3	4	7

SHOW CARD 22b

70d) Some people say the following things are important for being truly Irish. Others say they are not important. How important do you think each of the following is?

	Very Important	Fairly Important	Not very Important	Not at all Important	Can't Choose
A To have been born in Ireland	1	2	3	4	7
B To have Irish citizenship	1	2	3	4	7
C To have lived in the country for most of one's life	1	2	3	4	7
D To respect its political institutions and laws	1	2	3	4	7
E To be able to speak Irish	1	2	3	4	7
F To be Catholic	1	2	3	4	7
G To feel Irish	1	2	3	4	7

70e) Do you ever think of yourself as European?

A	**Yes**	1	➔ Go to Q70f
B	**No**	2	➔ Go to Q70g

70f) On a scale from 1 to 10 could you tell me how important it is to you that you are European?

1	2	3	4	5	6	7	8	9	10	77	99
Not Important								**Very Important**		**DK**	**NoAns**

70g) Generally speaking, do you think of yourself as a unionist, a nationalist or neither?

A	Unionist	1	➔ Go to Q70h
B	Nationalist	2	➔ Go to Q70h
C	Neither	3	➔ Go to Q71a
	Don't Know	7	
	No Answer	9	

70h) If Unionist or Nationalist would you call yourself a very strong (unionist/nationalist), fairly strong, or not very strong?

A	Very Strong	1
B	Fairly Strong	2
C	Not Very Strong	3
	Don't Know	7
	No Answer	9
	Not Applicable	0

71a) Individuals in Northern Ireland are entitled to claim both British and Irish citizenship.
In terms of your own personal choice, do your regard yourself as a citizen of Britain, the Republic of Ireland, or both Britain and the Republic of Ireland?

A	Britain	1	
B	Republic of Ireland	2	
C	Or, both Britain and the Republic of Ireland?	3	
D	Other (WRITE IN)	4	➔ Go to Q72
	Don't Know	7	➔ Go to Q72
	No Answer	9	➔ Go to Q72

71b) How proud are you of this [British/Irish/Joint] citizenship?

A	Very Proud	1
B	Quite Proud	2
C	Not very Proud	3
D	Not at all Proud	4
	Don't Know	7
	No Answer	9
	Not Applicable	0

SHOW CARD 32

72) If there was an election tomorrow in which only Northern Ireland parties were standing which political party would you be most likely to vote for?

Ulster Unionist Party (UUP)	1	→ Go to Q74
Social Democratic and Labour Party (SDLP)	2	→ Go to Q74
Democratic Unionist Party (DUP)	3	→ Go to Q74
Alliance Party	4	→ Go to Q74
Sinn Féin	5	→ Go to Q74
Progressive Unionist Party (PUP)	6	→ Go to Q74
Ulster Democratic Party (UDP)	7	→ Go to Q74
UK Unionist Party	8	→ Go to Q74
Women's Coalition	9	→ Go to Q74
Worker's Party	10	→ Go to Q74
Green Party	11	→ Go to Q74
Other political party (SPECIFY)	12	→ Go to Q74
I would not vote	96	→ Go to Q74
I would cast a blank ballot	97	→ Go to Q74
Response refused	99	→ Go to Q74
Don't Know	77	→ Go to Q73

SHOW CARD 23

73) If don't know in (a): Do you think of yourself as a little closer to one political party than the others?

Ulster Unionist Party (UUP)	1
Social Democratic and Labour Party (SDLP)	2
Democratic Unionist Party (DUP)	3
Alliance Party	4
Sinn Féin	5
Progressive Unionist Party (PUP)	6
Ulster Democratic Party (UDP)	7
UK Unionist Party	8
Women's Coalition	9
Worker's Party	10
Green Party	11
Other political party (SPECIFY)	12
I would not vote	96
I would cast a blank ballot	97
Response refused	99
Don't Know	77

References

Acheson, A., 2002. *A History of the Church of Ireland 1691-2001.* The Columba Press and APCK, Dublin.

Akenson, D.H., 1988. *Small Differences. Irish Catholics and Irish Protestants,* 1815-1922: *an International Perspective.* McGill-Queen's University Press, Kingston and Montreal.

Ashford, S. and Timms, N., 1992. *What Europe Thinks.* Aldershot, Darmouth.

Aughey, A., 2002. 'The Art of Political Lying in Northern Ireland.' *Irish Political Studies.* 17: 1-16.

Baker, K., Dalton, R. and Hildebrandt, K., 1981. *Germany Transformed: Political Culture and the New Politics.* Harvard University Press, Cambridge.

Bartolini, S. and Mair, P., 1990. *Identity, Competition and Electoral Availability: The Stabilisation of European Electorates 1885-1985.* Cambridge University Press, Cambridge.

Bellah, R.N., 1975. *The Broken Covenant.* University of Chicago Press, Chicago.

Bew, P., Gibbon, P. and Patterson, H., 1995. *Northern Ireland 1921-1994: Political Forces and Social Classes.* Sherif, London.

Biever, B.F., 1976. *Religion, Culture, and Values. A Cross-Cultural Analysis of Motivational Factors in Native Irish and American Irish Catholicism.* Arno Press, New York.

Bowen, K., 1983. *Protestants in a Catholic State. Ireland's Privileged Minority.* Gill & Macmillan, Dublin; McGill-Queen's University Press, Kingston.

Bradley, J., 1999. 'The history of economic development in Ireland, north and south,' *in Ireland North and South. Perspectives from Social Science,* A.F. Heath, R. Breen and C.T. Whelan (eds.), Oxford University Press, Oxford.

Breen, R. and Devine, P., 1999. 'Segmentation and Social Structure,' in *Politics in Northern Ireland,* P. Mitchello and R. Wilford (eds.), Westview Press, Colorado, pp. 52-65.

Breen, R. and Hayes, B.C., 1996. 'Religious Mobility in the UK', *Journal of the Royal Statistical Society,* Vol. 159, Series A, pp. 493-504.

Breen, R., 1996. 'Who Wants a United Ireland? Constitutional Preferences Among Catholics and Protestants,' in *Social Attitudes in Northern Ireland: The Fifth Report,* R. Breen, P. Devine and L. Dowds (eds.), Blackstaff, Belfast, pp. 33-48.

Breen, R. and Hayes, B.C., 1997. 'Religious Mobility and Party Support in Northern Ireland', *European Sociological Review*, Vol. 13, no. 3, pp. 225-239.

Brewer, J.D. and Higgins, G.I., 1998. *Anti-Catholicism in Northern Ireland 1600-1998.* Gill & Macmillan, London.

Brinkerhoff, M.B. and Mackie, M.M., 1993. 'Casting Off the Bonds of Organized Religion: A Religious Careers Approach to the Study of Apostasy', *Review of Religious Research*, Vol. 34, pp. 235-258.

Bronchi, C. and de Kam, F., 1999. 'The Income Taxes People Really Pay.' *OECD Observer*, April 2, 1999.

Bruce, S., 1986. *God Save Ulster! The Religion and Politics of Paisleyism.* Oxford University Press, Oxford.

Bruce, S., 1999. *Choice & Religion: A Critique of Rational Choice.* Oxford University Press, Oxford.

Bruce, S., 2002. *God is Dead: Secularization in the West.* Blackwell, Oxford.

Cairns, E., 1991. 'Is Northern Ireland a Conservative Society?' in *Social Attitudes in Northern Ireland*, P. Stringer and G. Robinson (eds.), Blackstaff, Belfast.

Central Statistics Office, 2003. *Census 2002. Principal Demographic Results.* Stationery Office, Dublin.

Christoph, B. and Noll, H-H., 2003. 'Subjective well-being in the European Union during the 90s.' *Social Indicators Research.* 64: 521-546.

Clark, N.E., 1986. 'The Future of Antitrust Enforcement', *Antitrust Bulletin*, Vol. 31, pp. 401-408.

Clarke, H.D., Kronberg, A., McIntyre, C., Bauer-Kaase, P. and Kaase, M., 1999. 'The effect of economic priorities on the measurement of value change: new experimental evidence', *American Political Science Review*, Vol. 93, pp. 637-647.

Coakley, J., 2002. 'Religion, National Identity and Political Change in Modern Ireland', *Irish Political Studies*, Vol. 17, pp. 4-28.

Coleman, D., 1999. 'Demography and Migration in Ireland, North and South,' in *Ireland North and South: Perspectives from Social Science,* A.F. Heath, R. Breen & C.T. Whelan (eds.), Oxford University Press, Oxford, pp. 69-116.

Compton, P., 1995. *Demographic Review, Northern Ireland.* Northern Ireland Economic Council, Belfast.

Conrad, K., 1999. 'Women Troubles, Queer Troubles: Gender, Sexuality, and the Politics of Selfhood in the Construction of the Northern Irish States,' in *Reclaiming Gender: Transgressive Identities in Modern Ireland,* M. Cohen and N.J. Curtin (eds.), Macmillan, London, pp. 53-68.

Corish, P.J., 1985. *The Irish Catholic Experience.* Gill & Macmillan, Dublin.

Coulter, C., 1994. 'The Character of Unionism', *Irish Political Studies*, Vol. 9, pp. 1-24.

Coulter, C., 1999. *Contemporary Northern Irish Society. An Introduction.* Pluto Press, London.

Dalton, R.J., 1996. *Citizen Politics: Public Opinion and Political Parties in Advanced Western Democracies* (2nd edn.). Chatham House, New Jersey.

Dalton, R.J., 1999. 'Political Support in Advanced Industrial Democracies,' in *Critical Citizens: Global Support for Democratic Governance*, P. Norris (ed.), Oxford University Press, Oxford, pp. 57-77.

Davie, G., 1992. 'God and Caeser: Religion in a Rapidly Changing Europe,' in *Social Europe*, J. Bailey (ed.), Longman, London, pp. 216-238.

Davie, G., 1994. *Religion in Britain since 1945.* Blackwell, Oxford.

Davis, D.W. and Davenport, C., 1999. 'Assessing the validity of the Postmaterialism index', *American Political Science Review,* Vol. 93, pp. 649-664.

Davis, E.E. and Sinnott, R., 1979. *Attitudes in the Republic of Ireland Relevant to the Northern Ireland Problem.* Economic and Social Research Institute, Dublin. Working Paper No. 97.

Davies, C. and Downey, A., 1993. 'Women's Rights or Responsibilities? Reconciling the Demands of Home and Work,' in *Social Attitudes: The Third Report*, P. Stringer and G. Robinson (eds.), Blackstaff, Belfast, pp. 49-64.

De Graaf, N.D. and Need, A., 2000. 'Losing Faith: Is Britain Alone?,' in *British Social Attitudes: The 17th report: Focusing on Diversity,* R. Jowell *et al.* (eds.), Sage, London, pp. 119-135.

de Moor, R., 1993. 'Epilogue,' in *The Individualizing Society. Value Change in Europe and North America,* P. Ester, L. Halman and R. de Moor (eds.), Tilburg University Press, Tilburg.

Diener, E., Suh, E.M., Lucas, R.E. and Smith, H.L., 1999. 'Subjective Well-Being: Three Decades of Progress', *Psychological Bulletin,* Vol. 125, no. 2, pp. 276-302.

Diener, E. and Suh, E.M., 2000. *Culture and Subjective Well-Being.* MIT Press, Cambridge Mass. and London.

Diener, E., 2000. 'Subjective Well-Being. The Science of Happiness and a Proposal for a National Index', *American Psychologist,* Vol. 55, no. 1, pp. 34-43.

Dixon, P., 2001. *Northern Ireland: The Politics of War and Peace.* Palgrave, Basingstoke.

Dobbelaere, K., 1985. 'Secularization Theories and Sociological Paradigms: A Reformulation of the Private-Public Dichotomy and the Problems of Social Integration', *Sociological Analysis,* Vol. 46, pp. 377-387.

Dobbelaere, K., 1987. 'Some Trends in European Sociology of Religion: The Secularization Debate', *Sociological Analysis,* Vol. 48, pp. 107-137.

Dobbelaere, K., 1993. 'Church Involvement and Secularization: Making Sense of the European Case,' in *Secularization, Rationalism and Sectarianism,* E. Barker, J.A. Beckford and K.

Dobbelaere (eds.), Clarendon Press, Oxford, pp. 19-36.

Duffy, M. and Evans, G., 1997. 'Class, Community Polarisation and Politics,' in *British Social Attitudes: The 7th Report,* R. Jowell *et al.* (eds.), Gower, Aldershot, pp. 102-136.

Dunlap, R.E. and Scarce, R., 1991. 'The Polls – Poll Trends: Environmental Problems and Protection.' *Public Opinion Quarterly.* 55: 651-672.

Dutch, R. and Taylor, M.F., 1993, 'Postmaterialism and the economic condition', *American Journal of Political Science,* Vol. 37, pp. 747-779.

Elliott, M., 2000. *The Catholics of Ulster.* Penguin, London.

Ester, P., Halman, L. and de Moor, R., 1993. *The Individualizing Society. Value Change in Europe and North America.* Tilburg University Press, Tilburg.

Evans, G., 1993. 'Is Gender on the "New Agenda"? A Comparative Analysis of Inequality Between Men and Women.' *European Journal of Political Research.* 24: 135-158.

Evans, G. and Duffy, M., 1997. 'Beyond the Sectarian Divide: The Social Bases and Political Consequences of Unionist and Nationalist Party Competition in Northern Ireland', *British Journal of Political Science,* Vol. 27, pp. 47-81.

Evans, G. and Sinnott, R., 1999. 'Political Cleavages and Party Alignments in Ireland, North and South,' in *Ireland North and South: Perspectives from Social Science,* A.F. Heath, R. Breen and C.T. Whelan (eds.), Oxford University Press, Oxford, pp. 419-456.

Fahey, T., 1992. 'Catholicism and Industrial Society in Ireland,' in *The Development of Industrial Society in Ireland,* J.H. Goldthorpe and C.T. Whelan (eds.), Oxford University Press, Oxford, pp. 241-263.

Fahey, T., 1999. 'Religion and Sexual Culture in Ireland,' in *Sexual Cultures in Europe, National Histories,* F.X. Eder, L. Hall & G. Hekma (eds.), Manchester University Press, Manchester, pp. 53-70.

Fahey, T., 2002. 'Is atheism increasing? Ireland and Europe compared,' in *Measuring Ireland: Discerning Values and Beliefs,* E.G. Cassidy (ed.), Veritas, Dublin, pp. 46-66.

Fahey, T. and Russell, H., 2001. *Family Formation in Ireland. Trends, Data Needs and Implications.* Policy Research Series No. 43, Economic and Social Research Institute, Dublin.

Fahey, T. and Smyth, E., 2004. 'Do subjective indicators measure welfare? Evidence from 33 European societies.' *European Societies.* 6, 1.

Farrell, M., 1976. *Northern Ireland: The Orange State.* Pluto Press, London.

Fogarty, M., 1984. *Irish Values and Attitudes. Report on the European Values Study.* Dominican Publications, Dublin.

Frank, D.J. and Mc Eneaney, E.H., 1999. 'The Individualization of Society and the Liberalization of State Policies on Same-Sex Sexual Relations, 1984-1995.' *Social Forces.* 77: 911-944.

Frey, B.S. and Stutzer, A., 2002. 'What Can Economists Learn from Happiness Research?', *Journal of Economic Literature,* Vol. 40, pp. 402-435.

Fuchs, D. and Klingermann, H.-D., 1995. 'Citizens and the State: A Relationship Transformed,' in *Citizens of the State,* H.-D. Klingermann and D. Fuchs (eds.), Oxford University Press, Oxford.

Fuller, L., 2002. *Irish Catholicism since 1950. The Undoing of a Culture.* Gill & Macmillan, Dublin.

Gaffikin, F. and Morrison, M., 1990. *Northern Ireland: The Thatcher Years.* Zen Books, London.

Gallagher, M., Laver, M. and Mair, P., 2001. *Representative Government in Modern Europe.* McGraw Hill, New York.

Girvin, B., 1999. 'Nationalism and the Continuation of Political Conflict in Ireland,' in *Ireland North and South: Perspectives from Social Science*, A. Heath, R. Breen and C.T. Whelan (eds.), Oxford University Press, Oxford, pp. 369-399.

Garvin, T., 1981. *The Evolution of Irish Nationalist Politics.* Gill & Macmillan, Dublin.

Greeley, A., 1999. 'The Religions of Ireland,' in *Ireland North and South. Perspectives from Social Science. Proceedings of the British Academy '98*, A.F. Heath, R. Breen and C.T. Whelan (eds.), Oxford University Press, Oxford, pp. 141-160.

Greeley, A., 2004. *Religion in Europe at the End of the Second Millennium.* Transaction Publishers, London.

Gudgin, G., 1999. 'The Northern Ireland Labour Market,' in *Ireland North and South: Perspectives from Social Science,* A. Heath, R. Breen and C.T. Whelan (eds.), Oxford University Press, Oxford, pp. 251-284.

Hadaway, C.K., 1989. 'Identifying American Apostates: A Cluster Analysis', *Journal of the Scientific Study of Religion,* Vol. 28, pp. 201-215.

Hadaway, C.K., Marler, P.L. and Chaves, M., 2003. 'What the Polls Don't Show: A Closer Look at US Church Attendance', *American Sociological Review,* Vol. 58, pp. 741-752.

Hagerty, M.R., Cummins, R.A., Ferriss, A.L., Land, K., Michalos, A.C., Peterson, M., Sharpe, A., Sirgy, J., & Vogel, J., 2001. 'Quality of Life Indexes for National Policy: Review and Agenda for Research', *Social Indicators Research,* Vol. 55, pp. 1-96.

Haller, M., 2002. 'Theory and method in the comparative study of values: critique and alternative to Inglehart', *European Sociological Review,* Vol. 18, no. 2, pp. 139-158.

Halman, L., 2001. *The European Values Study: a Third Wave. Source book of the 1999/2000 European Values Study Survey.* Tilburg University, Tilburg.

Halman, L. and Riis, O., 1999. *Religion in Secularizing Society. Europeans' Religion at the End of the 20th Century.* Tilburg University Press, Tilburg.

Hammer, T., 1990. *Democracy and the Nation State.* Hants., Avebury.

Harding, S., Philips, D. & Fogerty, M., 1986. *Contrasting Values in Western Europe.* Macmillan, London.

Hayes, B.C. and Hornsby-Smith, M.P., 1994. 'Religious Identification and Family Attitudes: An International Comparison', *Research in the Social Scientific Study of Religion,* Vol. 6, pp. 167-186.

Hayes, B.C., 1995. 'The Impact of Religious Identification on Political Attitudes: An International Comparison.' *Sociology of Religion*. 56: 177-194.

Hayes, B.C., and McAllister, I., 1995. 'Religious Independents in Northern Ireland: Origins, Attitudes and Significance', *Review of Religious Research*, Vol. 37, pp. 65-83.

Hayes, B.C. and McAllister, I., 1995. 'Social Class, Class Awareness and Political Beliefs in Northern Ireland and the Irish Republic', *Economic and Social Review*, Vol. 26, pp. 349-368.

Hayes, B.C., 1996. 'Gender Differences in Religious Mobility in Britain', *British Journal of Sociology*, Vol. 47, pp. 643-656.

Hayes, B.C. and McAllister, I., 1996a. 'British and Irish Public Opinion Towards the Northern Ireland Problem', *Irish Political Sudies*, Vol. 11, pp. 61-82.

Hayes, B.C. and McAllister I., 1996b. 'Public Support for Democratic Values in Northern Ireland,' in *Social Attitudes in Northern Ireland: The Fifth Report,* R. Breen, P. Devine and L. Dowds (eds.), Appletree Press, Belfast, pp. 13-32.

Hayes, B.C., 1997. 'The Influence of Gender on Public Attitudes Towards Homosexual Rights in Britain.' *International Journal of Public Opinion Research*. 9: 361-385.

Hayes, B.C. and McAllister, I., 1999a. 'Generations, Prejudice and Politics in Northern Ireland,' in *Ireland North and South: Perspectives from Social Science,* A.F. Heath, R. Breen and C.T. Whelan (eds.), Oxford University Press, Oxford, pp. 457-491.

Hayes, B.C. and McAllister, I., 1999b. 'Ethnonationalism, Public Opinion and the Good Friday Agreement,' in *After the Good Friday Agreement: Analysing Political Change in Northern Ireland,* J. Ruane and J. Todd (eds.), University College Dublin Press, Dublin, pp. 30-48.

Hayes, B.C. and Marangudakis, M., 2000. 'Religion and Environmental Issues Within Anglo-American Democracies.' *Review of Religious Research.* 42: 159-174.

Hayes, B.C., McAllister, I. and Donley, T.S., 2000. 'Gender, Postmaterialism and Feminism in Comparative Perspective.' *International Political Science Review*. 21: 425-439.

Hayes, B.C., 2000. 'Religious Independents Within Western Industrialized Nations: A Socio-Demographic Profile', *Sociology of Religion*, Vol. 61, pp. 191-207.

Hayes, B.C. and McAllister, I., 2001a. 'Who Voted for Peace? Public Support for the Northern Ireland Agreement', *Journal of Political Studies*, Vol. 16, pp. 73-93.

Hayes, B.C., and McAllister, I., 2001b. 'Sowing Dragons Teeth: Public Support for Political Violence and Paramilitarism in Northern Ireland', *Political Studies*, Vol. 49, pp. 901-922.

Hayes, B.C. and McAllister, I., 2004. 'Protestant Disillusionment With the Northern Ireland Peace Agreement'. *Irish Journal of Sociology*, Vol. 13, no. 1, pp. 107-123.

Heath, A., Taylor, B. and Toka, G., 1993. 'Religion, Morality and Politics,' in *International*

Social Attitudes: the 10th BSA Report, R. Jowell *et al.* (eds.), Darmouth, London, pp. 49-90.

Heath, A., Breen, R. and Whelan, C.T., 1999. *Ireland North and South: Perspectives from Social Science.* Oxford University Press, Oxford.

Heslinga, M.W., 1979. *The Irish Border as a Cultural Divide.* Van Gorcum, Assen, The Netherlands.

Hill, H., 2003. *Women in Ireland: A Century of Change.* Blackstaff Press, Belfast.

Hjerm, M., 1998a. 'National Identity: A Comparison of Sweden, Germany and Australia', *Journal of Ethnic and Migration Studies*, Vol. 24, pp. 451-469.

Hjerm, M., 1998b. 'National Identities, National Pride and Xenophobia: A Comparison of Four Western Countries', *Acta Sociologica*, Vol. 41, pp. 335-347.

Hornsby-Smith, M.P., 1992. 'Social and Religious Transformation in Ireland: A Case of Secularisation?,' in *The Development of Industrial Society in Ireland*, J. H. Goldthorpe and C.T. Whelan (eds.), Oxford University Press, Oxford, pp. 265-290.

Hornsby-Smith, M.P. and Whelan, C.T., 1994. 'Religion and Moral Values,' in *Values and Social Change in Ireland*, C.T. Whelan (ed.), Gill & Macmillan, Dublin, pp. 7-44.

Horowitz, D.L., 2001. 'The Northern Ireland Agreement: Clear, Consociational and Risky,' in *Northern Ireland and the Divided World,* J. McGarry (ed.), Oxford University Press, Oxford, pp. 89-108.

Hug, C., 1999. *The Politics of Sexual Morality in Ireland.* Macmillan, Basingstoke.

Hughes, J. and Donnelly, C., 2003. 'Community Relations in Northern Ireland: A Shift in Attitudes.' *Journal of Ethnic and Migration Studies.* 4: 643-661.

Hunter, J.D., 1991. *Culture Wars: The Struggle to Define America.* Basic Books, New York.

Hult, C. and Svallfors, S., 2002. 'Production regimes and work orientations: A comparison of six western countries', *European Sociological Review,* Vol. 18, no. 3, pp. 315-331.

Iannaccone, L.R., 1998. 'Introduction to the Economics of Religion', *Journal of Economic Literature*, Vol. 36, pp. 1465-1496.

Inglehart, R., 1977. *The Silent Revolution: Changing Values and Political Styles in Advanced Industrial Society.* Princeton University Press, Princeton.

Inglehart, R., 1990. *Culture Shift in Advanced Industrial Society.* Princeton University Press, Princeton.

Inglehart, R., 1995. 'Public Support for Environmental Protection: The Impact of Objective Problems and Subjective Values in 43 Societies.' *PS – Political Science and Politics*. 28: 57-72.

Inglehart, R., 1997. *Modernization and Postmodernization: Cultural, Economic and Political Change in 43 Societies.* Princeton University Press, Princeton.

Inglehart, R. and Baker, W.E., 2000. 'Modernization, Cultural Change and the Persistence of Traditional Values', *American Sociological Review*, Vol. 65, no. 1, pp. 19-51.

Jowell, R. and Central Co-ordinating Team, 2003. *European Social Survey 2002/2003: Technical Report*. Centre for Comparative Social Surveys, City University, London.

Inglehart, R. and Norris, P., 2003. *Rising Tide: Gender Equality and Cultural Change Around the World.* Cambridge University Press, Cambridge.

Inglehart, R. and Klingermann H-D., 1976. 'Party Identification, Ideological Preference and the Left-Right Dimension Among Western Publics,' in *Party Identification and Beyond,* I. Budge, I. Crewe and D. Farlie (eds.), John Wiley, London, pp. 243-273.

Inglehart, R., and Klingermann, H.-D., 2000. 'Genes, Culture, Democracy and Happiness,' in *Subjective Wellbeing across Cultures*, E. Diener and E.M. Suh (eds.), MIT Press, Cambridge MA, pp. 165-182.

Inglis, T., 1998. *Moral Monopoly. The Rise and Fall of the Catholic Church in Modern Ireland* (2nd edn.), University College Dublin Press, Dublin.

Jagodzinski, W. and Dobbelaere, K., 1995. 'Religious and Ethnical Pluralism,' in *The Impact of Values,* J.W. Van Deth and E. Scarbrough (eds.), Oxford University Press, Oxford, pp. 218-249.

Jarman, N., Bryan, D., Caleyron, N. and De Rosa, C., 1998. *Politics in Public: Freedom of Assembly and the Right to Protest – A Comparative Analysis*. Democratic Dialogue, Belfast.

Jones, F.L. and Smith, P., 2001a. 'Individual and Societal Bases of National Identity: A Comparative Multi-Level Analysis', *European Economic Review*, Vol. 17, pp. 103-118.

Jones, F.L. and Smith, P., 2001b. 'Diversity and Commonality in National Identities: An Exploratory Analysis of Cross-National Patterns', *Journal of Sociology*, Vol. 35, pp. 45-63.

Kaase, M. and Newton, K., 1995. *Beliefs in Government*. Oxford University Press, Oxford.

Kenny, M., 2000. *Goodbye to Catholic Ireland.* New Island, Dublin.

Klingermann, H-D. and Fuchs, D., 1995. *Citizens and the State*. Oxford University Press, Oxford.

Klingermann, H-D., 1999. 'Mapping Political Support in the 1990s: A Global Analysis,' in *Critical Citizens: Global Support for Democratic Governance,* P. Norris (ed.), Oxford University Press, Oxford, pp. 31-56.

Knutsen, O., 1995. 'Left-Right Materialist Value Orientations,' in *The Impact of Values*, J.W. van Deth and E. Scarbrough (eds.), Oxford University Press, Oxford, pp. 160-196.

Laver, M., Mair, P. and Sinnott, R. (eds.), 1987. *How Ireland Voted: The Irish General Election of 1987*. Poolbeg Press, Dublin.

Lechner, F.J., 1991. 'The Case Against Secularization: A Rebuttal', *Social Forces*, Vol. 69, pp. 1103-1119.

Lipset, S.M. and Rokkan, S., 1967. 'Cleavage Structures, Party Systems and Voter Alignments: an Introduction,' in *Party Systems and Voter Alignments*, S.M. Lipset and S. Rokkan (eds.), The Free Press, New York.

Listhaug, O., 1995. 'The Dynamics of Trust in Politicians,' in *Citizens and the State*, H.-D. Klingermann and D. Fuchs (eds.), Oxford University Press, Oxford.

Listhaug, O. and Wiberg, M., 1995. 'Confidence in Political and Private Institutions,' in *Citizens and the State*, H.-D. Klingermann and D. Fuchs (eds.), Oxford University Press, Oxford.

Lyons, F.S.L., 1979. *Culture and Anarchy in Ireland.* Claredon Press, Oxford.

Mair, P., 1987a. 'Breaking the Nationalist Mould: The Irish Republic and the Anglo-Irish Agreement,' in *Beyond the Rhetoric: Politics, the Economy, and Social Policy in Ireland*, P. Teague (ed.), Lawrence and Wishart, London, pp. 81-110.

Mair, P., 1987b. 'Explaining the absence of class politics in Ireland,' in *The Development of Industrial Society in Ireland*, J. Goldthorpe and C.T. Whelan (eds.), Oxford University Press, Oxford.

Mansergh, M., 2000. 'The Background to the Irish Peace Process,' in *A Farewell to Arms: From Long War to Long Peace in Northern Ireland*, M. Cox, A. Guelke and F. Stephen (eds.), Manchester University Press, Manchester, pp. 8-23.

McGarry, J. and O'Leary, B., 1995. *Explaining Northern Ireland: Broken Images*. Blackwell, Oxford.

McKay, S., 2000. *Northern Protestants: An Unsettled People*. Blackstaff, Belfast.

Mitchell, P., O'Leary, B. and Evans, G., 2002. 'The 2001 Elections in Northern Ireland: Moderating "Extremists" and the Squeezing of the Moderates', *Representation*, Vol. 39, pp. 23-36.

Moxon-Browne, E., 1983. *Nation, Class and Creed in Northern Ireland.* Gower, Aldershot.

Moxon-Browne, E., 1991. 'National Identity in Northern Ireland,' in *Social Attitudes in Northern Ireland*, P. Stringer and G. Robinson (eds.), Appletree, Belfast, pp. 23-30.

Muller, W., 1999. 'Class Cleavages in Party Preferences in Germany – Old and New,' in *The End of Class Politics? Class Voting in Comparative Perspective*, G. Evans (ed.), Oxford University Press, Oxford, pp. 137-180.

Murphy, C. and Adair, L., 2002. *Untold Stories: Protestants in the Republic of Ireland 1922-2002*. Liffey Press, Dublin.

Need, A. and De Graaf, N.D., 1996. 'Losing My Religion: A Dynamic Analysis of Leaving the Church in the Netherlands', *European Sociological Review*, Vol. 12, pp. 87-99.

Nic Ghiolla Phádraig, M., 1976. Survey of Religious Beliefs and Practices in Ireland. Moral Attitudes [3]. Research and Development Commission, Dublin.

Nic Ghiolla Phádraig, M., 1988. 'Ireland: The Exception that Proves Two Rules,' in *World Catholicism in Transition*, T. Gannon (ed.), Macmillan, New York.

Norris, P., 1999. 'Introduction: The Growth of Critical Citizens,' in *Critical Citizens: Global Support for Democratic Government,* P. Norris (ed.), Oxford University Press, Oxford.

Norris, P., 2003. *Democratic Phoenix: Reinventing Political Activism.* Cambridge University Press, Cambridge.

O'Connell, P.J., 2000. 'The Dynamics of the Irish Labour Market in Comparative Perspective,' in *Bust to Boom? The Irish Experience of Growth and Inequality*, B. Nolan, P.J. O'Connell and C.T. Whelan (eds.), Institute of Public Administration, Dublin, pp. 58-89.

O'Connor, F., 1993. *In Search of a State: Catholics in Northern Ireland.* Blackstaff Press, Belfast.

O'Connor, F., 2002. *A Shared Childhood: The Story of Integrated Schools in Northern Ireland.* Blackstaff Press, Belfast.

O'Connor, P., 1998. *Emerging Voices: Women in Contemporary Irish Society.* Institute of Public Administration, Dublin.

O'Duffy, B., 1995. 'Violence in Northern Ireland 1969-1994: Sectarian or Ethno-national?', *Ethnic and Racial Studies*, Vol. 18, pp. 740-772.

Ó Grada, C. and Walsh, B., 1999. 'Fertility and Population in Ireland, North and South', *Population Studies.*

O'Leary, B., and McGarry, J., 1993. *The Politics of Antagonism: Understanding Northern Ireland.* Athlone Press, London.

O'Leary, B., 2001. 'Comparative Political Science and the British-Irish Agreement,' in *Northern Ireland and the Divided World*, J. McGarry (ed.), Oxford University Press, Oxford, pp. 53-88.

O'Malley, P., 1995. 'The Question of Religion', *Fortnight*, Vol. 366.

O'Malley, P., 1990. *Biting at the Grave: The Irish Hunger Strikes and the Politics of Despair.* Blackstaff, Belfast.

OECD, 2001. *The Well-being of Nations. The Role of Human and Social Capital.* OECD, Paris.

Osborne, R.D., 2004. 'Education and the Labour Market,' in *Fair Employment in Northern Ireland: A Generation On*, B. Osborne and I. Shuttleworth (eds.), Blackstaff Press, Belfast, pp. 65-87.

Oswald, A., 1997. 'Happiness and Economic Performance', *Economic Journal*, Vol. 107, pp. 1815-1831.

Presser, S., and Stinson, L., 1998. 'Data collection mode and social desirability bias in self-reported religious attendance', *American Sociological Review*, Vol. 6, no. 1, pp. 137-145.

Putnam, R.E., 2000. *Bowling Alone. The Collapse and Revival of American Community.* Simon & Schuster, New York.

Robinson, G. and Heaton, N., 1997. 'Work, Marriage and Family: A Time of Change?' in *Social Attitudes in Northern Ireland: The Sixth Report*, L. Dowds, P. Devine and R. Breen (eds.), Blackstaff Press, Belfast, pp. 175-202.

Roof, W.C. and McKinney, W., 1989. *American Mainline Religion: Its Changing Shape and Future* (3 edn), Rutgers University Press, London.

Rose, K., 1994. *Diverse Communities: The Evolution of Lesbian and Gay Politics in Ireland.* Cork University Press, Cork.

Rose, M., 1985. *Re-working the Work Ethic*. Batsford, London.

Rose, R., 1971. *Governing Without Consensus: An Irish Perspective*. Faber and Faber, London.

Rottman, D.B., 1999. 'Problems of, and Prospects for, Comparing the Two Irelands,' in *Ireland North and South, Perspectives from Social Science, Proceedings of the British Academy '98*, Oxford University Press, Oxford.

Ruane, J. and Todd, J., 1992. 'Diversity, Division and the Middle Ground in Northern Ireland', *Irish Political Studies*, Vol. 7, pp. 73-98.

Ruane, J. and Todd, J., 1996. *The Dynamics of Conflict in Northern Ireland.* Cambridge University Press, Cambridge.

Russell, R., 2004. 'Employment Profiles of Protestants and Catholics: A Decade of Monitoring,' in *Fair Employment in Northern Ireland: A Generation On*, B. Osborne and I. Shuttleworth (eds.), Blackstaff Press, Belfast, pp. 24-28.

Ryan, M.R. and Deci, A.L., 2001. 'On Happiness and Human Potentials: a Review of Research on Hedonic and Eudaimonic Well-Being', *Annual Review of Psychology*, Vol. 52, pp. 141-166.

Sandomirsky, S. and Wilson, J., 1990. 'Processes of Disaffiliation: Religious Mobility Among Men and Women', *Social Forces*, Vol. 68, pp. 1212-1219.

Scott, J., 1998. 'Generational Changes in Abortion: A Cross-National Analysis.' *European Sociological Review*. 14: 177-190.

Sexton, J. and O'Leary, R., 1996. *Factors Affecting Population Decline of Minority Religious Communities in the Republic of Ireland.* Forum for Peace and Reconciliation, Building Trust in Ireland. Studies Commissioned by the Forum for Peace and Reconciliation. The Blackstaff Press, Belfast.

Sherkat, D.E. and Wilson, J., 1995. 'Preferences, Constraints, and Choices in Religious Markets: An Examination of Religious Switching and Apostasy', *Social Forces*, Vol. 73, pp. 993-1026.

Sherkat, D.E. and Ellison, C.G., 1999. 'Recent Developments and current controversies in the Sociology of Religion', *Annual Review of Sociology*, Vol. 25, pp. 363-394.

Shuttleworth, I. and Green, A., 2004. 'Labour Market Change in Northern Ireland: Unemployment, Employment and Policy,' in *Fair Employment in Northern Ireland: A Generation On,* B. Osborne and I. Shuttleworth (eds.), Blackstaff Press, Belfast, pp. 100-121.

Shirlow, P. and McGovern, M., 1997. *Who Are 'The People'? Unionism, Protestantism and Loyalism in Northern Ireland.* Pluto Press, London.

Simpson, A., 1995. 'Abortion in Northern Ireland: A Victorian Law,' in *Human Rights and Reproductive Choice*, Ann Foredi (ed.), Blackstaff, Belfast, pp. 6-15.

Sinnott, R., 1995. *Irish Voters Decide: Voting Behaviour in Elections and Referendums Since 1918.* Manchester University Press, Manchester.

Sinnott, R., 2002. 'Cleavages, parties and referendums: Relationships between representative and direct democracy in the Republic of Ireland', *European Journal of Political Research,* Vol. 41, pp. 811-826.

Smith, A., 1991. *National Identity*. Pengiun, London.

Smith, D.J. and Chambers, G., 1991. *Inequality in Northern Ireland*. Clarendon Press, Oxford.

Stark, R. and Finke, R., 2000. *Acts of Faith*. University of California Press, Berkeley.

Stephen, F., 2000. 'Promoting a Culture of Tolerance: Education in Northern Ireland,' in *A Farewell to Arms? From Long War to Long Peace in Northern Ireland*, M. Cox, A. Guelke and F. Stephen (eds.), Manchester University Press, Manchester, pp. 165-178.

Stringer, P., 1992. 'Environmental Concern,' in *Social Attitudes in Northern Ireland: The Second Report*, Peter Stringer and Gillian Robinson (eds.), Blackstaff Press, Belfast, pp. 18-38.

Taylor, R., 2001. 'Northern Ireland: Consociation or Social Transformation?,' in *Northern Ireland and the Divided World*, J. McGarry (ed.), Oxford University Press, Oxford, pp. 37-52.

Thomas, D.L. and Cornwell, M., 1990. 'Religion and Family in the 1980s: Discovery and Development.' *Journal of Marriage and the Family*. 52: 983-992.

Todd, J., 1995. 'Beyond the Community Conflict: Historic Compromise or Emancipatory Process?' *Irish Political Studies*, Vol. 10, pp. 161-178.

Trew, K., 1994. 'What it Means To Be Irish Seen From a Northern Perspective', *Irish Journal of Psychology*, Vol. 15, pp. 288-299.

Trew, K., 1996. 'National Identity,' in *Social Attitudes in Northern Ireland: The Fifth Report,* R. Breen, P. Devine and L. Dowds (eds.), Blackstaff, Belfast, pp. 140-152.

UNDP., 1999. *Human Development Report 1999*. Oxford University Press for the United Nations Development Programme, New York.

van Deth, J.W. and Scarbrough, E. (eds.), 1995. *The Impact of Values*. Oxford University Press, Oxford.

van den Akker, P., Halman, L. and de Moor, R., 1993. 'Primary Relations in Western Societies,' in *The Individual Society. Value Change in Europe and North America*, P. Ester, L. Halman and R. de Moor (eds.), Tilburg University Press, Tilburg.

Verba, S., Nie, N.H. and Kim, J., 1978. *Participation and Political Equality: A Seven-Nation Comparison*. Cambridge University Press, Cambridge.

von Tagen Page, M., 2000. 'A Most Difficult and Unpalatable Part – The Release of Politically Motivated Violent Offenders,' in *A Farewell to Arms? From Long War to Long Peace in Northern Ireland*, M. Cox, A. Guelke and F. Stephen (eds.), Manchester University Press, Manchester, pp. 93-103.

Weber, M., 1958. *The Protestant Ethic and the Spirit of Capitalism*. Charles Scribner's Sons, New York.

Whelan, C.T. (ed.), 1994. *Values and Social Change in Ireland*. Gill & Macmillan, Dublin.

White, R.W., 1997. 'The Irish Republican Army: An Assessment of Sectarianism', *Terrorism and Political Violence*, Vol. 9, pp. 20-25.

Whyte, J., 1983. 'How Much Discrimination Was There Under The Unionist Regime, 1921-68?' in *Contemporary Irish Studies*, J. Gallaghar and J. O'Connell (eds.), Manchester University Press, Manchester, pp. 1-35.

Whyte, J., 1990. *Interpreting Northern Ireland.* Clarendon Press, Oxford.

Widmar, E.D., Treas, J. and Newcomb, R., 1998. 'Attitudes Towards Non-Marital Sex in 24 Countries.' *The Journal of Sex Research.* 35: 349-358.

Wilcox, C., 1991. 'Support for Gender Equality in West Europe – A Longitudinal Analysis.' *European Journal of Political Research.* 20: 127-147.

Wilcox, C., 1991. 'The Causes and Consequences of Feminist Consciousness Among Western European Women.' *Comparative Political Studies.* 23: 519-545.

Wilford, R., 2001. 'Introduction,' in *Aspects of the Belfast Agreement*, R. Wilford (ed.), Oxford University Press, Oxford, pp. 1-10.

Wilford, R., 2001. *Aspects of the Belfast Agreement.* Oxford University Press, Oxford.

Wilson, B., 1982. *Religion in Sociological Perspective.* Oxford University Press, Oxford.

World Bank, 2001. *World Development Report 2000/2001.* Oxford University Press, New York.

Index

Note: f after a page number indicates a figure, n indicates a footnote and t a table.
Abbreviations: NI, Northern Ireland; RI, Republic of Ireland.